HAROLD NICOLSON
DIARIES AND LETTERS
1930–1964

Harold Nicolson and Vita Sackville-West in 1932

Harold Nicolson

DIARIES
AND LETTERS
1930 – 1964

Edited and Condensed by
STANLEY OLSON

ATHENEUM
NEW YORK
1980

Contents

Introduction by Nigel Nicolson 7

Part I   1930–1939   11

Part II   The War   161

Part III   1945–1964   295

Index   409

Introduction

Harold Nicolson's diaries, and some extracts from letters to his family, were edited by me and first published in three volumes annually from 1966 to 1968, the year when my father died. The volumes went out of print one by one, and rather than republish them entire, it was decided to compile a selection from them in a single volume, and this task has been admirably carried out by Stanley Olson.

The three earlier volumes were themselves a selection from the full diary, of which the typewritten original is in the library of Balliol College, Oxford, where historians can study and quote from it under certain conditions. In all, the original diary runs to some three-million words, covering the years 1930–64, and in my edition I reproduced only a twentieth part. Mr Olson has made his shortened version by reducing annotations and linking narratives to a minimum, and by omitting many passages likely to be of less interest to the general reader. He has included a number of unpublished passages from the diary and letters which seemed on re-reading to be amusing or historically valuable, or which I left out for reasons of discretion which has become less necessary with the passage of time, and has occasionally substituted diary entries for letters where the former conveyed much the same information in a shorter form. These new passages are marked in the text by asterisks. Finally, Mr Olson has added at the end a few extracts from the 1963–64 diaries, from which I made no quotation, being reluctant to reveal during my father's lifetime his failing health and his inconsolable grief at my mother's death in 1962.

A brief summary of Harold Nicolson's career and character may be found useful by a new generation to whom his name is not as familiar as it was to his contemporaries.

He was born in 1886, the youngest son of Lord Carnock, who

became head of the Foreign Office in the First War. Harold was educated at Wellington College and Balliol, and entered diplomacy in 1909. In 1913 he married Vita Sackville-West, the poet and novelist, and they had two sons. His work exempted him from military service, and he soon established a leading reputation among the younger Foreign Office officials, playing an important role in the Peace Conference of 1919, and subsequently in establishing the League of Nations. In the 1920s he was successively Counsellor in the British Legation in Teheran and in the Berlin Embassy. At the end of 1929, he resigned from diplomacy in mid-career, mainly because it separated him from Vita, who had better things to do than act the part of a diplomatic wife. After a year in journalism, he joined Oswald Mosley's New Party, leaving it when Mosley turned Fascist. In 1935 he was elected National Labour Member for West Leicester, and became spokesman for his Party on foreign affairs. In 1940–41 he was appointed a junior Minister under Winston Churchill, and for the remainder of the war acted unofficially as a link between the Government and de Gaulle's Free French. He lost his seat in the 1945 Election, joined the Labour Party, and stood unsuccessfully as its candidate at a by-election in 1948. He devoted the rest of his life to journalism, broadcasting and books. He had begun writing while still in diplomacy, and was seldom without a book in progress until a few years before his death. Among his best-remembered are *Some People*, his biographies of Tennyson, Verlaine, Curzon and his own father, his novel *Public Faces*, and his massive work on the reign of George V, for which he was knighted in 1953. His journalism included his weekly article for the *Spectator*, and his book-reviews for the *Observer*, which jointly established him as the leading critic of his day. As a lecturer and broadcaster he further widened his reputation.

He had a deep interest in the contemporary world, but temperamentally he was sometimes compared to an eighteenth-century Whig aristocrat, with a strong intellectual bent. He has been called a snob, but unfairly. He was an élitist, choosing his friends not for their birth, eminence or wealth, but because they shared his tastes and interests. He deplored the slow erosion, as he saw it, of the old cultural and humanistic values. He was at home in half-a-dozen foreign languages and literatures, loved France but England more, proving himself in the Second War a patriot of unremitting faith and courage. He was witty, gregarious and a tease, the most stimulating and responsive of companions. His personality had a certain feminine streak in it, and a Boswellian and Byronic capacity for self-scrutiny. His mind was extremely agile, his ability for hard work phenomenal, and his disposition kindly. If he had a fault, it was a certain softness in his make-up ("I have no combative qualities"), a tendency to sentimentality, but although his political reticence was often taken to be a sign of impotence, he brought to politics much that was admirable, decent, shrewd and wise, and to literature a buoyancy and irony that aerated his lightly classical style. It was sometimes held against him that he would never make up his mind what sort of man he was, a writer who dabbled in politics, or a man of action with a contemplative and literary base, and that he failed to achieve the highest of reputations in either field because he was regarded, as he wrote of himself, "by the Bohemians as conventional, and by the conventional as Bohemian". In fact, his very diversity of interests and activity made him unique among his contemporaries. His life tended to zigzag, but he extracted from it much pleasure, and gave much, particularly to his family, who formed the bone-marrow of his life. To him private pleasures were as important as public success, and his diary reflects both.

He did not write his diary for publication. He had a future reader vaguely in mind, whom he once identified as his great-grandson, but his main purpose in keeping it so conscientiously and fully for over thirty years was to give himself an entertaining literary exercise at the beginning of each morning, and to preserve one person's distillation of the daily cataract of events, thinking it a pity, like Francis Kilvert in his more modest diary, that so much experience should pass away without some record. Thus his diary became an essential accompaniment to his life, a receptacle for his delights and occasional unhappiness and self-reproach, a running self-investigation, but also a commentary on what he did, heard, read or wrote. He was so active socially and politically for the majority of the years covered by this volume, and wrote so vividly, that his diary became on publication more widely read than he had believed possible, both for its historical content and for the self-portrait it unconsciously drew. In the last year of his life, when two volumes of the diary had appeared, he said to me that he found it rather sad that he who had published forty books should be remembered only for the three that he hadn't realised he'd written.

His diary, therefore, should be read as much for the self it reveals as for the world it reveals. It has strong dramatic interest because he was involved in great affairs and had an unequalled gift for recording them. During these thirty years he watched an old world die, and tried to come to terms with the new. He was a marginal commentator, but had strong convictions and a streak of adventurousness and daring. Loveable as a friend, loving as a husband, caring and stimulating as a father, he was a more admirable man than the great diarists of the past, Pepys, Creevey, Greville. There was no meanness in him. He has left behind an incomparable record of what it was like to be alive during these most eventful years, and of his every mood from exhilaration to despair, in controversy and private happiness.

NIGEL NICOLSON
Sissinghurst Castle, Kent

PART I

1930–1939

Passages from the diary and letters
which were not included
in the original three published volumes
are marked by asterisks
at the start and finish of each passage.

On December 20, 1929 Harold Nicolson returned to England from Berlin where he had been Counsellor at the British Embassy since 1927. At the beginning of 1930 he resigned from diplomacy and joined the staff of Lord Beaverbrook's Evening Standard. *There he collaborated with Robert Bruce Lockhart in writing the Londoner's Diary – about fifteen paragraphs daily of social, literary and political gossip. He also began broadcasting a series of talks under the title "People and Things", and wrote book-reviews for the* Daily Express.

In January 1930 he was 43 years old. His wife Vita Sackville-West was 37, and their sons, Benedict and Nigel, were 15 and 13. H.N. lived for most of the week in his chambers at 4 King's Bench Walk, Inner Temple. At the weekends he went to Long Barn, their fifteenth-century house some two miles from Knole. In May the Nicolsons decided to leave Long Barn, and bought Sissinghurst Castle, a decrepit house near Cranbrook, Kent.

Diary   *January 1, 1930*

I feel glad that 1929 is over. Not a very happy year for me, since it has entailed being separated from Vita and living a rather hugger-mugger existence in Berlin. But there have been compensations. In the first place I have worked hard at father's book [the biography of his father, Lord Carnock, who died in 1928] and completed it before the year was out. In the second place I was able to perfect my knowledge of the German character: in other words, to make quite certain that I did not understand them in the least. In any case, for better or worse, the end of 1929 marks the end of my career as a diplomatist. What will 1930 bring?

Diary   *January 8, 1930*

Work fruitlessly superficially futilely upon the Londoner's Diary. The difficulty is that the only news I get is from friends and that is just the news that I can't publish.

Lunch with Sibyl Colefax [the well-known hostess who lived at Argyll House, Chelsea]. The Rudyard Kiplings there. Rudyard Kipling's eyebrows are really very odd indeed! They curl up black and furious like the moustache of a Neapolitan tenor. He has a slightly Anglo-Indian voice, with notes of civil service precision in it, and his conversation is twisted into phrases like his writing. He spoke of Cecil Rhodes and [Theodore] Roosevelt. Admired them both. *Told how once when on a yacht with Roosevelt and [Henry Cabot] Lodge and other pundits they talked of how many men carried mascots. They derided the practice until someone suggested that they should all empty their pockets on the table. It was found that all of them possessed some object, a bit of stick, a knife, or something, which they would hate to lose and always carried with them.* Kipling assured me incidentally that Rhodes did not drink: he looked as if he did, but that was due to a weak heart.

Diary   *January 23, 1930*

I was summoned by Lord Beaverbrook. I arrived at Stornoway House to find him alone writing a cross letter to his son about bills. In a few minutes Winston Churchill slouched in. Very changed from when I last saw him. A great round face like a blister. Incredibly aged. Looks like pictures of Lord Holland. An elder statesman. His spirits also have declined and he sighs that he has lost his old fighting power.

They talk the whole time about Empire free trade. Winston says that he has abandoned all his convictions and clings to the conviction of free trade as the only one which is left to him. But he is clearly disturbed at the effect on the country of Beaverbrook's propaganda. He feels too old to fight it. "Thirty years ago," he said, "I should have welcomed such a combat: now I dread it." He seems to think [Stanley] Baldwin [Leader of the Conservative oppo-

sition] absolutely hopeless, and no instructions have been given to
the provincial candidates and agents as to the line that decent Conservatives will adopt. Beaverbrook uses every wile to secure if not
his support then at least his agreement not to oppose. I must say,
he is rather impressive. Young and nervous he walks about the
room piling argument on argument and statistic on statistic. There
is no question but that he is passionately sincere and has really
studied his subject.

Diary   *March 8, 1930*

*Down to Long Barn. We go round the field at Westwood [the
neighbouring farm] with Mrs Taylour the lady who owns Cookes
[poultry farmers]. She will sell us the ridge fields at £150 an acre
when they are only worth £50. She will sell us the whole of Westwood for £21,000. Now this is absurd and beyond the dreams of
possibility. She is erecting huts and cottages on the field that over-
looks our garden. The view from Long Barn – its best point – will
be spoilt. Very gloomily we discuss migrating to Dorset.*

Diary   *March 26, 1930*

On to the *Daily Express* office about books. I see an intolerable man
who treats both me and literature as if they were dirt. I am so
depressed by the squalor of this interview that I return home in a
nerve-storm. To make it worse, I am sent out to represent the
Standard at the Knights of the Round Table dinner. There is no seat
for me and I creep away in dismay and humiliation. I never foresaw
that writing for the Press would be actually so degrading. What I
dread is that I might get to like it: the moment I cease to be unhappy
about it will be the moment when my soul has finally been killed.

Diary   *April 4, 1930*

Vita telephones to say she has seen the ideal house – a place in Kent
near Cranbrook, a sixteenth-century castle [Sissinghurst].

Diary   *April 5, 1930*

Go down to Staplehurst with Ben. We are met, after some delay, by
Vita, Boski [Audrey le Bosquet, V.S-W.'s secretary], Niggs [Nigel],

and all the dogs. We then drive to Sissinghurst Castle. We get a view of the two towers as we approach. We go round carefully in the mud. I am cold and calm but I like it.

H.N. to V.S-W.   *April 24, 1930*

My view is:

(a) That it is most unwise of us to get Sissinghurst. It costs us £12,000 to buy and will cost another good £15,000 to put it in order. This will mean nearly £30,000 before we have done with it. For £30,000 we could buy a beautiful place replete with park, garage, h. and c., central heating, historical associations, and two lodges r. and l.

(b) That it is most wise of us to buy Sissinghurst. Through its veins pulses the blood of the Sackville dynasty. True it is that it comes through the female line – but then we are both feminist and after all Knole came in the same way [Knole was given to Sir Thomas Sackville by his cousin Queen Elizabeth I]. It is, for you, an ancestral mansion: that makes up for the company's water and h. and c.

(c) It is in Kent. It is in a part of Kent we like. It is self-contained. I could make a lake. The boys could ride.

(d) We like it.

Diary   *May 6, 1930*

After dinner we are rung up by Beale [the land-agent]. He says that they accept our price. I sit there while Vita answers the telephone: "Quite" . . . "Yes, of course" . . . "Oh naturally!" She puts down the receiver and says, "It is ours." We embrace warmly. I then go and get the plans and fiddle. Vita thinks we had better build a small wing for ourselves abutting on to the tower and joined to the main building on the north side by a huge loggia. She has given up all ideas of leaving the courtyard open to the north.

Diary   *June 5, 1930*

Dine with Beaverbrook at Stornoway House. He is in a good temper. The chill of that house – no flowers, just newspapers and telephones

– is appalling. There is an air of sycophancy about it all which I find distressing. Have some talk with Beaverbrook after. I tell him I think the Londoner's Diary is getting dull. It is. He denies it – and gives some good suggestions. He thinks that the *Daily Herald* will only last a year. He says that once a modern paper begins to lose, it loses hand over foot.

Diary   *June 6, 1930*

I go to William Rothenstein [the portraitist] to have a drawing done. He tells me that Oscar Wilde had a red face, grey lips and very bad teeth. He was so ashamed of his teeth that he used to put his hand over them when he spoke giving an odd furtive expression to his jokes. Rothenstein did a drawing of Wilde which the latter always took with him. He lost it in Naples after the trial. It was probably stolen. That was about the only portrait of Wilde ever made.

Diary   *June 22, 1930*

Talk to Stephen Spender. He is an intelligent young man [aged 21] with wild blue eyes and a bad complexion. He takes his work and poetry with immense seriousness, and talks for hours about whether he is more fitted to be a poet than a novelist. He is not conceited so much as self-preoccupied. He is absolutely determined to become a leading writer. A nice and vital young man whom we both liked.

Diary   *July 2, 1930*

Dine at Sovrani's with Bob Boothby [Conservative M.P., later Lord Boothby]. Bob tells me that when someone asked Ramsay Mac-Donald whether he, Bob, was about to join the Labour Party, Ramsay replied, "No, Bob is no Labour man: it is merely that he has a deep personal admiration for myself." That is characteristic of the man's diseased vanity. I talk to [Harold] Macmillan. He says that the old party machines are worn out and that the modern electorate thinks more of personalities and programmes than of the pressure put upon them by an electoral agent. He thinks that the economic situation is so serious that it will lead to a breakdown of the whole party system. He foresees that the Tories may return with a majority of 20 and then be swept away on a snap vote. No other single party will form a Government and then there will be a Cabinet of young men. He was kind enough to include me in this Pitt-like Ministry.

Diary   *July 6, 1930*

Winston [at Wilton, the Pembrokes' house in Wiltshire] talks long and sadly about Beaverbrook's Empire Free Trade campaign which he sees is ruining the country. He says it will hand over South America to the Yanks, split the Empire for ever, and shatter the Conservative Party into smithereens. He is writing three books – one a last volume of the *World Crisis* – one a life of the Duke of Marlborough [in four volumes, 1933–1938] – one reminiscences of his own [*My Early Life*, 1930]. He is in gentle and intelligent form. He goes for a long walk with Vita and tells her his troubles and hopes. He spoke of his American tour. The difficulty of drink and food. One never got real food, only chicken.

Diary   *July 10, 1930*

Dine with Sir Henry Norman – a man's dinner. I sit next to Bernard Shaw. He is amazingly young looking [he was 73]: his shoulder blades at the back stick through his dinner jacket like those of a boy who has not finished growing. His hair is dead white but thick. His cheeks as pink as a girl's. His eyes as simple and unmalicious as those of an animal. And yet behind their simplicity is a touch of reserve. He talks with a faintly effeminate voice and a soft brogue. He had a special menu of excellent vegetables.

He talked of Laurence [Olivier]. Said he was a born actor. Spoke of him with real admiration. Afterwards we went upstairs and there were some young girls to amuse the old man.

> *In August the Nicolsons motored to Italy. While there H.N. wrote his only play* The Archduke *which was never produced or published, and V.S-W. wrote a large part of her novel,* All Passion Spent. *H.N. took the train back to England, leaving his wife and sons to follow by car.*

H.N. to V.S-W.   *August 22, 1930*
                                    en train, Bologna–Milan

Oh dear, that black and dusty bundle holds everything in life for
me, and shortly it will be humming along that very road under this
plate-glass sun. Darling, *why* did I consent to this bloody scheme?
I do so hate it for you. The road looks like white ashes, all hot. Dust
and ashes. But at least it looks straight, and when you get to where I
am looking now, you will be only a little way to Piacenza and can
sleep there.

Darling, I wonder if other people mind being separated quite
as much as we do? It's too silly. Today week we shall be reunited.
Exactly at this hour. Yet I feel as if we had been parted for ever. I
always retreat at such moments into the cool orchard of my gratitude. "For nearly seventeen years," I say, "we have been so happy.
Nothing, not even death, can take that away from us." If you died
or I died, we should not feel any wastage. We should merely feel
that we had been too happy for it to last.

Diary   *October 5, 1930*

We start off at 10 to motor to Chequers. We go through London.
On passing through Bromley we half-see a poster blown by the
wind which looks like "Airship destroyed". We stop later and buy
a paper. We find that the R.101 [airship] has crashed near Beauvais
and that [Lord] Thomson [Minister of Air] with 43 other people
have been burnt alive. We then drive on to Chequers.

When we arrive we find that the P.M. [Ramsay MacDonald] is
up in London and is expected back later. Ishbel [his daughter] says
he will be in a dreadful state. He arrives about 1.30. He looks very
ill and worn. [Richard] Bennett, the Prime Minister of Canada, is
there. Ramsay begins to introduce him to Vita but forgets his name.
He makes a hopeless gesture – his hand upon his white hair – "My
brain is going," he says, "my brain is going." It is all rather embarrassing. He then tells us that the bell beside his bed had rung that
morning and he had lifted the receiver. He was told it was the Air
Ministry. He was told of the disaster. He dashed up to London in
55 minutes and went to the Air Ministry. There were only a few
clerks about. Salmond [Air Marshal Sir Geoffrey Salmond] was
got hold of and sent across to France. Baldwin came to see him.
They agreed that no man's health could stand being Prime Minister.

The King was in a dreadful state. Ramsay seemed more worried about the King's dismay than about anything else.

We then go in to luncheon. All very beautifully and excellently done. Afterwards we go up to the long gallery. The women look at Cromwell's head [life-mask]. The P.M. pours out to Vita the miseries of his soul: he cannot sleep: two hours a night is all he gets: he can do no work: "the moment I distentangle my foot from one strand of barbed wire it becomes entangled in another. If God were to come to me and say 'Ramsay, would you rather be a country gentleman than Prime Minister?', I should reply, 'Please God, a country gentleman'. " He is a tired exhausted man. Bless him.

Diary   *October 18, 1930*

Feeling very depressed with life. Can't make out whether it is mere middle-aged depression or that I loathe journalism so much that it covers all my days with a dark cloud of shame. I feel that I have no time to add to my reputation by doing serious work and that my silly work day by day diminishes the reputation I have already acquired. I have become "famous" as a radio comedian, and I shall never be able to live down the impression thus acquired. I would give my soul to leave the *Standard* but I daren't risk it because of the money. Middle age for a hedonist like myself is distressing in any case but with most people it coincides with an increase of power and income. With me I have lost all serious employment, sacrificed my hopes of power, and am up against the anxiety of having not one penny in the world beyond what I earn. I have never been unhappy like this before.

Diary   *November 6, 1930*

Lunch with the Mosleys [Sir Oswald ("Tom") and Lady Cynthia Mosley]. Tom talks afterwards, when they have all gone, about the future. He is evidently thinking of leading some new party of younger Nationalists. He is not certain what to do or when to do it. If he strikes now he may be premature. If he delays he may be too late. "If," he says, "I could have £250,000 and a press I should sweep the country." By the press he means Beaverbrook. I warn him against the impulsive character of Lord B. I tell him that so long as there is battle on, B. will behave as a great and loyal fighter. But that once the battle is over and victory is assured, B. will get bored and will create battles, if necessary, in his own party. His pugnacity destroys both his judgement and his decent feeling. If they ally themselves with B. they must think of some bone to give him later which will keep him busy. He lives only by opposition: if he cannot find an opposition he creates one. Tom, I think agreed. I said I would be with him all the time. He begs me to do nothing till December. I shall hold my tongue, and hold my cards. I want to be in real things again, and not to feel that my batteries are wasted playing the spillikins of the Press.

Diary   *November 27, 1930*

To Noel Coward's *Private Lives* with Vita and on to supper with Noel at 17 Gerald Road. An elaborate studio. Noel very simple and nice. He talks of the days when his mother kept lodgings in Ebury Street and he himself had a top back room. Gradually he began to make money and took the top floor for himself, finally descending to the first floor and ejecting the lodgers. "As I rose in the world I went down in the house." Completely unspoilt by success. A nice eager man.

Diary   *November 30, 1930*

Tom Mosley tells me that he will shortly launch his manifesto practically creating the National Party. He hopes to get Morris [later Lord Nuffield] of Oxford to finance him. He hopes to get [Maynard] Keynes and similar experts to sign his manifesto. He hopes that [Oliver] Stanley and [Harold] Macmillan will also join. He hopes to get the support of Beaverbrook. I doubt whether many of these hopes will be realised, but his conversation is convincing enough to decide me to write to [Sir John] Tudor Walters declining his offer to stand for Falmouth [his seat, which he was resigning]. That is one boat burnt.

Diary   *December 22, 1930*

Bertram Mills gives a luncheon for 1,100 people at Olympia. I am about to enter when I hear a voice behind me. It is Ramsay Mac-Donald. He says, "Well, this is my one holiday in the year. I love circuses." At that moment they hand him a telegram. He opens it. He hands it to me with the words, "Keep this, my dear Harold, and read it if ever you think you wish to be Prime Minister." It is a telegram from some crank society abusing him for attending a luncheon in honour of a circus proprietor – since performing animals are cruel. He is disgusted and his pleasure spoiled.

Diary   *December 31, 1930*

Thus ends the year 1930. Such an odd year. We buy Sissinghurst; we make a vast sum of money from our books; we increase our fame and lower our reputation; we prepare for the future. Viti has been very well and happy except for her back. Ben has been unhappy at Eton but is doing better. Niggs is bored by his first half at Eton but will probably settle down. I have quite found my feet in the *Standard* office – and Beaverbrook likes me. But that is all very well. I was not made to be a journalist and do not want to go on being one. It is a mere expense of spirit in a waste of shame. A constant hurried triviality which is bad for the mind. Goodness knows what I shall do next year. I am on the verge of politics. I am on the verge of leaving the *Evening Standard* and either writing books of my own or sitting in the House of Commons. 1931 assuredly will be the most important year, for good or ill, in my whole life.

> H.N.'s dislike of journalism increased as his ambition to enter politics mounted. He joined Oswald Mosley's New Party in face of Lord Beaverbrook's disapproval and Vita's conviction that the whole Mosley venture was insane.

Diary   *January 28, 1931*

Walking across St Stephen's Yard I observe a small figure in front of me with collar turned up. He turns to see who is behind him and I see it is Ramsay MacDonald. I say, "Hullo, sir. How are you?" He greets me warmly. We walk across to Downing Street and people take off their hats as he passes. The traffic is stopped. He talks about Vita's broadcast on Persia: the best he has ever heard. He asks me to come in and have a drink. We reach the door of No. 10. He knocks. The porter opens and stands to attention. Ramsay asks him, "Is Berry in?" "No, sir, he has gone." "Is Ishbel in?" (not "Miss Ishbel"). "Yes, sir." "Would you ask her to bring two glasses to my room?" We then go upstairs. The room has an unlived-in appearance. Turners over the fireplace. Ishbel is there. He asks her to get us a drink. She goes out and returns with two tooth-glasses and a syphon. She says she can't find any whisky. Ramsay says it is in the drawer of his table. He finds it. "What about some champagne," he says, "to celebrate the victory?" [an unexpected Government majority on the Trade Disputes Bill]. I say I will not have champagne. Malcolm [MacDonald] comes in. "A cigarette?" I say I will. "Malcolm, we have got cigarettes, haven't we – in that Egyptian box?" Malcolm goes to search for the Egyptian box. Then there are no matches.

He complains of overwork and bother. He sees me out. Nothing will convince me that he is not a fundamentally simple man. Under all his affectation and vanity there is a core of real simplicity.

Diary   *February 15, 1931*

At Savehay [the Mosleys' country house]. Oliver Stanley, Harold Macmillan and other M.P.s come over including [David] Margesson [later Conservative Chief Whip]. Play rounders. I fall into the stream. Tom is organising his New Party. Poor Cimmie [Mosley] cannot follow his repudiation of all the things he has taught her to say previously. She was not made for politics. She was made for society and the home. He wants me to sit on the Party's publicity committee. I say that he must ask Beaverbrook, but as the latter is so busy with his East Islington Election he will not listen.

H.N. to Sir Oswald Mosley   *March 4, 1931*
                                                 Evening Standard

I spoke to Max [Beaverbrook] about joining your party. He was most appreciative. Striding about the room he explained to me how far, far more remunerative it would be for me to attach myself to some more established machine. He became eloquent on the constituencies and jobs which could be conquered and acquired under the tattered banners of the old parties. And when I, sitting there glum and obstinate, remarked that I did not care for the old parties, he said, "Go to Hell with ye – and God bless ye."

After which he expressed admiration for yourself and deep sympathy with me in my obstinacy and wrong-headedness. He said I had his blessing (his sorrowed blessing) in joining you. I might serve on any of your committees if I wished. I must not boost you unduly in the *Evening Standard*. Nor must I devote to the New Party the time that I ought to devote to the *Standard*. Nor must I proclaim on the housetops my conversion to the faith. But short of that I might do what I liked.

Diary   *April 29, 1931*

Lunch with Enid [Bagnold, novelist]. I ask her about Gaudier Brzeska [French sculptor, 1891–1915], whose life I have just been reviewing. She says that he was a hard, disagreeable little creature, with a curious, rattling voice like a machine-gun and a complete unawareness of when he was being a bore.

H. G. Wells talks to me after lunch about Beaverbrook. He says that he is really alarmed lest B. should have hardening of the brain. He contends that he is showing the first symptoms, namely a dislike of contradiction and an avoidance of all people who are likely to contest anything that he says. Wells had been down there lately and stated that he had returned with the determination never to visit Cherkley [Surrey] again, since one came away with a vague sense of humiliation and an acute sense of disquiet.

I drove back with Margot Oxford who, as usual, is very bitter about everything. She is furious with me for joining the New Party and tries to imply that this is a personal disloyalty to the memory of old Asquith [her husband]. When I said that it would be equally disloyal to my affection for that old man to have joined Lloyd George, she merely pinched me very hard with a long, claw-like hand and tells me not to become tiresome. "People," she said, "of your age get into the habit of saying tiresome things. You must break that habit."

Dined with Clive Bell and Keynes. Keynes is very helpful about the economics of the New Party. He says that he would, without question, vote for it. The attitude of the Labour Party on the Sunday Cinema Bill, as well as that on Free Trade, has disgusted him. He feels that our Party may really do an immense amount of good and that our Programme is more sound and certainly more daring than that which any other party can advance.

Diary   *May 19, 1931*

Go to the Chelsea Flower Show. The rock gardens are pretty poor owing to the late season, but the herbaceous plants are extremely good. We take notes of all copper and orange plants for our walls. Have tea in McLaren's tent. Harry McLaren [later Lord Aberconway] is president this year and Christabel [his wife] has been spending the afternoon taking the King [George V] and Queen [Mary] over. She said that ten minutes before the King arrived, an agitated equerry telephoned from the Palace to warn them that H.M. was in a furious temper. This did not diminish her anxiety at the prospect of taking a walk round the garden with him for over an hour. When he arrived, however, he appears to have quieted down and to have quite enjoyed himself. His remarks on being confronted with various plants are characteristic of the Royal mind. He was shown one hybrid of extreme delicacy and importance and after gazing at it for a minute in heavy-eyed silence, remarked: "What a large quantity of moss they have put round the roots. I wonder how they manage to get so much moss." At another point he was shown some very rare plants for which explorers have risked their lives. "Yes," he said, "people risk their lives for many curious objects. What, for instance, would happen to us if this tent came down upon our heads?" Christabel, unaware whether this was Royal humour or merely Royal sense of association, hedged by replying, "That, Sir, would indeed be terrible." "It would indeed," the King answered.

Diary   *May 28, 1931*

Shaw was at luncheon. He talked a great deal. He said that when he started to write a play, he never worked out the plot beforehand. What happened was that he had an idea for a play and started at once writing the first act. Subsequently, of course, he was aware, while writing, of the limitations of the stage and he presumed that some censor was at work within him modelling what he wrote into dramatic form. After *Methuselah*, he had determined to write no further plays, but one day he said to his wife that he was feeling growing pains and a desire to write further. "Why," she said to him, "do you not write about St Joan?" He replied, "I will," and started writing immediately. In the same way, *The Doctor's Dilemma* was taken entirely from a chance visit to a London hospital and a conversation with Dr Almroth Wright [originator of anti-typhoid inoculation]. He then spoke a great deal about St Joan saying that she was the first Protestant and the first nationalist in Europe.

Diary　　　　　　　　　　　　　　　　　　　　　　　*May 30, 1931*

Down to Oxford. Meet Harold Macmillan in the train. He takes the usual young Tory view that his heart is entirely with the New Party but that he feels he can help us better by remaining in the Conservative ranks. He does not hesitate to admit that if we could obtain a certain number of seats in Parliament, most of the young Tories, all the Liberals, and a large proportion of the youngish Labour people would come over to us. He anticipates the present Government being in power for another two years. He feels that five years from now, the New Party will have its great opportunity.

Diary　　　　　　　　　　　　　　　　　　　　　　　*June 13, 1931*

Down to Sissinghurst. Discuss future plans with Vita and decide that we shall make an enormous tree border run down to the lake. Also decide to run a lime-walk around the top of the moat. Draw designs in the evening for our new wing [eventually abandoned]. Our difficulty is that we do not wish to fake a Tudor reproduction and yet anything 18th-century must look too grand for the rest of the building.

Mosley offered H.N. the editorship of the New Party journal Action *– a post which he felt he could not accept because he was bound by contract to Beaverbrook until the end of 1932. Beaverbrook retaliated with the suggestion that if H.N. were to leave the New Party, he could edit the* Evening Standard.

Diary   *June 18, 1931*

After dinner, I discuss with V. the situation raised by my luncheon
with Beaverbrook. Clearly I am likely to fall between two stools.
Were I to enquire further into Beaverbrook's offer, I might well be
put in a position of authority on the *Evening Standard* which would
mean not merely a very high salary, but also an opportunity of
making a decent and influential paper out of it. There is no limit to
the possibilities opened by such a prospect. Alternatively, there is a
chance that the New Party within five years would be in such a
position as to force a coalition upon one of the other two parties.
In such a coalition, I should certainly be able to ask for the Foreign
Office, and here again, there is no limit to the avenue of extensive
power. For some time V.'s responses had become fewer and far
between. When I reach the point where I picture myself riding on
an elephant at Delhi, I find that for the last half-hour she as been
asleep.

Diary   *June 23, 1931*

Send a letter to Beaverbrook asking him to release me either wholly
or partially from my contract. I define the expression "wholly" as a
complete severance from the *Evening Standard*. I define "partially"
as continuing to review books but dropping all other work. I make
it quite clear that my purpose is to devote almost all my energies to
the New Party and the New Paper.

Lord Beaverbrook to H.N.   *June 25, 1931*
                                          Cherkley, Leatherhead

I am very sorry to hear that you are getting more deeply involved in
the New Party.

I think the movement has petered out. It might be saved by immense sums of money, and brilliant journalistic support, but of
course there is a conspiracy of silence in the newspapers, except for
the particular newspapers I am connected with.

I hope you will give up the New Party. If you must burn your
fingers in public life, go to a bright and big blaze.

Diary   *July 17, 1931*

I think that Tom at the bottom of his heart really wants a fascist movement, but Allan Young [secretary to New Party] and John Strachey think only of the British working-man. The whole thing is extremely thin ice and I raised it purposely to see whether the ice had become any thicker. I talk to him afterwards about the paper and we decide we must start immediately and go ahead within the next ten days.

Diary   *July 23, 1931*

I am working at the *Evening Standard* office when, at about 11 a.m., Tom rings me up and says will I come round at once. He had, at that moment, received letters from John Strachey and Allan Young resigning from the Party. I go round at 12.30 and find the Council gathered together in gloom. We try to get hold of our two delinquents but they are out and will not return till 6.0. As 6.0 is the hour at which they announced their intention of communicating their resignation to the Press, that is not of much value. We adjourn for luncheon.

   Back to the office. I begin drafting statements to the Press in order to meet John's impending announcement. While thus engaged a letter comes in containing that announcement. It says that they have resigned because Tom, on such subjects as The Youth Movement, Unemployment Insurance, India and Russia, was adopting a fascist tendency. On all these points except Russia (where John's memo was idiotic) they have had their way. I draft another statement.

   At 5.30 we at last find they have returned to 7 North Street. Bill Allen [New Party member] and I dash round in a cab. John is at the House but Allan Young is up with Esther. He descends to the dining room looking pale and on the verge of a nervous breakdown. We say that Tom suggests that they should not openly resign at this moment, but "suspend" their resignation until December 1, by which date they will be able to see whether their suspicions of our fascism are in fact justified. Allan might have accepted this, but at that moment John Strachey enters. Tremulous and uncouth he sits down and I repeat my piece. He says that it would be impossible for him to retain his name on a Party while taking no active direction of that Party's affairs. He would feel that in his absence we were doing things, with his name pledged, of which he would deeply disapprove. He then begins, quivering with emotion, to indicate some of the directions in which Tom has of late abandoned the sacred cause of the worker. He says that ever since his illness he has been a different man. His faith has left him. He is acquiring a Tory mind. It is a reversion to type. He considers socialism a "pathological condition". John much dislikes being pathological. His great hirsute hands twitched neurotically as he explained to us, with trembling voice, how unpathological he really was.

Undoubtedly the defection of John and his statement that we are turning fascist will do enormous electoral harm to the Party. Politically, however, it will place Tom in a position where, with greater ease, he can adhere to Lloyd George and Winston. I think that John and Allan are inspired with passionate sincerity. Subconsciously, however, Tom's autocratic methods and biting tongue have frayed their vanity and their nerves. I see us from this moment heading straight for Tory Socialism.

Diary *July 30, 1931*

To luncheon with the Huntingtons [Chairman of Putnam, the publishers] to meet James Joyce. We await the arrival of this mysterious celebrity in a drawing-room heavy with the scent of Madonna lilies. Suddenly a sound is heard on the staircase. We stop talking and rise. Mrs Joyce enters followed by her husband. A young looking woman with the remains of beauty and an Irish accent so marked that she might have been Belgian. Well dressed in the clothes of a young French bourgeoise: an art-nouveau brooch. Joyce himself, aloof and blind, follows her. My first impression is of a slightly bearded spinster: my second is of Willie King [authority on Sèvres porcelain] made up like Philip II; my third of some thin bird, peeking, crooked, reserved, violent and timid. Little claw hands. So blind that he stares away from one at a tangent, like a very thin owl.

We go down to luncheon. Gladys Huntington in her excitement talks to Joyce in a very shrill voice on the subject of [Italo] Svevo. She bursts into Italian. I catch the fact that Joyce is contradicting Gladys pretty sharply, and withal with bored indifference, Desmond [MacCarthy] weighs in with a talk about Charles Peace and the Partridge murder. I describe the latter with great verve and acumen.

"Are you," I say to Joyce, hoping to draw him into conversation, "are you interested in murders?" "Not," he answers, with the gesture of a governess shutting the piano, "not in the very least." The failure of that opening leads to Desmond starting on the subject of Sir Richard and Lady Burton. The fact that Burton was once consul at Trieste sends a pallid but very fleeting light of interest across the pinched features of Joyce. It is quickly gone. "Are you interested," asks Desmond, "in Burton?" "Not," answers Joyce, "in the very least." He is not a rude man: he manages to hide his dislike of the English in general and of the literary English in particular. But he is a difficult man to talk to. "Joyce," as Desmond remarked afterwards, "is not a very *convenient* guest at luncheon."

> *On August 22 H.N. left the* Standard *to edit Mosley's* Action, *the journal of the New Party. The first number appeared some six weeks later. On August 24 Ramsay MacDonald abruptly formed a Coalition Government, with himself as Prime Minister, to the consternation of the Labour Party, most of whose members split from him.*

H.N. *to* V.S-W.   *September 8, 1931*
                    Action, 5 Gordon Square, WC1

Madam,
I understand that you are prepared to contribute to this journal a weekly article containing hints to the amateur gardener.

This article should contain 650 words, and the ms of the first article should be received at this office not later than September 22nd.

The fee payable to you for this contribution will be £0.0.0.

Diary   *September 22, 1931*

Party meeting at 11.30. We discuss *fascismo*. Tom says the young Tories are forcing on an Election for October. He is being approached on all sides to join some combination. The increase in communism will be rapid and immense. But can we counter this by fascism? And will not the Conservative element be represented not by dynamic force but by sheer static obstruction? The worst of it is that the communists will collar our imaginative appeal to youth, novelty and excitement. We decide to call the Youth Movement the Volts (Vigour-order-loyalty-triumph).

Diary   *September 26, 1931*

Vita goes off by Folkestone this afternoon for a hiking tour of Provence. Going up in the train I think what it is that makes us so indispensable to each other. I think it is this. (a) That we each respect in the other some central core of reality. (b) Neither of us would find it easy to define that core, but we are aware of it and the other knows that it is there and recognised. This produces a feeling of not having to strive or to posture. It is not a question of insincerity or sincerity. It is merely that when with each other we relax completely. Thus we get the maximum satisfaction out of our static relationship. (c) Yet our relations are also dynamic. We stimulate each other. We are not merely intellectual chairs to each other, we are intellectual exercise. I think it is the perfect adjustment between these two elements, the static and the dynamic, which creates such harmony in our lives. No one else knows or understands.

*Find that we have had orders for 110,000 copies of *Action*. This of course is solely on the sale or return basis and does not mean a guaranteed circulation of even half that figure. But it does mean that the newsagents think *a priori* that there is a prospect of disposing of something like that number.*

Diary   *October 1, 1931*

Lunch with Sibyl Colefax. A good party. Lady Castlerosse, Diana Cooper, Charlie Chaplin, H. G. Wells, Tom Mosley. We discuss fame. We all agree that we should like to be famous but that we should not like to be recognised. Charlie Chaplin told us how he never realised at first that he was a famous man. He worked on quietly at Los Angeles staying at the Athletic Club. Then suddenly he went on a holiday to New York. He then saw "Charlie Chaplins" everywhere – in chocolate, in soap, on hoardings, "and elderly bankers imitated me to amuse their children". Yet he himself did not know a soul in New York. He walked through the streets where he was famous and yet unknown. He at once went to the photographer and had himself photographed as he really is.

Polling Day in the General Election of 1931 was on October 27th. Ramsay MacDonald asked the country to return him as the head of the National Government. He won the Election overwhelmingly.

The New Party's showing was abysmal. All of their 24 candidates lost, and 22 forfeited their deposits. H.N. stood as the New Party candidate for the Combined English Universities; he came last of five candidates, with a vote of 461. Mosley was also defeated, and at the bottom of the poll. Soon afterwards Action *ceased publication.*

Diary   *October 28, 1931*

Wake up to read the election returns. A panic swing towards the Tories. Henderson and most of the Labour ministers out. The whole thing is so absurd and sensational that there is little to be said about it. From the purely selfish point of view I am glad of the Tory land-slide since it will restore monetary confidence and its very immensity covers up our own discomfiture. Tom is out at Stoke and we have done hopelessly all along the line. Even the communists have done better than we have. The National Government will have a majority of some 500 and the Socialists are reduced to 50. Considering that the Labour Party have polled nearly seven million votes to the fourteen million of the National Government, this proportion is absurd. It really is most disquieting that at this crisis of our history we should have a purely one party House of Commons and no strong Opposition. I feel more than ever glad that I should have courted disaster with the New Party than achieved success under this Tory ramp.

Diary   *November 2, 1931*

Life is a busy but I am glad to say a mottled business. Hell! Heaven! I am going through a bad period. A period of ill success. I am so used to being successful that failure gives me indigestion. This does not arise from my forfeiting my deposit in the Election. I had foreseen that. It arises from my having been unable to control Hamlyn [General Manager of *Action*] or run the paper in a really efficient manner. The fact is that I am not a journalist and as such not well suited to be a man who runs a weekly. I see both sides of every question. That is a mistake. Yet I should like to make something of this paper. The difficulty is that I am backed and financed by a political party. And even then it is not a party but rather a sly little movement. I am loyal to Tom since I have an affection for him. But I realise that his ideas are divergent from my own. He has no political judgement. He believes in fascism. I don't. I loathe it. And I apprehend that the conflict between the intellectual and the physical side of the N.P. may develop into something rather acute.

Diary   *November 24, 1931*

Lunch with Tom and Cimmie over their garage, I beg Tom not to get muddled up with this fascist crowd. I say that in the first place fascism is not suited to England. He says he feels no resentment: that he had expected that the effect of his defeat would be to throw him into a life of pleasure: on the contrary, he feels bored now with night clubs and more interested than ever in serious things. I say that he must now acquire a reputation of seriousness at any cost. That he is destined to lead the Tory Party (at this, Cimmie, who is violently anti-Tory screams aloud) – and that he must rest in patience till that moment comes, and meanwhile travel and write books.

We go on to a Party Meeting. The accounts disclose that we have £1,000 left. That this sum will not suffice to pay the lease and other commitments due in March, and that therefore the Party will have to borrow or steal from the Newspaper fund. As our own circulation has dropped to 30,000 and we are running at a loss of £1,000 a month, the prospect is gloomy.

Diary   *December 23, 1931*

A gloomy day spent in giving notice to the [*Action*] staff. I only hope there will be money enough to pay them good compensation. Vita visits my bank and extracts an unwilling loan from them. My future financial prospects are so black that I groan to gaze into the abyss. I feel irreparably shallow.

Of all my years this has been the most unfortunate. Everything has gone wrong. I have lost not only my fortune, but much of my reputation. I incurred enmities: the enmity of Lord Beaverbrook; the enmity of the B.B.C. [Sir John Reith terminated his contract when H.N. praised *Ulysses* in a broadcast] and the Athenaeum Club; the enmity of several stuffies. I left the *Evening Standard*, I failed in my Election, I failed over *Action*. I have been inexpedient throughout. My connection with Tom Mosley has done me harm. I am thought trashy and a little mad. I have been reckless and arrogant. I have been silly. I must recapture my reputation. I must be cautious and more serious. I must not try to do so much, and must endeavour to do what I do with greater depth and application. I must avoid the superficial.

Yet in spite of all this – what fun life is!

> In January 1932 H.N. and Mosley went to Rome to study
> Fascism at close quarters, and H.N. went on alone to
> Berlin. He was horrified by what he saw, but Mosley was
> greatly stimulated. The New Party was approaching its
> end, and H.N. felt that he had made a fool of himself.

A fine cold morning. Walk up to the Arc de Triomphe through the Tuileries gardens. Memories of my past life: the toy shop in the Rue de Rivoli when we stayed at the Embassy in 1891 [when he was five and his uncle was British Ambassador]: the time that Reggie [Cooper, H.N.'s oldest friend] and I stayed at Versailles and bicycled into Paris every morning leaving our bicycles at the Gare St Lazare: then the successive times at Jeanne [de Hénaut's who presided over an academy for Foreign Office candidates]: the walk along the Avenue des Acacias learning French vocabularies: the Peace Conference. Thinking of these things I see little children scudding little chips of ice over the round pond. They swirl and tinkle. The fountain clears a space for itself on the pond, blowing sideways. *J'ai plus de souvenirs que si j'avais mille ans* [Baudelaire].

I walk thus, *parmi les avoines folles*, to the Hotel Napoleon. I am taken up to Tom's room. He is in blue pyjamas having only just arisen from sleep. He had spent *réveillon* at the Fabre-Luces and been kept up doing *jeux de société* till 8 a.m. He looks pale. Walk down again the Avenue Friedland and the Faubourg St Honoré. Again these incessant memories – the insistence of which show me how much I now regret the past. The tricolor in the January sun. The swept courtyard of the Embassy. The tug always at my heart of diplomacy in all its forms.

To the Gare de Lyons. The Rome Express, magnificently aligned, waits to receive me and me alone. I occupy the whole of one coach and a very little Frenchman occupies the whole of another coach. Read. Dine lonelily and well. Sleep.

Diary   *January 5, 1932*
                                               Rome

Tom talks to me about his impressions. He feels that one of our disadvantages as compared with these people is actual costs. In Italy you can run even a daily paper at a little loss. Our own compositors' union is so exacting that we can never compete with the great combines. He believes therefore in the future of our clubs. He feels that we should have two categories: one the Nupa [Youth Movement] clubs, and the other Young England clubs. The latter would be wholly unpolitical. The former would correspond to the S.S. or *Schutzstaffel* organisation of the Nazis. Christopher [Hobhouse, the author] insists that the movement should be working-class. I insist that it should be constitutional and that Tom should enter Parliament. He thinks he could do so with the backing of Winston and the Harmsworth press.

Diary   *January 6, 1932*
                                               Rome

Spend most of the day reading *fascisti* pamphlets. They certainly have turned the whole country into an army. From cradle to grave one is cast in the mould of fascismo and there can be no escape. I am much impressed by the efficiency of all this on paper. Yet I wonder how it works in individual lives and shall not feel certain about it until I have lived some time in Italy. It is certainly a socialist experiment in that it destroys individuality. It destroys liberty. Once a person insists on how you are to think he immediately begins to insist on how you are to behave. I admit that under this system you can attain to a degree of energy and efficiency not reached in our own island. And yet, and yet . . . The whole thing is an inverted pyramid.

Tom cannot keep his mind off shock troops, *the arrest of MacDonald and J. H. Thomas [Secretary of State for the Dominions], their internment in the Isle of Wight,* and the roll of drums around Westminster. He is a romantic. That is his great failing.

We dine up high by the Trinita dei Monti. A lovely flat with a view one way to the Villa Medici and the other way all over Rome. Signora Sarfatti is there. She is the friend of Mussolini whom we met at the Embassy yesterday. A blonde questing woman, the daughter of a Venetian Jew who married a Jew in Milan. It was there that she helped Mussolini on the *Popolo d'Italia* right back in 1911. She is at present his confidante and must be used by him to bring the gossip of Rome to the Villa Torlonia. She says that Mussolini is the greatest worker ever known: he rides in the morning, then a little fencing, then work, and then after dinner he plays the violin to himself. Tom asks how much sleep he gets. She answers, "Always nine hours". I can see Tom doing sums in his head and concluding that on such a timetable Musso cannot be hard worked at all. Especially as he spends hours on needless interviews.

Diary   *January 7, 1932*
                                                                    Rome

Tom off to Mussolini. He finds him affable, but unimpressive. He advises Tom not to try the military stunt in England.

Diary   *January 9, 1932*
                                                                    Rome

*Lunch with the Schuberts at the German Embassy, a bad villa near the Lateran Palace. They think that Hitler will agree to confirm Hindenberg in his presidency. This will give them another year free from internal disturbance and may lead to a coalition. I am glad to find myself again in the old diplomatic atmosphere – so calm, so quiet, so distinguished. Frau von Schubert stands for all that is best in the old life, and makes me homesick for it. This homesickness is increased by another bludgeon attack upon me in the *Times*. It all comes from me having mentioned [General] Gordon and Lytton Strachey. All I said was that to the modern generation it did not matter in the least whether Gordon was a dipsomaniac, but merely whether he was a real person or only a legend. They have caught on to this to say that I wished to slander Gordon, which was not my intention. I think he was a tiresome man, an egotist and a little mad, but I have no particular feeling against him one way or the other. And here I am being bashed over the head quite gratuitously by the *Times* and the *Morning Post*. No wonder I feel homesick for the orderly privacy of diplomacy. I loathe publicity in any form, as much as father loathed it, yet I seem always to be thrust into publicity of the most unenviable and damaging nature. I know that I have been reckless the last two years and that caution is not among my virtues. But I am not quite so scatter-brain as all that.*

Diary   *January 18, 1932*
                                                          London

Go to see Tom on his return from Italy. He was much inspired by Milan which he found Greek and bracing. He says that Mussolini sent him a message telling him to call himself Fascist. He does not want to do anything at present. What he would like would be to lie low till the autumn, write a book, then rope in Winston Churchill, Lloyd, Rothermere and if possible Beaverbrook, into a League of Youth. Then launch an autumn campaign. He fears, however, that the Harmsworths, being restless folk, cannot be "kept on ice" for so long as the autumn and that we may be forced to do something violent in the spring. It is a bore being thus dependent on the prima donnas of the Press.

H.N. arrived in Berlin on January 22, the very day that Hitler announced that he was a candidate for President, standing against Hindenburg. This time he was defeated.

There was a moment when Hitler stood at the crest of national
emotion. He could then have made either a coup d'état or forced a
coalition with Brüning. He has missed that moment. The intelligent
people feel that the economic situation is so complicated that only
experts should be allowed to deal with it. The unintelligent people
are beginning to feel that Brüning and not Hitler represents the soul
of Germany. In Prussia it is true Hitler is gaining ground. But he is
losing it in Bavaria and Würtemberg which are comparatively
prosperous. Hitlerism, as a doctrine, is a doctrine of despair. I have
the impression that the whole Nazi movement has been a catastrophe
for this country. It has mobilised and coordinated the discontented
into an expectant group: Hitlerism can never satisfy these expecta-
tions: the opinion they have mobilised may in the end swing
suddenly over to communism. And if that be a disaster (as to which
I am still not certain), then Hitler is responsible. The Ambassador
[Sir Horace Rumbold] feels that anything may happen and that the
only certain thing is uncertainty.

*Plant wistaria upon dead apple trees. Feeling depressed. Why? Is
it merely that after the debauchery of Berlin I have a liver reaction?
Or is it that while at Berlin I have been able to push from myself the
realisation of my own practical difficulties and these have swung
back upon me with sudden vigour?*

There is a dead and drowned mouse in the lily-pond. I feel like
that mouse – static, obese and decaying. Viti is calm, comforting
and considerate. And yet (for have I not been reading a batch of
insulting press-cuttings?) life is a drab and dreary thing. I had a
great chance. I have missed it. I have made a fool of myself in every
respect.

> Surely there was a time I might have trod
> The sunlit heights, and from life's dissonance
> Struck one clear chord to reach the ears of God? [Oscar Wilde]

Very glum. Discuss finance. Vita keeps on saying that we have
got enough to go on with. But when one goes into it, that enough
represents only two months. I must get a job. Yet all the jobs which

pay humiliate. And the decent jobs do not pay. Come back to Long Barn. Arrange my books sadly. Weigh myself sadly. Have put on eight pounds. Feel ashamed of myself, my attainments, and my character. Am I a serious person at all? Vita thinks I could make £2,000 by writing a novel. I don't. The discrepancy between these two theories causes me some distress of mind.

Diary   *February 2, 1932*

Go to see Beaverbrook at Stornoway House. He welcomes me with twin opening hands. "My dear Harold, it is good to see you again." He asks me about Germany. He asks me about Tom's personal finances. He says that Tom is an ambitious man whereas he (Beaverbrook) is not an ambitious man. He says that Tom committed errors of tactics which have done him harm. He does not think that this harm is permanent. He thinks I should write a biography of Curzon. He thinks that I exaggerate when I feel that I have lost prestige. He indicates that I might do books for the *Sunday Express*. He exercises his charm which is vital and vivid. He says that we must meet often and again.

Diary   *March 2, 1932*

Lunch with T. S. Eliot. He is very yellow and glum. Perfect manners. He looks like a sacerdotal lawyer – dyspeptic, ascetic, eclectic. Inhibitions. Yet obviously a nice man and a great poet. My admiration for him does not flag. He is without pose and full of poise. He makes one feel that all cleverness is an excuse for thinking hard. He does one good.

Diary   *March 6, 1932*

In the evening Vita and I discuss finance. Our discussion is interrupted by a sudden desire on her part to take the Blue Train to Biarritz, or why not Syracuse, or why, if one has got so far as that, not go to Greece, or the Lebanon? I point out that we CANNOT AFFORD IT – THAT WE ARE POOR PEOPLE THESE DAYS – she says she will make so much money in America [on a lecture tour], and she wants the sun. I long also to go off before I am chained again to an office stool, but it would be madness. We work out that our life costs us no less than £240 a month. That at present we have £600 and about £1,000 owing from America. We do not want to use the latter because of income tax.

Meanwhile Louise [V.S–W.'s lady's-maid] during the day has been spreading out the carpets Viti brought from Streatham [one of Lady Sackville's houses, now for sale]. They are moth-eaten but superb. It is typical of our existence that with no settled income and no certain prospects, we should live in a muddle of museum carpets, ruined castles, and penury. Yet we know very well that all this uncertainty is better for us than a dull and unadventurous security. After dinner we discuss the front of Sissinghurst. We decide to plant a wall of limes, framing the two gables and the arch, and following on to a poplar avenue across the fields. That is our life. Work, uncertainty, and huge capitalistic schemes. And are we wrong? My God! we are not wrong.

Diary   *March 14, 1936*

Feel more happy and healthy than I have felt in my life. This is due to the violet rays at Sissingbags [*sic*], plus lack of unsuccessful occupation. I am doing nothing, therefore I do not fail. I am about to do many things, therefore I am on the verge of success. I know that this verge will not be a very sharp or productive verge. But until I reach it, I feel it will be magnificent, remunerative and calm.

Diary   *April 19, 1932*

I go to the New Party meeting in Great George Street. Tom says that he has been asked by Margesson to rejoin the Tory Party, and that he has been asked to lead the Labour Party. He will do neither of these things. He wishes to coordinate all the fascist groups with Nupa and thus form a central fascist body under his own leadership. I say that I think this is a mistake. He says that it would be impossible for him to re-enter the "machine" of one of the older parties. That by doing so he would again have to place himself in a strait-waistcoat. That he has no desire for power on those terms. That he is convinced that we are entering a phase of abnormality and that he does not wish to be tarred with the brush of the old regime. That he thinks, as leader of the fascists, he could accomplish more than as a party back-bencher, and that in fact he is prepared to run the risk of further failure, ridicule and assault, than to allow the active forces in this country to fall into other hands. I again say that I do not believe this country will ever stand for violence, and that by resorting to violence he will make himself detested by a few and ridiculed by many. He says that may be so but that he is prepared to take the risk. I say that on such paths I cannot follow him. We decide to think it over.

The argument, though painful, is perfectly amicable. The ice cracks at no single moment. Nor do I think that Tom was hurt or imagined for one moment that I was deserting him.

Yet I hated it all, and with battered nerves returned to Cannon Street and took the train home.

Thus ended H.N.'s connection with Mosley's New Party and Mosley himself. At the beginning of April he began his novel Public Faces, *set in the not too distant future of 1939. It is a satirical account of a political crisis, conducted by many of his friends in new roles. It took him three months to write, at the rate of 5,000 words a day. As soon as he finished it, he began to write* Peacemaking.

Diary   *April 11, 1932*

I have been thinking during the last few days about my book. I have now had three good months of quarantine, and feel that I have at last got the poison of journalism out of my system. I can now settle down to write a book. What book? It comes down to doing either a sequel to *Some People* or a novel on a grand scale. I have toyed with the former idea. Yet I am not happy about it. Sequels are in every case bad things. I expended upon *Some People* the best of my autobiographical experience, and the sense of development which gave unity to that book could not be reproduced again in a book dealing only with my middle life. Again, the note of *Some People* is good-humoured irony plus a certain youthful irreverence: I could not, at my age, recapture the exact mood in which it was written, and if I did, the repetition of that mood might prove ungainly and false. In the third place, I have nothing to write about which interests me on the same scale of *Some People* things.

I shall try, therefore, to write a novel. About what? I think that it should be dramatic, even a romantic, novel. Dealing with diplomacy and character. A central figure, intense as Charles Siepmann [Director of Talks at the B.B.C.], who might be a Private Secretary. A dispute, say in Persia. A Secretary of State such as Joynson Hicks [Home Secretary 1924–1929, later Lord Brentford] – unctuous, evangelical, and insincere. A woman Under-Secretary of the type of Hilda Matheson [recently Director of Talks, B.B.C.]. All this could work up into a play eventually. So much for the scaffold: but I must choose a material and a design. There must be a central intellectual theme: and a central emotional theme. I must choose one out of many "ideas" and concentrate on that: the individual versus the democratic machine; something like that. But apart from all this, it is the *key* which I find difficult – whether ironical or romantic or angry.

Diary   *July 19, 1932*

This lovely summer is amazing. Work hard at Chapter 12. Finish *Secretary of State* [altered to *Public Faces* after the lines by W. H. Auden] at 10.40 p.m.

Diary   *July 29, 1932*

Rains. Start my book on the Peace Conference [*Peacemaking*].

Diary   *October 6, 1932*

Paving across the courtyard finished. They begin upon the windows in the porch. Viti and I plant lupins at the end of the moat walk. *Public Faces* published.

Diary   *October 19, 1932*

A lovely day. Round to the *New Statesman*. Kingsley Martin [editor, 1930–1960] indicates that he wants me to become literary editor. That is all very well. But I get £600 a year already from my articles and could not expect to make more than £1,000 a year as Lit. Ed. This would mean that I should gain only £400 a year net and that sum would be absorbed by loss of time and the need to live in London for four days a week. Besides, I think that Raymond [Mortimer] should have that £1,000 a year.

On to Constable's to see Michael Sadleir. He talks about my

Peace Conference book. He agrees that it should be in two parts and that the second part should be my diary as it stands. He says that *Public Faces* is going very well. I say, "How well?" He says that it sold 1,600 copies before publication. I say that Viti's *Family History* [published this year] sold 6,000 copies before publication. He says, "But then she has broken through." I say, "Broken through what?" He says, "The middle-class belt." Buy a pair of shoes at Fortnum and Mason.

Diary   *October 21, 1932*

Over to Churt to see Lloyd George. Motor there with Copper [chauffeur] at the wheel. Arrive at 1.0. Gate-piers with Welsh emblems. Cystus and rosemary. A small house. A parlour-maid. A puff of hot air as I enter. Ll.G.'s study. Ceiling up to the roof. Comfortable arm-chairs. Photograph of A. J. Balfour on his writing table, and an engraving of Bonar Law above it. He rises from his hard Windsor chair. He waddles powerfully as of old.

He talks of Tom Mosley. His lack of judgement, his wasted opportunities, his courage. He talks of his early speeches. "Nobody listened to him, but I did. I knew that that young man always had something to say." About fascism in England, he is not so sure it may not be possible. One doesn't know. "I do not know at this moment what our condition really is. On the surface all seems right enough. But what is happening underneath?"

We go into luncheon. He discusses bores: he says that a man who finds any other man a bore is a fool: no man, once you are alone with him, is a bore: he has always something which he knows better than other people: it is only when he interrupts other and more vital informants that he becomes a bore. He talks of Asquith; his inability to face facts except under pressure. Of [Sir Edward] Grey; his sham honesty. Of Edward VII; his dignity and his shrewdness; how he never treated Ll.G. as monarch to subject, but as old man to young man. "He was irresistible". Of Gladstone; his terrifying eyes. We talk Peace Conference. I go with him back to the study. I produce my thirty questions which I have prepared. He answers glibly. His answers will all be embodied in my book. Main new thing is that he thinks President Wilson had something like a stroke in March [1919]. After April 1 he fell entirely under the influence of Clemenceau.

Ll.G. is on the surface as hearty and brilliant as ever. But one feels it is an effort. I felt he was glad that I did not stay long.

Diary   December 9, 1932

To a party where I meet Mrs D. H. Lawrence. She is much less *hausfrau* than I had supposed. A sharp questing little nose, a bright inquisitive impression, a sense of silliness somewhere, and excess. She talks quite naturally about Lawrence and is clearly pleased at his being the hero of legend. She has a sort of *Egeria* look which must be put on. She says that Lawrence said, "Frieda, if people really knew what you were like, they would strangle you." I say, "Did he say that angrily?" She said, "No – very quietly, after several minutes of deep thought." She talked of how ghastly it was to see all this Lawrence worship now, and then realise that if only this fame had come to him in his lifetime he might have been spared. "We were so poor," she said. "So poor!" "Surely," I said, "you could not have been so very poor at the end?" She laughed. "No," she said, "that was not true what I said just now. We were not poor in the end." Anyway we are both invited to New Mexico.

> *During the first three-and-a-half months of 1933, H.N.
> and Vita went on a lecture tour of the United States and
> Canada. For H.N. it was the first of many visits; for her
> it was the first and last. Their schedule was exhausting,
> and it coincided with a grave economic crisis in America.
> They visited 53 cities, spent 63 nights in the train and
> covered over 30,000 miles.*

Diary   January 5, 1933
                                                                       New York

Wake up at 5.30. Dress and go on deck. It is warm with a faint rain. We are in the East River. By 7.30 it is quite light and two tenders come alongside. We file up for the medical examination and the passports. Having finished the passports we dash out to see the entry into New York. We are intercepted by reporters. We take them to the writing room and sit around a table. They ask us questions.

What do we think of American women? What do we think of the future of marriage?

We drive through Brooklyn in a car. A lovely morning. All very like Berlin. Suddenly as we reach Manhattan Bridge the skyline indents itself for us. Up Broadway and Madison to this hotel. Rooms 1852 1853. Nesting boxes. As we enter the room the telephone rings. Press people arrive. Bootleggers ring up. Social hostesses ring up. There are two telephones, one in each room, and three publicity agents, that of the hotel, that of Doubleday and that of Colston Leigh [lecture agent].

The afternoon is a further succession of journalists, flowers, bell-hops, photographers, telephones. We have no time to unpack and change our clothes.

We go to a suite at the Waldorf Astoria where we dine. Charles Lindbergh and his wife are there.

Lindbergh is a surprise. There is much more in his face than appears from photographs. He has a fine intellectual forehead, a shy engaging smile, windblown hair, a way of tossing his head un-happily, a transparent complexion, thin nervous capable fingers, a loose-jointed shy manner. He looks young with a touch of arrested development. His wife is tiny, shy, timid, retreating, rather inter-ested in books, a tragedy at the corner of her mouth. One thinks of what they have been through and is shy to meet them.

We go on to the Empire State Building. The lights of the great avenues sparkle like fire-flies. But there are great dark patches where there are no fire-flies at all. The great water spaces. The shadows of huge buildings. Little cabs creeping like lice. To bed at 1.0. Not tired. Oh brave new world!

Diary   *January 8, 1933*
                                                     New York

Lunch with Elizabeth Marbury [the author and literary agent who died a fortnight later] at 13 Sutton Place. Find Mrs Vanderbilt there representing society. [Hendrik] Van Loon [the historian] represent-ing literature. Wylie representing journalism – he is editor of the *New York Times*. Miss Marbury is enormous, emphatic, civilised, gay. She says she is 76 and has never been so happy as in the last fifteen years. All passion spent. She abuses all other agents. She wants [V.S-W.'s] *Seducers in Ecuador* put into a play. Van Loon is Dutch but very Americanised. Wylie is pure American.

Now, here were three people corresponding roughly to [James] Garvin, Ethel Smyth and Maynard Keynes. And this, with infinite slowness, was one of the many stories that Wylie told: "That," he said, "reminds me of a story I heard the other day down town. A man is taken from speak-easy to speak-easy. He returns to his wife after having music of negro orchestras drummed into his ears. She says, 'How are you feeling?' He says, 'Rather syncopated.' She looks up 'syncopated' in the dictionary and finds it says 'passing rapidly from bar to bar'." We laugh politely. But it is incredible that such a story should be told by people and to people who are really educated. It is this that I find so trying. They are so slow in conversation that it is like being held up by a horse-dray in a taxi. And then they never listen to what one says oneself.

The depression is dreadful. All the hotels are bankrupt. Most apartments are empty. The great Rockefeller buildings, and the two theatres, are to close down. Rockefeller will lose some £3,000,000 a year by this venture. Four thousand architects are out of work in New York alone.

Diary   *January 13, 1933*
                                                    New York

They do not give you wine to drink at meals. Always water. I gather that this was always more or less so, and that it is not a sign of Prohibition. But none the less it is a fact that we do get far less to drink than we do in Europe and that it is a great economy and a saving of health.

Diary   *January 14, 1933*
                                                     Boston

Stop at the Library [in Copley Square] and look at Sargent's pictures. They are in a bad narrow hall above a staircase and ill-lit. He has embossed some of them and there is a faint tinge about them of art nouveau. Very disappointing. Vita does not want to go to the Art Gallery as the Knole tapestry is there and she hates it.

Diary   *January 26, 1933*
Boston–Washington

Leave Boston by the "Senator" at noon. We take the coast route. The beauty of the Massachusetts coast line. Indented lagoons with little wooded islands and white houses and churches. Something hard and small and moving like early settlers. Not a trace of vulgarity or emphasis.

Luncheon in the train. Shrimp cocktail, mackerel, and salad. Water. I sit opposite a young financier. He says that the provincial banks are going smash by the hundred. He says that the depression is passing slowly westward like an epidemic and has now settled in all its intensity upon St Louis.

Get to Washington at 9.55. Drive to the Embassy. Viti has recovered from her cold. We retire and read accumulated letters.

Diary   *January 27, 1933*
Washington

Viti and I drive out to Mount Vernon. We stop on the way to let me see the Lincoln memorial and the statue. It is impressive with its sunken eyes and heavy working-man hands. But there is a look of angered despair in the face by which I am not surprised. The dramatic effect is heightened by flood lighting in the roof. Then along the grey Potomac in a gathering snow storm. Mount Vernon is impressive in its simple magnificence. There is a park-like farm with a big estate feel about it. The ceilings and the furniture indicate a high level of culture and taste.

Lunch at the Embassy. Then on to the Senate. The Vice President [Charles Curtis] presides. A bleary, tobacco drugged looking man. He has a wooden mallet which he holds by the hammer end tapping irritably with it against the wood of the desk. Around the tribune sit little boys like the elder sons of peers on the steps of the throne. They wear black plus fours with black woollen stockings and shoes. They giggle and pick their noses. From time to time a Senator beckons to them and they run messages giggling back at their fellows. The desks for the Senators are arranged in a rough semicircle with a gangway down the middle. The room itself is rectilinear and scarcely decorated at all. Two brown-wood roll-top desks are pushed against the wall. There is a hard top light from the glass ceiling and busts along the cornice. Under each desk is a spittoon of green glass. The Senators, when they speak, turn their back upon the President and address each other walking away from their desks. They all look stout, solid, blear-eyed and sulky. [William E.] Borah [Dean of the Senate] is there. He is not what I expected. I expected an ascetic, arrogant, enfevered face: it is just an untidy rather unimportant sort of face, shaking his invincible locks.

We are picked up there by Elizabeth Lindsay [wife of the British Ambassador] and she and Vita drive on to the White House. Negro footmen in dark livery with silver buttons. Aides-de-camp in white gloves and cigarettes. They are given tea. Two negroes stand behind Mr Hoover at attention like eunuchs.

Diary   *February 7, 1933*
Chicago

Wake up to find a blizzard proceeding outside. The whole place howls and whirls and boils. It is like smoke blowing upwards. Lake Michigan is frozen right up to the beach and in ridges in the shape of breakers. The lake further out, where it has always been frozen, is a dark scabby colour. A few cars struggle along Lake Shore Drive, twist and stagger and then get stuck. The snow banks against their mud guards and radiators. Vita has to catch the 11.30 for St Louis. She will not let me go to the station. She disappears into a revolving snow landscape through a revolving glass door.

H.N. to V.S-W. (in Wisconsin)   *February 16, 1933*
British Embassy, Washington

Lunched with Alice Longworth [eldest daughter of Theodore Roosevelt]. My word! How I like that woman! There is a sense of freedom in her plus a sense of background. That I feel is what is missing in this country – that sense of background. Nobody seems to have anything behind their front. Poor people, they feel it them-selves and hence all those pitiful gropings after manor-houses in Wiltshire and parish registers and the Daughters of the Founding Fathers. But Alice Longworth has a world position and it has left her simple and assured and human. Yes, there at least is an American who is unquestionably a woman of importance.

H.N. to V.S-W. (in Columbus, Ohio)   _February 17, 1933_
                                          Charleston, South Carolina

I feel rather guilty as I have been enjoying myself these days and
you must have been having an absolutely foul time. My poor sweet.
It isn't fair. That's what comes of being a celebrity and having a
husband and two children to support.

I went to the train [in Washington] having stolen a large bottle
of brandy.

_H.N. to V.S-W._   _February 18, 1933_
                                          Charleston, South Carolina

Charleston really is delightful. It has personality – which is a thing
most American towns and people lack. The whole place is old in
character and southern. The old atmosphere of lazy, untidy, dignified, lotus-eating, anti-noise and rush. Even their voices are soft.
*They loathe "taste" which they call _Lady's Journal_, and they keep
old Victorian things in their houses so as not to "become period".
Their servants are all black nannies like in magazine stories, but they
refuse to sentimentalize about them. They are infinitely less affected,
more proud, than the denizens of Rye and Broadway.*

Dubose Heywood – author of _Porgy_ [1925] – picked us up. A
very thin, quiet, interesting man. He motored us out to Middleton
Place, some fifteen miles away. We drove through avenues of huge
ilexes draped in Spanish moss. It isn't moss in the least but a hanging
creeper like old man's beard. The effect is as if every tree were
draped in widow's weeds of grey. In detail it is ugly and untidy: in
the mass it is strange and impressive.

Middleton Place was one of the great plantation seats. It is as
romantic in its way as Sissinghurst. Enormous ilexes, eighteen feet
round in the trunk, flank a wide lawn cut up into high beds of
camellias in flower. The terrace drops down to dark lakes 30 feet
below. In front stretches a wide marsh intersected by a broad river.
The marsh used to be a rice field. Six elderly Negroes in blue were
mowing the vast lawns with little tiny moxing machines. The
camellias blazed. The air was damp and heavy with the smell of
olea fragrans or scentive olive – a sprig of which I sent you. We went
into the little house. All very simple. Three rooms with Empire
furniture and shuttered off as if it were blazing hot. Not a touch of

Lady's Journal. The gardens were beautifully kept up and when the azaleas are out it must be amazing. I am not much of one for camellias even in the mass. But there was no nonsense about it.

We came back and I came face to face with Elizabeth Lindsay. We fell into each others arms. I said I had been to Middleton. She said, "Now what did it remind you of?" I said it had reminded me strangely of something but I could not say what. She said, "Well, it's Vita's poem *Sissinghurst.*" Of course it was. She is no fool, that Elizabeth.

I gave my lecture in a lovely Adam hall with old pictures. The whole thing is so effortless and unaffected here. No strain. No noise. I delight in it. We MUST come. They are all longing to see you. Great passion-spenters.

H.N. to V.S-W. (*in Newark, Delaware*)   *February 23, 1933*
                                                                        Cincinnati, Ohio

I confess that I myself find all this slushy adulation very trying – and irritating in the sense that all unrealities are irritating. Of course I know that you and I are very gifted and charming. Only we are not charming in the sort of way these people suppose.

One should remember, however, that if we were lecturing at Cheltenham, Roedean College, Bath and Harrogate we should be faced with just the same vapidity of compliment, by just the same uniformity of faces. I try to concentrate on the really nice people we have met. It is not that these people are really less civilised than similar sorts of people in England. It is just that at home we should be bored stiff by that sort of person, and that here we have the feeling (which may or may not be justified) that there simply does not exist the sort of other person whom we like. If you cut out the territorial aristocracy and the types which have gathered round them in England, and also cut out our scholars and our intellectuals – one would be left with a residue which would be no better than, and possibly worse than, our audiences.

Diary   *March 4, 1933*
Toledo, Ohio

We have luncheon with a Women's Club. Daffodils and wall-flowers on the table. The rest of the guests at little tables all around.

I sit next to a woman in purple silk. "Well, Mr Nicolson, and are you going right out to the coast?" "Yes, Mrs Scinahan, we go to San Francisco, Los Angeles and Pasadena. We then visit the Grand Canyon." "That is swell for you, Mr Nicolson. When I first saw the Grand Canyon I said, 'My, if only Beethoven could have seen this'. You see, I am very musical. I do not know how people can see life steadily unless they are musical. Don't you feel that way, Mr Nicolson?"

Meanwhile the inauguration of President Roosevelt was proceeding in Washington and a huge voice was braying out across the daffodils in their art-ware. *"And now,"* yelled the voice, *"the historic moment is about to arrive. I can see the President-Elect . . ."* The band strikes up at that moment *Hail to the Chief*. My neighbour pauses for a moment while we have the President's inaugural address. It is firm and fine. "It is such a pity," twitters Mrs Scinahan beside me, "that you are only staying such a short time in Toledo, Mr Nicolson. I would wish to have you see our museum here. We have a peristyle of the purest white marble – a thing of utter simplicity but of the greatest beauty. I always say that the really beautiful things in life such as the Sistine Madonna are beautifully simple." *"Small wonder,"* boomed the voice of President Roosevelt, *"that confidence languishes, for it thrives only on honesty, on honour, on the sacredness of obligation, on faithful protection, on unselfish performance . . ."* "You see," whispered Mrs Scinahan, "the peristyle is lit by hidden lights in the cornice. And they change colour, Mr Nicolson, from the hues of sunrise to those of midday and then to sunset. And at night it is all dark blue. Very simple."

I strive to catch the historic words of Roosevelt. "You see, Mr Nicolson," whispered Mrs Scinahan, "our peristyle is a dream in stone. Now I mean that literally. The architect, Mr J. V. Kinhoff, dreamt of that very peristyle. And one day . . ." "Mrs Scinahan," I say firmly, "do you realise that your new President has just proclaimed that he will, if need be, institute a dictatorship?" "My," she said, "now isn't that just too interesting? Not that I care for the radio, Mr Nicolson. We have one, of course, at home above the bathing-pool. It sounds so much better out of doors."

Afterwards, Viti and I have to stand up to say a few words. I get back on them by stating that they have just listened to the most important announcement in American history. We then go to the station and entrain for Detroit.

Diary   *March 13, 1933*
                                                                Cleveland, Ohio

The banks have opened in most places and the people are pouring in with their hoarded gold. Partly patriotism, partly fear of being shown up, but mainly the effect of Roosevelt's wireless address. No man has ever enjoyed such sudden prestige as Franklin Roosevelt. His stocks are right at the top. Even the Senate dare not delay his activity. This will lead to great jealousy on their part when once the crisis is over. They will never forgive him for appealing to the country across their heads.

Diary   *March 15, 1933*
                                                             en route to California

Traverse Illinois and Iowa. A ghastly succession of wooden farms, dump heaps, black soil and dreariness. In the afternoon get to Council Bluffs and then cross the Missouri. A disappointing stream. Enter Omaha. Get out. A magnificent station with Turkey rugs, palm trees, and olive green arm chairs. Why is it that the Americans and the Germans spread themselves in railway stations? Compare the railway station at Omaha with that of Paddington. Yet the latter represents something more important. It is all this desire to impress by externals.

Diary   *March 18, 1933*
                                                                San Francisco

*We are met on the landing by Mr Gaer of the *San Francisco Forum*, a representative of the *San Francisco Examiner*, and a stout gentleman with a carnation who I discover afterwards is the manager of the William Tylor Hotel. We drive off. Vita is silent, looking to right and left in order to catch sight of an earthquake up a side street before it reaches us. She holds her bag tightly in one hand and me in the other in order to jump out quickly with her two possessions once the tremors begin [there had been a serious earthquake a few weeks before]. We reach the hotel. A facade of brick. Now Vita had been told especially that we must go to a steel and not brick hotel. The porter begins to take off our bags, and the second taxi with the manager and his carnation arrives. I murmur feebly, "Is this hotel built of steel?" "Steel and brick," they answer. Dumb victims of an impending earth catastrophe, we enter the hotel. We are taken up to the thirteenth floor where there is a lovely view from a corner window. From there I observe the Pacific. Vita, however, has only observed that we are terribly far off from the ground. "Isn't," she says, "this very high up?" Being a tactful man, and having a bad cold, I do not press the two points which have arisen in my consciousness. I do not say "there is the Pacific" since that would have suggested stout Cortez and Vita at the moment is not feeling stout in the least. Nor do I suggest that it is very questionable whether in an earthquake it is better to be high up or low down. In the former case there is less to fall on top of one, in the latter case there is less distance for oneself, if it comes to the point, to fall. I avoid these controversial topics and seize the telephone. "Couldn't we have a room lower down?" We can have a room on the fifth floor if we want. I am thus robbed of my view of the Pacific Ocean, but we leave it at that, and the rooms are larger and nicer.*

Diary   *March 28, 1933*
                                             Smoke Tree Ranch, California

We reach Smoke Tree Ranch and are shown our cottage – an asbestos hut with bedrooms, shower room and kitchenette. Mr Doyle, the owner of the ranch, comes to visit us. The desert is all around us with sage bush and verbena in flower. The hills across the plain are pink and crinkled as in Persia. We are very happy. Unpack and write up this diary. We then go across the sand between the little tamarisk hedges and enter Mr Doyle's house. We are given mint julep. We then cross to dinner in the main cottage. Good food. I do not sleep well as the desert air is too exciting. The coyotes howl in the hills.

Diary   *April 1, 1933*
                                                   Grand Canyon, Arizona

We are woken by the conductor demanding tickets. Vita ticks him off proper. A bright fresh morning among pines. The train reaches the Grand Canyon at 8.10 mountain time. We walk to the hotel a few yards away and go on to the terrace from which the Grand Canyon opens before us. It is very like the Devonshire Cliffs near Dawlish only without the sea. It gets less like Dawlish as one looks at it after breakfast, and becomes more like the Grand Canyon in Arizona – twenty Matterhorns blazing with alpine glow and situated many thousand feet below one. We walk on further for a bit and sit under the pines. We find some seeds of unknown plants and a saxifrage. We then walk back to the hotel just in time for a dance of Hopi Indians.

A fat chief in feathers explains in that flat voice assumed by orientals when they know English very well, that the Hopis are a very peaceful tribe and as such have no war dance, but that he will show us the sort of war dance that they would have had had they been a less peaceful tribe. Having given us this bright explanation he starts to yell aloud and shake a cardboard shield and a bow and arrow. Being a stout man, and his assistant brave not being very well, the dance is defective in vigour. There is also an eagle dance and a cow dance – neither of which carry much conviction. A good deal of shuffling in mocassins and shaking of bells and feathers. Vita is deeply impressed by the Grand Canyon. So am I.

They returned home in the 'Bremen' in mid-April to the domestic felicities of Sissinghurst. H.N. began writing his book on Lord Curzon, and finished it by November. They were still worried by their financial problem, and by the continuing problem of H.N.'s future. Which was he to be – a writer who dabbled in politics, or a politician who enjoyed writing?

Diary   *May 9, 1933*

Storm and sun. Ben goes to Brighton to see B.M. [Lady Sackville, Vita's mother] who behaves with devilry by telling him things to put him against his mother and me. Luckily it doesn't work – but it will have been a shock to him and might have had very serious consequences. Feel sick with anger.

Diary   *May 27, 1933*

Go to tea with the Drummonds. [Lord] Eustace Percy there. He walks back with me. He says that the world does not realise how far the capitalist system has really broken down. I say that it is not the old question of rich versus poor, but of man versus the machine. He says that it is merely the old thing of consumption and production in another form. I say, "Is it, Eustace, seriously now?" He says, "No, Harold, it isn't. It is a new factor." We discuss whether economics are a science or an art. We agree that the Victorians regarded it as pat as Latin grammar. Now there is the something unknown. That has rendered economics more dynamic and far less respectable.

I ask him whether he thinks I am lotus-eating by living in the country and doing what I love. He says that serious people ought to withdraw from life nowadays as it is so transitional as to entail insincerity. I feel comforted by him: I am worried about Ben: I am worried about life: and this old friend is calm and sincere. He says what he likes is administration. He should be head of a great university [later he was – Rector of the Newcastle Division of Durham University, 1937–1952]. In spite of his pessimistic views I leave him feeling more confident. As long as we keep our intellectual integrity we shall be all right. I lost it in 1931: I have got it back today.

Diary   *June 16, 1933*

Work hard at *Curzon* [*Curzon, the Last Phase*]. Lady Curzon writes that she is going to write the life herself. That means that she will do his personal side and use all the letters she promised me. This is really not such a blow as it sounds since the book will be mainly a study of post-war diplomacy and I do not wish to cram it with personal detail. Moreover it leaves me free to say what I like. We decided yesterday quite suddenly at luncheon to go off to Italy for three weeks. These improvised excursions are the best. We shall leave on the 25th. [And they returned on July 13th.]

Diary   *June 21, 1933*

Have a long talk with Gladys Marlborough [the second wife of the ninth Duke of Marlborough] about Proust. She had known him for years. She said that his snobbishness was just snobbishness and that there was little more to say about it. He would repeat names to himself succulently. Once she said to him that she thought the Duke of Northumberland had a lovely name. He was very excited.

"Tiens," he explained, "je vais l'annoncer." And up he got, flung the door open and yelled, "Madame la Duchesse de Northumberland!" This brought on a fit of coughing and wheezing. She also said that Albert ["Albertine"] was not, as I had been told, a Syrian waiter, but a boy at the Lycée Condorcet. He deliberately made Proust jealous. Proust loved Hardy. He said that *A Pair of Blue Eyes* was of all books the one which he would himself most gladly have written.

Diary   *August 4, 1933*

Wystan Auden reads us some of his new poem in the evening. It is in alliterative prose and divided into Cantos. The idea is Gerald Heard as Virgil guiding him through modern life. It is not so much a defence of communism as an attack upon all the ideas of comfort and complacency which will make communism difficult to achieve in this country. It interests me particularly as showing, at last, that I belong to an older generation. I follow Auden in his derision of patriotism, class distinctions, comfort, and all the ineptitudes of the middle classes. But when he also derides the other soft little harmless things which make my life comfortable I feel a chill autumn wind. I feel that were I a communist, the type of person I should most wish to attack would not be the millionaire or the imperialist, but the soft, reasonable, tolerant, secure, self-satisfied intellectual like Vita and myself. A man like Auden with his fierce repudiation of half-way houses and his gentle integrity makes one feel terribly discontented with one's own smug successfulness. I go to bed feeling terribly Edwardian and back-number, and yet, thank God, delighted that people like Wystan Auden should actually exist.

Diary   *August 26, 1933*

After luncheon at Lympne [Sir Philip Sassoon's house] Colonel T. E. Lawrence, the uncrowned king of Arabia, arrives. He is dressed in an Air Force uniform which is very hot. Unlike other privates in the Air Force he wears his heavy uniform when he goes out to tea. He has become stockier and squarer. The sliding, lurcher effect, is gone. A bull terrier in place of a saluki.

Diary *October 11, 1933*

Go to see Tom Mosley at Ebury Street. He has had a bad back and is lying down. One of his fascist lieutenants is there but leaves us. He says he is making great progress in town and country alike. He gets very little money from the capitalists but relies on canteens and subscriptions. His aim is to build up from below gradually, and not to impose construction from above as we did in New Party days. Whenever anything happens to remind him of Cimmie [who died five months earlier aged 34], a spasm of pain twitches across his face. He looked ill and pasty. He has become an excellent father and plays with the children. Cimmie's body is still at Cliveden in the chapel, and he visits it once a week.

Then to the London Library. H. A. L. Fisher [the historian] in the chair. He talks to me afterwards about Curzon. He says he was above all a *savant* and an historian and not a man of action. That he would bore the Cabinet by endless discourses, and when asked for his policy would look disconcerted and astonished. Fisher never once knew Lloyd George to be rude to Curzon.

Diary *October 27, 1933*

Viti gets a letter from her French bank saying she has a balance there of £2,600. We decide on this that I shall NOT have to sell myself to Beaverbrook. I am immensely relieved. The dread of the ordeal and humiliation had been hanging over me like a sullen cloud. Work hard and cheerfully at Chapter IX [of *Curzon*]. Very cold and damp. In the afternoon plant irises and mark out the path in the kitchen garden.

Diary *November 23, 1933*

Read through the whole of *Curzon*. A most disappointing book. It falls between two stools. It is too detailed and historical for the ordinary reader, and not documented enough for the student or as a work of reference. If I could be certain of getting the papers out of Lady Curzon I should write the whole thing over again. She is a most tiresome and inconsiderate woman.

Diary   *December 24, 1933*

I have got into the way of taking my happiness for granted. Yet Viti is not a person one can take for granted. She really does not care for the domestic affections. She would like life to be conducted on a series of *grandes passions*. Or she thinks she would. In practice, had I been a passionate man, I should have suffered tortures of jealousy on her behalf, have made endless scenes, and we should now have separated, I living in Montevideo as H.M. Minister and she breeding Samoyeds in the Gobi Desert.

Diary   *December 31, 1933*

A year coloured by two anxieties, some disappointments and much pleasure. The first anxiety was Niggs' illness [appendicitis], which caused us agony at the time but which has left no traces. The second has been money worry. By giving up what B.M. ought to pay us under settlements we are flung back upon what we can make. It is quite clear that as long as B.M. lives and unless we begin to make more money by books, we are in for a very difficult time. This for me is a constant anxiety. Vita takes it more calmly. B.M. is likely to live five more years at least [Lady Sackville died two years later] and to become more and more paranoiac. No job that I could get in London would really make the difference unless I sold myself to Beaverbrook which I cannot face. Thus at the back of all our life is a sense of worry and possible disaster.

In addition to all this there is the sad feeling that I have not made the best of my life. I cannot write better than I write now, and my best is little more than hack-work. My three books on diplomacy will have a certain value since they represent experience, study, and a certain amount of practical reflection. But they are not good enough to justify my having cut adrift from public service. Had I remained in diplomacy I should have had at least the illusion of progress. The horrors of age would have been compensated for by material rewards. I should have been soothed by the fallacy that "Minister", "Ambassador" etc. did represent some sort of progression, some rising scale of achievement. Yet would I *really* have been lulled by such a fallacy? I do not think so. The constant work might have given me the illusion of creative activity, whereas the self-centred work that I do now seldom gives me that illusion. On the other hand, I should have ruined my domestic happiness and sacrificed much personal enjoyment. It would not be true to say that I "regret" having left diplomacy. What I regret is that I did not from the first devote my energy to some profession which could have been combined with my present sort of life.

H.N. and Vita, and his sister Gwen, went to Italy in February, and from there to Morocco, where he had spent much of his childhood. He conceived the idea of a six-volume autobiography, but did not pursue it. After a severe but short illness, he returned to Sissinghurst for the summer.

Diary   *January 1, 1934*

My New Year Resolutions are (1) Not to drink at luncheon any alcoholic beverages (2) Not to light a cigarette until a meal is over.

Diary   *January 13, 1934*

Go to Hackwood to stay with Lady Curzon. From Basingstoke I have to take a taxi. The hall, which in Curzon's day I remember bright with candelabra and tapestry, is lit by a single lamp. A bad butler; half the rooms shut up. I go through the photograph albums and find some good illustrations. Lady C. tells me stories about C. Few that I have not heard before. Says that his mother was very fussy and meticulous. Says that he took her down to the vault at Kedleston, and placing his hand on one of the niches, said "This, Gracie dearest, is reserved for you." In fact he had placed in the niche a large Foreign Office envelope on which he had scrawled in blue pencil "Reserved for the second Lady Curzon". After dinner I read to her the nicer passages in my book. It goes well.

Diary   *January 14, 1934*

Establish myself in the little library and go through the Curzon papers. I work at it all day. There are all the letters received by him during the period I cover. Very useful especially letters from Winston and Lloyd George. Finish just before dinner. Read after dinner the first chapter to Lady Curzon. I can see that she is hurt and furious. But she keeps her temper.

H.N. to V.S-W.   February 1, 1934
                                                    4, King's Bench Walk, EC4

Your telegram arrived saying that you have taken the Castello [at Portofino]. Well, I am all for that sort of thing, as you know. I liked being turned out of my dear little suburban home [Long Barn] and made to sleep in a ruined tower on a camp-bed [Sissinghurst]. And I see no reason why, in the present state of our finances, you did not buy the Castello outright. You might also lease the Carnarvon Villa in case Olive Rinder comes to stay with us. But I am glad all the same. It all comes from Gwen [St Aubyn] reading the Tauchnitz edition of the works of Elizabeth Russell [whose novel, *The Enchanted April*, was set in the Castello]. I hope you are both very uncomfortable and happy. Bless you both.

H.N. to V.S-W.   February 4, 1934
                                                  Munich, en route to Portofino

I found that Jim Lees-Milne was going over to Paris on the Friday, so I decided to go with him, as it was more or less on my way. I am glad I did, as I had finished everything off in London and we had an amusing and indeed curious day. The crossing was rather rough. I met my pal Sibyl Colefax (you know her I think) and sat and talked with her all the way across. She is a nice pal when one gets her alone like that with no other guests, potential or actual, in the offing. And then at Calais she left me because she travels second. I felt rich and foolish.

Jim had never been to Versailles so we went out there to lunch. It was quite empty and very cold and magnificent. We lunched at the Trianon Palace where the Treaty was presented to the Germans in 1919. Very odd it was after all these years. We walked to the Trianon and then up through the park to the Chateau. I picked up several hints for Sissinghurst. The *Basin de Neptune* would do well in Mr Nicolson's rondel.

Jim is such a charming person. He has a passion for poetry and knows masses about it. I like my friends to be well-read and well-bred. Jim is such an aristocrat in mind and culture. You would like him enormously.

I walked to [James] Joyce's flat in the Rue Gallilée. It is a little furnished flat and stuffy and prim as a hotel bedroom. The sitting room was like a small salon at a provincial hotel, and the unreal effect was increased by there being florists' baskets about with arranged flowers. Joyce glided in. It was evident that he had just been shaving. He was very spruce and nervous and natty. Great rings upon little twitching fingers. Huge concave glasses which flicked reflections of lights as he moved his head like a bird, turning it with that definite insistence to the speaker as blind people do who turn to the sound of the voice. Joyce was wearing large bedroom slippers in check, but except for that one had the strange impression that he had put on his best suit. He was very courteous as shy people are. His beautiful voice trilled on slowly like Anna Livia Plurabelle [in *Finnegans Wake*]. He has the most lovely voice I know – liquid and soft with undercurrents of gurgle.

He told me how the ban had been removed from *Ulysses* (Oolissays, he calls it) in America. He had hopes of having it removed in London also and was in negotiation with John Lane. He seemed rather helpless and ignorant about it all, and anxious to talk to me. One has the feeling that he is surrounded with a group of worshippers and that he has little contact with reality. This impression of something unreal was increased by the atmosphere of the room, the mimosa with its ribbon, the bird-like twitchings of Joyce, the glint of his glasses, and the feeling that they [Joyce and his son] were both listening for something in the house – a shriek of maniac laughter from the daughter along the passage. He told me that a man had taken Oolissays to the Vatican and had hid it in the cover of a prayer book, and that it had been blessed in such a disguise by the Pope. He was half-amused by this and half-impressed. He saw that I would think it funny, and at the same time he did not think it wholly funny himself. It was almost as if he had told me the story in the belief that it might help to lift the ban in England.

My impression of the Rue Gallilée was the impression of a very nervous and refined animal – a gazelle in a drawing-room. His blindness increases that impression. I suppose he is a real person somewhere, but I feel that I have never spent half-an-hour with anyone and been left with an impression of such brittle and vulnerable strangeness.

Drive up to Max Beerbohm's villa [at Rapallo]. He meets us. It is a
shock. He is quite round; his cheeks have chubbed round a scarlet
nose like two melons with a peppercorn between them. And his
head has sunk sideways a trifle – a very different thing from the neat
slim seductive person I first remember. Mrs Beerbohm appears
straw-coloured and *affairée*. Then Gerhart Hauptmann [the German dramatist] and his wife. He is more magnificent than ever. A
huge grey frock-coat of which the waistcoat buttons up almost to the
chin disclosing a little black stock from which hangs a huge *catena*
of tortoiseshell at the end of which is (as I later observe) a flat gold
watch.

We go up to the little house for luncheon. It is almost unbearably
hot, but the food and wine are excellent. Hauptmann talks a great
deal and very simply. He talks about the lack of harmony in the
German character. "But you," I say to him, "seem to be harmony
personified." "Yes," he answers, "*aber nach siebzig jahre be-
strebungen* [but after exerting myself for seventy years]." Max,
who speaks no German, says little, and in fact I scarcely had a word
with him.

*I leave the Castello; Vita and Gwen remaining on till tomorrow.
I take the train for Genoa and at Genoa I take a Pullman car which
provides an excellent luncheon and lands me at Beaulieu at 2.45 or
so. Met by Gerald Haxton [Somerset Maugham's secretary]. The
King of Siam is expected and there are people in uniform in front of
the waiting room and a red carpet. Drive to Villa Mauresaue
[Somerset Maugham's villa at] Cap Ferrat. Willy Maugham plays
billards with Gerald for a bit and I read my beloved Proust. The
house is all white and furnished with Chinese things of great value
and therefore very few. A lovely house.* We motor into Nice and
then on to Cannes where at the Carlton bar we meet Michael Arlen
and his wife. Dine with them. Willy Maugham tells me two stories
about Lily Langtry. They were crossing to America together and
one night on deck she mentioned a man called Eckmühl, or some-

thing like that. Willy said he had never heard of Eckmühl. "But," said Mrs Langtry, "he was famous on two continents." "And why was he famous?" asked Willy. "I loved him," she answered quite simply. Then there was another story. She had an affair with the Crown Prince Rudolf or Archduke Leopold or someone – anyway a potent potentate to be. They were sitting in front of the fire and had a row. She took off a huge emerald ring which he had given her and cast it into the flames. He immediately dropped down on his knees and began to rummage in the ashes. "Naturally," said Mrs Langtry, "I couldn't love him again."

Michael Arlen is one of the few writers who have had the sense to realize that his great vogue was not permanent, and that he must treat his income as capital. Thus although he was at one time making about £20,000 a year, I doubt whether he actually earns today more than £1,200. But he has investments. He is a decent companionable person, clever and intelligent. The two so seldom go together.

Diary   *February 11, 1934*
                                                              Cap Ferrat

Since I left Munich – and in this sunshine – an idea has been forming in my mind. "I shall," I said suddenly to myself, "write an auto-biography in six volumes. It will be called F.A. or *Fictional Auto-biography*. It will be dedicated to Viti."

Since then the thing has seldom been absent from my mind, and I see the whole scheme as a vast undertaking stretching over ten years. Primarily it will be a study in mutations. But I shall try and give to it a serious philosophical shape. I may be wrong, but I feel in the last year I have found myself. And if my present mood of energy and confidence persists, then I shall bring the whole thing off.

Curiously enough, the idea has shown me one thing clearly. I have been toying with the theory that when B.M. dies I shall go into politics, and many of my day-dreams have centred upon the picture of my returning to the Foreign Office as Secretary of State. But now that I am obsessed by The IDEA all of this seems perfectly trivial, and is disclosed as an attempt to solace myself for not writing better by the illusion that I am really a man of action. Thus I now see six volumes ahead of me – *à la recherche du temps perdu*. Tangier fits in beautifully for this.

Diary   *February 18, 1934*
                                                  Marrakesh, Morocco

Begin taking notes for my *magnum opus*. Rather appalled by its hugeness. After luncheon we go down to the town. The [Atlas] mountains are visible and it is very warm. Walk about the market. There are story tellers and snake-charmers and conjurers. The whole atmosphere is unchanged since thirty years ago. A lovely new moon in the evening. Please God make me able to do my *magnum opus*.

Diary   *February 19, 1934*
                                                  Marrakesh, Morocco

Is the book to be fictional or accurate? There is much I do not mind saying about myself but much which would, if truly told, cause trouble to other people. The only standard, I think, is to expose myself to any amount of shame but to disguise other people so that they will not get involved in my humiliations. Yet the book will be nothing if it is not true.

   Proust was not honest enough. If I do not possess his talent, I do possess far more courage. I have a good memory, an observant nature, and have lived through one of the most interesting fifty years in the history of human civilisation. If I can reproduce those years in a really sincere form I shall have contributed something to human understanding. But can I be sincere without wounding people less pachydermatous than myself? The only thing about which I know anything is myself. Yet I was not alone.

Diary   *March 10, 1934*
                                                              Tangier

My ear, which was stung at Fez, has begun to suppurate. I do not know how to treat it and send for the doctor. Spend the morning working on my proofs [of *Curzon*, published on May 10].

Diary   *March 19, 1934*
                                                              London

Go to see Knuthsen [H.N.'s doctor, Sir Louis Knuthsen]. As I enter he says, "You're ill!" "No," I answer, "I am not ill. In fact I have just eaten the largest luncheon I have ever eaten." "Sit down," he says, taking my pulse and at the same time thrusting a thermometer into my mouth. "Thought so," he says, releasing the pulse. "Over 100". "Thought so," he says, glancing at the thermometer, "101. Now let's look at the ear". He thinks I have got staphylococcus poisoning and tells me to go straight to bed. In the early morning my temperature goes down to 98°. I therefore get up intending to see him at 2.30. But by then I feel groggy, take my temperature again, and find it nearly 104. I telephone to Knuthsen saying this. He fixes me up with a room in a nursing-home in Manchester Street where I am to go at 4 p.m.

Spend the interval writing my Will, instructions to Christopher Hobhouse etc. These may be the last words I ever type on my beloved Tikki [typewriter]. I am not really jumpy, which is strange, rather excited and amused. I wish V. were here, but it would fuss her terribly to telegraph tonight when she is so far away [she was motoring home through Provence]. If I am not well, I shall telegraph to her tomorrow morning. But even if I am a corpse before she arrives, I have nothing to say to her which she doesn't know – immortal love, immortal gratitude. These cannot die.

Diary   *March 24, 1934*

In the night the crisis comes. I am sick and feverish and pour with sweat. Very apprehensive and nightmarey. Dim edges of consciousness flickering like a battlefield. Very horrible. In the morning I recover. My temperature drops to normal.

> *At the end of June, he was invited to write the life of the American Dwight Morrow (1873–1931), lawyer, financier, and diplomat; a man Walter Lippmann described as "a public figure of the first magnitude". H.N. had met him once at the London Conference in 1930. To gather material for the book, H.N. went to America in September and stayed with Mrs Morrow, whose daughter had married Charles Lindbergh.*

Diary   *June 26, 1934*

Lunch at Morgan, Grenfell at 23 Great Winchester Street [the finance-house associated with J. P. Morgan & Co. of New York, of which Morrow was a partner]. After luncheon Teddy Grenfell takes me into another room and shows me a letter to him from Mrs Dwight Morrow. "Will I write the biography of her husband?" I reply that the idea appeals to me. That, however, it will entail visiting New York and Mexico. That this means loss of income here and expenses there. I should have to be indemnified for these expenses. He asks me to think it over. I am attracted to the idea, as I admired Morrow and want to write a book about an American. It will have a small success here but should go well in America. But he was a fine man and I should like to do it. The difficulty is that if I have my expenses paid I shall lose something of my independence and that unless I have my expenses paid I can do nothing.

Diary   *August 13, 1934*

Finish the main skeleton of my Morrow notes. I can now begin on the bricks.

Diary   *August 22, 1934*

Dread going to America and being parted from Viti. It is like a dark cloud ahead. Yet if I say so, she will feel she ought to come with me which is impossible. Depressed also about the Morrow book. At the Garrick I met Constant Huntington who, as an American, gave me glum advice. He says I shall never be able to capture the American background and that if I try to do so they will think I am being patronising. I must expect great prejudice in the U.S.A. against my doing it at all. I felt diffident about that side from the first. God grant that I make a good book of it – mainly for Mrs Morrow's sake. It is so bold of her to suggest me and I know all too well that her friends and family will reproach her for it. I must try and make this the best book I have written.

　　I have left active life too soon. I could have done this biography business when 60, and devoted these thirteen years to real active work.

H.N. to V.S-W.   *September 16, 1934*
                                            Berengaria, one day out

It was slightly foggy as we approached Cherbourg. We swung into the outer harbour and I watched the tender approaching. I remember how in the *Bremen* I had leaned over and seen Ben and Niggs on that tender. *J'avais pitié de moi.* I entered the bar and ordered a martini. That made me feel better, and when I felt the throb of engines again I faced my departure with emotion but not in despair. For half an hour I paced the deck seeing the lights fling out sudden appeals. And then I said goodbye to my really beloved continent and retired to my cabin.

H.N. to V.S-W. *September 23, 1934*
Deacon Brown's Point, North Haven, Maine

*I pinched the blind [in the train] and pulled it up. A Scotch mist and by the railway embankment masses of stunted golden rod with rain drops hanging. We were met by the captain of the Morrow's [launch] *St Michael*, by a man I could not make out, by another man I could not make out and by a third man I could not make out. Anyhow I shake hands all round and if I include a chauffeur here and there what does it matter in this egalitarian country.

I walked across to the cable office and sent B.M. a many happy returns cable. The man there was helpful in the best American way. "Now see here," he said, "when exactly do you wish this dame to receive your message." I said that her birthday was September 23. "Is that so?" he commented. "But you see," I said, "I am not sure whether in England they deliver telegrams on a Sunday." "Is that so?" he said. "Well now you just leave it to me. With our deferred rate, we can make certain sure that the lady gets her message before she retires for the night." I must say, there is something about this side of American manners which attracts me strongly. It has nothing about it of the prim self-consciousness of the English petty official.*

We went down to the little pier where something between a yacht and a steam launch awaited us. The Scotch mist hung over the little harbour and the spars and the rigging of a little yacht at anchor was hung with heavy drops. We hummed out into a satin sea, accompanied by a soft circle of fog. The islands are some eight miles from the mainland and I enjoyed the forty odd minutes which it took to creep cautiously towards them. We swung between two islands and across to a third where there was a landing stage. A station car was waiting for us. We drove in and out of little bays with pines down to the water and eventually the pines became tidier and there were sweeps of mown grass between the plantations. Then we swept on to the house. It was built by [Chester] Aldrich and is charming. It is of wood and has shingle sides. Rocks and islands at every angle and the sea splashing in and out of the dahlias.

Mrs Morrow advanced to meet us at the gate. A little woman, neat and ugly. She was in quite a state of excitement at my arrival. She had not slept all night. I feel that this book means so very much to her. I pray that I shall not disappoint her. She worships her husband's memory, but is intelligent enough not to wish to control what I write.

The Lindberghs are in California and are coming back shortly. I gather they will be at Englewood [New Jersey] all through the time I am there.

H.N. to V.S-W.   *September 30, 1934*
                              Next Day Hill, Englewood, New Jersey

As we approached Epping Forest (since it is in such terms that you must visualise this place), a man at the gate waved us on with an electric torch. To be accurate, there is no gate, only two piers and a a little hutch in which the detectives group and grouse. Banks, the butler, was waiting. "Mrs Morrow," he said, "is dining out with Mr Lamont [Chairman of J. P. Morgan and Co.]. Colonel and Mrs Lindbergh are here." He led the way through the Home and Garden Hall to the Home and Garden boudoir. There was Anne and Charles. Anne like a Geisha – shy, Japanese, clever, gentle – obviously an adorable little person. Charles Lindbergh – slim (though a touch of chubbiness about the cheek), schoolboyish, yet with those delicate prehensile hands which disconcert one's view of him as an inspired mechanic. They were smiling shyly. Lindbergh's hand was resting on the collar of a dog. I had heard about that dog. He has figured prominently in the American newspapers. He is a police dog of enormous proportions. His name is Thor. I smiled at him a little uncertainly. Not for a moment did Lindbergh relax his hold on the collar. It is this monster which guards Lindbergh baby No. 2.

"What a nice dog!" I said.

"You will have to be a little careful at first, Mr Nicolson," he answered.

"Is he very fierce?"

"He's all that. But he will get used to you in time."

"Thor is his name is it not? I read about him in the papers."

I stretched a hand towards him. "Thor!" I said, throwing into the word an appeal for friendship which was profoundly sincere. He then made a noise in his throat such as only tigers make when waiting for their food. It was not a growl, it was not a bark. It was a deep pectoral regurgitation – predatory, savage, hungry. Lindbergh smiled a little uneasily. "It will take him a week or so," he said, "to become accustomed to you." He then released his hold on the collar. I retreated rapidly to the fire place, as if to flick the ash away from my cigarette. Thor stalked towards me. I thought of you and my two sons and Gwen and Rebecca [H.N.'s terrier], and my past life and England's honour. "Thor!" I exclaimed. "Good old man!" The tremor in my voice was very tremulous. Lindbergh watched the scene with alert, but aloof, interest. "If he wags his tail, Mr Nicolson, you need have no fear." Thor wagged his tail and lay down.

I had a stiff whisky-and-soda and talked to Anne. Feeling better after that, I turned to Lindbergh. "What happens," I asked, "if Thor does not wag his tail." "Well," he said, "you must be careful not to pass him. He might get hold of you." "By the throat?" I asked – trying, but not with marked success, to throw a reckless jollity into my tone. "Not necess*a*rily," he answered. "If he does that, you must stay still and holler all you can."

By the time you get this I shall either be front page news, or Thor's chum. I have a lovely suite here. Large sitting-room, superb bathroom, large bedroom. I shall be supremely comfortable. I am here all safe with a super police dog to protect me against gangsters and detectives behind every bush.

H.N. to V.S-W.   *October 1, 1934*
                                                                     Englewood

Lindbergh has an obsession about publicity and I agree with him. He told me that when Coolidge presented him with a medal after his Paris flight he had to do it three times over – once in his study which was the real occasion, and twice on the lawn of the White House for the movie people. "The first time," he said, "I was kind of moved by the thing. After all I was more or less a kid at the time and it seemed sort of solemn to me to be given that thing by the President of the United States. But when we had to go through the whole damned thing again on the lawn – me standing sideways to the President and looking an ass – I felt I couldn't stand for it. Coolidge didn't seem to care or notice. He repeated his speech twice over in just the same words. It seemed a charade to me."

An odd thing. We have breakfast together. The papers are on the table. The Lindbergh case is still front-page news. [The arrest of Bruno Hauptmann, for kidnapping the Lindbergh baby.] It *must* mean something to him. Yet he never glances at them and chatters quite happily to me about Roosevelt and the air-mail contracts. It is not a pose. It is merely a determined habit of ignoring the Press. I like the man. I dare say he has his faults, but I have not yet found them. She is a little angel.

H.N. to V.S-W.   *October 9, 1934*
                                                 Englewood

Yesterday Hauptmann was identified by Lindbergh as possessing the voice he had heard calling in the cemetery [where the ransom money was handed over in April 1932]. Yet this dramatic event did not record itself upon the life here. Lindbergh was at breakfast as usual and thereafter helped me to unload my Leica camera. He is very neat about such things and I am clumsy. He then said, "Well, I have got to go up to New York – want a lift?" I said no. Then I worked hard at my files and at luncheon there was only Anne and me. Towards the end of the luncheon Lindbergh arrived and we chatted quite gaily until coffee came. We had that in the Sun Parlour, and when it was over I rose to go. The moment I had gone I saw him (in the mirror) take her arm and lead her to the study. Obviously he was telling her what happened in the court. But they are splendid in the way that they never intrude this great tragedy on our daily lives. It is real dignity and restraint.

At 3 PM I went out for my walk in the garden. Anne and Jon [two years old] join me. Jon is bad at going down steps and has to turn round and do them on his tummy. He is a dear little boy with the silkiest fair curls. I think of his brother. It is a ghastly thing to have in one's life and I feel profoundly sorry for them. The best way I can show it is by manifesting no curiosity. But it is awkward and rather farcical when I take up the paper at breakfast and it is full of nothing else. "Things seem to be getting rather dangerous in Spain," I say. But I am sure that is the best attitude.

H.N. to V.S-W.   *October 26, 1934*
                                                          Englewood

My God! What a difficult job I have taken on. It seems more and more difficult as I get deeper. And therefore more and more fascinating. Morrow is a Protean figure. There was about him a touch of madness, or epilepsy, or something unhuman and abnormal. Very difficult to convey, but certainly there. He had the mind of a super-criminal and the character of a saint. There is no doubt at all that he was a very great man.

H.N. to V.S-W.   *November 7, 1934*
                                                          Englewood

There was a reception for the Englewood neighbours. In they poured, about eighty of them, and I was introduced to each single one. I got an ache in my face. But how undiscriminating are Americans! A sickly looking dotard in huge glasses assured me of the immense interest taken by Morrow in music. "But surely," I suggested, "he was not really musical." "So people have said, Mr Nicolson; but I assure you that is not true. He would come to our glee-club evenings and beat time with his hand. There was a song called *So Let's Have Another* – it went like this:" (dotard sings drinking-song in undertone with gestures of his right hand as if clinking tankard against tankard). "Not of course that Dwight was in favour of excessive drinking, but he liked the swing of the thing." (Further spectacle of dotard humming and carousing.) "And then he felt that it made people feel human, Mr Nicolson. He was always one for the human side. So that always at *alumni* dinners he would ask the glee-club to sing that song and he would always keep time with it with his fork and knife. I can tell you he was a real man right through." This sort of thing makes me loathe Morrow.

Finally they began to drift away. They went. Mrs Morrow, Miss Shiff [secretary], Anne and I were left alone in the big room. We agree that it had all gone very well. A sepulchral voice broke in on us from outside the window. "Have they all gone?" And in vaulted Lindbergh who had been watching outside. Miss Shiff gazed at him with lustre eyes. He handed her what remained of the caviare sandwiches. "You look all in, Miss Shiff. Have a bite". She bit lovingly.

H.N. to V.S-W.   *November 25, 1934*
                                                            Englewood

In the afternoon I sat with Anne in the Sun Parlour and she went through the notes she had prepared for me. You know, Viti, there is a great difference between an observant and non-observant person. 97% of humanity is non-observant. Anne is observant. She noticed every detail about her father and remembered it. She sat there graceful and shy upon the chintz sofa reading her notes slowly with precision. "He would rub his right forefinger over the back of his left hand as if feeling a lump. When he threw away his newspaper it never fell flat upon the carpet but always remained standing upwards." "He would tear off little bits of paper while talking, roll them into spills, and then work the spills into his ear. These spills would lie about the floor. We hated them." "On Sunday evenings we used to have family prayers. As we got older these prayers became more and more embarrassing and therefore fewer." And then there was a description of family breakfast which was so good that I told her to write it down and I shall produce it in the book just as I did your piece in father's book [*Lord Carnock*].

> *During the two months between his return to England in December 1934 and his next visit to America in February 1935, H.N. wrote ten of the eighteen chapters of "'Dwight Morrow", and on board ship completed a further five. He reached Englewood on the very day when Hauptmann was found guilty of the murder of the Lindbergh baby. Later he went with Mrs Morrow to Mexico, where her husband had been American Ambassador. He returned to England at the end of March, but was summoned back to America in June to deal with criticisms of his book.*

H.N. to V.S-W.   *February 14, 1935*
                                                            Englewood

Dinner yesterday evening was rather strained. You see, that morning Judge Trenchard had summed up in the Hauptmann trial. He did it very well and his statement was one of which even an English judge need not have been ashamed. Lindbergh tells me that it reads more impartial than it sounded. The jury had been in consultation for five hours when we sat down to dinner and a verdict was expected at any moment. They knew that the first news would come over the wireless, so that there were two wirelesses turned on – one in the pantry next to the dining-room and one in the drawing-room. Thus there were jazz and jokes while we had dinner, and one ear was strained the whole time for the announcer from the court-house. Lindbergh had a terrible cold which made it worse.

Then after dinner we went into the library and the wireless was on in the drawing-room next door. They were all rather jumpy. Mrs Morrow, with her unfailing tact, brought out a lot of photographs and we had a family council as to what illustrations to choose for the book. Then Dick Scandrett [Morrow's nephew] came to see me. It was about 10.45. The Lindberghs and Morgans with Mrs Morrow left us alone. We discussed Dwight for some twenty minutes. Suddenly Betty put her head round the huge Coromandel screen. She looked very white. "Hauptmann," she said, "has been condemned to death without mercy."

We went into the drawing-room. The wireless had been turned on to the scene outside the court-house. One could hear the almost diabolic yelling of the crowd. They were all sitting round – Miss Morgan with embroidery, Anne looking very white and still. "You have now heard," broke in the voice of the announcer, "the verdict in the most famous trial in all history. Bruno Hauptmann now stands guilty of the foulest . . ." "Turn that off, Charles, turn that off." Then we went into the pantry and had ginger-beer. Charles sat there on the kitchen dresser looking very pink about the nose. "I don't know," he said to me, "whether you have followed the case very carefully. There is no doubt at all that Hauptmann did the thing. My one dread all these years has been that they would get hold of someone as a victim about whom I wasn't sure. I am sure about this – quite sure. It is this way . . ."

And then, quite quietly, while we all sat round the pantry, he went through the case, point by point. It seemed to relieve all of them. He did it very quietly, very simply. He pretended to address his remarks to me only. But I could see he was really trying to ease the agonised tension through which Betty and Anne had passed. It was very well done. It made one feel that there was no personal desire for vengeance or justification; there was the solemn process of law inexorably and impersonally punishing a culprit.

Poor Anne – she looked so white and horrified. The yells of the crowd were really terrifying. "That," said Lindbergh, "was a lynching crowd."

He tells me that Hauptmann was a magnificent-looking man. Splendidly built. But that his eyes were like the eyes of a wild boar. Mean, shifty, small and cruel.

H.N. to V.S-W.   *February 16, 1935*
                                                              Englewood

I went through the book yesterday and am terribly discouraged. It is as heavy as lead. What was interesting about Morrow was his character and his method. But the actual things he did were very dull. I fear that the book falls between two stools. I have tried to make it the same sort of thing as my book on my father, but whereas father was dealing with great historical and dramatic events, Morrow was dealing with the New York Underground Railways. I am very disappointed in the book now that I read it *en masse*. I fear it will have largely to be re-written. I console myself by think-ing that one always goes through a stage of gloom and that re-writing is never as serious a business as it seems. The real work is getting the facts down on paper. It is not very hard work titivating them up a little once they are in some sort of form. It is odd, really; I was not conscious that the book was dull when I was writing it. I never felt stale or bored with it. But the resultant effect is something which does not live at all. It just crawls along in prose.

H.N. to V.S-W.   *February 22, 1935*
                                        Casa Mañana, Cuernavaca, Mexico

I cannot tell you the beauty of the mornings and the evenings in this place. My little cottage, which is only one room really and a bath-room, is at the bottom of the garden and the main house is three terraces higher. I have two little windows with blue shutters and little blue wooden bars. The centre of the room is taken up by large folding doors, which, when opened, turn the room into a loggia. I shut them at night.

When I wake I see a square of sunshine from the little east win-dow upon my wall. I then look at the clock. 7.30. I then wait till 8.15. I then rise, open my two doors. That is the excitement. The first impression is a puff of cool datura smell – not hot datura smell. The second is of ringing sunshine and blue sky. The third is tropical creepers tumbling up into that sky – magenta and scarlet and blue. In my own little walled garden there is a tree called Jacaranda, which is quite naked of leaves, but from which burst huge plumes of blue-like enormous wistaria blooms. On the wall, which must be twenty feet high, is a vast *Thunbergia* with blue morning-glory flowers. On the higher terrace I see plumbago, white oleander and hibiscus.

I put on my dressing-gown and soon I hear flip-flap on the steps and Carmencita appears carrying my shaving water in a tin cruche. I then shave and dress, walking towards the door the whole time and gazing out upon this piled and terraced Gauguin. (Bananas when fruiting are very rude. They hang like a stallion.) I then climb up the several flights of staircase, past the pool, to the upper loggia where there is breakfast. I then come down again to find my room swept and garnished and heavy with the scent of Bermuda lilies. I then write to you. I then work. I then lunch. I then sleep. I then work again. I then have tea. I then work again. I then have a bath. I then dine out on the terrace. I then play nap which is a good game. I then go up on the Mirador and look out over the view. I then go to bed.

I should like never to move out of this enchanted garden but I suppose I will have to. It is incredible that this should be in the New World. I cannot believe that I am not in Spain. But there is also a Tahiti flavour about it.

H.N. to V.S-W.
March 8, 1935
Cuernavaca

I have FINISHED THE BOOK! Morrow is dead. I have had to leave a tiny gap in the chapter on the Naval Conference as I cannot finish that part until I have seen Massigli. But it is only about 3,000 words of a gap in a book of 110,000. Yes – it is done. I am relieved.

Diary
May 16, 1935

Betty [Morrow] telephones at noon to ask me to come over at once. Evidently the House of Morgan are raising difficulties. Very annoyed and depressed – but I shall have to go. Book a berth on the *Aquitania* May 29.

H.N. to V.S-W. *June 1, 1935*
Aquitania, two days out

Well I tackled a large section of the Lamont [House of Morgan] dossier yesterday. It is easier to meet them on points of fact. But it is points of interpretation which will be difficult. It all boils down to the difference between my conception of banking and their's. There was one comment which amused me. I had written, in describing the immense expansion assumed by Morgan's bank at the outbreak of the war, "It ceased to be a private firm and became almost a Department of Government." I meant that as a compliment. Old J. P. Morgan appears to have regarded it as an insult. He has added a little note on his own, "I have no right to ask you to alter this, but it will be interpreted as if we were reduced to the status of a department subordinate to the Government." This is characteristic of both of us. *I* feel it the highest compliment to compare Morgan's to the Foreign Office. *They* regard it as an insult to suggest that they have any connection with the Government, or any Government. But, you see, the whole point of view is different. I regard bankers and banking as rather low-class fellows. They regard officials as stupid and corrupt. Anyhow I continued my emendations this morning and should finish the whole Lamont dossier before I reach New York.

H.N. to V.S-W. *June 2, 1935*
Aquitania

Having worked all morning at the beastly thing [Lamont dossier], and having emerged upstairs with my feathers all the wrong way, I sat down in a huge armchair in the lounge and started reading the letters of Proust before going down to luncheon. And while so engaged the smoking-room steward descended upon me with glee. "You've won, sir," he exclaimed. "Won what?" I asked. "The sweep." I was very British and imperturbable and went on with Proust's really appalling letters to Robert de Montesquiou. Then, all aloof, I strolled into the smoking-room to see the extent of my gain. £127 – exactly the cost of Ben's ticket there and back in July. Now it will have to be spent on that.

Diary   *June 4, 1935*
Englewood

In the car I discuss the thing with Betty. I find on arrival a memorandum by Reuben Clark [Legal adviser to the State Department who accompanied Morrow to Mexico] bitterly attacking the whole Mexican chapters and saying the thing will do harm. He has evidently been put up to this by Lamont. The result is that Betty has lost all confidence in the book and in me. I shall either have to withdraw the book or insist on its being printed as it stands. We sit up talking till 1.40 a.m. and I retire to my room only to lie awake in torments of rage. How seldom do I get as angry as this and how seldom do I feel unable to sleep! A horrible night.

Diary   *June 7, 1935*
Englewood

Devote today to revising the whole book in the light of final criticisms. As I read it again, it seems to me to be very sugary sort of stuff. The influence of American caution and sentimentality has pervaded my style. My fear of hurting Betty's feelings has made me a trifle sloppy. And then the excisions have removed from the book any tang it may have had. Thus the result is soft and flabby. But in spite of all this Morrow does emerge as a real person, not as a legend. I am not really discontented with the book.

Diary   *June 19, 1935*
London

Christopher [Hobhouse] tells me that I have "not got a political mind". I ask him to explain what he means. He says that I am too fastidious and too critical to have the essential faculty of belief in democracy. He is right.

I then lunch at the Travellers with Rex Leeper [later Ambassador to Athens] to discuss the book or article on Allen [Leeper, Rex's brother who died earlier that year]. He tells me that Michael Sadleir had said to him that he thought I would survive as one of the leading writers of this age. True it was that my public was at present small, but then a faithful minority was proof of permanent literary reputation.

Odd that these two remarks should have been made to me within an hour of each other. Not that I believe either. Yet they occur at a moment of acute hesitation and may well tip the balance. Christopher with his usual insight realises that my desire to go into politics is motivated by feelings other than real political ambition or aptitude. He knows that I wish to enter public life partly from a sense of curiosity, partly from a feeling of duty, and partly because I have not sufficient confidence in my own literary gifts.

Now all this coincides with a real perplexity. I think it odd that I who have worked so hard and have written so many books should not have a serious literary position. I have been thinking that this must be due to the fact that I do not possess essentially a literary gift. I therefore desire politics as a sort of alibi from literary failure. And then come these two chance remarks. I do not think I am conceited about myself. Vain and proud I am; but not conceited. The actual conjunction of these two remarks may in fact prove determinant in my future decision. If Michael and Christopher are both right, then there is only one alternative. I must devote such years as may remain to my *magnum opus* [the six volume autobiography]. And that is evidence of how little one knows oneself. Having left this finger of fate indicating in one direction, I realise that it was in that direction only that I have wished to go.

Diary   *June 25, 1935*

Charlie [Lord Sackville] telephones to say the Sevenoaks Conservative Association have not chosen me as a candidate [for Parliament]. Vita is in the room, but pays no attention at all, and merely plays with Martha the puppy whom I had brought from Uckfield. Nor does she ever refer to the matter again. It is as if she hadn't been aware in any sense that this may mean a final decision regarding politics versus literature. Strange, very strange.

In July H.N. went to America for the fourth time in less than a year, this time accompanied by his son Ben. "Dwight Morrow" was published in October.

H.N. to V.S-W.   *July 12, 1935*
                                                          North Haven, Maine

Already by breakfast it was very hot and the flag on the mast hung limp in a cloudless sky. We returned to our cottage and worked hard. Ben really does work when he get to it. Four hours at a time without a word and with neat and careful notes entered in a *cahier*. At 12.30 there was a knock at the door. Charles Lindbergh appeared. "It is a perfect day for flying: would you like to go up, Ben?" Ben said that he would, and we walked out to the front where the flying field had been cleared. There was a little aeroplane scarlet as sealing-wax. Ben was quite calm and brave and aloof and slow and distant and drawly and incompetent. They climbed in. Off they went over the sea and islands and then high, high up in the ringing air. I watched my poor son and heir up there, a tiny point in the stratosphere. In half-an-hour they came down and there was Ben safe and aloof and lethargic and drawly and incompetent. But even he expressed something which in someone else would have been indicative of slightly aroused interest but which in him was passionate enthusiasm. I did so envy him, damn you [H.N. had promised V.S-W. he would not fly again after a near-escape in 1923]. That perfect summer's day, that lovely island-studded sea, those distant mountains and that vault of blue above the scent of pines. Damn you.

H.N. to V.S-W.   *July 17, 1935*
                                                                North Haven

I worked and worked and at four-thirty there was the whole thing beautifully finished and at five-thirty there was the beach-wagon going down to the village with my final proofs for Harcourt, Brace. I watched it turning the corner with deep relief. No book has caused me such fuss and worry as this one. It is a relief to see it turn tail and go.

Ben leaves tomorrow for Boston, Washington and Philadelphia.

He has got museums opened for him all along the route. He gets on very well with Lindbergh who seems to enjoy talking to him. Lindbergh has a reputation for being an extremely silent man, yet with us he chatters the whole time.

Anne told me a story which I find strange. They were asked formally to the White House after their flight to China. Much against their will they went. Mr and Mrs Hoover were very polite. But Mrs Hoover called them "Mr and Mrs Lingrün" throughout. Now isn't that very odd indeed? What would Freud have said to that? That is the sort of story I really enjoy. An insoluble problem in human conduct. Now you see, that's what comes of foreign travel. Had I stayed at Sissinghurst I should never have learnt that Mrs Hoover called Lindbergh Lingrün.

Diary   *August 16, 1935*

I dreamt that Vansittart wrote and asked me to join the F.O. again. My disappointment when I woke up and found that this was only a dream is a measure of how much I really mind having severed my connection with the F.O. I must seriously consider, now that I have finished my diplomatic books, and now that politics offer no opening and journalism is horrible to me, if I could not creep back somehow into the Service.

Diary   *August 21, 1935*

I drive to Grosvenor Square to lunch with Emerald Cunard. Then a lovely lady arrives whom I afterwards identify as Lady Jersey. Then in comes Sir Arthur Wauchope, High Commissioner in Palestine. And then a slim young man of the name of Davison. And then Emerald herself very glad about everything. Then Anthony Eden [Minister without Portfolio for League of Nations Affairs, aged 38]. Then Walter Elliot [Minister of Agriculture]. We go into luncheon.

Emerald is at her best. She well knows that Anthony Eden and Elliot are not able to disclose what happened at the Cabinet this morning. Yet she also knows that by flagrant indiscretion she may get them to say something. "Anthony," she says, "You are all wrong about Italy. Why should she not have Abyssinia? You must tell me that." As the only guest I have not mentioned was de Castellane of the French Embassy, Eden's style was cramped. He just reacted flippantly. They therefore discussed English women and how they were no help to their husbands whereas the merest French cocotte at Toulon moved heaven and earth in favour of her *commandant de frégate*.

As I was one off Eden I was able from time to time to ask leading questions: e.g. "What attitude will Switzerland adopt?" "She has her constitutional difficulties, but we do not think that land frontiers matter very much." He then said that Lloyd George had been summoned that morning into conference. He had explained that Italy in 1919 had been offered far more than she could absorb. This is true about Eregli, Adalia and Albania. Eden asked me whether this was true. I said it was. I asked what other people had been called into consultation. He said old Lansbury, Herbert Samuel, and Winston. Also Bruce of Australia and other High Commissioners. He said that Winston was all out for blood and thunder. I referred to the unhelpful attitude of the French press, instancing the *Figaro* of yesterday. He said, "Yes, it would be simple enough if the French were really with us." From which I gather that he himself and the F.O. are out for sanctions but that the French and the Beaverbrook and the Rothermere Press over here are a doubtful quantity. Walter Elliot hinted that we might remove the embargo on the export of arms to Abyssinia and I suggested that this would not be understood in the U.S.A.

I felt that I had touched the fringe of the centre of the problem. But I also felt that in the F.O. I should have been in the centre of the problem. I was very sad.

Then back by the 5.42 to Sissinghurst. The posters of the evening papers bear headlines, "Ramsay MacDonald says, 'Worst crisis since 1914'." "Ll.G. and Lansbury summoned to F.O." "Opposition consulted" etc. etc. A general crisis atmosphere. It is very hot in the train. I read the silly books I collected at the *Daily Telegraph*. A guidebook to Morocco. A book on English phonetics for foreign readers. I feel more out of it all than ever.

Diary   *October 1, 1935*

*Our wedding day 22 years ago. I go out early and tie up for V. a little bouquet of rosemary. She has no idea what it is all about. Now this ought to have offended me. But it doesn't in the least. Our

love for each other is a thing which does not depend upon incidents
or Annie Versaries [*sic*]. But how like her to be completely unaware
of a thing which brings me back to Park Lodge when I dressed so
carefully to go up to Knole! I would not have her different one
single inch.*

Diary   *October 3, 1935*

Buck De La Warr [Parliamentary Secretary to the Ministry of Agri-
culture] telephones to say that if I will agree to contest West
Leicester in the National Labour interest he thinks he can give me a
safe seat. I answer that I must think it over.

> *West Leicester had been represented by a National*
> *Liberal since 1931. A few months after the Election, he*
> *crossed the floor and became an Opposition Liberal – an*
> *act that provoked the displeasure of his constituents.*
> *They were determined to replace him. H.N. agreed to*
> *stand as National Labour candidate, with Conservative*
> *and National Liberal support. The General Election took*
> *place at the height of the Abyssinian crisis, and both*
> *major parties backed the League of Nations' sanctions*
> *against Italy. H.N. was obliged to defend the National*
> *Government's home policy, which he knew little about,*
> *and his own peculiar political past. His ignorance of*
> *Leicester, or any town like it, added to his dislike of*
> *electioneering, and V.S-W. refused to make one single*
> *appearance at his side. H.N. said that she was ill.*

H.N. to V.S-W. (in France)   *October 11, 1935*

I went to see Buck yesterday. Jarvis [Chairman of the West Leicester
Conservative Association] is aged about 35; high colour; high
morals. He began by saying that it is most important that I should
stand as "The National Government Candidate" and not as
"National Labour". I let Buck answer that point as I am all at sea
about these labels. Buck said he agreed. I said, "But supposing
people ask me what party I belong to, what am I to say?" Buck said

that I must say that I was a follower of Ramsay MacDonald. The conversation went on this way with me sitting all good and quiet on the sofa. Then I realised that something must be done. I said that it was no use asking me about these things, but that what was important was that I should not get a single vote under false pretences. I would be anything they liked except all things to all men. I would not pretend to be a Tory to catch the Tory vote and so on. I would get muddled if my own position was not quite clear and straight from the start. "I am very bad," I said, "at *prolonged* deception." Anyhow they agreed and told me not to fuss about MY HONOUR.

As regards expenses, headquarters will pay one third, local organisation one third, and (what may strike you as unexpected) V.S-W. one third. (She does it by raising a mortgage on Long Barn.) I shall ask for £500 from you under this head, pay you interest on it, and repay the mortgage when I become First Lord of the Treasury. I made it quite clear you could take no part. I said that I much objected to the "Candidate's Wife" stunt, that you were not interested in politics and that it would be humbug to pretend that you were. They said that would be all right. It would go down very well if I explained that in advance.

H.N. to V.S-W.   *November 5, 1935*
                                                        Leicester

*I had two more meetings last night. The procedure is always more or less the same. I have a light supper of sandwiches and coffee at 6.30. Then I am taken on to my first meeting which is generally in some school house. There is a chairman and a local speaker who speak first. I then get up and the local speaker dashes off to start another meeting. When I have finished my first speech, I also dash off to the other meeting and when I arrive the local speaker stops talking and I start my little piece. Then there are questions and off we go.

It is not a pleasant experience. There are always two or three women who sing out the whole time "That's a bleeding lie" or "You ought to be ashamed of yourself" and remarks like that. These interruptions, which are organised, and constant, do in fact force one to concentrate against getting angry and are therefore exhausting.

The discouraging thing about it all is that one feels that what one says is not believed and that in any case only about 8% of the electors ever hear one.*

H.N. to V.S-W.   *November 7, 1935*
                                                           Leicester

I think that we may say that the position is more or less as follows:

(1) I have about a 48% chance – just a little below even chances. In other words, the odds are really against me, but there is just a chance I may scrape in.

(2) If I fail, I shall not feel that it was due to any mistakes on my part, to any lack of organisation or lack of energy.

(3) If I succeed, it will be a great personal triumph.

Were I a young man, it would be worth it. But of course I cannot pretend at my age it is pleasant to have a failure and to spend all this money and energy for nothing. Generally in experiences such as this there is something, some isolated moment, which one enjoys. I hate and loathe every moment of this Election. The evening meetings are such absolute HELL that they hang on one's soul all day like a lump of lead.

H.N. to V.S-W.   *November 13, 1935*
                                                           Leicester

I can see from the manner of my canvassers who have toured the streets that they do not believe for one moment that I shall be elected.

Diary   *November 14, 1935*

One of the strangest days of my life. It pours, the rainwater sluicing down the dark streets. At about 10 p.m. we go on to the de Montfort Hall and find the counting in progress. Long trestle tables with people counting in rows. The voting papers are separated into little bundles of fifty and I and my supporters stroll around the tables watching the size of the piles. By about 11.30 p.m. it is clear to us that Morgan [Labour] will be first, I second, and Crawfurd [Liberal] third. I go out into the lobby and listen on the wireless for other results. I return to the main rooms and find my supporters very glum and sad. Morgan is triumphant. "It's a bad system of counting this," he exclaims, "the first thing I shall do is to get some alteration in the ballot law." He says this openly, assuming that he will get in. Then come the announcements for East and South Leicester. Lyons and Waterhouse [both Conservative] both in. Applause and cheers, plus two short speeches. By that time my own tables are handing their bundles up to the platform. Jarvis comes to me in the hall and says "You ought to be up on the platform by now." So up I go. There is a group round the central counting table, including the returning officer and my agent Tuthill. Morgan sees me, and comes up to me. "Well," he says, "you have done splendidly – a rare fight for a first election – but do not be discouraged – we want men like you in the House of Commons." "What," I ask him, "is your majority?" "My tellers," he answers me, "estimate it at between 1,200 and 1,500." I shake his hand in congratulation.

I then walk to the back to think out my speech for seconding the vote of thanks. I catch Tuthill's eye as he stands there at the table. He winks at me and jerks his head. I imagine that he wants to ask me some question and go up to him. "You're in," he whispers, "by 150." My first thought is "Poor Morgan – I must show no sign of triumph." I return again to the back and I hear Morgan's voice, almost hysterical, "I claim a recount, I claim a recount." The bundles are then handed down again to the main room. I stand there looking up at a sea of excited faces, including my Benzie, my Niggs and Sam [his brother-in-law, Francis St Aubyn, later Lord St Levan]. I give them a slight affirmative motion of the head and see the colour rush to Niggs' face. Never shall I forget that second. The recount goes quickly. Waterhouse, imperturbable as always, comes up slowly to me smoking a cigarette in a long holder. "Well," he says, "you must be feeling pretty proud. The greatest fight of the whole election." The bundles are then returned and the Socialists query many defective papers. I give them all they want. That leaves me with [a majority of] 87. Tuthill moves away from the table very quietly. "Well," he says, "we're in."

The news communicates itself to the crowd in the hall below and there is a hum rising like a swarm of bees. The press buzz round me. The Clerk to the Council steps forward and makes his announcement. As my majority is announced, a wild yell goes up from the hall. People rush towards the platform. I step forward and make a short speech. Morgan follows, then Crawfurd. Then photographs outside and on to the Constitutional Club. They are waiting for me in the street in the rain and as I draw up there are shouts of "Here he is!" Out they drag me and hoist me up the stairs. Pandemonium let loose. I am dumped on the staircase and say a few words. Then back to the hotel – champagne with Waterhouse. To bed at 2.30 a.m.

V.S-W. to H.N.   *November 15, 1935*
                                                    Sissinghurst

I am *so* glad. What a triumph! My heart stood still when I heard "Leicester West" on the wireless. Oh darling, I do congratulate you.

> *H.N. was now the member for West Leicester, and he retained his seat for the next ten years. The National Government under Baldwin had won the Election with a huge majority, and the National Labour Party, led by MacDonald, had 8 seats. Soon after the Election there was a sudden crisis caused by the British Foreign Secretary (Hoare) who made a secret pact with the French (Laval) over the partition of Abyssinia, and it was on this subject that H.N. made his maiden speech on 19 December.*

H.N. to V.S-W.   *December 4, 1935*

There is something very strange about Stanley Baldwin. At first sight he is a solid English gentleman, but then one observes odd nervous tricks. He has an extraordinarily unpleasant habit of smelling at his notes and licking the edges slightly as if they were a flap of an envelope. He scratches himself continuously. There are russet patches across his head and face. And a strange movement of the head, with half-closed eyes, like some tortoise half-awake smelling the air – blinking, snuffy, neurotic.

I went to the smoking-room, which was an unwise thing to have done. I wanted to see if I could find [Sir] Ralph Glyn with whom I was supposed to be lunching today. But the smoking-room was full of old boys sitting round tables and drinking whisky. It is not in the least like the smoking-room at the Travellers Club. It is far more like the bar of a pub. Shouts and laughter and an almost complete absence of decorum. Having got in, I could scarcely get out, and I tried that business of walking rapidly through with head turning right and left and eyes bearing that far-away look which signifies, "I am not in the very least bit shy. I am merely looking urgently for someone of immense importance." Then to my horror from the extreme end of the room came yells of "Harold!" – and there was Winston Churchill and [Sir] Robert Horne and Oliver Stanley waving at me. I had to go towards them feeling stared-at and conspicuous.

Winston rose tubbily and stretched out great arms. "Welcome! Welcome!" he yelled. You know how overwhelming his charm can be, but I would rather it had occurred in great privacy. "Well," he shouted, "when I saw your result on the tape, I said to myself, 'That means he goes straight into the Cabinet', and then I remembered that all your Party were already in the Cabinet and that they must have at least one follower on the back benches. So I realised that you would be chosen as the single follower." This amused people all around and there was general laughter while I stood there looking a fool. But I do not suppose I really looked so foolish as I felt, and then I sat down with them for a moment and nothing could possibly have been so delightful as they were.

H.N. to V.S-W.   *December 10, 1935*

After luncheon I went round to the Privy Council Office for a meeting of our National Labour Party. It is a lovely room with a huge sculptured fireplace and many Queen Anne inkstands. Ramsay sat there in front of the fire and we others sat on either side. We discussed the future organisation and policy of our Party. It was a ridiculous and rather painful discussion. It boiled down to the question of Party funds. We had so much in hand which would enable us to keep on for such and such a time. How were we to get more money? Ramsay dismissed that question as secondary. "One can always get money," he said, "for great political purposes." Kenneth Lindsay, who is an impatient and able man, suggested that we might discuss what those purposes were. We all winced at that. "We shall," said Ramsay, "be neither red, white nor blue. We stand for Labour within the Baldwin organisation. We shall further the aims of the organisation but we shall remain OURSELVES." Having said that,

he struck the arm of his chair with a clenched fist and gazed upwards
to where, above the mantelpiece, God was most likely to be found.
"OURSELVES," he repeated fervently, like a Covenanter dedicating
his sword and buckler. We did not even like to look at each other so
awkward were our feelings. It was by then 3.30 p.m., and in acute
embarrassment we broke up.

H.N. to V.S-W.   *December 12, 1935*

I am really fussed about this Abyssinian business. It seems to me
that Sam Hoare has completely and absolutely let us down. I feel
very deeply about it and shall certainly not vote with the Government unless I am convinced that they have not done what they seem
to have done. But I believe they have. It is really disgraceful – Sam
Hoare was certified by his doctors as unfit for public business, and
on his way to the sanatorium he stops off in Paris and allows Laval
to do him down. My God! Were I on the other side of the House
what a chance for a crushing speech.

Diary   *December 13, 1935*

Dine with Sibyl Colefax. Diana Cooper, Mr and Mrs [Ernest]
Simpson, Bruce Lockhart and the Prince of Wales there. The latter
is very thin; his complexion has gone and he is brick-coloured,
against which background his fair eyelashes rise and fall. He talks
a great deal about America and diplomacy. He resents the fact that
we do not send our best men there. He knows an astonishing amount
about it all. "What can I do?" he says. "They will only say, 'Here's
that bloody Prince of Wales butting in'." One finds him modest and
a good mixer.

Diary   *December 19, 1935*

After questions Sam Hoare comes in with his nose plastered [broken
while skating] and sits on the third bench below the gangway. He
makes his statement in a precise voice. It is excellent. His voice just
breaks at the end: "I trust that my successor will have better luck
than myself." Then Attlee moves a vote of censure, and while he
does so Hoare creeps out a broken man. I do not like the man but
my whole sympathy went out to him.

The Speaker's Secretary taps me on the shoulder and says that I will be called after Macpherson and Maxton. It is getting near the dinner hour. I must confess that waiting is torture to me and I am afraid that my knees will knock together when I rise. But eventually Maxton finishes his speech and I find myself on my feet and beginning, "I crave the indulgence . . ." It all goes well enough and members crowd in from the dining-rooms. Baldwin remains on the front bench and leans forward appreciatively. Very friendly of him. When I sit down there is much applause and Eustace [Percy] comes and says it was the best maiden speech he has ever heard. He is followed by J. H. Thomas [Secretary of State for the Dominions] who sits down beside me: "You did fine, 'Arold, you did fine!" Thereafter many Members cross the House and congratulate me, and one way and another it is rather a sort of demonstration. Duff Cooper is particularly polite. Yet I know that I could have done it better if I had been less nervous. The manner was right enough but the matter was too thin. But it is good enough for a start.

Diary   *January 13, 1936*

Meet Sibyl Colefax at the Apéritif, then on to the Phoenix Theatre for the first night of Noel Coward's play [*Tonight at Eight-Thirty*]. Sibyl breaks to me the fact that the other two members of our party are the Prince of Wales and Mrs Simpson.

Mrs Simpson is bejewelled, eyebrow-plucked, virtuous and wise. I had already been impressed by the fact that she had forbidden the Prince to smoke during the entr'acte in the theatre itself. She is clearly out to help him. Our supper party at the Savoy Grill goes right enough, but I find the Prince gazing at my tie and [soft] collar in a mood of critical abstraction – the eye of Windsor blue surrounded by jaundice. Nobody pays any attention to him, and what is odd is that the waiters do not fuss unduly. The Prince is extremely talkative and charming. I have a sense that he prefers our sort of society either to the aristocrats or to the professed high-brows or politicians. Sibyl imagines that she is getting him into touch with Young England. I have an uneasy feeling that Mrs Simpson, for all her good intentions, is getting him out of touch with the type of person with whom he ought to frequent.

Go home pondering on all these things and a trifle sad. Why am

I sad? Because I think Sibyl is a clever old bean who ought to concentrate upon intellectual and not social guests. Because I think Mrs
Simpson is a nice woman who is flaunted suddenly into this absurd
position. Because I think the P. of W. is in a mess. And because I
do not feel at ease in such company.

> *On January 19, H.N. went to Dingwall, Scotland, where
> Malcolm MacDonald was standing as National Labour
> candidate. There he learned of King George's death, on
> January 20, 1936.*

Diary   *January 23, 1936*

At 2 p.m. the House meets. Prayers, and then Baldwin rises to propose a vote of condolence [to Queen Mary]. He speaks perfectly
with great simplicity and with great style. He refers to Kipling whom
he had been burying that morning at Westminster Abbey. The end
of another epoch.

At 3.20 we walk in procession to Westminster Hall. We enter by
our own side entrance. The centre of the hall is free but for a purple
catafalque. Four candles and four Beefeaters draped in black.
Behind a slight parapet which runs down the side of the hall are
grouped on the north side the House of Lords, with Bishops, on the
south side ourselves with the Speaker. The two maces glint in the
light. Upon the steps are grouped members of the Court and behind
them the choir of the Chapel Royal. A great cross is carried to the
entrance. Then the Princesses arrive shrouded in black and are
grouped near the steps. From outside one hears the words "Present
arms" and above the catafalque I can see the swing doors on to
Palace Yard open for a minute. I understand that the Queen has
come in with her sons. A hush again. Then Big Ben begins to strike
four and in the interval of these reverberations one hears the chink
and grating of a gun carriage outside. The doors swing open again.
Then I see something rising above the catafalque. It is the end of the
coffin with the crown upon it. Six huge guardsmen with bared
heads carry the coffin which slips quite easily onto the catafalque
although its Royal Standard gets caught for a moment underneath
it. The officer in command straightens the Standard, clicks his
heels, and marches off the steps which raise the catafalque. The

coffin remains there, just a wreath of flowers and the crown, its diamonds winking in the candle-light. It is at that stage that I notice that something has gone wrong with the crown. The Maltese Cross at the top is missing [it had fallen off during the procession from King's Cross station to Westminster Hall and was instantly retrieved by an escort]. A few very short prayers. A hymn. And then a pause while the Royal Family leave. As they pass the coffin they bow and curtsey. Then in the opposite direction the heralds pass and process up the steps – a sudden flash of gold and scarlet against all those black and dim figures. And then we all file past two by two, some of us bowing as we pass the coffin and others not. The place is then closed – I imagine in order that they may reaffix the cross on the crown. A most terrible omen.

Diary   *January 28, 1936*

The King's funeral. I stay in at K.B.W. [King's Bench Walk] all morning and do not hear more than the minute-guns firing dolefully in the distance.

Go to see Buck De La Warr and we discuss the future of National Labour and agree that there is none. Now that the two MacDonalds [Ramsay and Malcolm] have fought [by-elections] with the aid of the Tory Central Office we cannot claim any independence. He says that Baldwin is really keen to maintain the semblance of a National Government and wants us to help.

Diary   *February 5, 1936*

Ramsay MacDonald takes his seat amid much booing on the part of the Labour Opposition and only perfunctory cheers on our side of the House. I receive a chit to go down and see him. He asks me if I will be his Parliamentary Private Secretary. I suggest that were I to do this I should limit my freedom of action in the House. He says that on the other hand it would give me enormous insight into the working of the Parliamentary machine, into the functioning of the Privy Council Office, and into such schemes as Radium research; apart from this it would be very useful to our own group to have a Secretary (i.e. Whip) who would keep him in touch with lobby opinion and enable the group as a whole to put up a continuous and combative fight. I suggest that the group as at present constituted is not capable of putting up such a fight. Its able men are on the front bench; its back-benchers are not able, with the possible exception of [Richard] Denman. He says he is astonished at the amount of National Labour feeling in the country. Now this is simply dealing in unreality. There is no National Labour feeling in the country; there is only progressive conservatism. But Ramsay would sooner die than enter into a real alliance with the Tories based on any system of fusion.

Diary   *February 8, 1936*

Catch the 12.00 Victoria train for Brighton. It is a bitter cold day with a strong east wind. Am met by Cecil Rhind [secretary to Lady Sackville, who had died on January 30] and we lunch at the Metropole. We then go to the oyster shop of Mr English where B.M.'s [Lady Sackville] ashes have been preserved overnight. The reason for this strange procedure is that the Press had got hold of the story, and it was feared that they would picket the undertakers and take snapshots of us as we carried out the urn. *The latter is placed in the back of the car by Mr English who is slightly drunk but says he has a bad cold in the head.* He is anxious to come with us in the boat but I am very firm on that point. "No, Mr English, we really should prefer to be by ourselves." The boat is there on the shingle – a large open fishing boat with two sailors and a petrol engine. We are launched down the shingle in Homeric fashion and chug along the coast until we get opposite White Lodge [Lady Sackville's house]. Cecil and I sit there huddled in our coats with a most inadequate rug over our knees bending our heads from time to time as the spray lashes over us. Sun shining and an angry brown sea. "We're two miles out," says the boatman, at which I undo the string of the parcel. The urn or container is of gun-metal and one opens it by pressing up the lid with one's thumbs. I am terrified lest the ashes be caught by the wind and keep the lid on. The two men stand up and take off their hats. So does Cecil. I kneel by the gunwale and spill the ashes over into the sea saying, "B.M. – all who love you are happy that you should now be at peace. We shall remember always your beauty, your courage and your charm." It is merely a handful of dust which slides out of the container into the waves.

Diary   *February 10, 1936*

Dine with the De La Warrs in their mews. We are all very sorry for old MacDonald but feel that he is too vain to have any sense of reality. I tell them how he imagines his own election is a proof that the country believes in National Labour and that we have the ball at our feet. "And we know—" I say, "that it isn't a ball at all; it is only a Carters Little Liver Pill." Then back to the House.

Diary   *February 13, 1936*

Go to see Anthony Eden in his room; he is very frank. He says that his aim is to prevent another German war. To do that he is prepared to make great concessions to German appetites provided they will sign a disarmament treaty and join the League of Nations. I am all in favour of such a far-sighted plan.

H.N. to V.S-W.   *February 18, 1936*

I went to see Ramsay MacDonald. I told him I would not be his P.P.S. but would be glad to help him unofficially in any way I could. He asked me to "drop in on him" every morning. Well if it is only a drop, I don't mind. But I dread an orgy of vain outpourings. I fear that Ramsay is a vain and slightly vindictive old man. Why is it, darling, that I who am the least combative person on earth seem always to be attached to battle-cruisers – Curzon, Tom Mosley, B.M. – but I daresay it is good for me.

H.N. to V.S-W.   *February 20, 1936*

My new pal [Lady] Maureen Stanley asked me to come round and meet her father who is just back from hobnobbing with Hitler. Now I admire [Lord] Londonderry [Secretary of State for Air, 1931–35] in a way, since it is fine to remain 1760 in 1936; besides he is a real gent. But I do deeply disapprove of ex-Cabinet Ministers trotting across to Germany at this moment. Anyhow, when I got in, there was a dear little woman in black sitting on the sofa, and she said to me, "We have not met since Berlin." I sat down beside her and chattered away all friendly, thinking meanwhile, "Berlin? Berlin?

How odd. Obviously she is English, yet I do not remember her at all. Yet there is something about her which is vaguely familiar." While thus thinking, another woman came in and curtsied low to her and I realised it was the Duchess of York [by the end of the year she would be Queen Elizabeth, wife of King George VI]. Did I show by the tremor of an eyelid that I had not recognised her from the first? I did not. I steered my conversation onwards in the same course as before but with different sails; the dear old jib of comradeship was lowered and very gently the spinnaker of "Yes Ma'am" was hoisted in its place. I do not believe that she can have noticed the transition. She is charm personified.

Towards the end of February Charles and Anne Lindbergh took a two-year lease of Long Barn and the newspapers gave the incident unfortunate publicity.

H.N. to V.S-W.   *March 5, 1936*

*I am not in favour of bringing an action [against the *Daily Express*] as it would expose us to ridicule on the part of all the popular press and would do the Lindberghs no good at all. But I am in favour of making some sort of row.* I telephoned to dear Mrs Woods at the Weald Post Office and asked her to "use her influence" in the village to see that Charles and Anne were not bothered. She was very flattered at being roped in as an ally. "No, Sir, we shall not stare at the poor people."

Italy's continued invasion of Abyssinia, culminating in the capture of Addis Ababa in May, partly overshadowed the drama of Hitler's occupation of the Rhineland in March. He was acting in violation of the Treaty of Versailles and the Locarno Pact. Both Britain and France were outraged, but neither had the determination to act, and Hitler won the first of his bloodless victories.

Diary *March 9, 1936*

Vita's [44th] birthday. Great excitement about Hitler's coup. House crowded. Eden makes his statement at 3.40. Very calm. Promises of help if France attacked, otherwise negotiation. General mood of the House is one of fear. Anything to keep out of war.

H.N. to V.S-W. *March 12, 1936*

The French are not letting us off one jot or tittle of the bond. We are thus faced either with repudiation of our pledged word or the risk of war. The worst of it is that in a way the French are right. We know that Hitler gambled on his coup. If we sent an ultimatum to Germany she ought in all reason to climb down. But then she will not climb down and we shall have war. Naturally we shall win and enter Berlin. And what is the good of that? It would only mean communism in Germany and in France and that is why the Russians are so keen on it. Moreover the people of this country absolutely refuse to have a war. We shall therefore have to climb down ig- nominiously and Hitler will have scored. But it does mean the final end of the League and that I do mind dreadfully. Quite dreadfully.

Diary *March 17, 1936*

Meeting of the Foreign Affairs Committee in the House of Com- mons. It is packed. The debate is opened by [Victor] Raikes who urges that sanctions against Germany in any form would mean war and that the country is not prepared to fight for France. I reply by saying that we are bound morally by Locarno and that while we must restrain France from any rash demands we must never betray her.

Diary *March 23, 1936*

The feeling in the House is "terribly pro-German", which means afraid of war.

Diary   *April 2, 1936*

I dine with Mrs Simpson to meet the King. Black tie: black waistcoat. A taxi to Bryanston Court: an apartment dwelling; a lift; butler and maid at door; drawing room; many orchids and white arums. The guests consist of Lady Oxford, Lady Cunard, Lady Colefax, Kenneth Lindsay, the Counsellor of the U.S. Embassy at Buenos Aires plus wife, and Alexander Woollcott [American playwright and critic]. Mr Simpson enters bringing in the King. We all bow and curtsey. King looks very well and gay. It is evident that Lady Cunard is incensed by the presence of Lady Colefax and that Lady Colefax is furious that Lady Cunard should also have been asked. Lady Oxford appears astonished to find either of them at what was to have been a quite intimate party. The King passes brightly from group to group. Sibyl Colefax makes the mistake, to my mind, of talking very close to his ear, thus indicating that she knows how deaf he is. He asks me to tell Lindbergh to come and see him. I bow. Then dinner.

Something snobbish in me is rather saddened by all this. Mrs Simpson is a perfectly harmless type of American but her husband is an obvious bounder and the whole setting is slightly second-rate. Sibyl's excuse is that she makes him happy and that should be enough. But I do not myself want to be drawn into that set if I can help it.

> *H.N. gained in reputation. His industry was extra-*
> *ordinary: he played an active role in the House, wrote*
> *the main policy statement for his party, was elected*
> *Vice-Chairman of the Foreign Affairs Committee, and*
> *meanwhile he continued to write book-reviews for the*
> Daily Telegraph.
>
> *V.S-W. was no less active. Her* Joan of Arc *was pub-*
> *lished in June, and she had started* Pepita. *The house at*
> *Sissinghurst was finished, and the garden continued to*
> *expand.*

H.N. to V.S-W.   *April 28, 1936*

Luncheon alone with Robert Vansittart [Head of the Foreign Office] at his house. Van was extremely pleasant and friendly. His view is that a German hegemony in Europe means the end of the British Empire and that we have no right to buy Germany off for a generation by offering her a free hand against the Slav countries. Once she has established herself in an unassailable position she will turn round upon us and we shall be too weak to resist her. I think he is right in theory but in practice it would be quite impossible for us to get the British people to fight Germany for the sake of the Czechs.

Tell Gwen I do not need Sanatogen at present. What I need is a feeling that we shall avoid a war. And that feeling I do not have at the moment.

H.N. to V.S-W.   *May 5, 1936*

Eden made such a dramatic statement yesterday. Nobody knew exactly what had happened to the Emperor [of Abyssinia], and Attlee asked a private-notice question. Eden replied at length, ending by the statement that H.M.S. *Enterprise* had been sent to take him to Palestine. "He embarks," he added, glancing at the clock, "at quarter-to-four." It was then twenty minutes to four, and we had a sudden picture of the steaming heat of Djibouti, the untidy French officials, and the strange black family being saluted by midshipmen in white ducks and sailing away from Africa five minutes later.

H.N. to V.S-W.   *May 13, 1936*

The gentian-bed sounds very professional. I am all for gentians. What fun we are going to have! I do so love the garden. It is a sort of still backcloth to my rattley ruttley rottley (those words are meant to convey the impression of an elderly Ford lorry bumping along a pavé road. I am a master of language) life.

Diary   *May 21, 1936*

*There are rumours that the Government is to be reconstituted after Whitsun. *The Star* last night stated apparently that I should be given a Ministerial job if [J. H.] Thomas goes. Obviously this is being talked about in the lobbies, as when Winston came in and sat beside me in the House he grinned and said "I gather you are about to leave this comfortable bench." I have heard no direct news of any such offer, but my first inclination is to refuse it on the grounds (1) that it is not fair on older members that I should be given a Government job after only six months in the House, and (2) that it is not really fair on the Conservative back-benchers that a Government job should be given to National Labour. I may find that if the proposal is put to me it will be almost impossible to refuse it.*

Diary   *May 28, 1936*

Nancy Astor is terribly indignant at the King for having invited to his first official dinner Lady Cunard and Mr and Mrs Simpson. She says that the effect in Canada and America will be deplorable. She considers Lady Cunard and Chips Channon as "disintegrating influences", and she deplores the fact that any but the best Virginian families should be received at Court. I stick up both for Emerald Cunard and for Mrs Simpson, but I refrain from saying that after all every American is more or less as vulgar as every other American. Nancy Astor herself, by her vain and self-conscious behaviour in the House, cannot claim to be a model of propriety. In any case she is determined to tell the King that although Mrs Simpson may appear at Court, she must not appear in the Court Circular. I suggest to her that any such intimation would be regarded by H.M. as a gross impertinence. She says that when the dignity of the United States and the British Empire is involved, it is her duty to make such sacrifices.

H.N. to V.S-W.   *June 10, 1936*

*I went to see Ramsay [MacDonald] who was very down and out. He thinks of resigning – but why resign now when there is all that fuss and bother about an Election? How strange people are. I should have died sooner than endure the cadging and humiliations which that by-election entailed and now having undergone all this he throws it away four months later. I think I persuaded him to stay. I pointed out that he would be of great help to the King for the Coronation. I don't suppose he will be anything but a hindrance to that obstinate young man – but Ramsay was pleased by the idea.

Passing out through the Private Secretaries' room there was Jim Thomas [recently found guilty of leaking budget secrets]. He just clutched hold of me and sobbed. He must have lost two stone during the last fortnight; his face is white. He can scarcely walk – he staggers, and he cannot talk at all; just blubbers. Well, I am sorry for him, but I should die sooner than show such self-pity and degradation.*

Diary   *June 10, 1936*

*Dine with Sibyl Colefax. It is rather tragic, since we all feel that it represents the last big party she will ever be able to give. [Her husband had died on February 19.] I arrive to find the Lamonts [Thomas Lamont, Chairman of the Board J. P. Morgan & Co.], the Stanleys, the Brownlows, the Vansittarts, Bruce Lockhart and Buck De La Warr. After keeping us waiting for half an hour, the King arrives and we go into dinner almost at once.

After the women have gone out, the King talks at length to Tom Lamont about American conditions and impresses him deeply with his wide knowledge and intelligence. The King told me about his dinner with the Lindberghs. He said that Anne Lindbergh had been rather shy at first, but that "old S[tanley] B[aldwin] and I, with our well-known charm, quickly put her at ease." There is no doubt about it that he has infinitely improved since the old Prince of Wales days. He seems almost completely to have lost his nervousness and shyness, and his charm and good manners are more apparent than ever.

After dinner, [Arthur] Rubinstein plays some Chopin and a few extra people come in. After Rubinstein has played three times, the King crosses the room towards him and says "We enjoyed that very much, Mr Rubinstein." I am delighted at this, since I was afraid that Rubinstein was about to play a fourth time. It is by this time 12.30 and the King starts saying good-bye. This takes so long that at our end of the room we imagine that he has departed, and get Noel Coward to sing us one of his latest songs. The King immediately returns on hearing this, and remains for another hour, which is not very flattering to Rubinstein.*

Diary   *June 18, 1936*

The House is packed for the debate on sanctions [against Italy], and it is obvious during question-time that the Opposition are out for battle. Anthony Eden adopts a tone of regretful frankness which, however, rather suggests an embarrassed apology. He is followed by Arthur Greenwood [Vice-Chairman of the Parliamentary Labour Party], who makes a second-rate platform speech. It is so bad that one feels actually uncomfortable at the thought that so many foreign diplomatists should be in the Gallery. He is followed by Lloyd George, who speaks from the Opposition box. His is a brilliant performance, ending up with a very amusing elaboration on the theme of leadership. He makes one serious mistake by saying that the British people will not fight for Austria. In so saying he obviously abandons the League of Nations point of view.

H.N. to V.S-W.   *June 28, 1936*
                                                     Cliveden, Taplow

Cliveden [the Astors' home], I admit is looking lovely. The party also is lavish and enormous. How glad I am that we are not so rich. I simply do not want a house like this where nothing is really yours, but belongs to servants and gardeners. There is a ghastly unreality about it all. Its beauty is purely scenic. I enjoy seeing it. But to own it, to live here, would be like living on the stage of the Scala theatre in Milan.

H.N. to V.S-W.   *July 1, 1936*

When the House of Commons gets to know me better, they will know that I am a good old tea-cup really. I do not mind that for the moment they should suppose I am dynamite disguised as vitriol. I cannot maintain the position I have now acquired. My present reputation is fallacious and transitory. It is a March flower. But I shall bloom all right in June. And my roots are deep in energy and faith. You know that – and that is where you help me. Politics I can look after myself. But my faith (in life and integrity and human nature) is something which you alone really understand, and to replenish which I rush to you like a petrol-filling station. We never talk about it, since we never talk about the really vital links between us. But that is where you help.

Diary   *July 13, 1936*

See Ramsay MacDonald. He is busy already with papers regarding the Coronation, and was trying to work out whether stands could not be erected in Hyde Park. This brings him to the problem of the King's appalling obstinacy and to the unfortunate Court Circulars in which Mrs Simpson's name figures as a guest. *He says this is making a bad effect in the country. "The people," he says, "do not mind fornication, but they loathe adultery."* The only person who can remedy this situation is Mrs Simpson herself, but there is always the possibility that her head (which as a head is not exceptional) may become turned.

Diary   *July 16, 1936*

Foreign Affairs Committee. Winston argues from the premise, which everyone accepts, that our main duty is to defend the British Empire and the Rhine frontier. What we have got to ask ourselves is whether that task would in the end be facilitated by our telling Germany she could take what she liked in the east. Were we to say this, Germany, within the course of a single year, would become dominant from Hamburg to the Black Sea, and we should be faced by a confederacy such as had never been seen since Napoleon.

> *Just before the House rose for the summer recess at the end of July the Spanish Civil War broke out. During the recess H.N. travelled to Northern Ireland and Scotland to do research for* Helen's Tower, *his biography of the first Marquess of Dufferin and Ava, and later to Austria, Venice and the French Riviera.*

Diary   *August 8, 1936*

The Spanish situation is hell. Philip Noel-Baker writes to *The Times* pretending that the Madrid Government is one which should command the support of all democratic liberals. In fact, of course, it is a mere Kerensky Government at the mercy of an armed proletariat. On the other hand, Franco and his Moors are no better. The Germans are fussing outside Barcelona with their pocket-battleships "making themselves felt". It is serious in that it emphasizes the division of Europe between left and right. Which way do we go? The pro-German and anti-Russian tendencies of the Tories will be fortified and increased.

Diary   *August 31, 1936*
                                                    Clandeboye, near Belfast

Go round the house carefully noting past things and memories. This is the first time in my life that I have become fully conscious of how old I am getting. Up till now I have regarded myself more or less as a young man. This depresses me and I feel very modest and crushed. Ride up to the Tower [Helen's Tower] with Basil [the fourth Marquess of Dufferin and Ava]. A lovely view. The old man Bruce at the Tower remembers me. "And what have you been doing Mr Nicolson all this long while?" What indeed? What indeed?

Diary   *September 8, 1936*
                                                            Sissinghurst

The Lindberghs, Betty Morrow and Constance [Morrow] come over from Long Barn in the afternoon. Lindbergh has just returned from Berlin where he has seen much of German aviation. He has obviously been much impressed by Nazi Germany. He considers that they possess the most powerful air-force in the world, with which they could do terrible damage to any other country, and could destroy our food supplies by sinking even convoyed ships. He admits that they are a great menace, but he denies that they are a menace to us. He contends that the future will see a complete separation between Fascism and Communism and he believes that if Great Britain supports the decadent French and the red Russians against Germany there will be an end to European civilization. He does not see any real possibility of our remaining in the centre between the right and the left. I point out to him that we are on this point a disunited nation, and that to go wholly red or wholly swastika would split our opinion from top to bottom. He contends that we cannot continue to remain on the hedge. That the old political divisions have ceased to count. That the severance today is between fascism and communism and that we cannot possibly find a middle way between these two opponents. I very much fear that he is correct in this diagnosis, and that our passion for compromise will lead us to a position of isolation, internal disunity and eventual collapse. Yet I cannot bring myself to envisage any adherence either to right or to left. Isolation seems our only policy. But it is not really feasible. Never have we been faced before by so

appalling a problem, since always before we have had a comparatively united public opinion.

H.N. to V.S-W. *September 22, 1936*
Schloss St Martin, Upper Austria

*Chips [Channon, H.N.'s host] is not really a snob in an ordinary
way. I suppose everyone has some sort of snobbishness somewhere
just like everybody has a few keys somewhere. What makes Chips
so exceptional is that he collects keys for keys sake. The corridors
of his mind are hung with keys which open no doors of his own
and no cupboards of his own but are just other peoples keys which
he collects. There they hang – French keys, English keys, American
keys, Italian keys and now a whole housekeeper's truss of Central
European keys.*

Diary *September 27, 1936*
Villa Mauresque, Cap Ferrat

*To Monaco where I am met by Willy [Somerset] Maugham's
enormous car and vast chauffeur. It starts with a loud snort as of six
horsemen of the Apocalypse and roars through Monaco, through
Villefranche, through Cap Dail, shrieking round precipices, hurtling
through caverns, thundering through village streets. I sit back and
pray to God in heaven. Miraculously we arrive.*

Diary *October 5, 1936*

Dine with Bernard Berenson at Lady Horner's house. He is very
interesting about London in the 'nineties. He used to dine regularly
with Oscar Wilde. He said that when alone with him the mask of
affectation gradually (but only gradually) dropped off. But that in
public he posed deliberately. Mrs Berenson says that, having met
him five nights in succession, he said to her "Now you have exhausted my repertory. I had only five subjects of conversation prepared and they have run out. I shall have to give you one of the
former ones. Which would you like?" They said they would like
the one on evolution. So he gave them the one on evolution.
    Berenson asks whether there are any conversationalists of my

generation. I am bound to say there are not. Not that I know of. We have no time.

H.N. to V.S-W.   *October 6, 1936*

*I went to my Party Meeting. Ramsay was in great form, and he chaffed me for being a friend of Wallis Simpson's. I do not know how he learnt that I ever knew her. I walked away with him and he spoke seriously about it. It seems that the King drove himself to Aberdeen to meet the lady and then drove her out to Balmoral. It is a real infatuation. What would his dear great grandmother [Queen Victoria] have said! But Ramsay thinks it will do harm. It irritates me that that silly little man *en somme* should destroy a great Monarchy by giggling into a flirtation with a third-rate American.*

Diary   *November 4, 1936*

Go to see Parliament opened. It pours with rain. The King's accent is really terrible. He speaks of Ammurica. I then lunch at the snack bar and thereafter change into my [Diplomatic Corps] uniform. At three I go to the House where I join Florence Horsburgh in Margesson's room [she was to move the Address in reply to the King's Speech and H.N. to second]. She is in brown velvet. We then go and sit behind the P[rime] M[inister]. He is very nice to us. Then the Speaker reads the speech and Miss Horsburgh rises. She is very calm and does it quite beautifully. I then get up and start off not feeling nervous. When I get to the part when I refer to Winston not having been elected for W. Leicester he shouts out "They also rejected the Rt Hon Member for the Scottish Universities [Ramsay Mac-Donald]". This leads to a howl from the Opposition, and when I go on to praise Ramsay MacDonald they hoot and interrupt. The rest of my speech goes off all right.

Diary   *November 7, 1936*

Many press cuttings come in which suggest to me that my speech on Tuesday was really more of a floater than I had imagined. It is most unfortunate, as I gather that they really did mean to give me a job in the Government when the reshuffle comes in the spring and I may now lose the chance forever. Three minutes of blindness and a ruined career! But I do not seriously believe this, although I could kick myself for having exaggerated the Ramsay part. I could have easily fulfilled the requirements of loyalty and courage by a fleeting reference which would not have provoked the outburst it did.

H.N., who had been seeing much of King Edward VIII and Mrs Simpson, was now a spectator from the sidelines of the dramatic events which led up to the King's abdication on December 10.

Diary   *November 18, 1936*

Have a long talk with Sibyl [Colefax]. She had been spending last Sunday down at the Fort [Belvedere] with nobody else there beyond a new naval equerry and Mrs Simpson. She had a heart-to-heart talk with the latter and found her really miserable. All sorts of people had come to her reminding her of her duty and begging her to leave the country. "They do not understand," she said, "that if I do so, the King will come after me regardless of anything. They would then get their scandal in a far worse form than they are getting it now." Sibyl then asked her whether the King had ever suggested marriage. She seemed surprised and said "of course not." Sibyl then suggested that it would be a good thing if certain Cabinet Ministers were told of this and were in a position to deny the story of the impending marriage. Mrs Simpson readily agreed to this, and authorised Sibyl to see Neville Chamberlain [Chancellor of the Exchequer]. Unfortunately Neville was ill in bed with gout, but Sibyl was able to send him a message through Mrs Chamberlain and derived the distinct impression that Baldwin had been told by the King that he was determined to marry Mrs Simpson after the Coronation. Sibyl agrees with me that Mrs Simpson is perfectly straightforward and well-intentioned, and that it is quite possible for the King to have spoken to Baldwin before raising the matter with Wallis herself. Sibyl wants me to do something more about it; but I refuse mainly because I dislike gossip but also because I remember how badly everybody burned their fingers over Mrs Fitzherbert [wife of George IV].

Diary   *November 30, 1936*

Ramsay MacDonald talks to me in deep sorrow about the King.
"That man," he says, "has done more harm to this country than
any man in history." It seems that the Cabinet are determined that
he shall abdicate. So are the Privy Council. But he imagines that the
country, the great warm heart of the people, are with him. I do not
think so. The upper classes mind her being an American rather
than her being divorced. The lower classes do not mind her being
an American but loathe the idea that she has had two husbands
already. Ramsay is miserable about it. The effect on America, the
effect on Canada, the effect on our prestige. And in particular he
is furious because Malcolm [MacDonald] had almost succeeded in
persuading de Valera to accept Edward VIII as King, and now the
whole thing is torn to pieces. *I am distressed since I felt sorry for
Wallis Simpson and hoped that she was a decent person. But after
her having lied like that to Sibyl and allowing Sibyl to make a fool
of herself in going to see Chamberlain – I cannot feel that she can
be anything better than a fool or a minx.*

H.N. to V.S-W.   *December 7, 1936*

You will be wanting to hear the news, so I will write tonight instead
of waiting until tomorrow morning. All is settled for the King's
abdication, but Baldwin has given the King "a few more days" to
think it over. In the House today, Winston (whose line is, "let the
King choose his girl") suffered an utter defeat. He almost lost his
head, and he certainly lost his command of the House. It was
terribly dramatic.

   Oliver Baldwin came to see me this morning. He told me that
his father and the King walked round and round the garden at Fort
Belvedere discussing the business, and then returned to the library
having agreed that H.M. must abdicate. Stanley Baldwin was feeling
exhausted. He asked for a whisky-and-soda. The bell was rung: the
footman came: the drink was produced. S.B. raised his glass and
said (rather foolishly to my mind), "Well, Sir, whatever happens,
My Mrs and I wish you happiness from the depths of our souls." At
which the King burst into floods of tears. Then S.B. himself began

to cry. What a strange conversation-piece, those two blubbering together on the sofa!

Diary   *December 10, 1936*

The House is crowded and rather nervous and noisy. I am glad to have got my front row of the stalls so early. The Prime Minister comes in, pushing past the encumbered knees of his colleagues, and finds his place. He has a box with him, and on sitting down, at once discovers that he has lost the key. He probes and rummages for a bit and then finds the key. He unlocks the box, extracts some sheets of paper with the royal monogram in red, and with it some flimsy notes of his own, more squalid than a young Labour candidate would dare to produce at a Wapping by-election. He collects them hurriedly and the next minute seizes the red-monographed sheets, walks firmly to the Bar, turns round, bows, and advances to the Chair. He stops and bows again. "A message from the King," he shouts, "signed by his Majesty's own hand." He then hands the papers to the Speaker.

The latter rises and reads out the message of Abdication in a quavering voice. The feeling that at any moment he may break down from emotion increases our own emotion. I have never known in any assemblage such accumulation of pity and terror.

The Prime Minister then rises. He tells the whole story. His papers are in a confused state. He confuses dates and turns to Simon "It was a Monday, was it not, the 27th?" The artifice of such asides is so effective that one imagines it to be deliberate. There is no moment when he overstates emotion or indulges in oratory. The tragic force of its simplicity. It was Sophoclean and almost unbearable. There was no question of applause. It was the silence of Gettysburg.

On leaving the library, I bumped straight into Baldwin in the corridor. It was impossible not to say something. I murmured a few kind words. He took me by the arm.

"You are very kind," he said, "but what do you really think about it?" I detected in him that intoxication which comes to a man, even a tired man, after a triumphant success. "It was almost wholly unprepared. I had a success, my dear Nicolson, at the moment I most needed it. *Now is the time to go.*" I made no answer.

*"You see," he went on – still holding me by the arm, "the man is mad. *MAD*. He could see nothing but that woman. He did not realize that any other considerations avail. He lacks religion. I told his mother so. I said to her 'Ma'am, the King has no religious sense.' I do not mean by that his atheism. I suppose you are either an atheist or an agnostic. But you have a religious sense. I noticed it the other day. (That meant my sticking up for Ramsay.) You realize that there is something more than the opportune. *He* doesn't realize that there is anything beyond. I told his mother so. The Duke of York has always been bothered about it. I love the man. But he must go."*

Then he got on to Winston. He said, "Do you know, my dear Nicolson, I think Winston is the most suspicious man I know. Just now I said that the King said to me, 'Let this thing be settled between you and me alone. I don't want outside interference.' I meant to indicate by that the reason I had not made it a Cabinet question from the start. But Winston thought it was a thrust aimed at him, and has been at my Private Secretary within the last five minutes. What can one do with a man like that?"

I suggested that Winston had put himself in a false position. The P.M. flung up his hand. "We are all in false positions!"

No man has dominated the House as he dominated it tonight, and he knows it.

Diary   *December 31, 1936*

So ends a full and historic year. I have been well and happy. A happy year, a useful year, but clouded by menace on the Continent. I reach the age of fifty. That is a deep sorrow to me. I should not mind it so much. But I have dispersed my energies in life, done too many different things, and have no sense of reaching any harbour. I am still very promising and shall continue to be so until the day of my death. But what enjoyment and what interest I have derived from my experience! I suppose I am too volatile and fluid. But few people can have extracted such happiness from fluidity, and when I look back upon my life, it is as gay as an Alpine meadow patinated with the stars of varied flowers. Would I feel happier if I had stuck to a single crop of lucerne or clover? NO.

At the end of the year, H.N. left England for Uganda, as a member of a Parliamentary Commission to study and report on African education. He was away ten weeks. This experience confirmed his view that civilisation existed only in a few Western European cities, but he was fascinated by the journey, and described it at great length in his diary, from which only very few passages are reproduced here.

Diary   *January 13, 1937*
                                                  Entebbe, Uganda

After dinner last night we discussed the capacity of the African brain. Kauntze [the Director of Medical Services, H.N.'s host] said that it had been proved by Windt that the cells of the African brain were undeveloped. What he wanted to find out was whether these cells developed in the educated African. So we must cut up a Makerere [College] student and see.

Diary   *January 23, 1937*
                                                  Ujiji, Tanganyika

Drive in procession to Ujiji, the big native centre where Stanley met Livingstone [in 1871]. We go direct to the spot where this famous meeting took place. An old man is brought up in a net and deposited upon the spot – marked as it now is by a monument, the old mango tree having died – and is given an ebony and silver walking-stick by H.E. [Sir Harold MacMichael, Governor]. The reason for this is that as a boy he was Livingstone's servant. We ask him about Livingstone. He raises bleared eyes to us and fumbles in his purple toga, producing a stained piece of paper. It is only a news-cutting from some African paper saying that he (Jumbee Heri) is the sole survivor among Livingstone's servants. We can get no more out of him, and he is put back in his grass net and hoiked up on to a pole and carried off swaying slightly and grasping his stick between the meshes of his net.

Diary   *February 8, 1937*
                                                  Kampala, Uganda

Get up at dawn, the freshest dawn I have ever felt outside of

Switzerland. Great miles of dew and early sunshine. We motor to Nakuru [Kenya] aerodrome. The famous flamingo lake is quite near and we fly over it. It looks at first as if it had been edged in a coral necklace, but as we swooped down, the necklace dissolved into a million pelicans flying in wedges. Below us the lake, with this screen of pink flamingoes flying across it, and through them the wake of a vast hippopotamus. And around us plain and mountain in the early light. Probably the loveliest thing I have seen. We then turn west and after an hour we leave Rift Valley and drop down to Lake Victoria. We land at Entebbe at 10.30, having accomplished a two-day journey in two hours.

Diary   *February 13, 1937*
                                                      Entebbe, Uganda

I talk to the boys in the Big School. I am tired and feel a gap between my mind and my words. This missing on two cylinders is increased by the fact that the boys laugh at the wrong time. My jokes, poor little things, are met in black blank silence. My few patriotic allusions arouse a flash of white teeth and a cacchination throughout the hall. At the end they ask questions which are sensible and indicate that they really did understand the whole time.

Diary   *February 22, 1937*
                                                      Khartoum

*The A.D.C., Walker, takes Rob [Bernays] and me before breakfast to see the *Bordein*, General Gordon's little steamer in which he might have escaped, but which he sent up river with despatches on the last day but one. It ran aground and was seized by the Mahdi who used it for thirteen years. Then we recaptured it after Omdurman and it is now anchored in mid-Nile as a curiosity. It was once a Thames steamer and is now just a hulk. The old armour plating remains very battered and seared. Sanders, the Private Secretary, realising our interest in Gordon, manages to unearth some photographs of the Palace as it then was.* He produces Gordon's old servant who happened to have gone off the day before the Dervishes entered [Khartoum, March 1884], and who thus escaped alive. He was quite good on the subject of the photographs. He showed us that what we took to be a flowering shrub or something (since the photographs were really very faded) was in fact Gordon's elephant tied up to a palm tree. He then took us to the place where Gordon was murdered. He says that there is no doubt at all that he was murdered on the steps. He showed us exactly how the present steps and the original steps differ from each other. He says that the picture "The Death of General Gordon" is almost wholly accurate. He added that they did not find Gordon at first, not because he was in hiding, since he was in the dining room, but because they were chasing Coptic clerks in the garden, murdering them and making them squeal. Then they came to the Palace itself. Gordon came out from the dining-room on to the verandah and shouted to the Sudanese guard below in very bad Arabic, "Kill them! Kill them!" He was leaning over the rail of the balcony shouting, "Hit them! Hit them!" when a dervish flung a spear which made him spin round and stand for a moment on the top of the stairs before he toppled down. Then they cut off his head and almost cut him to pieces. The remains "were thrown into the river at the place where the soldiers used to wash", i.e. opposite the Palace gate. The old man was not in the least gaga and became quite excited in explaining it all. But he had small sense of proportion and seemed more anxious to explain to us that there were three lavatories on each floor of the Palace than to tell us the details of Gordon's death. He said that although he did not witness the scene, he had obtained full details the next day from someone who had. I expect that this is the most authentic account that can be derived.

Despite his promise to V.S-W., H.N. flew home to England on March 7. V.S-W. was touring Algeria with Gwen St Aubyn and returned to Sissinghurst in the middle of the month. The Coronation of King George VI was on May 12.

Diary   *March 17, 1937*

It is quite possible, without undue shame, to arrive at Buckingham Palace in a taxi even though one's taxi driver (in an orgy of democracy) insists upon throwing his cigarette down upon the red carpet of the steps; but it is difficult when the outer hall is filled with Beefeaters, Gentlemen-at-Arms, and Royal Watermen to dash past duchesses in their tiaras and to say to someone (who for all one knows, may be the Lord Chamberlain or the Master of the Horse) "please, do you think I could get a taxi?"

The dining table is one mass of gold candelabra and scarlet tulips. Behind us the whole of the Windsor plate is massed in tiers. The dinner has been unwisely selected since we have soup, fish, quail, ham, chicken, ice and savoury. The wine on the other hand is very excellent and the port superb. I discuss with David Cecil the reasons why we have been asked. He says, "I know why I have been asked. I have been asked as a younger member of the British aristocracy." I say that I have been asked as a rising politician, and I regret to observe that David is not as convinced by this explanation as I might have wished.

Afterwards the Queen goes the rounds. She wears upon her face a faint smile indicative of how much she would have liked her dinner party were it not for the fact that she was Queen of England. Nothing could exceed the charm or dignity which she displays, and I cannot help feeling what a mess poor Mrs Simpson would have made of such an occasion. It demonstrated to us more than anything else how wholly impossible that marriage would have been. The Queen teases me very charmingly about my pink face and my pink views in exactly the same words as Mr Baldwin had used previously, so that I felt sure that during dinner he had told her of the remark that he cast at me from the Front Bench.

I go back to the Stanley's house and have some beer while we discuss the strange legend of monarchy.

Diary   *April 4, 1937*

Victor [Cazalet] is very excited by hearing that instructions have been issued from Buckingham Palace that members of the Royal Family are in future to cut Emerald Cunard. This is apparently due to (a) her having encouraged Mrs Simpson to become Queen of England and (b) to her having denied Mrs Simpson thrice when the crash came.

Diary   *May 12, 1937*

The Coronation. We breakfast in the House, and I then show Copley [Amory] and Nigel their seats in Palace Yard. I go to see

Ramsay MacDonald for a moment and find him sitting in his room punching a hole in his sword belt and looking very distinguished in a Trinity House uniform. I tell him how well he looks: – "Yes," he answers, "when I was a visitor to a lunatic asylum I always noticed how well the worst lunatics looked." I then go across to the Abbey and find my seat in the South Transept. Almost before we are aware what is happening the ceremony begins. I am not going to describe it since the newspapers accounts are full and accurate and since I shall write something for the *Figaro* myself. I get away about 2.40 and have an excellent lunch at the House. The carriage arrangements for the Abbey have broken down completely, and the guests were stranded until nearly 7.

Diary   *May 27, 1937*

I arrive at the House just in time to hear Baldwin make his last statement amid loud applause. [He was succeeded as Prime Minister by Neville Chamberlain on May 28.] With characteristic subtlety he does it in the form of an answer to a question on Parliamentary salaries, so that his final words are to give us all £200 a year more. This means a lot to the Labour members and was done with Baldwin's usual consummate taste. No man has ever left in such a blaze of affection.

Ramsay also has to answer a question and does it well. He is greeted with cheers. I go to see him afterwards. He had had an interview that morning with the King and had been offered and refused an Earldom. He had also seen the Queen. Poor old boy, he was pleased by the kindness they had shown him. He had told the Queen that the King had "come on magnificently since his accession". She had been pleased. "And am I doing all right?" she asked. "Oh you . . ." Ramsay had answered with a sweep taking that all for granted. The King had told him that for long periods at the Coronation ceremony he was unaware of what was happening. There is no doubt that they have entered upon this task with a real religious sense.

H.N. to V.S-W.   *June 8, 1937*

You were such an angel to take trouble about my old women and it really was worthwhile [three days earlier fifty members of the

West Leicester Women's Conservative Association visited Sissing-hurst]. I do not know whether this story of a lovely castle will affect the Labour vote. People are so odd. They might say, "He is a hum-bug: he talks Labour and lives in a castle." But they might also say, "How splendid of him when he lives in a castle to come and worry about our little affairs."

Anyhow, never has Sissinghurst looked more lovely or been more appreciated. I must say, Farley [head gardener] has made the place look like a gentleman's garden, and you with your extra-ordinary taste have made it look like nobody's garden but your own. I think the secret of your gardening is simply that you have the courage to abolish ugly or unsuccessful flowers. Except for those beastly red-hot pokers which you have a weakness for, there is not an ugly flower in the whole place. We have got what we wanted to get – a perfect proportion between the classic and the romantic, between the element of expectation and the element of surprise. But the point of the garden will not be apparent until the hedges have grown up, especially (most important of all) the holly hedge in the flower garden. But it is lovely, lovely, lovely – and you must be pleased with your work.

Diary   *July 27, 1937*

The Foreign Affairs Committee is addressed by Anthony Eden. He gives a general review of the problems from Tokyo to Washington. He says that the French really did take the initiative on Non-Intervention [in Spain] and were not put up to it by us. He admits that Non-Intervention has largely failed, but he says that it has pre-vented the dispatch of organised consignments of men and that those who have indulged in it are now sorry that they spoke. He makes a great point of the fact that whereas the difficulties of the dictator states are hidden behind a steel curtain, all our own cards are on the table. We must never bluff. But in fact the position is better than formerly since both Germany and Italy are abating their former truculent attitude. The foundations of peace, he says, are firmer than we suppose, and our diplomatic position with the neutral countries in the Eastern Mediterranean and in the United States is stronger than ever before. In private conversation with him afterwards he says that he thinks the Spanish War will last another year, and he hopes it will end in a deadlock out of which some middle government will emerge. He points out that if Franco wins he will be able to hold Spanish Morocco but that if he loses the Government will not be strong enough to turn him out, and a very difficult situation will arise.

H.N. did not have a holiday abroad during the summer recess. During that period, from August until October 21st, he finished Helen's Tower, *which was published in the autumn with V.S-W.'s* Pepita.

Diary   *November 10, 1937*

Take the 8.53 to London [from Leicester]. The porter tells me as he puts in my luggage that Ramsay MacDonald is dead, and I am so shocked by this information that I tell the man to go to the Central Station instead of the L.M.S.

Otto Kyllman [of Constables] asks me to go and see him urgently and then suggests that I should do the official biography of Mac-Donald. I say that I don't admire him either morally or intellectually sufficiently to justify so much labour. One can never write a biography of anyone for whom one did not have real enthusiasm.

Diary   *November 15, 1937*

Have a long talk in the smoking room with Winston Churchill. He congratulates me on my intervention in the Foreign Affairs Committee on Thursday, saying that he has seldom seen so short a speech make so much effect in so short a time. I say that I feel terribly hampered in making up my mind about foreign politics, since I have actually no conception whatsoever as to our real defensive power. Obviously, if it is a question between complete defeat and the surrender of the German colonies, there can be no question whatsoever. But if we are in fact able to defend ourselves, I see no reason why we should make concessions without receiving something in return. Winston says that it is of course impossible for the Government to disclose our exact strength at the moment, but that "he takes it" Germany's air force is a little stronger than the

French and British air forces combined. If you add to that the Italian air force, which is a very excellent striking machine, we are indeed not in a position to go to war without very active Russian assistance. He is in a very quiet, sensible and chastened mood.

Diary   *November 25, 1937*

Henry [Chips] Channon asks my advice about his diaries which he has kept at great length since 1917. He says that they are very outspoken and scandalous, but that they record the lives of important people for the last twenty years. He has made a Will leaving them to me plus £500. I say that he must make another Will leaving them plus £1,000 to Christ Church Library, with instructions that thirty years after his death the four youngest fellows of the time should consider their publication. [They were, in fact, bequeathed to his son.]

Diary   *December 8, 1937*

Go to breakfast with Lord Baldwin at 69 Eaton Square. I arrive to find him seated at the breakfast table opening his letters. He is rather lame with arthritis but otherwise looks well. He said that he only got out just in time and that a few weeks more would have led to a real collapse similar to that of Ramsay MacDonald's. He said that he had always looked forward to his retirement to be able to read and think, but that for the first three months he had been quite unable to think and only able to read detective novels. He was now beginning to recover and was reading Froude on Erasmus.

He goes on to talk about his mother's family and the Burne Jones–Kipling circle. He said that when Morris died at 63, the doctor said "He has died of being William Morris." We then talk about the Abdication, and he says that there were patches in the King's brain which were those of a child of thirteen. He considers Mrs Simpson to be an admirable woman within her circle of conscience, but to have no conception of proportions outside that circle. He showed me the original of the little pencilled note that King Edward had sent him after the Abdication.

He talked of Winston Churchill and said he lacked soul. I suggested that Winston is very sympathetic to misfortune in others. He answered, "I don't deny that Winston has a sentimental side."

He then goes on: "And what is more, he cannot really tell lies. That is what makes him so bad a conspirator."

I was alone with him for over an hour, and nothing could have exceeded his mellow charm.

Diary   *December 31, 1937*

I have been conscious that my political career has suffered a decline. I do not possess sufficient combative instincts to impose my personality upon the House of Commons. Although I am a good platform speaker and a better lecturer, I am not at my ease in the Chamber.

The difficulty is that Foreign Affairs, which are my special subject, are not a subject on which I wish to speak. It only does harm. Thus I have remained largely silent and the impression is that I have "dropped out". By one good speech I could destroy that impression and recover the general expectation which they had of me before my unfortunate speech on the Address in 1936. But I feel somehow that I am not sufficiently virile to force myself upon the House and that I am too old to create a gradual impression as Baldwin did.

How much do I mind this? Probably more than I realise. I am so happy in my domestic and ordinary life that I do not notice much that I have not fulfilled high hopes.

Almost from the moment when he succeeded Baldwin, Neville Chamberlain assumed increasing control of Foreign Affairs. He by-passed the Foreign Office by sending his own emissaries to appease the Dictators. Anthony Eden, his Foreign Secretary, protested that this private diplomacy flattered enemies and offended allies. In January, when Eden was on holiday, Chamberlain brushed aside President Roosevelt's offer to mediate between the European powers, and Eden returned too late to repair the damage. At the moment when Hitler was openly threatening the independence of Austria, Chamberlain proposed to open discussions with Mussolini. The timing and tactics of these negotiations were the main cause of the disagreement between the Prime Minister and Foreign

*Secretary; their mutual distrust lay behind it. Eden re-
signed on February 20 and was succeeded by Lord Halifax. H.N. spoke up strongly for Eden in the House and
in the Foreign Affairs Committee. The National Labour
Party virtually disowned his conduct, but his Leicester
constituents gave him a unanimous vote of confidence.*

H.N. to V.S-W.   *January 7, 1938*

*I went to Wandsworth Jail yesterday morning. The Governor was
a splendid type of person. He took me round himself through every
cranny of the place. It is rather ghastly – not that they could make it
better, but that imprisonment is a ghastly thing. What is so touching
is their little possessions which they deliver up when they enter the
prison. They take off their clothes and never see them again until
they come out. But what is nice is that they clean and press the
clothes for them before they are coming out so as to give them back
their self-respect. I do not quite see how it could be more humane,
but of course I went away feeling a beast and a brute.*

Diary   *January 20, 1938*

*Take the train to Leicester. I have no time to dine and merely dress
and go on to a dance and reception given by Acton the Lord Mayor.
He is very Labour and disapproves of me. He is a ghastly Trades
Union type. I cruise about the dancing floor with my synthetic constituency smile, but am conscious that I do not recognize half the
people and merely blink.*

To the Club where I meet Bertie Jarvis. We go over future engagements and I see that he is rattled by [Barnett] Janner [Labour
candidate for West Leicester who eventually defeated H.N. in
1945]. He thinks he will turn me out, but does not express it in that
way. The way he expresses it is to say, "We will give him a fine run
for his money." In a way, I think that Janner will make a better
Member than I am.

Diary   *February 3, 1938*

Dine at St James' with Gladwyn Jebb. Characteristically we do not
touch on the centre of Foreign Affairs. Here I am, Vice Chairman of

the Foreign Affairs Committee of the House, and there he is, Private Secretary to the Permanent Under Secretary of State [Sir Alexander Cadogan] – and friends of long standing – yet such is the tradition of discretion that I dare not ask him a single question nor even why it is that he has to return to the Office after dinner. That would not be so in France.

Diary   *February 15, 1938*

The news arrives of the result of the Berchtesgaden conversations between Hitler and [the Austrian Chancellor] Schuschnigg. Guido Schmidt is to be made Foreign Minister and Seyss-Inquart is to be given the police. This means that Austria hands over the direction of her affairs to Berlin. She will retain nominal independence. Mussolini went off to the Abruzzi just in time so as not to be able to answer Schuschnigg's appeal. But what will he be given in return for Hitler's obtaining Austria? This is a bad first symptom of the axis.

Diary   *February 17, 1938*

Meeting of the Foreign Affairs Committee. I open the discussion by indicating that Hitler has now reestablished his legend and imposed the will of the party on the army. The cautious people have been proved wrong. I discuss the implication of the Austrian agreement and indicate that Mussolini must have known in advance and must have been bought with certain promises. What were those promises and why has he now 100,000 men in Libya? I conclude by suggesting that we should keep a stiff upper lip, not throw sops or slops about, wait, and above all arm. Winston takes a far more truculent attitude than I do. The whole feeling of the meeting is very different from that of a year ago. They no longer believe that we can buy Germany off with concessions.

Diary   *February 20, 1938*

The Cabinet meet three times today, and on the late news it is put out that Eden has resigned. We spend much of the morning listening to Hitler's Reichstag speech on the wireless. It is meant to be moderate, but his references to foreign countries, his talk of "steel and iron", are received with wild demoniac yells.

Diary   *February 21, 1938*

*Party meeting at Tufton Street. Malcolm [MacDonald] takes the chair and tells us what happened. He spoke calmly and quietly. He states that in his opinion Eden made a mistake. He goes on to say that Eden was his best friend in the Cabinet and in fact dined with him when he drafted his letter of resignation. He then explains that there was no difference as to the objectives of policy, and that Eden agreed with the Cabinet as to the necessity of talks with Italy and Germany. His recent disagreement with the P.M. turned upon a question of method. His resignation, owing to the gradual accumulation of these small differences, was inevitable sooner or later. He felt that assurances regarding Spain and propaganda should precede any official conversations. The P.M. felt that we should make a gesture, open negotiations and hope that the good feeling thus established would lead the Italian to behave kindly to us. Hence the split.

I say that I shall speak in favour of Anthony and against the P.M. They say that will be all right so long as I disassociate the Party. I then go down to the House. There are large crowds. Towards the end the P.M. comes in and is loudly cheered. I do not join in. Then Anthony and Bobbety Cranborne [Under Secretary of State for Foreign Affairs who resigned with Eden] come in shyly across the bar and sit in the famous seat below the gangway. They are cheered wildly by the Opposition. He [Eden] looks very pale and a trifle nervous. He makes a speech which was not really very good. There was just a sufficient note of recrimination to spoil the dignified effect and not enough to constitute an appeal.

Bobbety follows and is far more effective. He speaks of Italian blackmail which arouses vociferous cheers. The P.M. follows – he is halting, precise and grim. It goes very badly. Then the debate opens. I am called about 7.15. I speak for about twenty minutes. The House crowds in. That is very flattering. I attack Italy and the P.M. and defend Anthony – "butchered to make a Roman holiday." I am loudly cheered by the Opposition. Afterwards there is that scurry which one knows accompanies a successful speech. Lloyd

George says, "A fine Parliamentary performance." Winston Churchill says, "You spoke wonderfully. I envy you your gift." The others
fiddled about.*

H.N. to V.S-W.   *February 25, 1938*

When I arrived at Leicester station I was met by Jarvis who informed me that the opinion in the Conservative Association was all
on the side of Chamberlain and that I had better say nothing at all.
I said "Not at all. I have come up here to explain my action to my
constituents and explain it I shall."

My speech in fact went well. They did not understand most of
it but they agreed. They passed a unanimous vote of confidence
with real enthusiasm. I was, as the papers say, "visibly moved".
And this morning I got a note from Bertie Jarvis: "Sorry, Harold.
You were right and I was wrong. The speech was triumphant."

We had a most unpleasant meeting of the Foreign Affairs Committee. We heard that they were going to ask for our resignation as
Chairman and Vice Chairman. Or at least that Nancy Astor was
going to ask. Paul Evans [Chairman] and I therefore agreed that we
should resign on our own initiative. Thus when the meeting opened,
Paul got up and said that he and I and Jock McEwan [Secretary]
had determined to resign. The room was packed and there was one
great shout of "No!" That sounds splendid, but what it really meant
was that they thought our resignation would embarrass the Government, as indeed it would. Several people got up quite shamelessly
and suggested that we should not resign at once but merely do so
later when feeling had diminished. At this Winston in all his
majesty rose and said that they were being mean and petty. They
were not treating us fairly and he must insist on a vote, either Yes
or No. They then voted. Those in favour of our not resigning were
unanimous except for one little vicious hand against. That hand
was the hand of Nancy Astor.

We then adjourned in some excitement. In the corridor a friend
of mine called Alan Graham came up to Nancy and said, "I do not
think you behaved very well." She turned upon him and said, "Only
a Jew like you would *dare* to be rude to me." He replied, "I should
much like to smack your face." I think she is a little mad.

Diary   *March 8, 1938*

I work away with Nigel Law. He is a great friend of Eden's. He said that the P.M. had of late been definitely rude to Eden and that the latter had derived the impression that he was wanting to drive him out. The P.M. had returned a snubbing message to President Roosevelt. Eden had much resented this since it ruined his policy of close relations with America. The P.M. is bitterly anti-Russian and also anti-America. The soul of the ironmonger is not one which will save England.

H.N. to V.S-W.   *March 9, 1938*

I dined with [Sir Edward] Spears. Vansittart was there. He was most gloomy. He thinks that we can scarcely prevent Germany collaring Eastern Europe, and that when she has done so, she will turn round on us and demand our submission. Well, it may not work out like that. But opinion at the moment is as gloomy as in the days after Austerlitz. Nobody who is well-informed believes that there is any chance of negotiations with Germany leading to anything at all. We may get some scrap out of Italy, but it will be a mere crumb of comfort and quite unreliable.

> *On March 12 German troops crossed the Austrian frontier and entered Vienna unopposed. Austria was declared annexed and Schuschnigg was arrested. Hitler was triumphantly received in Vienna on March 14, the very day when Chamberlain told the House that only the combined forces of Europe could have prevented it.*

Diary   *March 15, 1939*

This sense of danger and anxiety hangs over us like a pall. Hitler has completely collared Austria; no question of an Anschluss, just complete absorption.

Dine with Sibyl. Desmond [MacCarthy] is in despair and says that the Government have betrayed the country and that the Tories think only of a Red danger and let the Empire slide. I am in grave doubts about my position. How can I continue to support a Government like this?

Diary *March 16, 1938*

Go to Pratt's [Club] with Winston Churchill. He doesn't fully agree with us about Spain [H.N. had told the P.M. earlier that day that Britain should "occupy Minorca"], but mainly because of his personal friendship with Spanish grandees. He says that never before has a man inherited a more ghastly situation than Neville Chamberlain, and he places the blame wholly on Baldwin. He says that in his long experience he has never known a Conservative Party composed of so many blind and obstinate men. He says that he will wait for a day or two in the hope that the negotiations which are now going on between Chamberlain, Attlee and Sinclair [a fact denied by Attlee] for a formula of policy which will command the assent of the whole House have either failed or come to fruition. But if no clear statement is issued between now and Wednesday next, he will refuse the whip and take some fifty people with him. This threat should in itself suffice to determine the Government. He says that the situation is worse than in 1914. "We stand to lose everything by failing to take some strong action. Yet if we take strong action, London will be a shambles in half-an-hour."

Diary *April 7, 1938*

Paul Emrys-Evans tells me that the Foreign Affairs Committee wish me to resign my post as Vice Chairman. I say I shall do so. I know that I cannot possibly continue since I disagreed with the Chamberlain policy. But I do not like being turned out.

> *In April H.N. went on a British Council speaking tour of the Balkans, and with a secret mission from the Foreign Office to attempt to restore some confidence among the Eastern Europeans. His visit was used in the Balkan capitals as an excuse for pro-Western demonstrations.*

H.N. to V.S-W. *April 17, 1938*
British Legation, Bucharest

At 12.30 I said that I must dress for luncheon. As I walked upstairs I felt strangely giddy. The staircase seemed to shift and wobble. I was appalled. Suppose I came over faint during my luncheon? That would be hell. I arrayed myself miserably in the tail-coat of Rex Hoare [the British Minister] which would not, I regret, meet in front. But it looked all right. Then I espied the bottle of Sal Volatile. I corked it tightly and put it into my pocket, in fact the only pocket which I could call my own, my trouser pocket. Then off I went.

At the Palace an aide-de-camp in stays and aiguillettes arrived and made polite conversation. Then a lift hummed and two pekinese darted in barking followed by the King [Carol] in naval uniform. I bowed. He greeted me with affection and respect. We passed into the dining-room. I sat on his right. The aide-de-camp sat on his left. The pekinese sat on his knee. We started conversation.

He had ordered, he said, a purely Rumanian luncheon. God, it was good! In spite of my feeling so faint, I gobbled hard. We talked agreeably. He is a bounder but less of a bounder than he seemed in London. He was more at ease. His Windsor blue eyes were wistful and he had something behind them. He spoke with intelligence about Chamberlain and Eden and the Italian Agreement and the French Cabinet and the League of Nations. He was well-informed and most sensible. We kept all debating topics away.

I was beginning to enjoy my conversation when I was aware of a cold trickle and the smell of ammonia. I thrust my hand into my pocket. It was too late. The Sal had indeed proved Volatile and my trousers were rapidly drenched. I seized my napkins and began mopping surreptitiously. My remarks became bright and rather fevered, but quite uninterrupted. I mopped secretly while the aroma of Sal Volatile rose above the smell of *gruzhenkoia*.

This was agony. I scarcely heard what he was saying. "Have you," he was asking, "recovered your land-legs yet? After three days in the train one feels the room rocking like after three days at sea." So that was it! Why on earth had he not told me before, and now it was too late. I recovered my composure and dropped my sodden napkin. The conversation followed normal lines. At 2.45 he rose abruptly. I rose, too, casting a terrified glance at the plush seat of my chair. It bore a deep wet stain. What, oh what, will the butler think? He will only think one thing.

H.N. to V.S-W. *April 22, 1938*
Sofia

I went to write my name upon the King [Boris of Bulgaria]. There were four books to write in: the King's; the Queen's; the Princess's; and the *Prince héritier*, who is eighteen months. I wrote my name very distinctly in the last as he must have difficulty, being so young, in reading foreign hand-writings.

Then to see the Prime Minister [Keosseivanoff] in the Foreign Office. It is the same as in my day and I thought how often father must have waited in that waiting-room [Lord Carnock was British Agent in Sofia in 1894–5, when H.N. was eight]. The Prime Minister was not an attractive man. An ex-diplomatist with those over-polished manners, that *boulevard extérieur* elegance, which always faintly annoys me.

Then came the Press in a band. I sat there and they fired questions at me. I was as discreet as I could be. Here again I am front-page news. It is pathetic how these people long for British friendship and how they exaggerate my importance and the meaning of my visit.

Diary   May 2, 1938

Luncheon to meet Baroness [Karen] Blixen [the author] of Kenya – a haggard wide-eyed wench of fifty. Ethel Smyth [the composer] comes in. She has a telephone box in order to hear but she puts it the wrong way round and is absolutely stone deaf. She blows her nose on her muffler. She is rather drunk and doddery. She had come up from Oxford and had spent an hour and a half at the Paddington Hotel reading P. G. Wodehouse and drinking sherry. Thus she is wobbly the poor old sweet.

Diary   May 6, 1938

Lunch with H. G. Wells at 13 Hanover Terrace. The other guests are Bernard Shaw and Mrs Brendan Bracken, Penelope Dudley Ward, and Moura Budberg. Shaw looks very frail and jaunty. We talked about T. E. Lawrence and Shaw says that his mistake was that he always tried to hide in the limelight. He says that he had a boyish mind and that his smile remained that of a public school boy. Wells teases him about his love of publicity and he is none too pleased. He talks about Barrie. Shaw says that Barrie would talk quite a great deal but it was always dull. He was not an attractive man. Like a spinster.

H.N. to V.S-W.   *May 17, 1938*

We had an excitement yesterday, Swinton [Air Minister] sacked. But how silly the whole thing is! Here we are in the gravest crisis in our history, with a genius like Winston doing nothing and Kingsley Wood as our Minister for Air with Harold Balfour (a mere lick-spittle) as his No. 2. It is all due to David Margesson [Chief Whip]. I admire David, since he is strong and efficient and kind. But I do not believe that he is a good Cabinet-maker. Much sickness left behind. Nobody understands why Euan Wallace is sent to the Treasury. Nobody understands why on earth [Lord] Stanley (who is amiable but stone deaf) is given the Dominions. Nobody understands anything. There is a real impression that the whole show is going to crack up.

Diary   *May 18, 1938*

On my way back I stop at Pratts' where I find three young Peers who state that they would prefer to see Hitler in London than a Socialist administration. I go to bed slowly, pondering upon the Decline and Fall of the British Empire.

Diary   *May 22, 1938*

Charles and Anne Lindbergh and Mrs Morrow come over from Long Barn. Lindbergh is most pessimistic. He says that we cannot possibly fight since we should certainly be beaten. The German Air Force is ten times superior to that of Russia, France and Great Britain put together. Our defences are simply futile and the [barrage-] balloons a mere waste of money. He thinks that we should just give way and then make an alliance with Germany. To a certain extent his views can be discounted, (a) because he naturally believes that aeroplanes will be the determinant factor in war; (b) because he believes in the Nazi theology, all tied up with his hatred of degeneracy and his hatred of democracy as represented by the free Press and the American public. But even when one makes these discounts, the fact remains that he is probably right in saying that we are out-mastered in the air.

Diary   *May 26, 1938*

Lunch with Maureen Stanley. The Halifaxes are there. Lord Halifax tells me that Goebbels said to him "You must realise how sensitive we are. You have a three hundred years tradition behind you. We have only four." That means that they regard themselves as something quite new. We regard them as a development of Prussian history. They regard themselves as a revolution. They are thus enraged when we suggest that Hitler might go to a better tailor. We are rather arrogant and insensitive regarding that aspect.

We discuss the question of conciliating Goering. Halifax says that he would be pleased by an invitation to Sandringham. I say that we should resent any such thing. It would affect American opinion. It would lower our dignity. No – ask Goering to Nepal as much as you like: but do not expect the Queen to shake hands with him. Halifax is rather startled by our vehemence.

Diary   *June 6, 1938*

Chamberlain (who has the mind and manner of a clothes-brush) aims only at assuring temporary peace at the price of ultimate defeat. He would like to give Germany all she wants at the moment, and cannot see that if we make this surrender we shall be unable to resist other demands. If we assuage the German alligator with fish from other ponds, she will wax so fat that she will demand fish from our own ponds. And we shall not by then be powerful enough to resist.

Yet if we provoke Germany now (when our defences are in a pitiable state), she will or may destroy us utterly. We all know that at the moment Germany is not prepared for a European War. But if we really oppose her, she may drive us into it. And if we do not oppose her she will become so strong that we cannot face it. There is some truth in the idea that every month gained is a month gained. The Italians are already distrusting Mussolini, and after our Czechoslovak success the Germans are distrusting Hitler. The spell may have been broken, and I know that it is little more than a spell. But what happens if the Japanese involve America in an Asiatic war, involve Russia as well, detach some of our ships – then Germany can strike in Europe.

We have lost our will-power, since our will-power is divided. People of the governing classes think only of their own fortunes, which means hatred of the Reds. This creates a perfectly artificial but at present most effective secret bond between ourselves and

Hitler. Our class interests, on both sides, cut across our national interests. I go to bed in gloom.

H.N. to V.S-W.   *June 17, 1938*

I met an Austrian yesterday who had just got away from Vienna, and what he said made me ill. There is a devilish sort of humour in their cruelty. For instance, they rounded up the people walking in the Prater on Sunday last, and separated the Jews from the rest. They made the Jewish gentlemen take off all their clothes and walk on all fours on the grass. They made the old Jewish ladies get up into the trees by ladders and sit there. They then told them to chirp like birds. The Russians never committed atrocities like that. You may take a man's life; but to destroy all his dignity is bestial. This man told me that with his own eyes he had seen Princess Stahremberg washing out the urinals at the Vienna railway-station. The suicides have been appalling. A great cloud of misery hangs over the town.

Dearest, what unhappiness there is in the world. I am glad I am in a position to do something, however slight, to help. I simply could not just remain idle and do nothing.

Diary   *June 27, 1938*

Anthony Crossley takes me to task for being so anti-Chamberlain. He says that I am working for his fall. He says that the Conservatives realise this and simply hate me. I say, "But surely, Anthony, they are always so polite when I meet them?" "Yes," he answers, "that is part of their technique."

H.N. to V.S-W.   *August 5, 1938*
                                                          Villa Mauresque, Cap Ferrat

I came down to the villa, had a bath, shaved, put on my best clothes. Because the late King of England was coming to dinner. Willy Maugham had prepared us carefully. He said that the Duke gets cross if the Duchess is not treated with respect.

*With infinite tact he told a story of how recently some old friend of the Duchess had opened the conversation at luncheon by saying "How lovely Wallis is looking, Sir!" "*WHO*???" snapped the Duke. In all innocence the poor trout repeated "I said, Sir, how lovely Wallis was looking." He turned his back on her and never spoke to her again throughout the meal. "Oh dear," said Sibyl [Colefax], "what then am I to call her?" "D-D-D-uchess," said Willy. "I shan't," said Sibyl. There then followed a long pause. "I-I-I- think I shall ask Eliza [his daughter] to c-c-c-urtsey to her," said Willy. "You won't get me curtseying," said Sibyl. "W-W-W-ell," said Willy, "perhaps if Eliza comes to the door with me, then she can get her curtsey over outside." "Yes," said Sibyl, "I don't mind that."*

Thus when they arrived Willy and his daughter went into the hall. We stood sheepishly in the drawing room. In they came. She I must say looks very well for her age. She has done her hair in a different way. It is smoothed off her brows and falls down the back of her neck in ringlets. It gives her a placid and less strained look. Her voice has also changed. It now mingles the accent of Virginia with that of a Duchess in one of Pinero's plays. He entered with his swinging naval gait, plucking at his bow-tie. He had on a *tussore* dinner-jacket. His face and the back of his neck are burnt brick red and his fair hair shows up against it as if it were stuck on with glue or were a wig or something. His eyes looked less like fried eggs than formerly. He was in very high spirits. Cocktails were brought and we stood round the fireplace. There was a pause.

"Oim sorry we were a little loite," said the Duke, "but Her Royal Highness wouldn't drag herself away from the Amurrican orficers." He had said it. The three words fell into the circle like three stones into a pool. Her (gasp) Royal (shudder) Highness (and not one eye dared to meet another).

Then we went into dinner. I sat next to the Duchess. He sat opposite. They called each other "darling" a great deal. I called him "Your Royal Highness' a great deal, and "Sir" the whole time. I called her "Duchess" sharplike.

We chattered a great deal. You know that tiresome way royalties have of pretending everything is being very amusing when it isn't. I do not think that ex-Kings are very good company. But of course one cannot get away from his glamour and his charm and his sadness. Though I must say he seemed gay enough. They have a villa here and a yacht and go round and round. He digs in the garden. *But it is pathetic the way he is sensitive about her. I heard him say, "I think that must have been when I was King." A strange remark to overhear at dinner.

She was loaded with magnificent jewels. It was quite clear to me from what she said that she hopes to get back to England. She was very bitter about the French, very bitter about the "politicians" by which I suppose she meant Baldwin. I should imagine she has great social ambitions and wants to return to England to play some sort of part.* I derive this from the fact that when I asked her why she didn't get a house of her own somewhere, she said "One never knows what may happen. I don't want to spend all my life in exile."

Diary   *August 22, 1938*
                                                            London

Lunch with the Russian Ambassador [Maisky] alone. I ask him what Russia would do if Germany pressed on to the Black Sea. He says that the old pan-Slav feeling is dead, that Russia has no sympathy for the semi-fascist systems, and that she is profoundly disillusioned with the western democracies. If we and France went to war on behalf of the Czechs, then Russia would help. But if we abandon Czechoslovakia, then Russia will become isolationist. She is unconquerable and has her own unlimited territory and resources. But she would not consent to Germany establishing her influence over Turkey.

Diary   *August 23, 1938*

I explain to Vita, Ben and Nigel that this diary, of which they know the industry and persistence, is not a work of literature or self-revelation, but a mere record of activity put down for my own reference only.

Diary   *August 26, 1938*

I tell Buck [De La Warr] about my conversation with Maisky. He thinks it is so important that he forces me to sit down there and then and write a record of it for Vansittart. The point being that if Maisky can be induced to promise Russian support in the event of our taking a strong line over Czechoslovakia, the weak will of the P.M. may be strengthened.

Diary　　　　　　　　　　　　　　　　*September 1, 1938*

We may just squeak through. On the other hand we may get into the same mess as in 1914 – namely, give the Czechs the impression that we shall fight for them, and the Germans the impression that we shall not.

The month of September 1938 culminated in the Munich settlement, by which Hitler gained most of what he had demanded. It is unnecessary to do more than summarise here so famous an event, particularly as H.N. himself deals with it fully in his diary. In brief, Hitler claimed that the western territories of Czechoslovakia (the Sudetenland) were ethnically German, and he demanded their secession to Germany. Chamberlain was determined to avoid war, and put pressure on the Czech Government to give way. He had two meetings with Hitler at which he attempted to modify the German claims, but at the last moment it seemed that Hitler was too intransigent even for Chamberlain. Czech troops moved to the German border, and the British fleet was mobilised. On September 28 war was averted by Hitler's invitation to Britain, France and Italy to meet him in Munich. An agreement was signed which ended the crisis, and Chamberlain was hailed on his return as a great peace-maker. H.N., and many others like him, took a different view. He regarded the Munich Pact not only as a betrayal of the Czechs, but as an irremediable surrender to Hitler. He spoke up strongly against it both in Parliament and in his constituency.

Diary　　　　　　　　　　　　　　　　*September 4, 1938*

*Work at my [B.B.C.] talk for tomorrow. I try to tell people why it is vital that we have to fight for Czechoslovakia. I say (1) Because it is of vital interest to the British Empire to prevent Germany dominating Europe, becoming invincible and holding us at her mercy. (2) Because it is a test case in the spiritual conflict between liberty and the Nazi theory.

Bob Boothby told me how he persuaded Winston to see Halifax and to urge that some show of friendship or solidarity should be made with Russia. Halifax made no great objection. The P.M. regards it as a bitter pill but is prepared to swallow it. He [Boothby] regrets bitterly that Anthony [Eden] should remain away during this time and do nothing. He thinks he has "sunk himself" by so doing. He also thinks that Duff Cooper has sunk himself by going yachting in the Baltic at a moment of crisis. Here I agree.*

Diary   *September 11, 1938*

Several people ring me up during the day begging me "to do something". They have no idea what they want me to do but they are getting hysterical and it is some relief to them to bother other people on the telephone.

Oliver Stanley's point of view is typical I suppose of the better type of Cabinet opinion. What the worst type of opinion may be passes my comprehension. Thus Oliver on the one hand agrees that the conflict has nothing really to do with Czechoslovakia but is the final struggle between the principle of law and the principle of violence and that the two protagonists in this struggle are Chamberlain and Hitler. He also agrees that if Germany were to make an attack on Czechoslovakia and if France were to be drawn in it would be practically impossible for us to abstain. Yet his incidental remarks show me that at heart he is longing to get out of it. At the same time any reference to Russian assistance makes him wince, and at one moment he sighed deeply and said, "You see, whether we win or lose, it will be the end of everything we stand for." By "we" he means obviously the capitalist classes.

Diary   *September 14, 1938*

The news is even worse. Japan and Italy have announced that they stand by Germany. The Russian fleet is mobilised. The Sudetens refuse to negotiate and maintain their ultimatum. We feel we are on the very edge of the railings lining the cliff. I have not the heart to listen to the 9.40 news. Then Viti comes in and says the P.M. is flying tomorrow to [see Hitler at] Berchtesgaden. My first feeling is one of enormous relief.

Diary   *September 15, 1938*

How difficult it is to decide! Vita takes the line that the Sudeten Germans are justified in claiming self-determination and the Czechs would be happier without them in any case. But if we give way on this, then the Hungarians and the Poles will also claim self-determination, and the result will be that Czechoslovakia will cease to exist as an independent state. Vita says that if it is as artificial as all that, then it should never have been created. That may be true, although God knows how we could have refused to recognise her existence in 1918. It all seemed such a reality in those days. Hitler has all the arguments on his side, but essentially they are false arguments. And we, who have right on our side, cannot say that our real right is to resist German hegemony. That is "imperialistic". Never have conflicting theories become so charged with illusions.

Diary   *September 19, 1938*

I go to see Anthony Eden in Fitzhardinge Street. I find him in the depths of despair and ask him what attitude he will adopt. He says that it is very difficult to make any formal decision until the full facts are in his possession. He says that probably if he had been in Halifax's place he might have done the same as he did. Only he adds, with a smile, "but I do think I should not have put myself into Halifax's place". He says that it is very difficult to criticise one link in the chain of events when the whole chain is in itself vicious. He doesn't wish to lead a revolt or to secure any resignations from the Cabinet.

We then discuss the effect of our surrender. He takes the very gloomiest view, feeling the leadership has now passed completely from our hands into that of Germany.

We talk of what small comfort it is to have been proved right, and how terrible has been the influence of the Cliveden set. As I leave him he says, "well, we shall not be able to avert war now".

I dine at the Marlborough with Buck De La Warr and Walter Elliot. The latter very ingeniously states the Government point of view. He makes a great point of the desertion of France, saying that when one army runs away the other army can scarcely maintain its position. He denies absolutely that the Prime Minister was given an ultimatum at Berchtesgaden and in fact he says that Chamberlain told Hitler that if, pending negotiations, the Czech frontier were violated he would himself regard it as "an intolerable affront". He claims that the Russians never promised really to help and that we could not have asked the country to go to war merely to prevent a few Germans joining their fellow citizens. He is very charming and plausible but my heart is no lighter and my anger in no way diminished as I make my way to the B.B.C.

Diary   *September 21, 1938*

The news is gloomy. Poland and the Hungarians have asked for similar secessions. The Berlin Press say that what remains of Czechoslovakia must adopt a more "positive" attitude to Berlin. That means she must subordinate her foreign policy to that of the Wilhelmstrasse. Chamberlain goes to Godesberg tomorrow. I pity him.

Diary   *September 22, 1938*

Winston Churchill telephones. Would I come up to London for a meeting at 4.30 in his flat? I say that I shall be there.

I go to 11 Morpeth Mansions. As I approach the door, I see the vulture form of Bob Cecil slipping into the flat. While I wait for the lift to descend Winston appears from a taxi. We go up together. "This," I say, "is hell." "It is the end of the British Empire."

Winston had just been to Downing Street. He says that the Cabinet are at last taking a firm stand. Chamberlain is to demand from Hitler (a) early demobilization (b) agreement that the transfer of the Sudeten territories should be undertaken gradually by an international commission (c) that there must be no nonsense about the Polish and Hungarian claims (d) that what remains of the Czechs shall be guaranteed. We say at once "But Hitler will never accept such terms." "In that case," says Winston, "Chamberlain will return tonight and we shall have WAR." We suggest that in that event it will be inconvenient having our Prime Minister in German territory. "Even the Germans," flashes Winston, "would not be so stupid as to deprive us of our beloved Prime Minister."

We then get down to business. It is interrupted, first by a telephone message from Jan Masaryk [Czech Ambassador in London] saying that the Germans have occupied Asch and that the Czechs are withdrawing gradually from the Sudeten areas. Also [Prime Minister] Hodza has resigned, and a "Ministry of Concentration" has been appointed. Secondly, by a telephone call from Attlee saying that the Opposition are prepared to come in with us if we like. That is vague.

We continue the conversation. We conclude (a) that we shall support the P.M. if it means war or a firm line (b) that if he runs away again we shall join with the Opposition (c) that we shall be summoned by Winston again if things go wrong.

Dine at the Beefsteak. This is, I suppose, a more or less Tory Club and they are all in despair about their Government. They admit that at the moment half of the Cabinet will resign. I believe no such thing. The fact remains that they feel Chamberlain has behaved with great optimism and some conceit. The Berchtesgaden visit has been shown to have been a gesture of weakness. Then there is the secrecy side. Everybody was prepared to agree to Chamberlain's secret diplomacy, provided that it would let us out: they are furious with it now that it has let us in. My opinion is that these Tories are appalled by the force of opinion in the provinces.

Diary   *September 23, 1938*

I finish my book [*Diplomacy*] at 4.45. So that's done. But I doubt whether it will be published. We listen to the 6 o'clock news. Chamberlain has not resumed negotiations with Hitler: all they have done is to exchange letters. Meanwhile Reuter reports that the *Freikorps* have begun to invade Czechoslovakia. War is almost on us.

At 9 the telephone rings. It is Bob Boothby. "I have just come back from Geneva and I thought you might want a word." "What were they feeling there?" "Complete demoralization, but I had a good talk with Litvinov [the Soviet Foreign Commissar]. The Russians will give us full support." "Well, what about Godesberg?" "Haven't you heard? Chamberlain is returning." "That means war?" "Yes, it has taken the Germans in their idiocy to push us into this. We gave them all they asked for. Now they go to the point where they will push even us into it, and we are in for four years."

I suppose that Ribbentrop has convinced Hitler that whatever happens we shall stay out. We cannot stay out now that Chamberlain has sacrificed everything (even our honour) to secure a peace which he has broken. How sorry I feel for the German people! All the Cliveden set and *The Times* people prevented us from taking a strong line while it could have made for peace. But we must support the Government without vituperation or criticism. We are all in the same boat now.

Diary   *September 26, 1938*

Winston gathers that the memorandum or letter which Horace Wilson [Chamberlain's emissary] is to give to Hitler is not in the least a retreat. It is merely an attempt to save Hitler's face if he wants to climb down. It offers a conference to decide the means of carrying out the Franco–British plan. It warns him that we do not accept his own post-Godesberg plan and that if he insists, we shall go to war. He had urged the P.M. to mobilise the Fleet at once and call up all reserves. He says he will do so at 9 p.m. this evening if Hitler's speech at 8 p.m. tonight is not conciliatory.

Winston says (and we all agree) that the fundamental mistake the P.M. has made is his refusal to take Russia into his confidence. Ribbentrop always said to Hitler, "You need never fear England until you find her mentioning Russia as an ally. Then it means that she is really going to war!" We therefore decide that Winston shall go at once to Halifax and tell him to put out some notice before Hitler's speech. "We have only got till nine," says Winston grimly.

My first sight of the War of 1938 was a poster in the Strand: – "City of Westminster: Air Raid Precautions: Gas Masks Notice", followed by instructions where to get yourself fitted for masks. My second sight was workmen digging trenches feverishly in Green Park.

Diary   *September 28, 1938*

Hitler has announced that unless he gets an affirmative reply by 2 p.m. today he will mobilise tomorrow. I presume it means that he will try to cross the frontier some time this evening. President Roosevelt has issued an eleventh hour appeal for a conference. We have mobilised the Fleet.

I walk down to the House at 2.15 p.m. passing through Trafalgar Square and down Whitehall. The pigeons are clustered round the fountains and children are feeding them. My companion says to me "Those children ought to be evacuated at once, and so should the pigeons." As we get near the House of Commons there is a large shuffling, shambling crowd and there are people putting fresh flowers at the base of the Cenotaph. The crowd is very silent and anxious. They stare at us with dumb, inquisitive eyes.

The Speaker began by announcing the death of previous Members, and he had hardly finished with the obituary list before the Prime Minister entered from behind his chair. He was greeted with wild applause by his supporters, many of whom rose in their seats and waved their order-papers. The Labour Opposition, the Liberal Opposition and certain of the National supporters [among them H.N.] remained seated.

Chamberlain rose slowly in his place and spread the manuscript of his speech upon the box in front of him. The House was hushed in silent expectancy. From the Peers' Gallery above the clock the calm face of Lord Baldwin peered down upon the arena in which he himself had so often battled. Chamberlain began with a chronological statement of events which had led up to the crisis. He spoke in calm measured tones and the House listened to him in dead silence. The only interruption was made by the Messengers of the House who, as always happens, kept on passing along the benches the telegrams and pink telephone slips which were pouring in upon Members. Winston Churchill who sits at the end of my row, received so many telegrams that they were clipped together by an elastic band. Attlee sat opposite Chamberlain with his feet on the table looking like an amiable little bantam. The first burst of applause occurred when Chamberlain mentioned Lord Runciman's great services, and as he did so, he removed his pince-nez between his finger and thumb, raised his face to the skylight and spoke with friendly conviction. Being an experienced Parliamentarian, he would abandon his manuscript at moments and speak extempore.

The chronological method which he adopted increased the dramatic tensity of the occasion. We all knew more or less what had happened in August and the early weeks of September, and we were waiting for his statement of what had occurred during the last few hours. He reached the point where he described the fourth plan of President Benes. The mention of this plan was received with loud cheers, and he described it in precise terms, having taken off his pince-nez and holding them between his finger and thumb. "On Friday, 23rd September," he said, "a Cabinet meeting was held again . . ." The House leant forward, realising that he was passing from that part of the story which we already knew to the part that had not yet been divulged. He went on to describe his negotiations with the Czechs and the French and to tell us how he felt it necessary himself to visit Herr Hitler "as a last resort". When he said these words, "as a last resort", he whipped off his pince-nez and looked up at the skylight with an expression of grim hope. He then described his visit to Berchtesgaden. "It was," he said with a wry grin, "my first flight," and then he described the whole visit as "this adventure." He said that his conversation with Hitler had convinced him that the Führer was prepared, on behalf of the Sudeten Germans, "to risk world war". As he said these words a shudder of horror passed through the House of Commons.

"I came back," he added, "to London the next day." The House was tense with excitement. He then told us how the Anglo-French plan was described by Hitler at Godesberg as "too dilatory". "Imagine," he said, "the perplexity in which I found myself." This remark roused a murmer of sympathetic appreciation from all the benches.

"Yesterday morning," began the Prime Minister, and we were again conscious that some revelation was approaching. He began to tell us of his final appeal to Hitler and Mussolini. I glanced at the clock. It was twelve minutes after four. The Prime Minister had been speaking for exactly an hour. I noticed that a sheet of Foreign Office paper was being rapidly passed along the Government bench. Sir John Simon interrupted the Prime Minister and there was a momentary hush. He adjusted his pince-nez and read the document that had been handed to him. His whole face, his whole body, seemed to change. He raised his face so that the light from the ceiling fell full upon it. All the lines of anxiety and weariness seemed suddenly to have been smoothed out; he appeared ten years younger and triumphant. "Herr Hitler," he said, "has just agreed to postpone his mobilisation for twenty-four hours and to meet me in conference with Signor Mussolini and Monsieur Daladier at Munich."

That, I think, was one of the most dramatic moments which I have ever witnessed. For a second, the House was hushed in absolute silence. And then the whole House burst into a roar of cheering, since they knew that this might mean peace. That was the end of the Prime Minister's speech, and when he sat down the whole House rose as a man to pay tribute to his achievement. [Later H.N. added: I remained seated. Liddall behind me, hissed out, "Stand up, you brute!"]

Diary *September 29, 1938*

The papers are ecstatic about Chamberlain. Raymond [Mortimer] rings me up and says, "Isn't this ghastly?" Eddy [Sackville-West] rings me up and says "Isn't this hell?" Margot Oxford rings me up and says "Now Harold you must agree that he is a great man?" I say "Not at all." "You are as bad as Violet [Bonham Carter]," she snaps, "He is the greatest Englishman that ever lived."

It seems that my refusal to stand up yesterday when all the rest of the House went hysterical has made an impression. Everybody has heard of it. I was ashamed of the House yesterday; it was a Welsh revivalist meeting.

I had meant to go down to Sissinghurst but Winston asked me to stay on in London. At 7 p.m. we meet again at the Savoy. The idea had been to get Winston, Cecil, Attlee, Archie Sinclair and Lloyd to join in a telegram to the P.M. begging him not to betray the Czechs. We had been busy at that all afternoon. But Anthony [Eden] had refused to sign on the grounds that it would be interpreted as a vendetta against Chamberlain. Attlee had refused to sign without the approval of his party. There was thus no time. We sat there gloomily realizing that nothing could be done. Even Winston seemed to have lost his fighting spirit. Afterwards I go to Brooks' to look at the tape. So far as I can see, Hitler gets everything he wants.

Diary *September 30, 1938*

Wake up feeling wretched. Usually I wake up feeling life is worth living. Today I woke up with iron in my soul. The terms as published seem to me to be little better than Godesberg although one must wait to see the map before deciding. Violet Bonham Carter rings me up. She had been seeing Jan Masaryk. He told her that our Minister in Prague had presented the Munich scheme to Benes and demanded an acceptance in two hours. Benes and the Government will resign. So Hitler has achieved even that. A terrible humiliation.

Diary *October 1, 1938*

I go back to London [from Manchester]. The posters say "Cabinet Minister Resigns". I assume that it is Buck – but not at all. It is Duff

Cooper and his resignation is accompanied by a nasty letter. He has no money and he gives up £5,000 a year plus a job he loves.

Diary   October 2, 1938

Buck says that he tried to persuade Duff not to resign until they could all resign together. He feels that if he himself goes there will be nobody left in the Cabinet to fight the good fight. The Czech thing is over now. It is no use crying over spilt milk. He will remain in order to force Chamberlain to introduce National Service.

Diary   October 5, 1938

I keep on rising in my place from 3 p.m. till 9.25. This is a good thing. I have achieved a prominence in the House which is unjustified by my juniority. Thus when I am called, there is a burst of applause and people flock in. My speech goes well. I get approbation and notes from many people. I know that it made its effect.

Diary   October 6, 1938

Our group decide that it is better for us all to abstain, than for some of us to abstain and some to vote against. We therefore sit in our seats, which must enrage the Government, since it is not our numbers that matter but our reputation. Among those who abstained were Eden, Duff Cooper, Winston, Amery, Cranborne, Wolmer, Roger Keyes, Sidney Herbert, Louis Spears, Harold Macmillan, Richard Law, Bob Boothby, Jim Thomas, Duncan Sandys, Ronald Cartland, Anthony Crossley, Brendan Bracken and Emrys-Evans. That looks none too well in any list. The House knows that most of the above people know far more about the real issue than they do.

It was clear that the Government were rattled by this. In the first place, the P.M. gave a pledge that there would be no General Election. In the second place he made the astounding admission that his phrase about "peace in our time" was made under the stress of emotion. The House breaks up with the Tories yelling to keep their spirits up. But they well know that Chamberlain has put us in a ghastly position and that we ought to have been prepared to go to war and smash Hitler. Next time he will be far too strong for us.

H.N. found himself out of sympathy not only with the Government, but with his party (and its leaders Malcolm MacDonald and Lord De La Warr). He considered re-signing. Instead he allied himself with thirty other Members led unofficially by Anthony Eden.

He also began to write his weekly "Marginal Comment" for the Spectator, *and would continue to do so for the next fourteen years.*

H.N. to V.S-W.   *November 9, 1938*

I went to a hush-hush meeting with Anthony Eden. Present: Eden, Amery, Cranborne, Sidney Herbert, Cartland, Harold Macmillan, Spears, Derrick Gunston, Emrys-Evans, Anthony Crossley, Hubert Duggan. All good Tories and sensible men. This group is distinct from the Churchill group. It also includes Duff Cooper. We decided that we should not advertise ourselves as a group or even call ourselves a group. We should merely meet together from time to time, exchange views, and organise ourselves for a revolt if needed. I feel happier about this. Eden and Amery are wise people, and Sidney Herbert is very experienced. They are deeply disturbed by the fact that Chamberlain does not seem to understand the gravity of the situation. Unless we pull ourselves together and have compulsory registration [for military service] in the next few months, it will be too late. It was a relief to me to be with people who share my views so completely, and yet who do not give the impression (as Winston does) of being more bitter than determined, and more out for a fight than for reform.

H.N. to V.S-W.   *November 11, 1938*

Anthony Eden's speech last night created a sensation. Nobody quite knew what he was talking about. Was he trying to split the Government? Or angling for a Coalition? Or what? I know what he is doing. He is trying to wake up the country to real energies and sacrifice.

V.S-W. to H.N.   *November 14, 1938*

I know you will never forgive me, but I *can't* go to this party [a dinner at Buckingham Palace for the King of Rumania]. If I went to this party I should be being false to myself. I am writing this letter with my jewels littered all around me – emeralds and diamonds, just taken out of the bank – and they make me feel sick. I simply can't subscribe any longer to the world which these jewels represent. *I can't* buy a dress costing £30 or wear jewels worth £2,000 when people are starving. I *can't* support such a farce when people are threatened that their electric light or gas may be cut off because they can't pay their arrears.

H.N. to V.S-W.   *November 15, 1938*

You are quite right, as usual. It is wrong to spend all that money merely to go to a party. That sort of world is dead today. How can a person of your sensitiveness and imagination doll yourself up in expensive clothes when there are cultured Jewish women and men hiding like foxes in the Grunewald? I do admire you so, my Viti! You are so sound in your values. I shall never forget what you meant to me during the [Munich] crisis. You were all that was spiritually perfect during those days. I could not have stood them had you not been there as a sort of completely selfless person, right above all petty fears and jangles.

Diary   *November 21, 1938*

Up to Leicester with Anthony Eden. He tells me that Edward Halifax has been urging him to sink his differences and to get back into the Cabinet, thus admitting quite frankly that the split over foreign policy is so serious that the Party organisers are alarmed. Anthony says that he cannot go back if the policy is still to be directed towards a Four Power Pact.

Diary   *November 24, 1938*

A meeting of the group at Ronnie Tree's house. [Austin] Hopkinson is there and tells us the reasons for which he refused the Government whip. It seems that Chamberlain is trying to put all the blame for our disarmament on Thomas Inskip, and as Hopkinson was Inskip's [Minister of Defence] P.P.S., he is leaving him in order to defend him against attacks which he will not counter himself. His

account of our unpreparedness is appalling. He says that if we had
gone to war in September our air-force would have been wiped out
in three weeks and our pilots would have gone to certain death.
Things may be a little better in a few weeks but nonetheless we are
terribly at Germany's mercy and shall remain so. The Government
are really not telling the country the truth.

Diary   *December 5, 1938*

Winston starts brilliantly and we are all expecting a great speech.
He accused Hore-Belisha [Minister of War] of being too compla-
cent. The latter gets up and says, "When and where?" Winston
replies, "I have not come unprepared," and begins to fumble among
his notes, where there are some press cuttings. He takes time. The
ones he reads out excuse rather than implicate Hore-Belisha. Winston becomes confused. He tries to rally his speech, but the wind has
gone out of his sails, which flop wretchedly. He certainly is a tiger
who, if he misses his spring, is lost.

Diary   *December 13, 1938*

To a grand party given by Barbie [Mrs Euan] Wallace. Some of the
Cabinet had come on from the dinner given by the Foreign Press
Association to the P.M. They were all agog. The 40 German guests
(including the Ambassador) had not attended in view of Chamberlain's polite protest against their having called Lord Baldwin a
gutter snipe. There were forty empty seats and all this created wild
excitement. Then came Chamberlain's speech. He catalogued his
achievements. Treaty with Eire (slight applause); Treaty with
United States (loud applause); Anglo-German Treaty (you could
have heard a pin drop so icy was the silence). With France we had
relations which transcended all legal instruments since our interests
were the same (a wild ovation lasting for several minutes). As Buck
said, it was almost a vote of censure on the P.M.'s policy.

Diary   *December 31, 1938*

I go to bed at the usual time and just let the old year die. It has been
a bad year. Chamberlain has destroyed the Balance of Power. A
foul year. Next year will be worse.

On March 15, 1939 Hitler invaded Czechoslovakia and occupied Prague without a fight. It was the virtual end of Chamberlain's policy of appeasement. On March 31 he announced that Britain and France would guarantee Poland against German attack. It was a sad triumph for H.N. He was still very active, speaking frequently in Parliament and abroad, as well as broadcasting and writing weekly for the Spectator *and* Daily Telegraph.

Diary   *January 15, 1939*

Wind and rain. Finish my reviews and my article. V. and I go to the new cuttings and examine the willows which Niggs and I planted. Freya Stark [the writer] comes to dinner. She is anti-Chamberlain and thinks we should intervene in Spain at once. It is too late. Franco is almost within sight of Barcelona and once he gets there he will cut communications with France and obtain the munitions works of the Republicans. I fear it is all over. Chamberlain announces that "he is returning from Rome convinced of the good faith and of the good intentions of the Italian Government". How can he say such a thing at a moment when Italian troops are advancing on Barcelona? It is as bad as his "peace with honour" after Munich. Either he believes it, in which case he has no conception of the real proportions of the situation, or else he does not believe it in which case he is lying. How can he be so obstinate?

Diary   *January 17, 1939*

The tragedy of Europe seems to come closer to us in ever diminishing circles. Dear little Giles [St Aubyn, H.N.'s 14 year old nephew] chatters about Sir Humphrey Davy for whom he has a passion. His sensitive nervous face and his intelligence make me even more unhappy. What will that delightful boy have to create in the world which will be his adult world? To me it does not matter. I can just die. But he and Niggs and Ben have got to live, and all the delicacy of life will have gone. All the truthfulness, all the outspokenness, all the easiness of life will have gone. They will never know *la douceur de vivre*.

Diary   *January 25, 1939*

*Lunch at Bedford Square with Margot Oxford and Elizabeth
Bibesco. An incongruous party. Emil Ludwig [the biographer],
Attlee, Leon Blum's nephew and a Harley Street doctor. Attlee is
very silly and charming. A delightful man of course, but not a pilot
in a hurricane. Ludwig almost cuts me dead. I avoid him. He says
he is writing a book about the Windsors. Margot says, "Dear me,
that's very vulgar of you." He is much taken aback.*

Diary   *February 4, 1939*

V and I go round to the Beales' [farmers at Sissinghurst] where
there is a Television Set lent by a local radio-merchant. We see a
Mickey Mouse, a play and a Gaumont British film. I had always
been told that the television could not be received above 25 miles
from Alexandra Palace. But the reception was every bit as good as
at Selfridge's. Compared with a film, it is a bleary, flickering, dim,
unfocused, interruptible thing, the size of a quarto sheet of paper as
this on which I am typing. But as an invention it is tremendous and
may alter the whole basis of democracy.

H.N. to V.S-W.   *February 7, 1939*

Really Chamberlain is an astonishing and perplexing old boy. This
afternoon (as you will have heard) he startled the House and the
world by proclaiming something like an offensive and a defensive
alliance between us and France. Now that is the very thing that all
of us have been pushing for, working for, writing for, speaking for,
all these months. And the old boy gets up and does it as if it were
the simplest thing on earth. The House was absolutely astounded.
It could not have been more definite.

    Now what does it all mean? Is he really so ignorant of diplomacy
as to assume that this means little? I cannot believe that. He spoke
so resolutely and so deliberately. The House cheered loudly. It was
superb. I felt happy for the first time in months. But this is a complete negation of his "appeasement" policy and of his Rome visit.
He has in fact swung suddenly round to all that we have been
asking for. What does it mean? I think that it can only mean that he
realizes that appeasement has failed. It is at this stage that his value

as a diplomatic asset becomes operative. No ordinary German or Italian will ever believe propaganda telling him that Chamberlain is a "war-monger".

Diary   *February 9, 1939*

Lunch at the Russian Embassy. A strange party. Bob Boothby, Dick Law, Vernon Bartlett and J. B. Priestley. We start by talking rather shyly about food. Gradually, as the vodka circulates, we approach the less sure ground of politics. Maisky [Russian Ambassador] asks us (with his little Kalmuk eyes twinkling round the table), "What is going to happen now?" We all hope that someone else is going to answer. I suggest gaily that the moment may be approaching when Russia will be forced to join the anti-Comintern Pact. Maisky says that Russia was obviously much wounded by Munich and that we can expect no advances from her side. But (and here he becomes serious) if *we* made approaches, we should not find Russia as aloof or offended as we might have supposed. Bob Boothby and I have an eye-meet like a tennis-ball across a net.

Diary   *March 15, 1939*

Frederick Voigt [Editor, *Nineteenth Century*] telephones to say that Hitler has occupied Prague. Go round to Mark Patrick's house for a meeting of the group. Eden says that he is going to speak today, and what is he to say? We all agree that the one thing not to do is hoot and jeer. We agree that we must support the Government, and that Anthony should speak, and that only our lesser fry should speak also. The rest to keep silent.

   The *Manchester Guardian* today carried a leader headed "The Gift of Prophecy". There is a passage from my Munich speech.

Diary   *March 17, 1939*

The feelings in the lobbies is that Chamberlain will either have to go or completely reverse his policy. Unless in his speech tonight [in Birmingham] he admits he was wrong they feel that resignation is the only alternative. All the tadpoles are beginning to swim into the other camp and we find ourselves in the odd position of being Mr Chamberlain's loyal supporters. The difficulty is that he himself

cannot introduce conscription because he can only do so with a
Coalition Government. The Opposition refuse absolutely to serve
under him.

Diary   *March 31, 1939*

Down to the House. The P.M. says he will make a statement shortly
before three. The general feeling is that he will announce that if
Poland and Rumania are attacked we shall go to war. There is some
uneasiness about in the corridors. People fear lest Chamberlain may
not stay put.

Chamberlain arrives looking gaunt and ill. The skin above his
high cheek bones is parchment yellow. He drops wearily into his
place. David Margesson proposes the adjournment and the P.M.
rises. He begins by saying that we believe in negotiation and do not
trust in rumours. He then gets to the centre of his statement, namely
that if Poland is attacked we shall declare war. That is greeted with
cheers from every side. He reads his statement very slowly with a
bent grey head. It is most impressive.

Diary   *April 3, 1939*

The House rises at 10.50 p.m. and I am seized upon by Winston and
taken down to the lower smoking-room with Maisky and Lloyd
George. Winston adopts the direct method of attack. "Now look
here Mr Ambassador, if we are to make a success of this new policy,
we require the help of Russia. Now I don't care for your system and
I never have, but the Poles and the Rumanians like it even less. Although they might be prepared at a pinch to let you in, they would
certainly want some assurances that you would eventually get out.
Can you give us such assurances?" Lloyd George, I fear, is not really
in favour of the new policy and he draws Maisky on to describe the
deficiencies of the Polish Army. Apparently many of their guns are
pre-Revolution guns of the Russian Army. Maisky contends that
the Polish soldiers are excellent fighters and that the officers are
well-trained. Winston rather objects to this and attacks Lloyd
George. "You must not do this sort of thing, my dear. You are
putting spokes in the wheel of history." The relations between
these two are very curious. They have had bitter battles in the past
and have emerged from these combats with great respect for each

other's talents and an affectionate sharing of tremendous common memories. It is curious that little way that Winston has when he speaks to Lloyd George of calling him "my dear".

Diary   *April 9, 1939*

In the afternoon Viti and I plant annuals. We sow them in the cottage garden and then in the border and then in the orchard. We rake the soil smooth. And as we rake we are both thinking, "What will have happened to the world when these seeds germinate?" It is warm and still. We should have been so happy were it not for the thought which aches at our hearts as if some very dear person was dying in the upstairs room. We discuss whether we might be defeated if war comes. And if defeated, surely surrender in advance would be better? We ourselves don't think of money or privilege or pleasure. We are thinking only of that vast wastage of suffering which must surely come. All because of the insane ambitions of one fanatic, and of the vicious theory which he has imposed on his people.

> *The Western attitude was stiffening. The Anglo–Polish Pact of mutual assistance was signed in response to Germany's threat to Danzig. Britain and France signed equivalent guarantees to Greece and Rumania after Mussolini invaded Albania on April 7.*

Diary   *April 10, 1939*

The Mediterranean Fleet has been assembled. Italy warns us that if we attack by sea she will drive towards Salonica through the Vardar Valley. Does Mussolini seriously suppose that he could defeat ourselves and France? Or is he still relying upon the defeatist and the pampered group in London who have for so long been assuring him that the capitalists of England are on his side? I do not believe that an intelligent man such as Grandi [the Ambassador in London] could have left him under any illusion that the will-power of this country is concentrated in Mrs Ronald Greville. The harm which these silly selfish hostesses do is really immense. They convey to foreign envoys the impression that policy is decided in their own drawing-rooms. That is always what happens with us. The silly people are regarded as representative of British opinion and the informed people are dismissed as "intellectual". I should be most unhappy if I were Lady Astor. She must realise that her parrot cries have done much damage to what (to do her justice) she must dimly realise is the essence of her adopted class and country.

Diary   *April 11, 1939*

Harold Macmillan is enraged that Chamberlain should remain on. He thinks that all we Edenites have been too soft and gentlemanlike. That we should have clamoured for Chamberlain's removal. That no man in history has made such persistent and bone-headed mistakes, and that we still go on pretending that all is well.

There is a theory that the appeasers (Simon, Hoare and Horace Wilson) have regained their influence and that Chamberlain is preparing to overlook the rape of Albania and to enter into a new Mediterranean pact with Mussolini, under which we agree not to make an alliance with Greece and Turkey in return for Mussolini agreeing all over again to withdraw troops from Spain and Libya. I do not believe that Halifax would agree to anything so nonsensical, and if Halifax resigns the Government will fall.

Diary   *April 21, 1939*

The *Spectator* this week suggests that I should be sent as Ambassador to Washington. It amuses me to observe my own reactions to such a suggestion. My first fear is that it will expose me to ridicule, since all we Nicolsons are morbidly sensitive to being placed in a false position. My second impulse is to realise how much Vita would hate it. My third is to feel how much I should loathe the pomp and publicity of an Embassy. My fourth is to agree with the *Spectator* that I might do the job rather well. But it will not occur.

Diary   *April 23, 1939*

I talk to Gafencu [the Rumanian Foreign Minister]. He had been thrilled by his visit to Berlin. He said that Hitler had been quite polite and had not tried to bully him in the least. He had spoken quite calmly at first, but when he touched on ideology he began to scream. He had spent the whole time abusing this country. He had

complained that there was no British statesman of sufficient magnitude or vision to agree with him to divide the world between them.
He had no desire to possess the British Empire. All that he wanted
was that we should not thwart his destiny in Eastern Europe. It was
at this stage that he began to scream. He had said that it was gro-
tesque to imagine that he wanted to invade Holland or Belgium.
The only small countries that he wants to dominate were those of the
East. Gafencu asked him whether these included Rumania, and then
he stopped screaming and began to be polite. He said that if war
came we might be able to destroy three German towns, but that he
would destroy every single British town.

Diary   *April 29, 1939*

I feel pretty glum and devote myself to reviewing. There is Joyce's
Finnegan's Wake. I try very hard indeed to understand that book but
fail completely. It is almost impossible to decipher, and when one or
two lines of understanding emerge like telegraph poles above a
flood, they are at once countered by other poles going in the opposite direction. I see that at the back of it all there is some allegory
turning around the Tristan saga. But the research involved in working out this loose mosaic is greater than any ordinary reader can
possibly undertake. I truly believe that Joyce has this time gone too
far in breaking all communication between himself and his reader.
It is a very selfish book.

H.N. to V.S-W.   *May 17, 1939*

*I went to dine with [Leo] Amery to meet [Chaim] Weizmann [the
Zionist leader]. He is more like Lenin than ever, but a Lenin who has
been betrayed by those in whom he trusted. I fear our Palestine
settlement is a terrible act of treachery and will do us great harm
during the Royal Visit [to the U.S. and Canada in June]. We are just
handing the Jews over to the Arabs and giving up our mandate.
That is what it amounts to. He was calm, dignified, and wretched.
Even thus must Job have looked when he cursed the day he was
born. We sat round feeling so helpless and ashamed.*

Diary *May 31, 1939*

Jack Macnamara told me an interesting thing. He is an intimate friend of one of the more decent Whips and had discussed with them the Eden Group. It seems that they respect Eden, Duff Cooper, Amery and the big bugs. But they are terribly rattled by the existence and the secrecy of the group itself. They know that we meet, and what they do not like is that we do not attack them in the House. If we came out in the open they would know where they stood. What they hate is this silent plotting. They start from the assumption that we wish to upset the present Government, to force them to take our leaders in, and that we juniors imagine that we shall get some pickings from the victory of our leaders. They regard me, it seems, as an able man gone astray. They do not understand how I can be National Labour, regarding that as treachery to my class.

Diary *June 14, 1939*

Dine with Kenneth Clark. The Walter Lippmanns are there: also the Julian Huxleys and Winston Churchill as the guest of honour. Winston is horrified by Lippmann saying that the American Ambassador, Jo Kennedy, had informed him that war was inevitable and that we should be licked. Winston is stirred by this defeatism into a magnificent oration. He sits hunched there, waving his whisky-and-soda to mark his periods, stubbing his cigar with the other hand.

"It may be true, it may well be true," he says, "that this country will at the outset of this coming and to my mind almost inevitable war be exposed to dire peril and fierce ordeals. It may be true that steel and fire will rain down upon us day and night scattering death and destruction far and wide. It may be true that our sea-communications will be imperilled and our food-supplies placed in jeopardy. Yet these trials and disasters, I ask you to believe me Mr Lippmann, will but serve to steel the resolution of the British people and to enhance our will for victory. No, the Ambassador should not have spoken so, Mr Lippmann; he should not have said that dreadful word. Yet supposing (as I do not for one moment suppose) that Mr Kennedy were correct in his tragic utterance, then I for one would willingly lay down my life in combat, rather than, in fear of defeat, surrender to the menaces of these most sinister men.

It will then be for you, for the Americans, to preserve and to maintain the great heritage of the English-speaking peoples. It will be for you to think imperially, which means to think always of something higher and more vast than one's national interests. Nor should I die happy in the great struggle which I see before me, were I not convinced that if we in this dear dear island succumb to the ferocity and might of our enemies, over there in your distant and immune continent the torch of liberty will burn untarnished and (I trust and hope) undismayed."

We then change the subject and speak about the Giant Panda.

H.N. to V.S-W.   *June 19, 1939*

Why can we not be left alone? We are doing no harm. We care for fine and gentle things. We wish only to do good on earth. We are not vulgar in our tastes or cruel in our thoughts. Why is it that we are impotent to prevent something which we know to be evil and terrible? I would willingly give my own life if I could stop this war. I am so unhappy about the outside, and so happy in my own little orbit.

H.N. to V.S-W.   *July 18, 1939*

It looks as if we might make a compromise over Danzig and so long as the Poles really agree to it that is all right. But I have a nasty feeling that we have allowed the Germans to entrench themselves in the city and that by wishing to compromise we have again sold the fort. Moreover I am convinced that Hitler wants to come out at the next Nuremberg rally as the angel of peace and that he will be enraged if he is not able, before then, to present his country with some further spectacular gain. That means if he is diverted from Poland, he may strike at Hungary and the Near-East. But do not allow me to be always pessimistic. Things are on the surface looking better these days. It is what is happening under the surface that terrifies me.

Diary   *July 24, 1939*

Go to tea at the Russian Embassy and find a strange collection of left-wing enthusiasts sitting round in the Winter Garden with a huge tea-table spread with delicious cakes and caviar sandwiches, plus a samovar. The Ambassador is however so interested in convincing them how right is the Soviet definition of "indirect aggression" that he forgets to offer them any tea and they all go away casting regretful glances at the untouched table. Maisky asks me to go into his study where I have a long talk, plus a large quantity of the sandwiches which the other guests have not been offered.

He says that he believes that Chamberlain hopes to get a compromise on the Danzig question, and that if he does that, he will allow the [Anglo–]Russian negotiations to lapse. He says that he has a definite impression that the Government do not really want the negotiations to go through.

Diary   *August 2, 1939*

To the astonishment of the House the Prime Minister gets up and after saying that he will not give way an inch [on adjourning the House for the summer recess], he adds that certain Members had thanked the Whips for not putting on a three-line whip, but that he wished it to be clearly understood that he regarded the vote as a vote of confidence in himself. Ronnie Cartland says that the Prime Minister has missed a great opportunity by not showing his faith in this great democratic institution. He goes on, "We are in the situation that within a month we may be going to fight and we may be going to die." At this Patrick Hannon laughs, and Cartland turns upon him with a flame of indignation and says, "It is all very well for you to laugh. There are thousands of young men at this moment . . ." The effect is galvanic and I have seldom felt the temperature rise so rapidly. He is then followed by Macmillan who extracts some sort of promise from the Prime Minister that he will call Parliament should a situation arise similar to that which arose in September last year.

H.N. to V.S-W.   *August 2, 1939*

We have a debate today about whether we should adjourn or not. I had hoped that Anthony Eden was going to take a strong line, but he is now suggesting that we should all toe the line. I would do so were it not that Winston refuses, and I cannot let the old lion enter the lobby alone. But apart from this I do feel very deeply that the

House ought not to adjourn for the whole of the two months. I regard it as a violation of the constitutional principle and an act of disrespect to the House.

Why is it that I am always in a minority? Is it wrong-headedness? I simply don't know. Or is it really that I am not a trimmer by nature and hate discipline?

> *As a result of Britain's (and France's) hesitation, Stalin approached Berlin and negotiated the Russo-German non-aggression pact which provided that neither country would attack the other or come to the help of a Third Power which attacked them. It was signed by Ribbentrop on August 23.*
>
> *During the first weeks of the Adjournment, H.N. was sailing to France on his new yacht "Mar". On returning to Plymouth he heard of the emergency meeting of Parliament on the 24th. He immediately rushed to London.*

Diary   August 22, 1939
                                                          "Mar", Plymouth

I have a feeling that I shall not have much more of my beloved yacht. At six I listen to the News. The Germans and Russians have announced that they propose to sign a non-agression pact and that Ribbentrop is on his way to Moscow for the purpose. This smashes our peace-front and makes our guarantees to Poland, Rumania and Greece very questionable. How Ribbentrop must chuckle. I feel rather stunned by this news and sit on the deck in bewilderment with the fishing smacks around me. I fear that it means that we are humbled to the dust.

Diary   August 23, 1939

Round to the Travellers and meet Archie Sinclair there. He asks me to dine with him and the Bonham Carters. We discuss what the Russo–German agreement really means. There are those who take the view that the Russians have been extraordinarily clever and are forcing the Axis Powers to lay their cards upon the table. These people imagine that Ribbentrop (who has already arrived in Moscow) will be kept hanging about and will be humiliated. I doubt it. I doubt whether Ribbentrop would have been such a fool as to go to Moscow unless he was pretty certain that he would be exposed to no humiliating delays. Archie had seen the Prime Minister this morning and found him very depressed and resolute. He leaves us to ring up Winston Churchill. The latter has just returned from Paris and is in high fettle. The French are not at all perturbed by the Russo–German Pact and are prepared to support Poland nonetheless. They are half-mobilising. Winston has just rung up [Minister of Finance] Paul Reynaud, who asserts that all is going well: by which he means war, I suppose.

As I drive back to the Temple, I pass a motorcyclist in a steel helmet. A sinister sight.

H.N. to V.S-W. *August 24, 1939*

Just a scribble in the intervals of this debate. The P.M. was dignified and calm, but without one word which could inspire anybody. He was exactly like a coroner summing up a case of murder.

I see mighty little chance of peace. It may be that Colonel Beck [Polish Foreign Minister] will lose his nerve and fly to Berchtesgaden. But even that would be a bad catastrophe.

I gather that the P.M. has offered to resign, but the King won't accept it.

V.S-W. to H.N. *August 24, 1939*
Sissinghurst

What ghastly hours. If only you were not in London. It makes me physically sick to think of air-raids. I was rung up in the middle of my luncheon and asked if the Buick would take an eight-foot stretcher or "only sitting-cases or corpses". I feel sick with apprehension, but I find that I get braver as the day goes on, a curious psychological working which I wish I could analyse.

Diary *August 28, 1939*

*All international train traffic has been stopped. All British ships have been told to leave Italian and German ports. Lights are to be extinguished in aerodromes. The pound is falling on the New York Exchange. The *Europa* has scuttled back to Hamburg and the *Bremen* is taking refuge in New York.* It looks as if war would burst upon us tomorrow.

Again the curious contrast with August 3, 1914! Then we were excited by all these events and there was a sense of exhilaration. Today we are merely glum. It is not merely my age and experience which silences me under this leaden cope of gloom.

Diary   *August 30, 1939*

Lunch with Sibyl Colefax. Lady Cunard and Ivone Kirkpatrick [First Secretary in Berlin, 1933–38] there. He is interesting about Hitler. He says that to meet socially, and when he is host in his own house, he has a certain simple dignity, like a farmer entertaining neighbours. All very different from the showy vulgarity of Mussolini. But that once one begins to work with him, or sees him dealing with great affairs, one has such a sense of evil arrogance that one is almost nauseated. Evil and treachery and malice dart into Hitler's mystic eyes. He has a maddening habit of laying down the law in sharp, syncopated sentences, accompanying the conclusion either with a sharp pat of his palm upon the table, or by a half-swing sideways in his chair, a sudden Napoleonic crossing of his arms, and a gaze of detached but suffering mysticism towards the ceiling. His impatience is terrific. We asked Kirkpatrick what gave him a sense of actual evil. He said that after Hitler had flown from Godesberg to Munich to murder Roehm [in 1934], he returned in the very highest spirits, mimicking to his secretary the gestures of fear which Roehm had made. This was told to Kirk by one of those who were present.

Diary   *August 31, 1939*

The *Bremen* has left New York after having been held up for twenty-four hours by American customs. The *Europa*, after disguising itself and creeping round by Iceland, has reached Bremerhaven. The 1 o'clock news announces that we have decided to evacuate three million mothers and children tomorrow from menaced areas. It is rather grim. Historic names such as Rochester, Chatham, Southwark come over at us in the calm cultured voice of the announcer. The flag hangs limply on its flag-staff. It is odd to feel that the world as I knew it has only a few hours more to run.

Diary   *September 1, 1939*

I take a deck-chair and sit at the door of the South Cottage so that I can hear the telephone if it rings. Viti comes along the path walking quickly. "It has begun," she says. It seems that last night Förster [Nazi Gauleiter of Danzig], with Hitler's approval, announced the incorporation of Danzig in the Reich, and that hostilities between Germany and Poland have already begun. The House has been summoned for 6 o'clock tonight. It is exactly 10.45 that I get this news. Miss Macmillan [secretary] appears with my gas-mask in a box.

Motor up to London. There are few signs of any undue activity beyond a few khaki figures at Staplehurst and some schoolboys filling sand-bags at Maidstone. When we get near London we see a row of balloons hanging like black spots in the air.

Go down to the House at 5.30. They have already darkened the building and lowered the lights. The lobby is extremely dark, and the Chamber, which generally seems to be a dim aquarium, appears quite garish by comparison. The Speaker arrives punctually at 6 and we all bow to him. Lloyd George and Winston are already in their places facing each other. We have prayers. The Chaplain adds a little special prayer saying, "Let us this day pray for wisdom and courage to defend the right." The Prime Minister and Greenwood [Leader of the Opposition] enter together and are received with a loud cheer. People crowd into the Distinguished Strangers Gallery. The Polish and Russian Ambassadors find themselves next to each other. I grin up at Maisky and he grins back. The Dukes of Kent and Gloucester sit above the clock.

Chamberlain rises immediately. He begins by saying that the time has arrived when action rather than speech is required. He then, with some emotion, reminds the House how he prayed that it would never fall upon him to ask the country to accept the "awful arbitrament of war". "I fear," he continued, "that I may not be able to avoid that responsibility." He then goes on to say that we have neglected no means of making it crystal clear to the German Government that if they use force we should reply by force, and he raises his voice and strikes the box with a clenched fist as he says, "The responsibility for this terrible catastrophe lies on the shoulders of one man, the German Chancellor, who has not hesitated to plunge the world into misery in order to serve his own senseless ambition." This met with a loud cheer from all benches. He then continues calmly explaining the recent course of negotiations, resting the back of one hand upon the palm of the other, and every now and then pinching off his pince-nez between his finger and thumb. When he reveals the fact that the sixteen points which Hitler claims to have been rejected were never even communicated to the Poles, a gasp of astonishment rises and Lady Astor exclaims in ringing tones, "Well, I never did!" He then reaches the climax of his speech, and after saying that the two Ambassadors have been instructed "to hand to the German Government the following document," he fiddles with his papers for some time and then produces a document which he reads very slowly. He is evidently in real moral agony and the general feeling in the House is one of deep sympathy for him and of utter misery for ourselves.

I am afraid that the Lobby opinion is rather defeatist and they all realise that we have in front of us a very terrible task. The Prime Minister's speech is generally approved, although the Opposition mind very much his having brought in that friendly reference to Mussolini.

Diary   *September 2, 1939*

The House is packed and tense and we wait there exactly like a court awaiting the verdict of the jury. At 7.42 the Prime Minister enters with Greenwood. He gets up to speak. He begins with the chronological method: "On Wednesday night Sir Nevile Henderson, our Ambassador in Berlin, handed to Herr von Ribbentrop . . ." – that sort of thing. His voice betrays some emotion as if he were sickening for a cold. He is a strange man. We expected one of his dramatic surprises. But none came. It was evident when he sat down that no decision had been arrived at. The House gasped for one moment in astonishment. Was there to be another Munich after all? Then Greenwood got up. The disappointment at the P.M.'s statement, the sense that appeasement had come back, vented itself in the reception of Greenwood. His own people cheered, as was natural; but what was so amazing was that their cheer was taken up in a second and greater wave from our benches. Bob Boothby cried out, "*You* speak for Britain." It was an astonishing demonstration. Greenwood almost staggered with surprise. When it subsided he had to speak and did so better than I had expected. He began to say what an embarrassing task had been imposed on him. He had wanted to support and was obliged to criticise. Why this delay? We had promised to help Poland "at once". She was being bombed and attacked. We had vacillated for 34 hours. What did this mean? He was resoundingly cheered. The tension became acute, since here were the P.M.'s most ardent supporters cheering his opponent with all their lungs. The front bench looked as if they had been struck in the face.

The House adjourns. The lobby is so dark that a match struck flames like a beacon. There is great confusion and indignation. We feel that the German ships and submarines will, owing to this inexplicable delay, elude our grasp. The P.M. must know by now that the whole House is against him. He might (had he been a more imaginative man) have got out of his difficulty. It was not his fault but that of Georges Bonnet [French Foreign Minister]. But he is too secretive by nature to be able to create confidence. In those few minutes he flung away his reputation. I feel deeply sorry for him.

Diary   *Sunday, September 3, 1939*

The papers announce that we are sending an ultimatum which expires at 11 this morning.

To Ronnie Tree's house. The usual members of our group are enlivened by the presence of Bob Boothby and Duncan Sandys of the Churchill group. We discuss first whether Anthony [Eden] is to accept the offer to join the Cabinet, although he is not included in the inner Cabinet. Some people think that he must refuse to join except as a member of the War Cabinet. Anthony rather writhes and wriggles, from which I gather that he has already committed himself to join and does not relish these suggestions [in the afternoon he was, in fact, offered the Dominions Office without a seat in the War Cabinet]. I watch the minute hand of my watch creeping towards 11 a.m., when we shall be at war. When the watch reaches that point, we pay no attention. The Prime Minister is to broadcast at 11.15 and we have no wireless. The housemaid has one and she comes and fixes it up in a fumbling way. We listen to the P.M. He is quite good and tells us war has begun. But he puts in a personal not which shocks us. We feel that after last night's demonstration he cannot possibly lead us into a great war. At the end of his speech are official announcements and notably one which says that from this moment no factory sirens are to sound and that any we hear are to be taken to be air-raid warnings. One of the group who had come back into the Chamber after the adjournment says that Chamberlain remained on the bench with Margesson. The latter was purple in the face, and the former was white as a sheet. It must be clear to them that if it had come to a vote at the time, he would have been defeated.

At noon we return to the Chamber [after an air-raid warning]. The Speaker takes his seat with the usual calm procedure. We have prayers. The Prime Minister then makes a speech which is restrained and therefore effective. He looks very ill. Winston intervenes with a speech which misses fire since it is too like one of his articles. The sirens continue during the debate, but we pay no attention to them. They are sounding the all-clear. We learn afterwards that the whole air-raid warning was a mistake. But the effect of this alarm was that nobody was really attuned to listen with any real receptiveness to the speeches that were made.

At 1.50 I motor down with Victor Cazalet to Sissinghurst. There are many army lorries along the road and a few pathetic trucks evacuating East End refugees. In one of those there is an elderly woman who shakes her fist at us and shouts that it is all the fault of the rich. The Labour Party will be hard put to it to prevent this war degenerating into class warfare.

When I reach Sissinghurst I find that the flag has been pulled down.

PART II

The War

The outbreak of war found H.N. in a gloomy mood. He feared defeat. When Hitler conquered Poland in less than a month, he and his colleagues in the 'Eden Group' were convinced that the British war-effort would only stiffen if Winston Churchill succeeded Chamberlain as Prime Minister.

Diary   *September 4, 1939*

Vita has instituted a system under which people keep watches to listen for the siren at night. I do not think it is a very good system since it will be a strain on the nerves. Eventually she will abandon it.

Two things impress themselves upon me. (1) Time. It seems three weeks since yesterday morning and it is difficult to get one's days of the week in chronological order. (2) Nature. Even as when someone dies, one is amazed that the poplar should still be standing quite unaware of one's own disaster, so also when I walked down to the lake to bathe I could scarcely believe that the swans were being sincere in their indifference to the Second German War.

Up to London. The posters carry the words "British Liner Torpedoed". It is the *Athenia* out from Liverpool to Canada or the United States which was torpedoed off the Hebrides [112 lives were lost; 28 of them American]. Many Americans must have been drowned. How insane the Germans are at the very moment when Roosevelt has put out his neutrality proclamation. It is a bad proclamation from our point of view. He says that nothing on earth will induce the Americans to send forces to Europe. But he also says that no man can remain neutral in mind and that he knows where the right lies.

Diary   *September 5, 1939*

I am in a mood of deep depression. I do not really see how we can win this war, yet if we lose it, we lose everything. It may be that I am old [52] and sad and defeatist. But one thing I do know and it comforts me. I would rather go down fighting and suffering than creep out after a month or two at the cost of losing our pride. That may be the only thing left to us.

Diary   *September 7, 1939*

The papers report a serious German advance in Poland. We drop more pamphlets on Germany. Miss Niggeman (who is a good barometer of opinion) asks why we are letting the Germans have it all their own way. Chamberlain must go. The full list of the re-constituted Cabinet is published. Apart from the inclusion of Winston [First Lord of the Admiralty] and Eden [Dominions Office] it is a reformed Munich front.

H.N. to V.S-W.   *September 14, 1939*

The Opposition are getting somewhat restive, especially about the Ministry of Information. The latter has been staffed by duds at the top and all the good people are in the most subordinate positions. The rage and fury of the newspapermen passes all bounds. John Gunther [the American writer, then war-correspondent] for instance, told me that he had asked one of the censors for the text of our leaflet which we dropped over Germany. The request was refused. He asked why. The answer was, "We are not allowed to disclose information which might be of value to the enemy." When Gunther pointed out that two million of these leaflets had been dropped over Germany, the man blinked and said, "Yes, something must be wrong there."

Diary   *September 15, 1939*

*The *Daily Telegraph* are giving up book reviews which means a serious financial loss [for H.N.]. I hear a story of an old lady at Brighton who heard the air-raid warning at 11.30 on Sunday and only heard the all clear on the Monday afterwards. "That *was* a long raid," she said on emerging. More stories about the confusion and ill-feeling created by the evacuation scheme.*

Diary   *September 16, 1939*

My appalling depression may be due to the fact that I am living my former life with all the conditions altered. Rob Bernays told me yesterday that all the front-bench people keep exclaiming, "I wish I were twenty. I cannot bear this responsibility." What they really mean is, "I wish I did not know how bad things are!" The whole world is either paralysed or against us.

Diary   *September 17, 1939*

Write my *Spectator* article. At 11 a.m. (a bad hour) Vita comes to tell me that Russia has invaded Poland and is striking towards Vilna. We are so dumbfounded by the news that there is a wave of despair over Sissinghurst. I do not think that the Russians will go beyond her old frontier or will wish to declare war on us. But of course it is a terrific blow and makes our victory even more uncertain.

Let me review the situation. It may be that within a few days we shall have Germany, Russia and Japan against us. It may be that Rumania will be subjugated and that the Greeks and Yugoslavs will succumb to Germany. The Baltic and the Scandinavian states will be too frightened to do anything. Holland, Belgium and Switzerland will have to capitulate. Thus the Axis will rule Europe, the Mediterranean and the Far East. Faced by such a combine, France may make terms. Hitler is then in the position of Napoleon after Austerlitz, with the important difference that whereas we were then in command of the seas, our command of the seas is not now absolute. It is not so much a question of them encircling and blockading Germany; it is a question of us encircling and blockading them. Japan might threaten our position in Australia and the Far East. Russia might threaten us in India. Italy might raise the Arab world. In a few days our whole position might collapse. Nothing could be more black.

And yet and yet, I still believe that if we have the will-power, we might win through. The Germans, who are diffident by nature, can scarcely believe in this fairy-tale. A single reverse and they will be overcome with nervous trepidation. Our position is one of grave

danger. A generous offer of an immediate truce with the prospect
of an eventual conference might tempt us sorely. But we will not
have a generous offer. What will happen? I suppose there will be a
German ultimatum and a Coalition Cabinet. Chamberlain must go.
Churchill might be our Clemenceau or our Gambetta. To bed very
miserable and alarmed.

Diary   *September 20, 1939*

Lloyd George [then 76] says that he is frankly terrified and does not
see how we can possibly win the war. He contends that we should
insist immediately upon a Secret Session of Parliament in which we
should force the Government to tell us exactly how they estimate the
prospects of victory. If our chances are 50/50, then it might be
worthwhile organising the whole resources of the country for a
desperate struggle. But if the chances are really against us, then
we should certainly make peace at the earliest opportunity, possibly
with Roosevelt's assistance. He indulges in a fierce onslaught on the
stupidity and lack of vigour of the present Government. He contends
that to have guaranteed Poland and Rumania without a previous
agreement with Russia was an act of incredible folly and one which
was due to the essential weakness of Chamberlain's character.

The House is in one of its worst moods. The Prime Minister
rises to make his weekly statement. He reads it out from a manuscript and is obviously tired and depressed. The effect is most discouraging and Members drop off to sleep. The Prime Minister has
no gift for inspiring anybody, and he might have been the Secretary
of a firm of undertakers reading the minutes of the last meeting.

Diary   *September 25, 1939*

Allen Lane [Chairman of Penguin Books] comes to see me, and it is
agreed that I do a Penguin Special for him on why Britain is at War.

Diary   *September 26, 1939*

The Prime Minister gets up to make his statement. He is dressed in
deep mourning relieved only by a white handkerchief and a large
gold watch-chain. One feels the confidence and spirits of the House
dropping inch by inch. When he sits down there is scarcely any

applause. During the whole speech Winston Churchill had sat hunched beside him looking like the Chinese god of plenty suffering from acute indigestion. He just sits there, lowering, hunched and circular, and then he gets up. He is greeted by a loud cheer from all the benches and he starts to tell us about the Naval position. He began by saying how strange an experience it was for him after a quarter of a century to find himself once more in the same room in front of the same maps, fighting the same enemy and dealing with the same problems. His face then creases into an enormous grin and he adds, glancing down at the Prime Minister, "I have no conception how this curious change in my fortunes occurred." The whole House roared with laughter and the Prime Minister had not the decency to raise a sickly smile. He just looked sulky. His delivery was amazing. One could feel the spirit of the House rising with every word. In those 20 minutes Churchill brought himself nearer the post of Prime Minister than he has ever been before. In the lobbies afterwards even Chamberlainites were saying "we have now found our leader". Old Parliamentary hands confessed that never in their experience had they seen a single speech so change the temper of the House.

Diary   *September 27, 1939*

Lunch with Sibyl Colefax. The people are H. G. Wells, G. M. Young [the historian and novelist], Victor Cazalet and Jan Masaryk. The Duke and Duchess of Windsor appear although I had imagined that he was over in France. He is going there shortly. He is dressed in khaki with all his decorations and looks grotesquely young. H. G. Wells, who is a republican with a warm sympathy for the Duke of Windsor, refuses to bow to him but treats him with great friendliness. *The Duchess tells me that on the day before war he sent a private telegram to Hitler urging him to do his best for peace. At 2 a.m. the next morning they were rung up by the night watchman saying that a most important telegram had arrived. The local postmaster insisted upon delivering this telegram in person and when it arrived they discovered that it was merely an acknowledgment by Hitler in perfectly polite terms of the telegram the Duke had sent. The postmaster was so impressed by the signature that he had felt it necessary to rouse the household.*

I have seldom seen the Duke in such cheerful spirits and it was rather touching to witness their delight at being back in England. There was no false note.

Walking away with H. G. Wells I said to him, "You must admit the man has got charm?" "Glamour," he said. "Charm," I said. "Oh very well," he said, "have it your own way."

Diary   *October 3, 1939*

I go with Duff Cooper to the Carlton Grill, where Diana [Cooper] has a supper party in honour of Burckhardt, the former League of Nations High Commissioner in Danzig. He is rather a dapper, smart, fresh-coloured Swiss aristocrat speaking the most beautiful French. I sit next to him and find him most intelligent and amusing. He talks a great deal about Hitler. He says that Hitler is the most profoundly feminine man that he has ever met, and that there are moments when he becomes almost effeminate. He imitates the movements of his white flabby hands. He says that Hitler has a dual personality, the first being that of the rather gentle artist, and the second that of the homicidal maniac. He is convinced that Hitler has no complete confidence in himself and that his actions are really governed by somnambulist certainty. He says that the main energy in Hitler is an energy of hatred, and that he never met any human being capable of generating so terrific a condensation of envy, vituperation and malice. Yet now and then there is a pathetic side to him. For instance, he once heard Hitler say, "It is a great sorrow to me that I have never met an Englishman who speaks German well enough for me to feel at ease with him." It was evident to Burckhardt that he was fascinated, "as so many Germans are fascinated", by the problem of our easy-going self-assurance.

On October 28, H.N., with eight other back-bench M.P.s, flew to Paris to visit the Maginot Line, which impressed them greatly, and to exchange views with French politicians.

The closing months of 1939 only increased the strain of the war by inactivity; there was no fighting on land. The British were waiting for Hitler's move west through Holland and Belgium. The only major incident was Russia's invasion of Finland on November 30, following

Finland's rejection of Soviet territorial demands. To everyone's astonishment, the Finns repulsed the Russian advance.

Diary   *November 2, 1939*

The Prime Minister makes his weekly statement. It is dull as ditch-water. I admit that there was little for him to tell us but he need not have done it in so glum and gloomy a form. I hear that Halifax said recently, "I wish the P.M. would give up these weekly statements. It is as if one were in East Africa and received the *Times Weekly Edition* at regular intervals." It is certainly very bad. Archie [Sinclair] and Attlee are little better. I am ashamed, as there are Dominion representatives recently arrived who are crowded in the Gallery. They had come expecting to find the Mother of Parliaments armed like Britannia. They merely saw the old lady dozing over her knitting, while her husband read the evening paper aloud.

Diary   *November 25, 1939*

How curious are the moods through which one passes! I sit here in my room at Sissinghurst thinking back on the days since September 3. The acute depression and misery of the first weeks have passed. I have accepted the fact that we are at war and I suppose that I am physically relieved by the fact that there are not likely to be any raids during the winter upon London and that the Germans have not made a dash through Holland. Yet the fact that this war is costing us six million pounds a day and that I am not really certain that we shall win it fills me with acute sadness at times. We shall keep up a brave face and refuse to admit that defeat is possible. But my heart aches with apprehension.

Diary   *November 26, 1939*

It is odd that I should have written the above paragraph last night. For this morning at five I woke up with such a load of depression upon me as I have not had since the first days of the war. The wind yelled round the cottage and the windows were lashed with rain. I thought of people in open boats in the North Sea.

Diary   *November 30, 1939*

The Russians send an ultimatum to Finland and start bombing
Helsinki and Vyborg. The P.M. makes a statement. The Labour
Party are enraged with Russia. There are cries of "Shame!" from
all the benches. I was amused at Question time to watch a discussion
between the Whips as to whom they should put up from the back-
benches to answer [Hugh] Dalton. I saw them pointing at me, at
which [David] Margesson shook his head in fierce negation. He
never forgives nor forgets.

Diary   *December 9, 1939*

Read Cyril Connolly's new paper *Horizon*. The editorial note says
that in this war we are not inspired by "pity or hope" as in the
Spanish war. No pity. No hope. Glum. Glum. Glum. All this business about our having lost what we used to describe as "patriotism"
must be thought out carefully. The old national theory has been cut
horizontally by class distinctions. We used to cut it like a cake in
perpendicular wedges. Now we cut it sideways. This is a difficult
alteration.

Diary   *December 14, 1939*

*The *Bremen* has got back to Hamburg after having been sighted
by one of our submarines. We put out that "of course we did not
torpedo the ship because that would have been against the rules of
war". The Germans at once put out that our real reason was that
our submarine was spotted by an aeroplane. We then put out that
the *Bremen* didn't matter much anyhow. Now this is bad handling
of propaganda. Luckily it does not matter much since in the course
of the day the same submarine sinks another submarine and
damages a German cruiser.*
    Talk to Paul Evans. He agrees that yesterday's sitting [the first
Secret Session] was a great blow to the Party machine. They must
have realised the underlying force of the opposition on our side.
The effect of the Secret Session was not to divulge secrets which
could not have been divulged in public. It was to show the Whips
what their supporters really felt. The tremendous reception given
on our benches to Archie Sinclair's speech must in itself have

shown the Whips how precarious is their hold on their own party. This marks a stage in the end of this administration. They will try to placate us by appointing Amery Minister of Economics. But our implacability remains. We have got them.

Diary   December 18, 1939

Have a long talk with Rab Butler. He tells me that my book [*Why Britain is at War*] is a work of art and perfectly correct. He thinks that I am right about Chamberlain and Horace Wilson in so far as diplomacy is concerned, but that Horace is really a gifted man nonetheless. He says that his influence over Chamberlain is something extraordinary and that the latter simply cannot move without him. He says that Chamberlain is tough without being strong. There is a weakness somewhere.

Diary   December 31, 1939

Cyril Joad [the philosopher and broadcaster] expounds pacifism after dinner. His line is that the ordinary person in England would be less unhappy after a Nazi victory than if he or she lost their sons, lovers, or husbands. He thinks only of the greatest unhappiness of the greatest number, and accuses me of national and spiritual pride. It is a pleasure talking to him. He stirs up the mind. He is extremely imaginative about physical pain, and the picture of young men being gored by bayonets is so terrible to him that he would prefer sacrificing liberty to prevent it happening.

I do not stay to watch the New Year in or the Old Year out. I write this diary at 11.45 and shall not wait. The old year is foul and the new year terrifying.

As a speaker, writer and member of many Committees, H.N. was very active in what Churchill called "these months of pretended war". Aid to the Finns was under discussion when the Russians broke their resistance in mid-March. Chamberlain's leadership was still reluctantly accepted, until great events revealed its inadequacy.

Diary   *January 1, 1940*

A pleasant dinner with Cyril Joad and Vita. We listen to Lord Haw Haw [William Joyce, who broadcast anti-British propaganda from Germany]. Joad does not think that he will have any effect on his young pacifists. It is upon the middle, uncertain people that he will have an effect, the untrained mind. He simply must be answered. Joad teases me for being self-depreciative. He says that I lack the competitive instinct and that I never throw the whole of myself into what I believe. He is, in a way, right about this. But what does it come from? Do I lack courage? But in the House I have been brave enough. It cannot be fear of responsibility or hard work, since I enjoy both. It is, I suppose, a profound disbelief in myself coupled with a rather self-indulgent and frivolous preference for remaining an observer.

Diary   *January 3, 1940*

In the evening we hear Roosevelt's message to Congress. He begins by saying that the United States will never enter this war, and having said that, he delivers the most crushing attack upon our enemies that I have ever heard. It is superb. What a great man!

Diary   *January 6, 1940*

We dine with Victor Cazalet who has Eddy [Sackville West] and the Anthony Eden family staying with him. Anthony is in good form. I can see that he still loathes the Prime Minister whom he regards as obstinate, opinionated, rather mean, and completely ignorant of the main issues involved. He also dislikes Sam Hoare [Lord Privy Seal], whom he calls "Aunt Tabitha". He feels that Kingsley Wood [Secretary of State for Air] is a help since he is truthful.

Diary   *January 7, 1940*

I am amused by the effect of Hore-Belisha's dismissal [as Minister of War]. We in the House would assume that it was due to the fact that having told so many lies he had sactificed the confidence of the country. But not at all. It seems that the country regard him as a second Haldane and a moderniser of the Army. The line is that he has been ousted by an intrigue of the Army chiefs, and there is a general uproar about being ruled by dictators in brass hats. The Germans could make great capital of this consternation, were it not that Belisha is a Jew. Yet the general effect will be (a) among the unknowing that Belisha has been sacked because he supported the private against the officer; (b) among the *cognoscenti* that he has been ousted because he told lies, but that Chamberlain managed the thing clumsily; (c) a vague suspicion that the press are really anti-Chamberlain and are exaggerating this incident in order to attack him. My own feeling is that this is less a pro-Belisha than an anti-Chamberlain outburst.

Diary   *January 13, 1940*

This afternoon, as we walked through the frozen woods together, Vita said, "It is not as if we were fighting to preserve the things we care for. This war, whatever happens, will destroy them." We imagine that we are fighting for liberty and out standards of civilization. But is it perfectly certain that by these phrases we do not mean the cultured life which we lead? I know that such a life, as lived by Vita and myself, is "good" in the philosophical sense. We are humane, charitable, just and not vulgar. By God, we are not vulgar!

Diary   *January 20, 1940*

We listen to Winston Churchill on the wireless after dinner. He is a little too rhetorical and I do not think his speech will really have gone down with the masses. He is too belligerent for this pacifist age, and although once anger comes to steel our sloppiness his voice will be welcome to them, at the moment it reminds them of heroism which they do not really feel.

Get a letter from Walter Lippmann. He says that the American people want us to win but wish to keep out. Thus there is a conflict in their desires, and they want to be assured that they OUGHT to keep out. It is this gap between one desire and the other which offers so wide a fissure for German propaganda.

Diary   *February 20, 1940*

The P.M. makes a statement about Finland which is loudly applauded. Also one about Norway and the *Altmark* [which had been intercepted by a British ship in a Norwegian fjord]. Winston, when he comes in, is loudly cheered. I talk to Roger Keyes who was in the Admiralty while it was all going on. He says that our flotilla commander was assured by the Norwegians that there were no prisoners aboard the *Altmark*. He was shaken by this and telegraphed home. Winston replied, "Well, find out from the Captain of the *Altmark* what he has done with the prisoners." They tried to get the Norwegians to play up and to examine the ship themselves but they were too frightened of Germany. Finally, it was clear that the Norwegians would not cooperate and the final decision had to be made. Winston rang up Halifax and said, "I propose to violate Norwegian neutrality." Halifax replied, "Go ahead." The message was sent and they waited in the Admiralty anxiously for the result. What a result! A fine show. Winston, when he walks out of the House, catches my eye. He gives one portentous wink.

Diary   *February 29, 1940*

I see Vansittart. He is very worried by the return of Jo Kennedy, the American Ambassador. He says that Kennedy has been spreading it abroad in the U.S.A. that we shall certainly be beaten and he will use his influence here to press for a negotiated peace. In this he will have the assistance of the old appeasers of Maisky and the left-wing pacifists, *and the Henry Channon type. The latter has been entertaining the Kaiser's grandson and it is wrong that he as an ex-American should have such power.*

> On March 6th, H.N. went to France for twelve days, lecturing on British war aims for the Ministry of Information. He visited Chalon-sur-Saône, Grenoble, Lyons, Besançon and Paris.

H.N. to V.S-W.   *March 10, 1940*
                                                 Grenoble

I am introduced by the senior tutor in literature. I ascend the tribune. I make my speech, or rather I give my talk, which lasts fifty minutes. Again I abandon my prepared text, and talk just as if I were speaking in English. The audience listen with evident attention. At the end there is applause. The people in the front rows clap and murmur discreetly, "Well done." Suddenly, from the gallery where the students are seated, comes a second wave of applause accompanied by the stamping of feet. Everyone takes it up. It becomes a demonstration. I say a few words of thanks. And then the young people in the gallery rise to their feet and begin to shout. It becomes an ovation. I was much moved.

They talked about you at the meeting. Professor Blancagard said that you were one of the most admired poets in England. That gave me great pleasure and produced in me a wave of vague nostalgia. I leave for Lyons tomorrow.

Diary   *March 14, 1940*
                                                                                              Paris

Finland appears to have surrendered completely, and loses one-tenth of her territory and her strategic independence. I go to see Georges Mandel [Minister for the Colonies] at the Colonial Ministry. I find him seated at his desk on which the papers are piled as if they had just been spilled out of a suitcase. He asks me about the effect of the Finnish collapse upon British opinion. I say that I cannot tell from the newspapers and must wait till I get back to the lobbies. He says the effect on France will be tremendous. "You see," he says, "our government decided upon war as the only alternative to admitting German domination. Yet when one decides on war one also decides to sacrifice many lives, to run many risks, and to endure many defeats. We are at present trying to conduct a war of appeasement which means that Hitler may win." He asks me what they think of the French Government in England. He also is very anxious to know about our coming men. What of Eden? Is he a strong man? What about Herbert Morrison? *"Il nous faut des hommes!!"* he says.

Diary   *March 19, 1940*

The House is very crowded. Chamberlain makes a good debating speech, putting the whole blame for the Finnish collapse on the Scandinavian powers [Norway and Sweden refused to allow British troops to pass through their territory to aid Finland], and claiming that we had "answered" all Finland's demands and had done all we could. Dick Law makes his speech. He says that the P.M.'s arguments are all very fine, but we have seen again and again a Minister stand up "at that box" and explain the reasons for failure: people who have made so many mistakes should not remain in power. Harold Macmillan also makes a fine attacking speech, pointing out the discrepancy between what we sent to Finland and what she actually received. Chamberlain, who sat through the whole debate, replies vigorously. He is a remarkable man: there is no doubt about that. There is also no doubt that he wants to win the war. He gave the impression of great obstinacy and has enhanced his reputation. One thing that strikes drama is that he announces that at that very moment we are attacking the German air-bases at Sylt.

Diary   *March 26, 1940*

Vita and I discuss the war. She says that she sees no logical reason why we should retain Gibraltar, Malta, India or Aden. This enrages me since it is due to loose thinking. People do not understand that it is our independence and not imperialism which depends on such areas of communication. I go to bed with a sad heart.

Diary   *April 2, 1940*

Dine with Kenneth Clark [then Director of the Film Division of the Ministry of Information]. Willie Maugham, Mrs Winston Churchill, and Leslie Howard [the film star] are there. We have an agreeable dinner and talk mostly about films. Leslie Howard is doing a big propaganda film and is frightfully keen about it. We discuss the position of those English people who have remained over in the United States. The film stars claim that they have been asked to remain there since they are more useful at Hollywood, but we all regret bitterly that people like Aldous Huxley, Auden and Isherwood should have absented themselves. They want me to write a *Spectator* article attacking them. That is all very well but it would lose me the friendship of three people whom I much admire. I come back with Leslie Howard and he continues to talk excitedly about his new film. He seems to enter into such things with the zest of a schoolboy and that is part of his charm.

Diary   *April 5, 1940*

I lunch at the Beefsteak. Harold Macmillan tells us Peter Fleming's [the writer and traveller] *mot* about the Cabinet reshuffle: "I do not understand why they bothered to exchange Ministries; surely it would have been simpler to exchange names?"

It is curious to think back upon my moods since September 3. I recognise the first stage of acute depression, due I suppose to fear of the immediate Blitzkrieg and to hatred of war. Then there comes the second stage, trying to sort out my own ideas in order. And now there comes a third stage when I feel we CAN win the war but that we may fail to do so. My attitude towards the future is one of acute interest rather than acute dismay. My fear about what may happen to Nigel and Ben remains as an ulcer which winces at the thought. But my anger is increased. I want to win. I want to win. My God! I am prepared to sacrifice my whole happiness to victory. I feel resolute and well. I shall have my chance. I feel that in my odd fiddling, marginal, way I am helping. The *Spectator* articles have their effect. I feel combatant.

Diary   *April 8, 1940*

Come up in the early train with Walter Elliot [Minister of Health], Rob Bernays, Raymond Mortimer and Paul Hyslop [the architect] who have been staying at Swifts [Victor Cazalet's house]. We do not for once discuss politics, but we do discuss why I should hate T. E. Lawrence so much. After all, he was a friend of mine and our personal relations were never strained. I say that I feel for him that distaste that I feel for Sir James Barrie and John Galsworthy, namely that he acquired a legend without deserving it: he was fundamentally fraudulent. Walter Elliot asks did I really think the Arab campaign fraudulent? I say "no" but the whole after-time. The *Pillars of Wisdom* book and that inane translation of Homer. He says that I must be jealous of a man of action who achieved more than I did and a man of letters who attempted more than I did. That may be true. But I am not a jealous person and I feel that there must be some other explanation of my antipathy.

Two tremendous months followed. April was the month when German troops overran Denmark and Norway.

May the month of Hitler's attack in the West. As a consequence of the first campaign, and almost coincident with the second, Neville Chamberlain fell and Churchill became Prime Minister on May 10.

H.N. to V.S-W.   April 9, 1940

Well darling, the war seems to have begun. I am sad about it and apprehensive. But that is probably because I am an old pacifist at heart. But poor Denmark!!!

Diary   April 9, 1940

I go down to the House. The Prime Minister, who is looking very haggard, makes a statement. It is rather well done and he admits quite frankly that the Fleet is out and that we do not exactly know what is happening. He discredits the rumour that Narvik has been occupied.

The House is extremely calm and the general line is that Hitler has made a terrible mistake. I feel myself that I wish that we could sometimes commit mistakes of such magnitude. *I dine with Somerset Maugham and Raymond Mortimer at the Café Royal. It is very agreeable to get away from politics. We talk about the emigrés [to America], namely Aldous Huxley, Gerald Heard, Auden and Isherwood. They still want me to write a *Spectator* article attacking them. I don't quite see why they should put this burden upon me but they say that they are much greater friends with them than I am and that the act of treachery had better be committed by myself.*

H.N. to V.S-W.   April 10, 1940

I think the general opinion is that it is a bore but not a disaster. It means of course that Hitler gets Sweden as well and all the other neutrals will be terrified out of their lives. But it also means an advantage for us in so far as the blockade is concerned, and extension of the front.

Diary   *April 14, 1940*

I am fascinated by this crucial stage, since it really boils down to the incessant problem whether mastery of the sea is more important than mastery of the air. The early stages of the Scandinavian campaign seem to have shown that the air was the more important. The later stages have suggested that sea-power in the end prevails. It is too early to decide which of these two theories is correct. But it may prove that Narvik is one of the decisive battles of history.

Diary   *April 23, 1940*

Lord Salisbury tells us that he had been to see Winston Churchill and had asked him quite frankly whether he believed he could carry on concurrently the job of First Lord and Co-ordinator of Defence [he had been appointed on April 4]. Winston told him that he is feeling in perfect health, that he would die if the Admiralty were taken away from him, and that the Press had much exaggerated his role as Co-ordinator of Defence, which was little more than Chairman of a Committee of the fighting services. He had no right to initiate suggestions or make decisions.

Diary   *April 30, 1940*

The news begins to creep through that the Germans have occupied Stören [30 miles south of Trondheim]. That means that we are done. I talk to Harold Macmillan who has heard that we shall begin to evacuate Norway this evening. Others think that this will be the fall of Chamberlain, and Lloyd George as P.M. The Whips are putting it about that it is all the fault of Winston who has made another forlorn failure. This is hell.

Diary   *May 4, 1940*

I find that there is a grave suspicion of the Prime Minister. His speech about the Norwegian expedition has created disquiet. The House knows very well that it was a major defeat. But the P.M. said that "the balance of advantage rested with us" and that "Germany has not attained her objective". They know that this is simply not true. If Chamberlain believed it himself, then he was stupid. If he did not believe it, then he was trying to deceive. In either case he loses confidence. People are so distressed by the whole thing that they are talking of Lloyd George as possible P.M. Eden is out of it. Churchill is undermined by the Conservative caucus. Halifax is believed (and with justice) to be a tired man. We always say that our advantage over the German leadership principle is that we can always find another leader.

Diary   *May 5, 1940*

I read Dylan Thomas' *Portrait of the Artist as a Young Dog*. I am slightly disgusted by all the urine and copulation which occurs. I have a feeling that these people do not believe that they can write powerfully unless they can drag in the latrines. And yet it is quite clear that this young Thomas is a writer of great merit.

The lovely day sinks to sunset among the flowering trees. The Italian news is bad. It seems incredible to us that Italy should really come in. If she does it means that Mussolini is convinced of our early defeat. He is no fool and must have reasons for this belief. That is what fills me with such depression. Not Italy as an enemy, but Italy convinced as an intelligent and most admirably informed nation that Germany is going to win this war.

Diary   *May 7, 1940*

The House is crowded [for the Norwegian debate], and when Chamberlain comes in, he is greeted with shouts of "Missed the bus!" [the words Chamberlain used about Hitler a month before]. He makes a very feeble speech and is only applauded by the Yes-men. He makes some reference to the complacency of the country, at which the whole House cheers vociferously and ironically, inducing him to make a little, rather feminine, gesture of irritation. Attlee makes a feeble speech and Archie Sinclair a good one. When Archie sits down, many people stand up and the Speaker calls on Page Croft. There is a loud moan from the Labour Party at this, and they practically rise in a body and leave the House. He is followed by [J. C.] Wedgwood who makes a speech which contains everything he ought not to have said. He gives the impression of being a little off his head. At one moment he suggests that the British Navy has gone to Alexandria since they are frightened of being bombed.

A few minutes afterwards [Admiral Sir] Roger Keyes comes in, dressed in full uniform with six rows of medals. I scribble him a note telling him what Wedgwood has just said, and he immediately rises and goes to the Speaker's chair. When Wedgwood sits down, Keyes gets up and begins his speech by referring to Wedgwood's remark and calling it a damned insult. The Speaker does not call him to order for his unparliamentary language, and the whole House roars with laughter, especially Lloyd George who rocks backwards and forwards in boyish delight with his mouth wide open. Keyes then returns to his manuscript and makes an absolutely devastating attack upon the naval conduct of the Narvik episode and the Naval General Staff. The House listens in breathless silence when he tells how the Naval General Staff had assured him that the naval action at Trondheim was easy but unnecessary owing to the success of the military. There is a great gasp of astonishment. It is by far the most dramatic speech I have ever heard, and when Keyes sits down there is thunderous applause.

Thereafter the weakness of the Margesson system is displayed by the fact that none of the Yes-men are of any value whatsoever, whereas all the more able Conservatives have been driven into the ranks of the rebels. A further terrific attack is delivered by [Leo] Amery, who ends up by quoting from Cromwell, "In the name of God, go!"

Diary   *May 8, 1940*

Winston winds-up [the Norwegian debate]. He has an almost impossible task. On the one hand he has to defend the Services; on the other, he has to be loyal to the Prime Minister. One felt that it would be impossible to do all this after the debate without losing some of his own prestige, but he manages with extraordinary force of personality to do both these things with absolute loyalty and apparent sincerity while demonstrating by the brilliance of his personality that he has really nothing to do with this confused and timid gang.

Up to the last moment the House had really behaved with moderation, and one had the sense that there really was a united will to win the war. During the last twenty minutes, however, passions rose, and when the Division came there was great tensity in the air. Some 44 of us, including many of the young Service Members, vote against the Government and some 30 abstain. This leaves the Government with a majority of only 81 instead of a possible 213, and the figures are greeted with a terrific demonstration during which Joss Wedgwood starts singing *Rule Britannia*, which is drowned in shouts of "Go, go, go, go!" Margesson signals to his henchmen to rise and cheer the Prime Minister as he leaves, and he walks out looking pale and angry.

Diary   *May 9, 1940*

Lunch at the Beefsteak and find that all are unanimous in feeling that Chamberlain must go. Admiral Hall tells me that the whole Navy are absolutely insistent upon it and that it is even worse in the Army. Walk down to the House with Barrington-Ward [Editor] of the *Times* who has come completely round and agrees with me (a) that the Germans may attack at any moment; (b) that we cannot have a prolonged Cabinet crisis; (c) that Chamberlain ought therefore to resign immediately within the next few hours.

Diary   *May 10, 1940*

Salisbury says that we must maintain our point of view, namely that Winston should be made Prime Minister during the course of the day. I am still at the Travellers when the wireless news comes telling us that the invasion of Belgium and Holland is complete, that both countries have mobilised and appealed for our assistance. Alec Dunglass [later Alec Douglas-Home, then P.P.S. to Chamberlain] comes in looking rather white about the gills and we tell him that our Group will never allow Chamberlain to get away from the reconstruction [of the Cabinet] owing to this invasion. He says that the reconstruction has already been decided upon, but that the actual danger of the moment really makes it impossible for the Government to fall. The situation is really one of *videant Consules*, and that we must have a triumvirate of Chamberlain, Churchill and Halifax to carry us over these first anxious hours.

I go back to K.B.W. and on the way I see posters saying "Brussels bombed, Paris bombed, Lyons bombed, Swiss Railways bombed." We are all most anxious regarding the position of our Army on the Belgian frontier, since we dread it being caught in the open. What makes it worse in a way is that it is a beautiful spring day with the bluebells and primroses in flower everywhere.

I go down to Sissinghurst. Met by Vita and Gwen. It is all looking too beautiful to be believed, but a sort of film has obtruded itself between my appreciation of nature and my terror of real life. It is like a tooth ache. We dine alone together chatting about indifferent things. Just before nine we turn on the wireless and it begins to buzz as the juice comes through and then we hear the bells [of the B.B.C.]. Then the pips sound nine and the announcer begins: "This is the Home Service. Here is the Right Honourable Neville Chamberlain M.P. who will make a statement." I am puzzled by this for a moment and then realise that he has resigned. He has tendered his resignation and Churchill is Prime Minister. For the moment, acting Ministers will carry on. He will agree to serve under Churchill. He ends with a fierce denunciation of the Germans for invading Holland and Belgium. It is a magnificent statement, and all the hatred that I have felt for Chamberlain subsides as if a piece of bread were dropped into a glass of champagne.

Diary   *May 13, 1940*

When Chamberlain enters the House, he gets a terrific reception, and when Churchill comes in the applause is less. Winston sits there between Chamberlain and Attlee, and it is odd to see the Labour Ministers sitting on the Government Bench. Winston makes a very short statement, but to the point [the famous "blood, sweat and tears" speech]. Lloyd George gets up and makes a moving speech telling Winston how fond he is of him. Winston cries slightly and mops his eyes.

Harold Macmillan told me that Brendan Bracken [P.P.S. to the Prime Minister] had given him a vivid description of Cabinet-making. He sat up till three in the morning with David Margesson going through lists. Winston was not in the least interested once the major posts had been filled, and kept on trying to interrupt them by discussing the nature of war and the changing rules of strategy. Meanwhile they would come back to their list, and Brendan would say, "Well what about So-and-So?" Margesson would reply, "Strike him out. He's no good at all." "Why then," Brendan would ask, "did you appoint him?" "Oh well," Margesson said, "he was useful at the time." Macmillan had asked Brendan what was Winston's mood. "Profound anxiety," he replied.

Diary   May 15, 1940

The Dutch have capitulated and the Italians may be in by this evening. We have breakfast out of doors in brilliant sunshine with butterflies flitting in and out. I feel physically sick with anxiety. All through it the cuckoos cluck at us with their silly reiterant note. In other days this would have caused pleasure. Today it causes pain.

> H.N. *was appointed Parliamentary Secretary to the Ministry of Information in Churchill's Government, with Duff Cooper as his Minister. After Dunkirk, he was made responsible for coordinating Government advice to the public in case of invasion, and in many other directions was very active.*

Diary   May 17, 1940

I fear that it looks as if the Germans have broken the French line at Mezières and Sedan. This is very serious. These surely are the saddest moments of my life and I do not know how I could cope with it all were it not for Vita's serene and loving sympathy. *While we are at breakfast the telephone rings. It is a message from Sibyl. She says "I hear Harold is in the Government." I have heard nothing and shall believe nothing until it is confirmed.*

At 12.40 the telephone rings again and Mac [Miss Macmillan, the secretary] in an awed voice says, "The Prime Minister's Private Secretary." I lift the receiver and wait without hearing anything. Then after about two minutes silence a voice says, "Mr Nicolson?" I say "Yes". "Hold on please, Mr Asquith here." I tell Asquith that I was on to Downing Street and that would he mind ringing off. So on I get again and this time I hear the Private Secretary who says, "Please hold on. The Prime Minister wishes to speak to you." Another long pause and then Winston's voice. "Harold! I think it would be very nice if you joined the Government and helped Duff [Cooper] at the Ministry of Information." "There is nothing I should like better." "Well fall in tomorrow. The list will be out tonight. That all right?" "Very much all right." "O.K." says Winston and rings off. Of course I am pleased and what makes it better is that the 1 p.m. news is not as bad as we feared.

H.N. to V.S-W.   *May 19, 1940*
                                                              Ministry of Information

Our War Room is perfectly thrilling. It is kept going night and day, and there are maps with pins and different coloured bits of wool. The chiefs meet in conference twice a day at 10.30 and 5.30, and the Press Conference is at 12.30. I have to attend all these, and in addition I shall be given specific branches of work to take over. I have a nice sunny little room, and if bombing starts, I shall sleep here. They say the shelter under our tower is proof even against a direct hit.

Diary   *May 20, 1940*

We discuss the problem of wireless while an attack is on. If we remain on the air we definitely assist enemy bombers, but they are frightened that if we go off the air, the Germans will use our wavelength to issue false messages which will much alarm the public. A clever impersonator might imitate Winston's voice sufficiently well and give instructions that all troops are to lay down their arms. Duff will take this problem up in the Cabinet.

Diary   *May 25, 1940*

They have discovered that one of the American Ambassador's Confidential Clerks is a spy and has been furnishing Miss Wolkoff [Russian agent] with photostatic copies of all Kennedy's most confidential correspondence, including the Prime Minister's personal messages to President Roosevelt. Kennedy begs us to keep this out of the press but the American journalists have already got the scent of something of the sort.

The Germans occupy Boulogne and Calais. Our communications are almost completely severed, and it is possible that the B.E.F. [British Expeditionary Force] may be cut off.

H.N. to V.S-W.   *May 26, 1940*

The Government may decide to evacuate Kent and Sussex of all civilians. If, as I hope, they give orders instead of advice, then those orders will be either "Go" or "Stay". If the former, then you know what to do. If the latter, we are faced with a grave predicament. I do not think that even if the Germans occupied Sissinghurst they would harm you in spite of the horrified dislike they feel for me. But to be quite sure you are not put to any humiliation I think you really ought to have a "bare bodkin" [code name for suicide pill] handy so that you can take your quietus when necessary. I shall have one also. I am not in the least afraid of such sudden and honourable death. What I dread is being tortured and humiliated. But how can we find a "bodkin" which will give us our quietus quickly and which is easily portable? I shall ask my doctor friends. I think it will be a relief to feel, "Well, if the worst comes to the worst there are always those two little pills."

If I believe in anything surviving I believe in a love like ours surviving – it is so completely unmaterial in every way.

Diary   *May 28, 1940*

The Policy Committee meets rather grimly and we are told of Reynaud's [French Prime Minister] broadcast at 8.30 this morning. He claims that the King of the Belgians surrendered against the wishes of his Government and army and makes it clear that this means that the B.E.F. is lost. He says he will reform a line on the Marne and the Somme and fight to the death. From the purely cynical point of view, breaking the news to the British public in this way is not a bad thing. It will at least enable them to feel that the disaster was due to Belgian cowardice as indeed to some extent it was.

Diary   *June 1, 1940*

We have now evacuated 220,000 men [from Dunkirk], which is amazing when I recall how we feared we should lose 80%. But there are few grounds for enthusiasm really, except moral grounds. We have lost all our equipment. The French have lost 80% of their forces and feel that we deserted them. It will constitute a real problem to recreate good relations between the forces. Lord Gort [Commander-in-Chief of the B.E.F.] says that he offered to take more French off but that they were too dead beat to move and that all those who could be galvanized into marching a few miles further were in fact rescued. This may be true, but the French with their tendency to attribute blame to others will be certain to say that we thought only of rescuing the B.E.F. and let them down.

Diary   *June 4, 1940*

The Prime Minister makes his speech about the evacuation of Flanders. He pays warm tribute to all concerned and rejoices at the great "deliverance" which we have been accorded. He admits, however, that we have suffered a "colossal military disaster" and that it will take us time to replace the vast equipment which we have lost. He then passes on to the invasion and ends with a magnificent peroration on the lines that we shall fight in our fields, fight in our streets, fight in our hills, and if necessary fight alone. He ends by saying that if this country is starved into submission we shall continue the struggle from our Empire and call the New World in to rescue the Old.

Diary   *June 10, 1940*

I give my draft of the Invasion pamphlet to the Director-General, who takes it down to the meeting of the Home Defence Ministers. The War Office, to my mind, do not seem to have faced the problem that the Germans will treat as saboteurs any civilians who obstruct them. If we encourage sabotage, a tremendous responsibility will rest upon our heads and only the Cabinet can decide.

H.N. to V.S-W.   *June 12, 1940*

What a joy it is for me to be so busy at this moment and in so central a position. I really feel that I can do some good, and I am *embattled*. I did not know that I possessed such combative instincts. Darling, why is it that I should feel so *gay*? Is it, as you said, that I am pleased at discovering in myself forces of manliness which I did not suspect? I feel such contempt for the cowards. And such joy that you and I should so naturally and without effort find ourselves on the side of the brave.

H.N. to V.S-W.   *June 17, 1940*

*We still do not know what terms the Germans intend to impose on France. If they were wise they would give good terms and treat the

French population very well. This will not only enable them to exploit French resources but also increase defeatism over here. I fear that among some people defeatism is spreading.* I think it is practically certain that the Americans will come in in November and if we can last till then all is well. Anyhow as a precaution I have the bare bodkin. I shall bring down your half on Sunday. It all looks very simple.

How I wish Winston would not talk on the wireless unless he is feeling in good form. He hates the microphone and when we bullied him into speaking last night he just sulked and read his House of Commons speech over again. Now as delivered in the H. of C. that speech was magnificent, especially the concluding sentences. But it sounded ghastly on the wireless. All the great vigour he put into it seemed to evaporate.

Diary   *June 21, 1940*

Today the French delegates were received by Hitler in the dining coach at Compiègne in which the Armistice of 1918 was signed. Hitler gave them an allocution scolding them for having been so wicked as to win the last war [this was not true]. Poor people, my heart bleeds for them.

H.N. to V.S-W.   *July 10, 1940*

I told the Queen today [with whom he lunched] that I got homesick and she said, "But that is right. That is personal patriotism. That is what keeps us going. I should die if I had to leave." She also told me that she is being instructed every morning how to fire a revolver. I expressed surprise. "Yes," she said, "I shall not go down like the others." I cannot tell you how superb she was. But I anticipated her charm. What astonished me is how the King has changed. I always thought him rather a foolish loutish boy. He is now like his brother [the Duke of Windsor]. He was so gay and she was so calm. They did me all the good in the world. How I wish you had been there. [Lord] Gort was simple and modest. And those two resolute and sensible. WE SHALL WIN. I know that. I have no doubts at all.

H.N. to V.S-W. *July 11, 1940*

I had about eleven people to see me today. I wish I were a Cabinet Minister and could keep these people off by a barrage of private secretaries. All this means that I do not see Duff enough. We take taxis together and devise all sorts of dodges. But the result is that he is seeing the Alpha Plus people all day and I am seeing the Beta Plus people whom he throws onto me. But that is the right system. I am there to take things off from him and to collect Parliamentary opinion.

I dined with Sibyl [Colefax] who is broke poor dear, and for whom we will have to take up a subscription. But she feels she is Madame de Pompadour which irritates me. I like calm people like Duff. Sibyl is too fussy to be of real help in these days.

The German bombings of some of our ports are already pretty bad. God knows what they will be when they start full out. But our morale is perfect. I am cocky about the war. Cocky. All our reports show that Hitler funks invading us and yet is pledged to do so. They expect an invasion this week end. That is Hitler's last horoscope date. After that the stars are against him. I feel like a doctor watching a dangerous case of illness. But I like being a doctor. I am so busy that my beloved diary is getting to be no more than an engagement book.

Diary *July 13, 1940*

Ben has bought a Picasso portrait of a woman entirely composed of grey cubes. It was very expensive. It is a determined portrait and it says what it thinks. But I do not like these affirmations in art. I like art to be a relief and not a challenge. But Ben, who is far more expert than I am, regrets this sentimental approach. I am sure he is right.

Diary *July 18, 1940*

Brendan Bracken says that the moment the war is over, Winston will want to retire. He says that Winston is convinced that he has had all the fun he wants out of politics, and that when this is over he wants to paint pictures and write books. He adds that in the twenty years he has known Winston, he has never seen him as fit as he is today, and his responsibilities seem to have given him a new lease of life. He adds that he is very determined not to become a legendary figure and has the theory that the Prime Minister is nothing more than Chairman of the Cabinet.

H.N. to V.S-W.   *July 31, 1940*

We had a Secret Session today. Mm. Hush. All that I can say is that Winston surpassed even himself. The situation is obscure. It may be that Hitler will first bomb us with gas and then try to land. At the same time, Italy and Japan will hit us as hard as they can. It will be a dreadful month. On the other hand, Hitler may feel that he cannot bring off a successful invasion and may seek to gain new, easy but sterile conquests in Africa and Asia. Were it not for this little island under a great leader, he would accomplish his desires.

Diary   *August 3, 1940*

I am feeling very depressed by this attack upon the Ministry of Information. What worries me is that the whole Press, plus certain pro-Munich conservatives, have planned and banded together to pull Duff Cooper down. He may be able to survive for a few weeks with Winston's support. But now that they have pledged themselves to his destruction, it becomes for them a matter of prestige. At present the Ministry is too decent, educated and intellectual to imitate Goebbels. If propaganda is a vital weapon as it seems, it must be entrusted to less scrupulous hands.

> *The Battle of Britain began on August 13 when the Luftwaffe started the air offensive on south-east England. On September 7 the Germans began to concentrate their bombing on London in an attempt to destroy civilian morale. Ten days later Hitler postponed the invasion of England.*

H.N. to V.S-W.   *August 14, 1940*

How I wonder if the invasion of England is really to begin. We do not understand what is really happening. The German attacks are more serious than mere reconnaissance, but not serious enough to justify the heavy losses they receive. They lost certainly more than 100 pilots yesterday which is more than they can afford. I cannot make it out nor can they. (By they I mean our experts.)

Diary *August 15, 1940*

Everyone is in high spirits about our air triumphs. In fact the superiority shown by our men is a miracle. Duff told me today that the only explanation is the lack of German training. Our triumph today was superb.

Diary *August 17, 1940*

Wimbledon was bombed yesterday with 18 killed. We brought down 75 of their planes. For the moment everything is over-shadowed by what seems to be the failure of the German air offensive against this island. They have done some damage here and there: they have killed and wounded many people, but they have not dealt us a really serious blow and our confidence rises.

Diary *August 18, 1940*

A lovely day. While we are sitting outside [in the garden at Sissinghurst], the siren sounds. We remain where we are. Then comes the sound of aeroplanes and looking up we see thin streamers from the exhaust of the German planes. Another wave follows, and we see it clearly – twenty little silver fish in arrow formation. There is no sound of firing but while we are at luncheon we hear planes quite close and go out to see. There is a rattle of machine gun fire and we see two Spitfires attacking a Heinkel. The latter sways off, obviously wounded. We then go on with our luncheon. After that Ben talks to us about Roger Fry and Virginia [Woolf]. He had written to the latter saying that Fry was too detached from life and she had written a tart letter in reply. He feels that Roger Fry and his set were too ivory tower.

Diary *August 20, 1940*

Winston says, in referring to the air force, "never in the field of human conflict has so much been owed by so many to so few". It was a moderate and well-balanced speech and he did not try to arouse enthusiasm but only to give guidance. He made a curious reference to Russia's possible attack on Germany and spoke about our "being mixed up with the United States" ending in a fine peroration about Anglo–American cooperation rolling on like the Mississippi.

Diary   *August 26, 1940*

A lovely morning. They raided London yesterday and we raided Berlin. I work at my broadcast talk. At noon I hear aeroplanes and shortly afterwards the wail of the siren. People are really becoming quite used to these interruptions. I find one practices a sort of suspension of the imagination. I do not think that the drone in the sky means death to many people at any moment. It seems so incredible as I sit here at my window [at Sissinghurst] looking out on the fuchsias and the zinnias with yellow butterflies playing round each other, that in a few seconds above the trees I may see other butterflies circling in the air intent on murdering each other. One lives in the present. The past is too sad a recollection and the future too blank a despair.

Dine at the Beefsteak. An air-raid warning sounds. I wait till 10.45 and then walk back to K.B.W. It is a strange experience. London is as dark as the stage at Vicenza after all the lights have been put out. Vague gleamings of architecture. It is warm and stars straddle the sky like grains of rice. Then there are bunches in the corners of searchlights, each terminating in a swab of cotton wool which is its own mist area. Suburban guns thump and boom. In the centre there are no guns, only the drone of aeroplanes which may be enemy or not. A few lonely footsteps hurry along the Strand. A little nervous man catches up with me and starts a conversation. I embarrass him by asking him to have a cigarette and pausing lengthily while I light it. His hand trembles. Mine does not. I walk on to the Temple and meet no one.

When I get into my rooms, I turn the lights off and sit at the window. There is still the drone of planes and from time to time a dull thump in the distance. I turn on my lights and write this, but I hear more planes coming and must darken everything and listen. I have no sense of fear whatsoever. Is this fatalism or what? It is very beautiful. I wait and listen. There are more drones and then the search lights switch out and the all-clear goes. I shut my shutters, turn on my lights and finish this. The clocks of London strike midnight. I go to bed.

Diary   *September 2, 1940*

In the evening V and I discuss the high-spots in our life. The moment when I entered a tobacconist's shop in Smyrna, the moment when we took Ebury Street, our early days at Long Barn, the night that Niggs was born so easily, the night at Kermanshah and so on. Viti says that our mistake was that we remained Edwardian for too long and that if in 1916 we had got in touch with Bloomsbury we should have profited more than we did by carrying on with Mrs George Keppel, Mrs Ronald Greville and the Edwardian Relics. We are amused to confess that we had never even heard of Bloomsbury in 1916. But we agree that in fact we have had the best of both the plutocratic and the bohemian world and that we have had a lovely life.

Diary   *September 7, 1940*

At Tonbridge, where we change trains, there are two German prisoners. Tiny little boys of sixteen they are, handcuffed together, and guarded by three soldiers with fixed bayonets. They shuffle along sadly, one being without his boots, shuffling in thick grey socks. One of them looks broken-down and saturnine; the other has a superior half-smile on his face, as if thinking, "My Führer will pay them out for this." The people on the platform are extraordinarily decent. They just glance at them and then turn their heads away, not wishing to stare.

Diary   *September 19, 1940*

I get sleepy and go back to my room. I turn out the lights and listen to the bombardment. It is continuous, and the back of the museum opposite flashes with lights the whole time. There are scudding low clouds, but above them the insistent drone of the German 'planes and the occasional crump of a bomb. Night after night, night after night, the bombardment of London continues. It is like the Conciergerie, since every morning one is pleased to see one's friends appearing again. I am nerveless, and yet I am conscious that when I hear a motor in the empty streets I tauten myself lest it be a bomb screaming towards me. Underneath, the fibres of one's nerve-resistance must be sapped. There is a lull now. The guns die down towards the horizon like a thunderstorm passing to the south. But they will come back again in fifteen minutes. We are conscious all the time that this is a moment in history. But it is very like falling down a mountain. One is aware of death and fate, but thinks mainly of catching hold of some jutting piece of rock. I have a sense of strain and unhappiness; but none of fear.

One feels so proud.

Diary   *September 24, 1940*

I detect in myself a certain area of claustrophobia. I do not mind being blown up. What I dread is being buried under huge piles of masonry and hearing the water drip slowly, smelling the gas creeping towards me and hearing the faint cries of colleagues condemned to a slow and ungainly death.

Diary   *October 8, 1940*

Go round to see Julian Huxley [then Secretary of the Zoological Society] at the Zoo. He is in an awkward position since he is responsible for the non-escape of his animals. He assures me that the carnivores are pretty safe although a zebra got out the other day when its cage had been bombed and bolted as far as Marylebone. While we were at supper a fierce raid begins and the house shakes. The raid gets very bad and at 8.30 he offers to drive me back. It is a heavenly moon-lit night and the search-lights are swaying against a soft mackerel sky and a clear calm moon. The shells lit up their match flares in the sky. A great star shell creeps slowly down over the city under a neat parachute. We hear loud explosions all round but he gets out his car and drives me back bravely to the Ministry.

Diary   *October 17, 1940*

I go to the smoking-room with Harry Crookshank [Financial Secretary to the Treasury] and Charles Waterhouse. Winston is at the next table. He sits there sipping a glass of port and welcoming anyone who comes in. "How are you?" he calls gaily to the most obscure Member. It is not a pose. It is just that for a few minutes he likes to get away from being Prime Minister and feel himself back in the smoking-room. His very presence gives us all gaiety and courage. People gather round his table completely unawed. They ask him questions. Robert Cary makes a long dissertation about how the public demand the unrestricted bombardment of Germany as reprisals for the raids on London. Winston takes a long sip at his port gazing over the glass at Cary. "My dear sir," he says, "this is a military and not a civilian war. You and others may desire to kill women and children. We desire (and have succeeded in our desire) to destroy German military objectives. I quite appreciate your point. But my motto is 'Business before Pleasure'." We all drift out of the room thinking, "That was a man!"

Diary   *October 22, 1940*

There is a Press Conference for Lord Lothian [British Ambassador in Washington]. He sits there quire placidly under the glare of arc lamps and the barrage of questions. He manages the thing with consummate ease. He says that in the early stages America had felt that this was merely a European war. They had rather despised us for our muddle in Norway. Then came the collapse of France and the sudden realisation that the British Fleet was their first line of defence. In July they were really terrified that we should go the same way as France. Then came Dunkirk, the triumph of the R.A.F., the abandonment of invasion and the [German] Pact with Japan. These four things swung American opinion over in six weeks. They were still averse to any European commitments, but they had come to understand that our interests and the strategic points of the Commonwealth were essential to themselves.

H.N. to V.S-W.   *November 6, 1940*

I was so happy this morning when I heard of the Roosevelt result [elected for his third term]. I had steeled myself to pretend not to mind either way and I think it is true that three months ago it would not have mattered so much if Wee Willy Winkie [Wendell Willkie] had got in. But in the last month Roosevelt had become identified with our cause and Willkie (unfairly perhaps) with the German cause. Although the German papers have been very cautious about it all, the French papers in occupied France have not been so cautious at all. They have openly rejoiced at the apparent decline in Roosevelt's popularity and said that it shows that America has no faith in our victory. Now they all have to swallow their words.

Diary   *November 20, 1940*

We go to the Prime Minister's Room to be told of the King's Speech. We hang about in the corridor while the Chiefs of Staff creep out after a conference. Then we all troop in and there are glasses of sherry about. The P.M. reads the speech ("It is cuthtomary to thand up when the Kingth thpeech is read") and thereafter we have a sort of party. I see out of the corner of my eye that Winston is edging in my direction and I am embarrassed. He slouches up. "I see you have been speaking in Scotland?" "Yes" "Was it a good meeting?" and so on. He seems better in health than he has ever seemed. The pale and globular look about his cheeks has gone. He is more solid about the face and thinner. But there is something odd about his eyes. The lids are not in the least weary, nor are there any pouches or black lines. But the eyes themselves are glaucous, vigilant, angry, combative, visionary and tragic. In a way they are the eyes of a man who is much preoccupied and is unable to rivet his attention on minor things (such as me). But in another sense they are the eyes of a man faced by an ordeal or tragedy, and combining vision, truculence, resolution and great unhappiness.

Diary   *November 22, 1940*

Ronnie Tree says that someone complimented Winston upon his obituary oration on Neville Chamberlain [who died November 9]. "No," said Winston, "that was not an insuperable task, since I admired many of Neville's great qualities. But I pray to God in his infinite mercy that I shall not have to deliver a similar oration on Baldwin. That indeed would be difficult to do."

Diary   *December 20, 1940*

Go down to Nether Wallop [the R.A.F. station] to lecture to the Air Force about the German character. I do not feel that the young men really like it. They are all fascists at heart and rather like the Germans. I am taken into the operations room afterwards where I watch girls moving sinister discs over a great map. It all seems very efficient. I go to bed as soon as I can and am later joined by a scientist who snores and snores.

H.N. to V.S-W.   *December 23, 1940*

*I have luck. It is not only you and the garden and the boys and the zest in life and being here at this moment, but it is also little things. For instance today people came and bothered me in Duff's absence to prevent Winston speaking tonight. What they wanted him to do was to speak on the Italian broadcast and to have the substance of his speech relayed on the Home programme. "We have," they said, "read the script and it will be an absolute flop on the Home programme and in the U.S.A. You *must* stop him."

I said that I would do nothing of the sort. That I trusted Winston not to make that sort of mistake.

Well then, in some trepidation, I listened to his message to the Italian people. And you will agree that it was superb, not merely for Italian opinion (and we are pumping the Italian version into them without stopping for 24 hours) but also in America and here.*

H.N. to V.S-W.   *December 31, 1940*
                            en train from Bristol to Cardiff

I have found a new pleasure in life – travelling with a Private Secretary. One just walks along in a fur coat and things get done. Moreover he keeps the purse and gives mean little tips such as I should never dare to give for fear of being scolded. But it is him they scowl at, not me. I just walk away and gaze at the show cases in the hall.

    During the first few months of 1941 H.N. was busy with the problems of civilian morale, now that the provincial cities were bearing the brunt of German air-attacks, and with British relations with neutral and defeated countries. In early January he toured his Ministry's centres outside London. His own rooms in the Temple were badly shaken by a bomb.

Elvira Niggeman to H.N. [in Birmingham]   *January 2, 1941*

I regret to say that they had either a land-mine or a heavy bomb in the Temple again last night and the windows and the window frames in no. 4 have gone, and some of the panelling is completely out. I will get some stuff to patch over the windows since you could not sit there at all to have breakfast as it is, and the shutters would be too grim and also do not go right to the top.

H.N. to V.S-W.   *January 7, 1941*
                                                         Leeds

I dined with Billy Harlech, the Regional Commissioner [and later, High Commissioner in South Africa]. He had been spending the day with the Queen visiting Sheffield. He says that when the car stops the Queen nips out into the snow and goes straight into the middle of the crowd and starts talking to them. For a moment or two they just gaze and gape in astonishment. But then they all start talking at once. "Hi! Your Majesty, look here!!" She has that quality of making everybody feel that they and they alone are being spoken to. It is I think because she has very large eyes which she opens very wide and turns upon one. Billy Harlech says that these visits do incalculable good.

Diary   *January 20, 1941*

I lunch with General de Gaulle at the Savoy. De Gaulle looks less unattractive with his hat off since it shows his young hair and the tired out but not wholly benevolent look in his eyes. He has the taut manner of a man who is becoming stout and is conscious that only the exercise of continuous muscle power can keep his figure in shape. I do not like him. He accuses my Ministry of being "Pétainiste". "Mais non!" I say, "Monsieur le Général." "Enfin, Pétainisant." "Nous travaillons," I said, "pour la France entière." "La France entière," he shouted, "ce'est la France Libre. C'est MOI!!!" Well,

well, I admit that he made a great Boulangist gesture. But the spectre of General Boulanger passes across my mind. He begins to abuse Pétain, saying that once again he has sold himself to Laval, saying that Weygand showed cowardice when bombed at the front. Osusky [Czech Ambassador in Paris before the fall of France] says that French opinion imagines that de Gaulle and Pétain are at heart as one. "C'est une erreur," he says sharply. I am not encouraged.

To change the subject I say that I have received telegrams from unoccupied France which I was surprised had passed the censor. He said that he had received a long letter of the most de Gaullist nature, the writer of which had written on top "I am sure the Censor will stop this." Underneath in violet ink was written "La censure approuve totalement."

I turn on Roosevelt's inaugural address from Washington. I am still young enough to be amazed at hearing a voice from Washington as if it were in my own room. It is a good speech.

We discuss the infinite complexity of arranging the reception of Halifax [new Ambassador in Washington], who should arrive tomorrow at Baltimore in the *King George V*. How I wish I were with him. Except that I simply could not bear to leave London or England these days. One's patriotism, which has been a vague family feeling, is now a flame in the night. I may have felt arrogant about the British Empire in past years: today I feel quite humbly proud of the British people.

Diary   *January 21, 1941*

I go to the House. We are meeting in our dear old building. We cannot go to the cloakroom which has been smashed by the Nazis. In the Members' Lobby there are steel girders and scaffolding keeping the thing together. But the rest is just the same. I sit on the bench for a bit. They are discussing man power. Winston comes in and has a long whispered conversation with the Speaker. His second chin has swollen as if a goitre: it is a real Chinese paunch. But he is as acute and gay as ever.

Diary   *January 22, 1941*

Winston refuses again to make a statement on war aims. The reason given in Cabinet is that precise aims would be compromising, whereas vague principles would disappoint. Thus all those days of work [H.N. and Halifax had drafted the statement] have led to nothing. Winston replies to the debate on man power. He is in terrific form. Authoritative, reasonable, conciliatory and amusing. In the course of his speech he uses the phrase "primus inter pares". The Labour people cry out, "Translate!" Winston, without a moment's hesitation, goes on, "Certainly I shall translate," then he pauses and turns to his right, "for the benefit of any old Etonians who may be present."

Diary   *February 4, 1941*

I go to the Dorchester where Rebecca West is giving a dinner party for Wendell Willkie. They have reached the coffee stage when I arrive. Rebecca, Lady Rhondda [Editor of *Time and Tide*], Sibyl, Kingsley Martin, Wilson Harris [Editor of the *Spectator*], Huxley, Namier, Lord Horder, [J. B.] Priestley and others. I sit next to Willkie. He is not tired but he is evidently bored. He turns his charm on but drums with his fingers. We go up to his room and then he settles down to be interviewed. He has had a busy day. He has flown to Dublin to see De Valera and is flying tonight to America. I am amused to notice that during the discussion Priestley is ignored and resents it. He is in a stuffy wounded mood. He is really the most prima donna man that I have ever met.

Diary   *February 6, 1941*

To the Civil Defence Sub-Committee. We begin by discussing the new invasion leaflet and Herbert Morrison says that he is so dissatisfied with the present liaison that he will ask the Cabinet today to appoint a special committee. I insist that we be represented since unless we know what to say we shall get caught short. He agrees. He says, "These points should have been settled months ago; they should have been settled before the war." For instance nobody is quite clear whether the public should be asked to store food or not to store food. I gather they do not expect invasion before February 25. The area east of Ashford will be evacuated. I tremble for my poor Viti.

Diary   *February 14, 1941*

Dear London! So vast and unexpectant, so ugly and so strong! You have been bruised and battered and all your clothes are tattered and in disarray. Yet we, who never knew that we loved you (who regarded you, in fact, like some old family servant, ministering to our comforts and amenities, and yet slightly incongruous and absurd), have suddenly felt the twinge of some fibre of identity, respect and love. We know what is coming to you. And our eyes slip along your old untidy limbs, knowing that the leg may be gone tomorrow, and that tomorrow the arm may be severed. Yet through all this regret and dread pierces a slim clean note of pride. "London can take it." I believe that what will win us this war is the immense central-dynamo of British pride. The Germans have only assertiveness to put against it. That is transitory. Our pride is permanent, obscure and dark. It has the nature of infinity.

H.N. to V.S-W.   *February 18, 1941*

I had the dreaded meeting of the National Labour Party. Malcolm [MacDonald] was in the chair. He told us exactly what had happened about his being bumped off to Canada [as High Commissioner]. He had said to Winston, "But you are condemning me to exile. All the lights will be on in Ottawa and I shall yearn for the dark of London." He refused to go. He said that he would much rather join up. Winston was evidently touched by his attitude and asked him not to decide till next day. And after sleeping over it "I saw," Malcom said, "that if Winston asked me to go to Timbuctoo I should have to accept."

All this sounds awful bunk when one writes it down afterwards, but if you had been there and heard Malcolm speak so simply and frankly you would have know that the whole thing was true, and that it reflects great credit on both the P.M. and Malcolm.

Then the leadership question came up. They wanted me to be leader [in place of MacDonald]. But I knew that they did not want it very much. So I said, "But it is absurd that a Party which began under the leadership of Ramsay MacDonald should end under the leadership of the Parliamentary Secretary to the Minister of Information. I have neither false pride nor false modesty. But you, as sensible people will agree that such a solution would make both the

Party and myself seem ridiculous." They agreed with that and thus we have left the leadership in suspense and only pray that there will be no Press publicity.

How silly and out of proportion it all is!

Diary February 26, 1941

I am rather fussed about this diary. It is not intimate enough to give a personal picture. The really important things that I know I cannot record. And thus it gives a picture of someone on the edge of things who is so certain that he knows what is really happening that he does not dare to say so. The day to day impressions of a greengrocer in Streatham would really be more interesting. I must try henceforward to be more intimate and more illuminating. It is half that I feel that if I survive this diary will be more a record from which I can fill in remembered details. And half that I find some relief before I go to bed in putting down on paper the momentary spurts and gushes of this cataract of history.

Diary February 27, 1941

I attend the Anglo-French Parliamentary Association's lunch to de Gaulle and [Admiral] Muselier. I sit bang opposite to de Gaulle and have much talk with him. I dislike him less than I did at first. He has tired, ruminating but not unkindly eyes. He has curiously effeminate hands (not feminine hands but effeminated hands without arteries or muscles). He abuses the paper "France" [published by the Ministry of Information] which he says is not "avec moi". Otherwise he says nothing at all interesting. He is off to Africa soon.

Diary March 1, 1941

The Bulgarian Ministers went to Vienna yesterday and signed a pact adhering to the Axis. At the same time German mechanized forces thundered into Sofia. This is bad for Yugoslavia and Greece and will have a depressing effect here. People do not care so much how many square miles we occupy in Eritrea so long as Germany is creeping ever closer to our jugular arteries. We know that in a few weeks we shall be exposed to a terrific ordeal.

Diary   March 2, 1941

Viti asks me how we are going to win this war. Hitler will shortly
have the whole of Europe under his control and how are we to turn
him out? It will require all our strength to resist the appalling
attacks by air and submarine which are shortly coming to us. We
shall be shattered and starved. Yet how are we to tell our people
how they can win? The only hope is that America and Russia will
come in on our side. I think we can resist the worst.

Diary   March 3, 1941

*[John Gilbert] Winant the new American Ambassador arrived
yesterday and was met by the King. At the Press Conference afterwards he was much embarrassed and fiddled with his glasses, as
Fred Kuh told me, "like a school-girl at commencement exercises".
Somebody asked what he thought of Jo Kennedy. He writhed in
agony. Finally he said "You better ask someone else that."*

Diary   March 4, 1941

I dine with Louis Spears in his upstairs room at the Ritz. Mary Spears
is there, also Ned Grigg and Monsieur and Madame Jean. The latter
was diplomatic Chef de Cabinet to Reynaud with Roland de
Margerie. Since then he has been in Morocco and brings back disturbing news. The Germans are gradually infiltrating into Morocco
and unless we do something within the next few months he fears
they will have it in their power as they have Rumania and Bulgaria.
    He tells us the full story of Hélène de Portes [Reynaud's mistress].
He admits that it is "inénarrable et inavouable". But after all he was
there and he knew. He said that she really believed that Reynaud
would become the dictator of France and she the power behind the
throne. She was passionately anti-British since she felt that our
democratic ideas would prevent this strange pattern of state govern-
ance. The extent of her influence and interference cannot be
exaggerated. It was not so much that she dictated policy but that she
surrounded Reynaud with fifth columnists and spies. For instance
he and Roland de Margerie had managed at a crucial moment to
convince Reynaud that he should send the fleet and what remained
of the army and material to North Africa. All the plans were made.

But it was Madame de Portes who made him change his mind and accept Baudouin as Foreign Minister.

We discuss how it came that this frowsty soiled woman with the dirty fur tippet managed to sway the destiny of a great nation. He said it was because Reynaud had an inferiority complex about his small stature and that she made him feel tall and grand and powerful. "Had Reynaud been three inches taller the history of the world might have been changed." He and Spears talk together about the final *débandade*. Those hurried rushes through the night from château to château only to find that there was only one telephone in the butler's pantry and that France could not communicate with its Prime Minister. Madame de Portes was always there and keeping away from Reynaud anybody whom she felt might spur him to resistance. "C'est moi," she used to scream, "qui suis la maîtresse ici." And my God she was right.

Then the final scene in the two-seater car. Reynaud was driving. The luggage was piled behind. He was always a bad driver and he crashed into a tree. A suitcase hit Madame de Portes on the back of the head and killed her instantly. Reynaud was hit by the steering-wheel and rendered unconscious. When he recovered in hospital they broke the news to him that Madame de Portes was dead. "Elle était la France," he said. Dejean thought he really felt it. *La fausse Marianne.*

H.N. to V.S-W.   *March 5, 1941*

*I hope you got my ration card. That ought to enable you to get a little more meat. But the meat ration is going to be further reduced. It seems we have got heaps of tea, sugar and oil but that meat is very short as also food stuff for cattle. It is a serious position.

The news from the Balkans is very bad and we are telling the Press not to expect anything dramatic from Eden's visit. In fact things are looking rather murky today.*

H.N. to V.S-W.   *March 17, 1941*

I lunched with James [Pope-Hennessy] and he took me to see the devastation round St Paul's. It is unbelievable. A great space as wide as Trafalgar Square laid low. I feel that at any cost we should retain it as a memorial to London's civilians. They deserve it, and it gives a magnificent vista of St Paul's such as Wren would have given his soul to achieve. It is as if St Paul's stood where the National Gallery now stands. To get that permanently cleared is worth £40 million in site-value and should be done.

Diary   *March 31, 1941*

Go to see Maisky. He sits there in his ugly Victorian study like a little gnome in an arm-chair, twiddling his thumbs, twinkling his eyes and giving the impression that his feet do not reach the floor. He says that he takes an objective view of all this. We shall not be beaten. Our Navy is the finest in the world and perhaps our Air Force also. But what about our Army? Is it good for anything but a colonial war? Shall we be able to resist the Germans in Greece or even in Cyrenaica? We cannot afford another Norway. And how on earth do we imagine that we shall ever defeat the Germans? Italy we may knock out. But Germany never. I reply that I rely on my instinct and my knowledge of the German character. They will assuredly crash before we do. He says that this may be so: "Time will show," he says, grinning mischievously. He thinks that the Labour people here are not strong enough. They do not force the Government to come to terms with Russia. "The Labour people are as bad as Chamberlain." I ask him whether he sees any prospect of a Yugo-slav–Greek–Turkish alliance. He says that Turkey is too cautious. I ask him whether he has any fear that Russia will be attacked. He says, "Germany is too cautious."

H.N. to V.S-W.   *March 31, 1941*
                                                     Ministry of Information

It is always a gloomy moment for me when I unpack the *panier* which we packed together. I take out the flowers sadly and think of you picking them and putting the paper round them. But today it was worse, as I feel such a failure as a help to you. I do not know what it is, but I never seem to be able to help you when you are in trouble. I loathe your being unhappy more than I loathe anything. But I just moon about feeling wretched myself, and when I look back on my life, I see that the only times I have been really unhappy are when you have been unhappy too.

I wonder whether you would have been happier if married to a more determined and less sensitive man. On the one hand you would have hated any sense of control or management, and other men might not have understood your desire for independence. I have always respected that, and you have often mistaken it for aloofness on my part. What bothers me is whether I have given way too much to your eccentricities. Some outside person might imagine that I should have made more of my life if I had had someone like Diana De La Warr to share my career. There are moments when I think you reproach yourself for not having been more interested in my pursuits and for not having pushed against my diffidence. I never feel that myself. I have always felt that the struggle in the market-place was for me to fight alone, and that you were there as something wholly different.

But what has always worried me is your dual personality. The one tender, wise and with such a sense of responsibility. And the other rather cruel and extravagant. The former has been what I have always clung to as the essential you, but the latter has always alarmed me and I have tried to dismiss it from my mind – or, rather, I have always accepted it as the inevitable counterpart of your remarkable personality. I have felt that this side of you was beyond my understanding, and when you have got into a real mess because of it, you have been angry with me for not coping with the more violent side in yourself.

I do not think that you have ever quite realised how deeply unhappy your eccentric side has often rendered me. When I am unhappy I shut up like an oyster. I love you so much, darling. I hold my head in my hands worrying about you. I was nearly killed by a taxi today. I only missed an accident by a hair's breadth. And my first thought was, "If I had really been taken to hospital in a mess, then Viti would have been shaken out of her muzzy moods." I love you so much.

V.S-W. to H.N.   *March 31, 1941*
                                                            Sissinghurst

I have just had the most awful shock: Virginia has killed herself. It is not in the papers, but I got letters from Leonard [Woolf] and also from Vanessa [Bell] telling me. It was last Friday. Leonard came home to find a note saying that she was going to commit suicide, and they think she has drowned herself, as he found her stick floating on the river. He says she had not been well for the last few weeks and was terrified of going mad again. He says, "It was, I suppose, the strain of the war and finishing her book, and she could not rest or eat."

I simply can't take it in. That lovely mind, that lovely spirit.

Diary April 9, 1941

I go down to the House to hear Winston make his statement [on the invasion of Greece]. It had been devised as a motion congratulating the fighting services on their victories [in Africa] and I remember a few days ago how Winston promised that he would say "Fly the flags in celebration." These victories are now dust and ashes.

The P.M. comes in at 11.56 and is greeted with cheers. He sits between Greenwood and Attlee, scowls at the notes in his hand, pulls out a gold pencil and scribbles an addition to the last sheet. He then gets up to speak in a grim and obstinate voice. He throws out news incidentally. We have taken Massawa [chief port in Eritrea]. The Germans entered Salonika at 4 a.m. this morning. At this news there is a silent wince of pain throughout the House. He discloses that the U.S. Government have given us their revenue cutters. His peroration implies that we are done without American help. He indulges in a few flights of oratory. He evidently feels that even graver news is ahead of us. The House is glum and sad.

Diary April 13, 1941

From the propaganda point of view, all that the country really wants is some assurance of how victory is to be achieved. They are bored by talks about the righteousness of our cause and our eventual triumph. What they want are facts indicating how we are to beat the Germans. I have no idea at all how we are to give them those facts. Fundamentally (although they are unaware of the fact) the British public have lost confidence in the power of the sea. Norway was a nasty knock. "How," they ask, "was Germany able to land four divisions in Libya?" There are many explanations of this feat but none of them really disposes of the question, "But if they can land four divisions in Libya, what prevents them obtaining mastery of Africa and Asia?" I see no ostensible answer to that terrible question. I have no doubt that we shall win in the end. But we shall have to learn a new technique, the secret of mobile warfare, and only when we have learnt it will the efficacy of our sea-power be brought to bear.

H.N. to V.S-W.   *April 16, 1941*

*I dined tonight with Sibyl at the Dorchester. Dinner was all right although I question the propriety of such meals in war time. I sat between Irene Ravensdale and Mary [Mrs St John] Hutchinson. Irene is worried about Tom [Mosley] and his wife. They are treated as common prisoners and not allowed to wash much or have a change of clothes. They are thus actually dirty and that shocked me. I must see what can be done about it.

I left my dinner early and stepped out into a first class blitz. There was a glow over Westminster as red as an Egyptian dawn. Of course I could get no taxi and had to walk the whole way here [Ministry of Information, Malet St.]. It is really no fun. I could not put on my torch and the Messerschmitts droned overhead and the guns crashed. I did not mind over much until I fell over a brick and rolled about like a huge rabbit, breaking my glasses.*

Diary   *April 21, 1941*

We are evacuating from Greece. The Americans will take this badly and there is a wave of defeatism sweeping that continent. Lindbergh has been proclaiming that we are in a desperate position. I confess that my mind goes back to my last talk with Maisky when he said, "You cannot stand another Norway." Another Norway is now upon us, and the news from Spain is equally bad [Hitler planned to capture Gibraltar with Spain's help]. Hitler is evidently determined to turn us out of the Mediterranean.

Diary   *April 28, 1941*

*The swastika flies over the Acropolis. Not a pleasant thought. I gather that we have lost at least ¾ of our B.E.F. from Greece but the bombing is bad and the Germans are on the Gulf of Corinth. I fear I have a cold coming on and feel pretty glum all around.

I go back to K.B.W. but it is too gloomy. I then go to the Garrick which is gloomier still. I then go to the Etoile where I meet Sibyl dining with Roger Senhouse [publisher and translator]. The latter makes little Bloomsbury hints about "What I should like to know is from where is this war being directed?" All this is subtle underground anti-Winston propaganda.*

Diary May 7, 1941

To the House. Lloyd George makes a speech. Very gloomy and realistic he is – pointing his forefinger constantly and speaking about "dark chasms". His main theme is that the public must be told the truth. About Turkey for instance. Why were we not told that Turkey has let German ships through the Dardanelles? Of course from one point of view it was a damaging speech, since he made it abundantly clear that we are in danger of being starved and defeated. But from another point of view my pride swelled to think that nowhere except in our own beloved House of Commons could such a speech have been made and received with calm and even with welcome. When he criticised the Prime Minister he gazed across at him with a firm aggressive chin of combat and opposition, but his little eyes twinkled with admiration and (I am not in the least exaggerating) with love. It was a good day for Parliament.

Diary May 8, 1941

This is the eighth day of my renunciation of smoking. It gets more difficult rather than less difficult. But I do observe that it is a thought which suggests a pang rather than a pang which suggests a thought. Thus an aching tooth twitches into consciousness and says "I have a toothache". But this nicotine hunger is only stimulated by some outside occurrence such as the sight of someone else smoking or an advertisement of Craven A. Then the pang lights up. Apart from that it is a vague feeling of something missing as if one had had no breakfast.

H.N. to V.S-W. May 13, 1941

*You will be puzzled by the Hess thing [Rudolf Hess's solo flight to Scotland two days earlier]. My own impression is that he was rather mad in any case but a fine fellow. He really believed in Hitler and was disgusted by the people whom Hitler had around him.

Years ago he had made friends with [Lord] Clydesdale and

Nigel Douglas Hamilton. They had discussed the possibility of an alliance between Germany and Britain. The memories of these conversations came back to him. He took his aeroplane, looked out the Hamilton place on the map, and headed straight for it. His machine caught fire in the neighbourhood and he baled out. The first thing he did when the military came was to ask to see the Duke of Hamilton. The latter was much embarrassed. You can imagine what a difficult publicity problem that entails.*

Diary   *May 14, 1941*

Defence Committee. There is the usual complaint that the newspapers will insist upon publishing defence details. The present grumble is that they say half the House of Commons remains intact [it was bombed on May 10]. Walter Elliot is very keen that the House should now sit in St Stephen's Chapel. That after all is the historic place [where the Commons sat from 1547 to 1834]. But the Prime Minister, when I suggest it to him, says "Too narrow – that would not do at all. We must have the Royal Gallery."

I lunch with the Prime Minister and Mrs Churchill in the flat which has been constructed for them in the Office of Works. It is not very large, but it is well done and comfortable. Winston has brought some of his pictures in and the general effect is very gay. Winston beams there with his ugly watch-chain and his ugly ring. I try to get directives out of him about Hess, but he will go no further than to say we must not make a hero out of him. We have white wine and port and brandy and hors d'oeuvres and mutton. All rather sparse. Winston had been seeing the film *Comrade X* [about a fictional Russian spy] and simply loved it. I told him that Maisky had tried to get it suppressed. He was overjoyed that it had not been. He is in a good purring mood.

Diary   *May 17, 1941*

There are two Hess jokes about. The first says that Salisbury Plain is being cleared of troops in case Göring also wishes to land. The second is that Hess was ill and came here to consult a really good German doctor.

Diary   *May 22, 1941*

Before midnight I am picked up by Kenneth Clark and we go on to the B.B.C. where we are met by Ed Murrow [European Director of the C.B.S.]. It is rather a curious experience. K. and I sit opposite each other and have earphones. Then we hear that we are linked up to New York and Kenneth starts doing his piece. He is opening the exhibition of British War Artists at the Museum of Modern Art in New York. While he talks I listen in with my earphones and can hear Kenneth talking opposite to me and a fraction of a second later Kenneth saying the same thing from New York. The distance of 6,000 miles does not exactly give a time pause but merely a faint duplication of what I hear him say in London and what I rehear him say from New York. I then do the same and then we both listen to Halifax [from New York].

Diary   *May 27, 1941*

Winston comes in and rises to give the latest news. He passes on to the battle of the Denmark Straits. He does it beautifully. He builds up the whole picture from the moment we heard that the *Bismarck* and the *Prinz Eugen* were driving westwards against our convoys to the moment when we came into contact with them and the *Hood* was sunk. After paying tribute to the loss of these men, he passed on to the further pursuit. The *Prinz Eugen* had disappeared, but the *Bismarck* was followed closely and bombed. This bombing slowed down her escape. Further arrangements were made to intercept, but then the weather changed and the visibility diminished, and by a sudden change of course the *Bismarck* managed to elude our vigilance. The whole House felt at that moment that Winston was about to break it to us that the ship had escaped. There was a hush of despair. At dawn next morning (Winston continued) we again resumed contact. He told us how the Fleet Air Arm then fired torpedoes at the ship, destroying her steering gear and forcing her to go round and round in immense circles in the ocean. From all sides our fleet approached to destroy her. Such is the innate sporting feeling of the House that we all began to feel sorry for the *Bismarck*. The P.M. went on to say that our ships had established contact; that they had begun to fire; that their shells had not made any effect; and that the only hope was to fire torpedoes. "That process," he said, "is in action as I speak." He then went on to speak about conscription in Northern Ireland and left the House with a sense of *coitus interruptus*. I saw one of the secretaries in the official gallery

make a violent sign with a small folded sheet to Brendan Bracken.
He took the missive and passed it up to Winston. The latter rose at
once and interrupted Griffiths. "I crave your indulgence, Mr
Speaker," he said, "I have just received news that the *Bismarck* has
been sunk." Wild cheers, in which I do not join.

Diary   *June 10, 1941*

Duff tells us that the P.M. is under the impression that the anxiety
which exists is purely a House of Commons anxiety and is not
shared by the country as a whole. We all say that this is not true, and
that the country is deeply anxious and shocked.

The Middle East have no sense of publicity. The Admiralty is
even worse. We complain that there are no photographs of the
sinking of the *Bismarck*. Tripp [Navy spokesman] says that the
official photographer was in the *Suffolk* and that the *Suffolk* was
too far away. We say, "But why didn't one of our reconnaissance
machines fly over the ship and take photographs?" He replies:
"Well you see, you *must* see, well upon my word, well after all, an
Englishman would not like to take snapshots of a fine vessel sinking." Is he right? I felt abashed when he said it. I think he is right. It
reminds me of Arthur Balfour when Brockdorff-Rantzau refused to
stand when he was handed the Treaty [at Versailles]. "Did he remain seated?" said someone to Balfour afterwards. "I did not notice.
I do not stare at a gentleman in distress."

> *The German Army, having cleaned up the Balkans, now*
> *launched its massive campaign against Russia, and*
> *within three weeks had advanced 450 miles and captured*
> *Smolensk. Few considered that the total defeat of*
> *Russia could be avoided. It was at this moment that*
> *H.N. lost his ministerial job. Churchill asked for his*
> *resignation so that the office could be given to another*
> *Member. He was deeply shocked and saddened. In partial*
> *compensation, Churchill made him a Governor of the*
> *B.B.C.*

Diary   *June 22, 1941*

We have breakfast outside. Vita arrives to say that the 7 o'clock news announced that Germany has invaded Russia. Goebbels has declared that Hitler's patience was exhausted and that the frontier has been crossed in Poland and Rumania.

Most people in England will be delighted. I am not so optimistic. It will have a bad effect on America, where many influential people do not like to see themselves as the allies of Bolshevism. It will have a bad effect on Conservative and Catholic opinion here. And if, as is likely, Hitler defeats Russia in three weeks, then the road to the oil is open, as also the road to Persia and India.

At 9 Winston broadcasts. He says that he is on the side of the Russians who defend their homes. He does not conceal that Russia may be beaten quickly, but having indicated to us the approaching collapse of India and China, and, in fact, of Europe, Asia and Africa, he somehow leaves us with the impression that we are quite certain to win this war. A masterpiece.

Diary *June 24, 1941*

Walk to the Beefsteak with Ned Grigg [Parliamentary Under-Secretary of State for War]. He says that 80% of the War Office experts think that Russia will be knocked out in ten days. They are not at all pleased by this new war, which will give great triumphs to Hitler and leave him free to fling his whole force against us.

H.N. to V.S-W. *July 1, 1941*

The battle of Bloomsbury has been fought and lost. We [the Ministry of Information] have not been given control of the news and I fear that most of our best men will resign. The P.M. asked Duff not to resign on "a mere matter of administration" and I have a feeling that he knows very well that nobody else would accept the job. I fear lest the attack will now develop against Duff for not resigning and it is all going to be most unpleasant. My own task is primarily to be loyal to Duff and to stay put till I am turned out. What will infuriate me is if all the others go off in a blaze of virtue and glory and I stick by Duff's side feeling at the bottom of my heart that he should go also – and then I am sacked to give room for someone else. But even if that happens I am sure I must stick by Duff.

Diary   *July 8, 1941*

I drive down to White's Club with Duff and beg him to treat the P.R.O.s this afternoon with all gentleness. They are a touchy lot. There are 21 of them, and we meet after luncheon in the Chancellor's Hall. Duff glowers at them as if they were coolies in some Cingalese copper-mine. He then tells them an angry story about how he had been brought up from Bognor on false pretences. He then scowls at them and says that this is all he has to say. He then stalks out of the room. We are left ashamed and wretched and do not know which way to look. I cannot make out what happens to Duff on such occasions. He seems to lose all power over himself. I think it is a sort of shyness.

Diary   *July 18, 1941*

When I get back to the Ministry after lunch, I get a message from the Prime Minister's Private Secretary to say that he wants to see me at No. 10 at 5.30. I discuss this with Duff. He says that he is to be made Chancellor of the Duchy of Lancaster and to go to Singapore to coordinate. The P.M. had just mentioned me, and said that the Labour Party wanted a Labour man in my job. Duff thinks that if I am offered something as good, I should accept it, but if something worse, I should refuse and go back to my writing. A later message comes that the interview is cancelled and that I shall receive a communication "in another form".

At 5.55 it arrives in the shape of a black box from Downing Street. I get Sammy Hood to open it for me, and I find a letter inside. I think it might have been more politely worded. Could I afford it I should not accept a Governorship of the B.B.C. But both Duff and Walter [Monckton] urge me to accept. I realise that this means the end of any political ambitions which I may ever have cherished. I am hurt and sad and sorry. The P.M.'s Secretary telephones to say that he wants a reply at once, and could I send it by taxi. Well, I send it.

Diary   *July 19, 1941*

I wake up feeling that something horrible has happened, and re-member that I have been sacked from the Government. Go to the Ministry and start clearing out some of my private possessions. Then attend the Duty Room, probably for the last time.

I come back to the bench below the gangway having had my chance and failed to profit by it. Ever since I have been in the House I have been looked on as a might-be. Now I shall be a might-have-been. Always up till now I have been buoyed up by the hope of writing some good book or achieving a position of influence in politics. I now know that I shall never write a book better than I have written already, and that my political career is at an end. I shall merely get balder and fatter and more deaf as the years go by. This is an irritating thing. Success should come late in life in order to compensate for the loss of youth; I had youth and success together, and now I have old age and failure. Apart from all this, I mind leaving the Ministry where I did good work and had friends.

Diary   *July 28, 1941*

There is a rude article about me in *Truth* saying that I have "the mincing manner of a French *salon*", that I lack virility and should retire from public life and bury myself in my books. All rather true, I suppose. But I happen to enjoy public life. I could never be merely an observer.

Diary   *August 13, 1941*

Dine with Camrose at the Dorchester. The guest of honour is Dorothy Thompson [the American journalist].

She talks a great deal about the difficulty of welding American opinion together up to the point where they will be prepared to enter the war on our side. She says that we must always remember that America is composed of many millions of people who left Europe because they hated it, and that there are many millions of Italian and Germans whose hearts go out to their mother countries. Although these emotions pull America apart, they feel at the same time a strong longing to remain together. What we don't fully understand in this country is the actual dread of the American soul at being split. There is always the fear that they will cease to be a nation, and this is the fear which Roosevelt understands so perfectly and which he guides with such genius.

Diary   *September 9, 1941*

The House meets. The Prime Minister makes a long and optimistic review. He stands there very stout and black, smoothing his palms down across his frame – beginning by patting his chest, then smoothing his stomach and ending down at the groin. He does not attempt any flight of oratory but he quotes Kipling's lines about the minesweepers, and is so moved by them that he chokes and cannot continue. His speech has a good effect, and the slight anti-Churchill tide which had begun to be noticeable was checked.

Diary   *September 12, 1941*

Dylan Thomas comes to see me. He wants a job on the B.B.C. He is a fat little man, puffy and pinkish, dressed in very dirty trousers and a loud checked coat. I tell him that if he is to be employed by the B.B.C., he must promise not to get drunk. I give him £1, as he is clearly at his wits' end for money. He does not look as if he had been cradled into poetry by wrong [Shelley]. He looks as if he will be washed out of poetry by whisky.

Diary   *September 23, 1941*

I go to see my doctor, Sir Kenneth Goadby. He has had the results of my x-ray and other analyses. It seems that my skull is thicker than that of most people and that this has inhibited the full expansion of the pituitary gland. It may be owing to this excess of calcium in babyhood that I became homosexual. He takes my blood pressure again and it is excellent. He tests my urine again and there are faint traces of albumen but not pathological. He measures and weighs me. The former discloses that my upper part is out of proportion to my lower part and that my legs ought to be 1½ inches longer. My weight is just below fourteen stone. That is bad. He prescribes thyroid capsules and sends me off to Bell and Croydon [chemists] to present the prescription.

Diary   *October 6, 1941*

Dine with Sibyl [Colefax] in Lord North Street. The American Ambassador, R. A. Butler, the Master of the Rolls, and the Kenneth Clarks. Winant is one of the most charming men that I have ever met. He has emphatic eyes and an unemphatic voice. Rab says that he was dining the other night with Winston, Eden and Beaverbrook, and that Winston spoke with deep sympathy of Baldwin. Winston has no capacity of meanness, and that is why we love him so. A great soul in a great crisis.

They bother me to write a book about the British Empire. I am tempted. Winant adds his persuasion. It was a lovely dinner, and we walked away in the mist with the moon, and felt so pleased to be in London in October 1941.

Diary   *October 9, 1941*

There is deep gloom about the Russian news. It looks as if Moscow might be taken and the Russian armies divided. Hitler will then declare that the Russian war is over and turn to the south-east. There will be great resentment in this country that we did not strike while the iron was hot, and Winston will be blamed. I have complete confidence, however, that everything strategic will be done: it is in administration and tactics that we are so weak.

Diary   *October 10, 1941*

Vita comes up in the morning, the first time she has been in London for two years. I have always tried to explain to her that the destruction of London is very bad in the places where it is bad, but not very bad in the places where it is not very bad. That sounds a dull way of putting it. She now agrees that it is absolutely right. She cannot conceive why St Paul's is still standing, or why our dear Temple should have been banged so badly about the head.

H.N. to V.S-W.   *October 21, 1941*

My luncheon at the Prunier's was divine. Madame Prunier is not in the very least what one expects a restaurateur to be. She is slim and fair and very neatly dressed. She has lovely hands. She speaks a very Duc d'Aumale French. We had oysters, and coquille St Jacques, and pheasant all done up funny, and fruits refraichis and good wine. I rather enjoyed it. We agreed to form a club. This will enable me to invite my friends to an excellent French luncheon at Madame Prunier's expense.

Diary   *October 28, 1941*

Roosevelt last night made an address in which he pledged the U.S.A.
to bring supplies to British ports in their own bottoms and escorted
by their own Navy. This is a tremendous advance. He said, "We
know who fired the first shot!" A great date. A very great date.
Probably the turning point of the war. I walk the streets in silent
elation. What a master he has been! I am cheered when I think of
the aged and bewildered Mussolini (for whom I have a growing
sympathy) and the neurotic genius of Berchtesgaden – and then of
dear Winston and that consummate politician of Hyde Park.

Diary   *November 17, 1941*

I go to Pratts and find Harold Macmillan there. He talks about
Beaverbrook. He thinks him half mad and half genius. He says that
he thinks only of his present work [Ministry of Supply], and that
all his old fortune, newspapers and women are completely forgotten. But he also says that Beaverbrook gives no man his complete
confidence. Thus, although there is great enthusiasm among the
staff, and a feeling that they are important and useful, there is also
a sort of uneasiness at not knowing what is really happening.

Diary   *November 20, 1941*

The papers and even the B.B.C. take a very optimistic view of our
Libyan offensive. This distresses me, since if things go wrong (as
they well may) public opinion will have a bad shock. Winston in
the House today, while warning us against premature exultation
and making it clear that the real fighting has not yet begun, makes
the error of proclaiming that this is the first time that we have met
the Germans on equal terms. I dread these forecasts. Moreover, in
his Order of the Day to the troops, he said that the battle might prove
the equal of Blenheim or Waterloo. The 1 o'clock news announces
progress in almost hysterical terms. At the B.B.C. Board I bring up
the question of the Libyan bulletins, and we damp them down.

Diary   *December 4, 1941*

Aneurin Bevan says an interesting thing. He says that we intellectuals are in a difficult position. Our tastes attract us to the past, our

reason to the future. Hitherto we have been able to appease this conflict since our tastes were still able to find their outlets, whereas our reason could indulge in the picture of the shape of things to come. Now, however, the future is becoming very imminent and we are faced with the fact that our tastes can no longer be indulged. Gone are ease and income and travel and elegance. There is a tendency therefore for the weaker souls to escape to mysticism. Their reason tells them that the future is right, but it is agony for them to lose the past. This is what has happened to Aldous Huxley and Joad. I pray to God it will not happen to me. "I don't think it will, Harold," says Aneurin, "your intellectual courage is great."

> On December 7 the Japanese attacked the American fleet in Pearl Harbor, and sank four of their finest battle-ships. "A mad decision", Churchill later called it. But he also reflected, "So we had won the war after all." He crossed the Atlantic to confer with his ally. But the new war began badly for Britain with the loss of their battle-ships Prince of Wales and Repulse, and Hong Kong was captured on Christmas Day.

Diary   *December 7, 1941*

After dinner we listen to the 9 o'clock news. The Japanese have bombed Pearl Harbour. I do not believe it. We then turn on the German and French news and get a little more information. Roosevelt has ordered the mobilisation of the American Forces and instructed the Navy to carry out their sealed orders.

I am dumbfounded by the news. After all, Roosevelt was still in negotiation with Kurusu [the Japanese envoy], and had dispatched a personal letter to the Mikado. While these negotiations were still in progress, the Japanese deliver a terrific air-attack 7,000 miles away from Japan. The whole action seems as insane as Hitler's attack on Russia. I remain amazed.

The effect in Germany will be bad. They will not say, "We have a new ally." They will say (or rather they will think in the recesses of their anxious souls), "We have outraged the most formidable enemy in the world." Their sense of destiny will begin to hover again as a sense of doom.

Diary   *December 8, 1941*

The House has been specially summoned. Winston enters the Chamber with bowed shoulders and an expression of grim determination on his face. The House had expected jubilation at the entry of America into the war and are a trifle disconcerted. He makes a dull matter-of-fact speech. He has a great sense of occasion. The mistake he makes is to read out his message to the Siamese Prime Minister. The Siamese are bound to capitulate, and it was a mistake to expect them to do anything else.

Diary   *December 9, 1941*

Lunch with de Gaulle at the Connaught Hotel. I cannot make out whether I really like him. His arrogance and fascism annoy me. But there is something like a fine retriever dog about his eyes. He challenges me on my defence of Weygand. He says that he was a bad strategic ally. He asks what I meant by saying the French in England should "compose their differences". What he wanted me to say was that I had meant that they should all join de Gaulle. I am not prepared to say that as yet. I say that I was cross at having one Frenchman telling me that de Gaulle was surrounded by Jews and Freemasons, and another that he was surrounded by Jesuits and *cagoulards*. He does not like this at all, and his A.D.C. blushes. But it was not a bad thing to say.

Diary   *December 11, 1941*

The House is depressed. I have a feeling that our nerves are not as good as they were in July 1940, and that we are tired of defeat. We still face the central issue with courage and faith, but in minor matters we are getting touchy and irritable.

Germany and Italy have declared war on the United States. The B.B.C. gives us extracts from Hitler's and Mussolini's speeches in the Reichstag and the Palazzo Venezia respectively. An admirable performance. But the main factor of this declaration (which should have filled us with the springing hope and aroused tumults of exultation) is ignored. We take it flatly. The loss of the *Prince of Wales* [the day before] has numbed our nerves.

H.N. to V.S-W. *December 11, 1941*

Winston this morning was very grim and said we must expect
"heavy punishment". I like him best when he makes that sort of
speech. I am full of faith. We simply can't be beaten with America in.
But how strange it is that this great event should be recorded and
welcomed here without any jubilation. We should have gone mad
with joy if it happened a year ago.

I bet de Gaulle that Germany would declare war on the United
States. He said, *"Jamais de la vie."* I said, "But will you take my
bet?" He said, "No, since you may be right."

Not an American flag flying in the whole of London. How odd
we are!

Diary *December 19, 1941*

Go up to Leicester. I find them all rather depressed. The sinking of
the *Prince of Wales* has made an impression out of all proportion.
They ignore the Russian victories, the Libyan advance and the
entry of America. They are faced with the fact that two of our greatest battleships have been sunk within a few minutes by the monkey
men, and that we and the Americans have between us lost command
of the Pacific. I try to cheer them up.

Diary *December 28, 1941*

Feeling much better. I do a *Spectator* article on keeping diaries, in
which I lay down the rule that one should write one's diary for one's
great-grandson. I think that is a correct rule. The purely private
diary becomes too self-centred and morbid. One should have a
remote, but not too remote, audience.

*The new year began disastrously. Japan gained almost
all her objectives in the Far East. Singapore was lost,
with the surrender of 60,000 British troops; the sinkings
in the Atlantic neared their climax; Rommel threw the
British out of Cyrenaica; and Churchill's leadership was
challenged at home.*

Diary   *January 1, 1942*

Mr Auren of a Stockholm newspaper comes to see me. He asks
how I explain the British love of self-criticism. I say it is partly pride
and partly our love of fresh air. He says it does our propaganda
harm abroad. I say that it is worth it from our point of view since it
keeps our public opinion healthy. We should die if we were not able
to abuse our institutions and public men. Moreover in the end it is
good long-term policy even from the propaganda point of view.
He says that all Swedes know that they will come in in the end. I
do not suggest that "the end" means the moment when it is quite
clear which side is going to win.

  *I then go round the House to fire-watch. I have my bread and
butter and sausages and then read Rebecca West's Yugoslav book
[*Black Lamb and Grey Falcon*] in the library. I am not sure it is not
a masterpiece.*

Diary   *January 2, 1942*

Dine at Brooks' with Jim Lees-Milne, James Pope-Hennessy and
Guy Burgess. We discuss everything and mainly the question of
success. James says, "It is ridiculous of you, Harold, not to realize
that it does not matter your having been a failure at the M. of I.,
since you have written such good books." This annoys me, since I
was not a failure at the M. of I. but merely politically inconvenient.
I say that I would rather be able to send 100 tons of grain to Greece
than write an immortal work. That impresses them since they
agree. What does even the *Symposium* matter compared to the
death by hunger of 200 Greeks a day?

Diary   *January 20, 1942*

Bitterly cold. Go down to the House. I arrive a bit late and do not
hear the reception given to Winston at his entry [he had just returned
from America]. Some say it was most enthusiastic; others say it had
about it a note of reserve. I ask Randolph Churchill how it struck
him. He said, "Nothing like the reception which Chamberlain got
when he returned from Munich."

  *When I get there Winston is being heckled regarding the
debate on the Far East. He had promised the House three days

debate next week culminating in a vote of confidence. He had indicated that the House would be asked whether his speech might be recorded for broadcasting. The House did not like the postponement; they did not like that bit about the vote of confidence; they hated the idea of the speech being broadcast. The newspapers will hate it even more.

Winston has a bad cold and is pink about the gills. I go off, after Winston has sent condolences on the death of the "Duke of Coddaught", with Randolph to the smoking room. The latter is on leave from Egypt.* He says that Rommel is getting reinforcements, but only half of what is sent ever reach him. He thinks Germany may well attack Turkey. Oil is now essential to them; they cannot run their mechanized transport on synthetic oil since it freezes.

Diary   *January 27, 1942*

Down to the House. Winston speaks for one hour and a half and justifies his demand for a vote of confidence. One can actually feel the wind of opposition dropping sentence by sentence and by the time he finishes it is clear that there is really no opposition at all – only a certain uneasiness. Winston does nothing to diminish that uneasiness. He says that we shall have even worse news to face in the Far East and that the Libyan battle is going none too well. He thrusts both his hands deep into his trouser pockets and turns his tummy now to the right, now to the left in evident enjoyment of his mastery of the position.

Diary   *January 29, 1942*

Third day of the Vote of Confidence Debate. Winston winds up. He is very genial and self-confident. He does not gird at his critics, but compliments them on the excellence of their speeches. When he reaches his peroration he ceases to be genial and becomes emphatic. "I have finished," he says, "I have done," and he makes a downward gesture with his palms open as if receiving the stigmata. He then crouches over the box and strikes it. "I offer no apologies, I offer no excuses, I make no promises. In no way have I mitigated the sense of danger and impending misfortunes that hang over us. But at the same time, I avow my confidence, never stronger than at this moment, that we shall bring this conflict to an end in a manner agreeable to the interests of our country and to the future of the world."

Loud cheers. It takes a long time to count the votes and finally they are recorded as 464 to 1. Huge cheers. Winston gets up and we rise and cheer him. Then he joins Mrs Winston and arm-in-arm and beaming they push through the crowd in Central Hall.

As I pass the tape I find it ticking imperturbably. It tells us that the Germans claim to have entered Benghazi, and that the Japs claim to be only eighteen miles from Singapore. Grave disasters indeed. A black day for a vote of confidence.

Diary　　　　　　　　　　　　　　　　　　　*February 2, 1942*

Lunch at the Beefsteak. George Peel tells me a curious story. When he was a boy he went out to Florence some time in 1887 or 1888. The façade of the Duomo had been repaired and the new frontage had been revealed. He saw policemen clearing the way for a little carriage. In it sat an old lady with a companion. It was Queen Victoria. She stopped the carriage, fumbled in her corsage, and drew out a locket which she held up to the façade. The Lady-in-Waiting afterwards told Peel that it was a miniature of the Prince Consort. She thought it would interest him to see how the Duomo looked after being repaired. Peel had been so impressed by the incident that he wrote a long account of it to Mr Gladstone. He had himself forgotten all about it, but his letter was recently found among Gladstone's papers and returned to him.

Diary　　　　　　　　　　　　　　　　　　　*February 12, 1942*

What has saddened me is not merely the bad news from Singapore and Libya, but a conversation with Violet [Bonham-Carter]. She had been to see Winston yesterday and for the first time in their long friendship she had found him depressed. He was querulous about criticism, unhappy at [Sir Stafford] Cripps not consenting to take office [Minister of Supply], worried about the absence of alternative Ministers whom he could invite into the Government. But underneath it all was a dreadful feeling, she felt, that our soldiers are not as good fighters as their fathers were. "In 1915," said Winston, "our men fought on even when they had only one shell left and were under a fierce barrage. Now they cannot resist dive-bombers. We have so many men in Singapore – so many men – they should have done better." It is of course the same in Libya. Our men cannot stand up to punishment. WE ARE NOT FIGHTING WELL. That is the sadness in my heart. There is something wrong with the whole morale of our army."

Diary   *February 13, 1942*

*A bad date. The *Scharnhorst* and *Gneisenau* [German battle cruisers] nipped out of Brest yesterday in broad daylight and steamed through the Channel to Wilhelmshaven. We sent out our Air Force and lost 20 bombers without, apparently, doing any harm. Altogether we lost 42 aircraft on this venture. Singapore is still holding out and Rommel is massing for another attack in Libya.*

Diary   *February 15, 1942*

Winston Churchill tells us that Singapore has fallen. He is grim and not gay. Unfortunately he appeals for national unity and no criticism in a manner which recalls Neville Chamberlain. Moreover, though he is not rhetorical, he cannot speak in perfectly simple terms and cannot avoid the cadences of a phrase.

Diary   *February 16, 1942*

I fear a slump in public opinion which will deprive Winston of his legend. His broadcast last night was not liked. The country is too nervous and irritable to be fobbed off with fine phrases. Yet what else could he have said? A weaker man would have kept away from the wireless and have allowed someone else to tell us the bad news.

Diary   *February 24, 1942*

In the House Ralph Rayner makes a speech in which he accuses the B.B.C. of issuing soft-soap bulletins. I interrupt him to say that they put out what they get. This is the first time I raised my voice in the House since I was sacked.

Diary   *February 27, 1942*

I do a talk on Winston for the Empire programme. I cannot bear the thought that this heroic figure should now be sniped at by tiny little men.

This Singapore surrender has been a terrific blow to all of us. It is not merely the immediate dangers which threaten the Indian Ocean and the menace to our communications with the Middle East. It is dread that we are only half-hearted in fighting the whole-hearted. It is even more than that. We intellectuals must feel that in all these years we have derided the principles of force upon which our Empire is built. We undermined confidence in our own formula. The intellectuals of 1780 did the same.

Instead of the much needed victory, Britain suffered another defeat. Tobruk fell on June 20. Churchill returned from Washington to face another Vote of Confidence at the beginning of July.

H.N. to V.S-W.   *March 6, 1942*

I had a long meeting of the B.B.C. board yesterday. We are trying to rearrange the news completely and are having great difficulty with our news editors. They are about as obstinate as can be. But we simply must put the thing on a new basis since we get cursed all the time for "sunlight" stuff when we are really only repeating the official communiqués.

Diary   *March 11, 1942*

To the House. Churchill announces that Cripps is to be sent to India. As he refers to him as "my Rt. Hon. friend the Lord Privy Seal", the House imagines at first that he means Attlee and a most conspicuous chill follows. But the word goes round "he means Cripps" and everyone is delighted.

H.N. to V.S-W.   *March 16, 1942*
          Farmhill, Dundrum, Co. Dublin

I gave a lecture in Dublin in the evening. It went well. There was one man afterwards who made an impassioned speech saying that there was only one thing that should be subject to Government censorship, and that it began with the letters "c.o.n.". I imagined, of course, that he was attacking the cruelty of Great Britain and all the wrongs that we were still doing to Ireland. I looked down my nose. I merely said, when, panting with passion, he had resumed his seat, that I do not wish to comment on controversial matters. It was only when I was walking away with one of the Professors that I was told that what he meant was "contraceptives".

Diary   *March 18, 1942*
                                                                    Dublin

I go to see De Valera in his office. He is not what I expected. I expected a thin sallow man with huge round spectacles, a thin mouth, great lines from nose to lip-corner, and lank black Spanish hair [inherited from his Spanish father]. But he is not thin, pale rather than sallow, not a bit haggard, benevolent cold eyes behind steel-framed glasses, hair that is soft, and almost brown, no great lines in his face anywhere. An unhealthy look about the gills, and faint indications of white puffiness. A firm gentle voice with a soft Irish accent. An admirable smile, not showing teeth, but lighting up the eyes and face very quickly, like an electric bulb that does not fit and flashes off and on. Yet not an insincere smile. A happy smile.

His conversation is uninteresting. He talks rather in a monologue. He asks me about things at home and sympathises much with Churchill's difficulty in having to cheer up the country and yet not give us bright and optimistic forecasts. "I know that difficulty – I know it all too well." He talks about the "partition", but in a stereotype way and I do not feel much fire behind it. He regrets the presence of American troops [in Northern Ireland], "since they won't understand our people as well as the Tommy does." He thinks that if we in Britain were beaten, America would not carry on an Atlantic war, but would compromise with Germany and Japan. He is indignant with Churchill for not supplying Ireland with arms. I say that it is due to our shortages. He taps thick whitish fingers on the table. "No, it is something more than that." I fear he is right about this. He then touches on the Press. I tell him that he only gets the disagreeable cuttings, and that on the whole our Press is good about Ireland.

He is a very simple man, like all great men. He does not look like a strong man, nor are there any signs in his face of suffering and endurance. Rather he reminds me of Lothian in his last years. Deep spiritual certainty underneath it all, giving to his features a mask of repose.

Diary　　　　　　　　　　　　　　　　　　　　　　*March 30, 1942*

The wireless booms out the Indian agreement. "Under Article Six it is provided that the States and Provinces . . ." I feel so enraged that the Cabinet did not listen to Leo Amery a year ago and did not give India Dominion status then. Now we have done it under threats from the Japanese. Our whole Eastern Empire has gone. Australia has as good as gone. Poor little England. But I should not have minded all this so much if we had fought well.

　　Start work on my Search of the Past, Vol. II. I think I shall call it *The Other Side* [*The Desire to Please*].

H.N. to V.S-W.　　　　　　　　　　　　　　　　　　*April 14, 1942*

I was busy yesterday. Winston in the House was not at his best. He feels deeply the loss of naval units and becomes like a surly buffalo – lowered head – eyes flaring right and left. He becomes angry and not triumphant.

Diary　　　　　　　　　　　　　　　　　　　　　　*April 15, 1942*

We are addressed by Harry Hopkins [Roosevelt's personal representative] in the large Committee Room. He is very astute and makes a good impression by telling us amusing stories such as how Winston was introduced to Mrs Roosevelt in his pyjamas. The implication was that we should be made to get rid of Winston since he is the only man who really understands Roosevelt. It was cleverly done. He talks of Anglo-American relations and tells us that there are many people in the U.S.A. who say today that we are yellow and can't fight. It is true that we have been beaten in everything we do. Somebody asks him whether America can advise us on the sort of propaganda we ought to conduct. He gets out of it well. He says,

"Well, we are the worst propagandists in the world and you are the next worst. Why not consult someone better?"

Diary   *April 23, 1942*

Secret Session in the House. I am not allowed, even in my diary, to give all the details of what passed, but I can at least give an outline. Cripps, on his return from India, was received with a cheer stronger than that accorded to Winston. The latter when he rose (and after all the strangers had been spied and harried from the House) adopted his stolid, obstinate, ploughman manner. He tells of Singapore, where the conduct of our large army "does not seem to have been in harmony with the past or present spirit of our forces". He tells us of our present dangers and prospects and dwells at length upon the heavy sinkings we are sustaining in the eastern Atlantic. It is a long and utterly remorseless catalogue of disaster and misfortune. And as he tells us one thing after another, gradually the feeling rises in the packed House. "No man," Members begin to feel in their hearts, "no man but he could tell us of such disaster and increase rather than diminish confidence." And as this feeling rises, there rises with it a feeling of shame at having doubted him. The House gives him a great ovation and the debate thereafter peters out.

H.N. to V.S-W.   *April 29, 1942*

I went to the House to hear Cripps on India. I know nothing about India and just cut it out of my interests. He was very competent, very clear, very straightforward, very tactful. But he is so dry and inhuman; he lacks fire; he lacks sympathy. I do hate the way philanthropists are so cold in their affection for their fellow human beings. I do not think that Cripps will ever make a leader. He at present enjoys a legend, but it is a false legend. He is a perfect Lord Chancellor.

I lunched with Victor Cazalet to meet [Admiral] Muselier [recently dismissed from his command of the Free French Navy by de Gaulle]. Victor cannot see a pie without wishing to have his finger in it. I wish I could get a clear map of Victor's soul. I think you would find much swamp and little firm ground, and round the edges there would be a vague area labelled *terra incognita*. Anyhow, Muselier told his whole sad story. He was dressed in civilian clothes and seemed ill and miserable. He ate nothing, but kept on reading us telegrams exchanged with de Gaulle. There is no doubt that he has been abominably treated.

Diary   *May 11, 1942*

I have a long talk with Ed Murrow who has just returned after three months in the United States. He says that the anti-British feeling is intense. I ask him why. He says partly the hard-core anglophobes (Irish, Italians, Germans and isolationists); partly the frustration produced by war without early victory; partly our bad behaviour at Singapore; and partly the tendency common to all countries at war to blame their allies for doing nothing. He feels moreover that we have sent the wrong type of person over there. Halifax is not popular with the people although he has gained the esteem and confidence of the administration. The problem is largely one of proper boasting. I tell him that it is profoundly repugnant for us to boast, and he replies that it is taken by the Americans either as feebleness or as arrogance. It is in fact a major element in the *superbia Britannorum*.

Diary   *May 19, 1942*

Debate on the Adjournment. Attlee opens with a long and rambling statement which is so dull and so badly delivered that the House can scarcely refrain from yawning. The only interesting thing about it was the fact that the Deputy Prime Minister, at such a crisis in our history, *could* make a dull speech. But Attlee succeeded where lesser men would have failed.

Diary   *June 11, 1942*

B.B.C. Board. We discuss whether the clergy should use the microphone to preach forgiveness of our enemies. I say I prefer that to the clergy who seek to pretend that the bombing of Cologne was a

Christian act. I wish the clergy would keep their mouths shut about the war. It is none of their business.

Diary   June 21, 1942

The six o'clock news tells us that the enemy claim that Tobruk has surrendered "with 25,000 men and many generals". The news crashes on us as a thunderstorm in the lovely evening.

I do some work on Chapter IV [*The Desire to Please*], but have not the heart to continue. Our losses must have been serious indeed if we could not defend Tobruk for twenty-four hours.

Diary   June 22, 1942

Another lovely day and I bathe before breakfast. I have not slept well as I kept on waking up with the word "Tobruk" echoing in my ears, and rolling from side to side with gigantic apprehensions.

The *Chicago Sun* ring up to ask me whether I feel the fall of Tobruk will lead to a major political crisis. I think it may but do not say so. Had Winston any alternative he might be severely shaken by this event. There must have been either serious miscalculation or else our tank and anti-tank guns are very inferior.

Diary   June 23, 1942

Victor Cazalet comes to me. He says, "Let's have a word . . ." We sit on a retired bench. "What do you feel?" he asks. I say, "Well, Victor, there is one thing about which I am certain – we must all get together." "I am glad to hear you say that, Harold." "Yes, we have kept silence too long. We must now speak out with courage and together." "That is exactly my view." "You see," I continue, "you see, Victor, none of us who know what Winston did in 1939 and 1940 have really spoken out. We must now close the ranks to defend him." Victor's jaw drops. "You are pulling my leg again!" he says and walks away.

Diary   *July 2, 1942*

The second day of the Vote of Censure Debate. Aneurin Bevan opens with a brilliant offensive, pointing his finger in accusation, twisting and bowing. Then comes Walter Elliot and then Hore-Belisha.

Winston sits there with a look of sullen foreboding, his face from time to time flickering into a smile. He rises stockily. His hands in his trouser pockets. He makes a long statement which really amounts to the fact that we had more men and more tanks and more guns than Rommel, and that he cannot understand why we were so badly beaten. In the end, after one hour and thirty minutes, he is quite fresh and gay. He gets his vote of confidence by 475 votes to 25, plus a great ovation afterwards. But the impression left is one of dissatisfaction and anxiety, and I do not think it will end there.

Diary   *July 4, 1942*

For the first time an American squadron joined us in a raid on occupied France. This is the beginning of a great air offensive which will go on and on.

Diary   *July 8, 1942*

I go to the House. A Scottish debate. I like these family affairs. What a good Parliamentarian was lost in me!! I am too busy with other interests to give the House that passion for trivialities, that constant assertion of an individual.point of view, which leads to power. I feel sometimes that my failure is due entirely to myself; I have had every opportunity and have missed them. But I am a happy, honest, loving man and I don't care – not one hoot. When I think of Nigel I don't care about success. When I think of Viti I do not care even about death. Few men have achieved that certainty of love.

Diary   *August 7, 1942*

I dine at Pratts and find Pug Ismay [General Ismay, Chief of Staff to the Prime Minister] next to me. He talks about Winston. He calls him a "child of nature". He says that when things are going well, he is good; when things are going badly, he is superb; but when things are going half-well, he is hell on earth. He says that he has the deepest veneration for the House of Commons. One day he found Winston in distress at having to prepare a speech. He said to him, "But why don't you tell them to go to hell?" Winston turned round on him in a flash and said, "You should not say those things – I am a servant of the House."

Diary   *August 18, 1942*

A perfect summer day. After tea, at 7 p.m., I finish my book. I call it *The Desire to Please*.

We are told on the wireless in the evening that Claude Auchinleck has been succeeded by Alexander and that Montgomery is to have the 8th Army.

Diary   *August 28, 1942*

I go to see William Beveridge who has been charged by the Government to make a report upon social insurance. We [the National Labour Group] had put in to him a memorandum urging (a) that the medical services should be completely taken over by the State. He evidently doesn't think much of this. (b) That there should be an increase in old age pensions on the theory that people should be bribed to retire from industry and thus to leave more employment for the young people. He takes exactly the opposite point of view. At present one person in twelve is over 65. By 1961 one in six of the total population will be old people. Therefore we must provide for them. He hopes to create a contributory scheme which in the end will enable all old people to have a really life-giving benefit. He thinks that this self-supporting scheme will become practicable "in my own life-time". He foresees also a comprehensive family allowance giving people 7/6 a week for "large families". But when does a family become large? And if the allowance begins only for the third child, will that child not come to have a different status in the family from the others, and lose that atmosphere of sacrifice-gratitude which is the best parent–child relationship? He is optimistic about grappling with the unemployment problem after the war, and looks forward to a simplified all-in system of insurance. I come away more cheerful and encouraged than I have been for weeks.

H.N. to V.S-W.   *September 9, 1942*

Winston was splendid yesterday. He reduced the art of understate-
ment to a virtuosity such as I have never seen equalled. People were
meaning to speak about the changes in command in Egypt, about
the [Canadian] Dieppe raid, about the Second Front. But he took
the wind so completely out of their sails that they tore up their
notes and remained seated. The debate therefore collapsed. This
would have been all right if Cripps had not profited by the occasion
to give the House a rather sharp talking-to and to accuse them of
preferring their luncheon to their duties. This has enraged everyone.

Diary   *September 9, 1942*

To the House. They are still enraged by Cripps having rebuked
them for not attending the debate yesterday in sufficient numbers.

Guy Burgess [then attached to the Foreign Office] has heard
from his friends who are in close touch with Cripps that the latter
is so discontented with the conduct of the war that he proposes to
resign. Guy and I agreed that Cripps' attitude was probably wholly
disinterested and sincere. That he really believed that Winston was
incapable of dealing with the home front and that his handling of
the minor problems of production and strategy was fumbling and
imprecise. We had agreed also that Cripps would find the atmosphere
of Downing Street, with its late hours, casual talk, cigar smoke and
endless whiskey, most unpalatable. Whereas Winston never regards with affection a man of such inhuman austerity as Cripps, and
cannot work with people easily unless his sentiments as well as his
respect is aroused. We also agreed that Cripps (who in his way is a
man of great innocence and narrow vision) might be quite seriously
unaware that his own resignation would shake Winston very
severely, that around him would gather all the elements of opposition, and that in the end he would group around him an "alternative
Government" and take Winston's place. We agreed that Cripps was
actually too modest a man to realize what an immensely disturbing
effect his resignation would produce, and too simple a man to see
how it would be exploited by evil men to their advantage. There
was a hope that if Winston would show real consideration to
Cripps, and give him a vital part in the direction of the war, then
something might be done to avert this disaster.

Violet Bonham Carter is the only outside person I know who is on terms of intimate friendship with Winston and also has the confidence of Stafford and Lady Cripps. We told her the story. She said that she was in an awkward position as Lady Cripps had taken her into her confidence and told her much the same. She could not betray this confidence, much as she agreed with our point of view. We arranged therefore (a) that Violet should see Cripps or his wife and ask if she might say a word to Winston – a word of warning. (b) that failing this I should go and see Bracken.

H.N. to V.S-W.   *September 24, 1942*

I do not think that, except for Winston, I *admire* anyone as much as I admire you.

I remember your saying (years ago) that you had never established a complete relationship with anyone. I don't think you ever could – since yours is a vertical and not horizontal nature, and two-thirds of you will always be submerged. But you have established, with your sons and me, a relationship of absolute trust and complete love. I don't think that these things would be so fundamental to the four of us were it not that each one of the four is a private person underneath.

I have often wondered what makes the perfect family. I think it is just our compound of intimacy and aloofness. Each of us has a room of his own. Each of us knows that there is a common-room where we meet on the basis of perfect understanding.

H.N. to V.S-W.   *October 12, 1942*

Ben told me a story about Cyril Connolly that amused me. Peter Quennell was complaining that he had to do fire-watching. "Can't you get out of it," asked Cyril, "on the ground that you have a child and three wives to support?"

Diary   *October 14, 1942*

We repeal an Act of 1536 under which Welsh is not allowed in the courts in Wales. Herbert Morrison [the Home Secretary] makes an amusing speech but flatters the Welsh Members unduly. "I would rather be blown up," says Lady Astor to me, "than suck up." I believe this to be true – and it is one of her good points.

Diary   *October 21, 1942*

Duff Cooper tells me some of his experiences as head of the Cabinet Security Committee. Most of the indiscretions are due solely to an inability to make conversation or write letters. Young men having no power of invention fall back in despair upon talking shop. There have been grave cases lately: two staff-majors have been cashiered and one imprisoned for indiscretion. He told me of a letter from a young Air Force officer to his girl-friend. "The ops," he wrote, "which I told you about on my last leave, has been put off because some idiot of a man wrote and gave the exact date. I cannot understand how people can be so careless after all the warnings we have had. This particular op has been put off till October 22nd."

Diary   *October 24, 1942*

A new offensive has started at El Alamein [at 10 p.m.].

Diary   *November 4, 1942*

I reach K.B.W. at 11.40 p.m. and turn on the wireless. The announcer says, "I advise listeners to hold on as in the midnight news we are giving the best news we have heard for years." Then it comes. It is Alexander's communiqué. The Germans are in retreat in Egypt. We have captured 9,000 prisoners and are pursuing "their disordered columns". It is a great victory.

> *The victory at El Alamein was the turning point in the war. It was the end, in the words of A. J. P. Taylor, of Britain's "strategic independence". On November 8, American and British troops landed in Northern Africa, and by the end of the month, the Russians closed behind the German 6th Army in Stalingrad.*
> *H.N.'s sons left England for military service abroad.*

*Every Sunday for the next two and a half years, he wrote
to them, expanding (and censoring) his diary entries.*

Diary   *November 6, 1942*

At 1.15 I stroll across to Downing Street where I am to lunch. I
waved my blue pass and was not interrupted. The War Cabinet
were breaking up when I got there. I go downstairs to the basement
where the Churchills are living, since the upper floors have been
knocked about [by a bomb that had fallen nearby]. They made it
very pretty with chintz and flowers and good furniture and excellent
French pictures – not only the moderns, but Ingres and David.

We go into luncheon: sea-kale, jugged hare and cherry tart.
Not well done. In a few minutes Winston comes in. He is dressed
in his romper suit of Air Force blue and carries a letter in his hand. It
is a long letter from the King written in his own handwriting, and
saying how much he and the Queen have been thinking of Winston
these glorious days. Winston is evidently pleased. "Every word,"
he mutters, "in his own hand."

He gazes round the table with his curious eyes. They are glaucous
and look dead. When he gazes at people like that, there is no light
either of interest or intelligence in his eyes. There is a faint expression
of surprise, as if he were asking, "What the hell is this man doing
here?" There is a faint expression of angered indignation, as if he
were saying, "What damned cheek coming to luncheon here!"
There is a mask of boredom and another mask or film of obstinacy,
as if he were saying, "These people bore me and I shall refuse to be
polite." And with it all, there are films of stubbornness, perhaps
even a film of deep inner thought. It is very disconcerting. Then
suddenly he will cease thinking of something else, and the film will
part and the sun comes out. His eyes then pucker with amusement
or flash with anger. At moments they have a tragic look. Yet these
passing moods and phases do not flash across each other: they move
slowly and opaquely like newts in a rather dim glass tank.

He turns to me and thanks me for my article on his oratory. I say
I hope that I was right in saying that he was not a born orator.
"You are perfectly right," he mumbles. "Not born in the very least –
just hard, hard work." He then talks to us about the battle. He begins
with the first two battles of Alamein [in July 1942]. "I refuse," he

says, "to call it El Alamein. Like those asses who talk about Le Havre. *Havre* [pronounced to rhyme with carver] the place is to any decent man. Now this third battle must not be called Alamein. It must be called 'The Battle of Egypt'. Harold, see to that at once. Tell your people henceforward to call it the Battle of Egypt." He tells us at length how he decided to remove Auchinleck and how he broke the news to him. "It was a terrible thing to have to do. He took it like a gentleman. But it was a terrible thing. It is difficult to remove a bad General at the height of a campaign: it is atrocious to remove a good General." He admits that he wanted Gott [Lt-Gen E. H. E. Gott] for the 8th Army. "I made my decision. I telegraphed to the Cabinet. I then took off all my clothes and rolled in the surf. Never have I had such bathing. And when I got to Cairo, I heard at the Embassy that night that Gott was dead [shot down over the desert]. I sent for Montgomery."

Brendan Bracken comes in and Winston tells him to arrange for all the bells in England to be tolled on Sunday. Some hesitation is expressed by all of us. "Not at all," says Winston, "not at all. We are not celebrating final victory. The war will still be long. When we have beaten Germany, it will take us two more years to beat Japan. Nor is that a bad thing. It will keep America and ourselves together while we are making peace in Europe. If I am still alive, I shall fling all we have into the Pacific."

H.N. to V.S-W.   *November 9, 1942*

My first intimation that the American invasion of North Africa was imminent came from Fred Kuh, the United Press correspondent. I never imagined, however, that it would be on so large or far-flung a scale. I got up yesterday morning and turned on the wireless. When I heard that they had landed at Algiers, I held my breath. That means, eventually, Tunis, and brings us within eighty miles of Sicily and closes the Western Mediterranean. The Italians must be in a grave state of alarm. Nor can they be feeling very pleased with their allies. Six Italian Divisions (the whole Italian Army in fact) have been cut off [at Alamein] and will have to surrender. There has been no such military disaster since Sedan.

Diary December 2, 1942

The Lobbies are buzzing with comments on the Beveridge Report [on national insurance]. The 1922 Committee were addressed by Beveridge and gave him a cordial reception. The Tory line seems to be to welcome the report in principle and then to whittle it away by detailed criticism. They will say that it is all very splendid and a Utopian plan, but that we can only begin to know whether we can afford it once we have some idea of what our foreign trade will be like after the war. They also suggest that in many ways it is an incentive to idleness, that some people are better off under present arrangements and that in fact it is the old Poor Law immensely magnified.

Diary December 10, 1942

To the House where there is a Secret Session on North Africa and Darlan. It is opened by Winston who speaks for an hour and I have never heard him more forceful, informative, or convincing. He convinces us that (a) we were never consulted about the Darlan move [to make him political head of French North Africa, in place of Giraud]; (b) when it happened he himself realised at once what trouble would be caused and warned Roosevelt accordingly; (c) it is purely temporary. I cannot say more than that.

I see that it illustrates the difficulty of all Secret Sessions. Winston could not have convinced us as he did convince us unless he had been able to quote telegrams and documents which it would have been wholly impossible to quote in public. But some public statement can be made, and must be made.

Diary December 11, 1942

I go shopping at the [Army and Navy] Stores. It is a heartbreaking process. There is nothing to buy and the shelves, where filled at all, are filled with stuff which was put away as unsaleable in 1874.

H.N. to his sons   *December 20, 1942*

The military arrived at Sissinghurst. It consisted of the Headquarters of a Tank Brigade on excercise, heralded by a young officer.
He told us that his Brigadier, plus five officers plus cook plus bat-
man, would appear by tea-time and wanted to stay the night. He
departed to inform his Headquarters what a pleasant little welcome
was being prepared.

It was at that moment that Mummy remembered the onions
stored on the floor of the loft. They number between two and three
thousand. She said that the Army always stole onions and that we
must remove them at any cost before they arrived. I said we were
only having a Brigadier and his officers, and that (a) they would
probably not want to steal more than three onions each, and (b) we
shall not miss them much if they did. She said that you could never
tell with officers nowadays, so many of them were promoted from
the ranks. So we got three sacks and two shovels and all afternoon
till darkness came we carried the sacks across to the Priest's House
and spread them on the floor. We had scarcely finished with the last
onion when the Brigadier appeared. He was a nice well-behaved
man and looked so little like an onion-stealer that Mummy at once
asked him to dinner.

Diary   *January 1, 1943*

*I see the New Year in lying upon my truckle bed in the House of
Lords [currently occupied by the House of Commons] and listening
to the snorting and snoring of my companions. I hear Big Ben boom
out the twelve strokes – and some distant singing.

Lunch at the Beefsteak. Rothermere tells me that the Americans
have even now not told us the real identity of Darlan's assassin
[Darlan was shot in Algiers on December 24]. Some say he was a
Gaullist; others say he was Pétainist; others that he was in the pay
of the axis. The fact that he was executed so hastily causes uneasiness. The fact that Giraud arrested twelve people is also disturbing.
Harold MacMillan has been hurried out [to Algiers] immediately
by aeroplane. He will have a difficult job.*

H.N. to his sons   *January 7, 1943*

I had an appointment to conduct some American doughboys round
the Palace of Westminster. In they slouched, chewing gum, conscious

of their inferiority in training, equipment, breeding, culture, experience and history, determined in no circumstances to be either interested or impressed. In the Chamber we bumped into another party, of Dominion heroes this time, being shown round by no less a person than the Lord Chancellor of England. I have never cared for John Simon, but I must confess that on this occasion he displayed energy and even charm. Embarrassing he was, to be true. For having stood at the Prime Minister's place and lifted up the dust-cloths from the box and table, he asked me to go opposite to show them the relations between the Government and Opposition benches. Fifty blank faces, their jaws working at the gum, turned in languid interest in my direction. "Now Harold . . ." But I was firm. "No," I said, "I am no good at amateur theatricals." So then we went into the House of Lords [then sitting in the Robing Room] and Simon sat on the Woolsack and showed them how the Lord Chancellor behaves. "The Amendment standing in the name of the noble Marquess . . ." Jaws chewed unflinchingly in silence. "Now," he said briskly, "come to my room, boys – or should I call you doughboys? – and I will show you the Great Seal." Through the corridors they slouched apathetically, expecting to be shown a large wet animal such as they had seen so often at the Aquarium in San Francisco. But not at all. All they were shown were two cylinders of steel with a pattern inside. And then a man fetched the mace for them to see. "I must now ask you, my friends, to leave me to my labours. Even a Lord Chancellor sometimes has work to do. Harold, perhaps you will conduct our friends to the exit?" Harold did. We slouched along to Central Hall. To my surprise and pleasure one of the doughboys suddenly ceased chewing, flung his wad of Wrigley into his cheek with a deft movement of his tongue, and said, "Say, Sur, who was that guy?"

H.N. to V.S-W.   *January 20, 1943*

*I went to the House. We had a tribute to Lloyd George [who was celebrating his eightieth birthday] and the poor old man was much moved. He stood there, very pale and white, unable to find his words. What is tragic is that he retains all his old manner of impressive oratorical pronouncements. But nothing comes. It is like an old Rolls Royce back-firing and spluttering. We then had a Secret Session. Merely to give us a piece of information. And then

Attlee got up to make his war statement. He is so dull and puny that if he had told us about the fall of Bizerta, we should have been bored. Everybody filed out.*

Diary   *January 23, 1943*

On the 1 o'clock news we hear that our troops [the 8th Army] entered Tripoli at dawn today after having pursued Rommel for 1,400 miles. Lord Haw Haw [William Joyce] at 10.30 says, "May I quote the picturesque if slightly vulgar phrase used by General Montgomery? He said his object was 'to put Rommel in the bag'. In fact his aim was not to take Tripoli, but to take Rommel. He has failed."

Diary   *January 29, 1943*

Kingsley Martin and Aneurin Bevan start a hare by saying that Ll.G. was a finer man than Churchill. Churchill is "adolescent", which is suitable in times of emotional strain. Ll.G. is the wise statesman. I say that Ll.G., if he had not been so gaga, would have been our Pétain. They agree to this, but still say he is a great man. We also agree that the main quality demanded of a politician is not that he should be gifted or honest or wise – but "formidable". But to be formidable implies the capacity to bring votes into the lobby.

Diary   *February 2, 1943*

The whole country is under floods. On the midnight news we hear that the last of the Germans at Stalingrad, including Field Marshal Paulus, have surrendered.

H.N. to V.S-W.   *February 2, 1943*

What fools the Germans must feel about Paulus!! They obviously imagined he would commit suicide. They therefore made him a Field Marshal. But he has not committed suicide. He has surrendered. And that means for the first time in history a German Field Marshal has been taken prisoner. I do not know how they will explain it away.

Diary   *February 18, 1943*

We have the Division [on the Beveridge Report]. 338 to 121. This means that if one deducts the Cabinet Ministers, Parliamentary Secretaries and the P.P.S.s, practically all the Labour Party have voted against. They may now ask their Ministers to retire from the Government. A major political crisis would then arise.

I met Beveridge in the lobby, looking like the witch of Endor. I said, "Well, are you enjoying this?" He said, "I am having the fun of my life." "Upsetting Governments and wrecking constitutions?" He said, "My two previous reports [on coal in 1925 and unemployment insurance in 1936] led to the fall of two Ministers; this one may bring down a Government." He is a vain man.

Diary   *February 22, 1943*

In the evening I dine with our Monday Evening Club, which is a group of British and Americans. We dine at the Connaught. I have to address them afterwards. I say that a difficult diplomatic situation may arise between us and Russia and the U.S.A. The Russians will demand a gigantic reward which may entail the suppression of the independence of ten smaller powers. America's missionary spirit will resent this, and her isolationist spirit will do nothing to help us resist it. Anti-British opinion will concentrate on the theme that America was again ensnared by British propaganda and that so far from making the world safe for democracy, we have made it safe for Jo Stalin. It would have been better to take Germany's side. Ed Murrow refers to my "soul-satisfying pessimism" and agrees with what I say.

H.N. to his sons   *March 18, 1943*

We had a debate on the reform of the Foreign Service. The main idea is to fuse the Diplomatic with the Consular and Commercial Services. I have been in favour of this for thirty years. But the debate went wrong as usual. The women Members felt that their rights were being trampled on, and staged a full-dress attack on the exclusion of women from the Service. Nancy Astor, as the senior woman Member, insisted on voicing their complaint. She has one of those minds that works from association to association, and therefore spreads sideways with extreme rapidity. Further and further did she diverge from the point while Mrs Tate beside her kept on saying, "Get back to the point, Nancy. You were talking about the 1934 Committee." "Well, I come from Virginia," said Lady Astor, "and that reminds me, when I was in Washington . . ." I was annoyed by this, as I knew I was to be called after her. It was like playing squash with a dish of scrambled eggs. Anyhow I made my speech and it went well enough. Lady Astor had said that women had never been given any chance to show their capacity in foreign politics. I said that they might not have been *given* chances, but from the days of Helen of Argos to the days of the Noble Lady the Member for the Sutton Division of Plymouth they had *taken* chances, and that the results had been disastrous. "You mean mistresses," shouted Lady Astor. I said No, I was thinking of women's virtues and not their frailties. Intuition and sympathy were the two main feminine virtues, and each of these was of little value in diplomacy.

H.N. to V.S-W.   *March 25, 1943*

I bought an evening newspaper on my way to the House and read with pleasure the headlines "EIGHTH ARMY POURS ON TO- WARDS GABES". But after questions Winston, looking his most bulldog, got up and growled that we had had a knock on the Mareth Line and that the Germans had recaptured the positions we took on Saturday. It was like a douche of cold water.

Diary   *April 14, 1943*

I go to the Aeolian Hall for the poetry reading organised by Osbert and Edith Sitwell for the benefit of the Free French. The Queen arrives accompanied by the two Princesses. The poets file in – Mase- field, T. S. Eliot, Gordon Bottomley, Arthur Waley, Edmund Blunden, and Viti. Masefield pays a tribute to Laurence Binyon [who died on March 10], and then the readings start. I cannot hear most of them as I am in the gallery and they are impeded by a lectern which Osbert found in the Caledonian Market and which impedes voice and sight. I am impressed by Eliot's reading and rather moved by the Poet Laureate [Masefield]. Then there is an interval during which the Poets are received by the Queen in an ante-room. Then the second series begins and Viti reads her piece. She stands there looking magnificent and modest and recites *The Land* quite perfectly. I hear a low murmur of delight passing through the audience. She was by streets the best of the lot and I am so proud of her. She is as serene as a swan.

H.N. to V.S-W.   *April 20, 1943*

I was talking in the Smoking Room to Duff. He was beginning to say all again that lovely piece [about V.S.W.'s poetry reading] when I saw an odd expression of embarrassment in his eyes and at the same time I felt an arm on my shoulder. "May I join you?" said a voice. It was Winston. OH MY GOD what a man he is!!!! Two of his incidental remarks picked out from the whole sea of delight. I told him of Niggs's hope that the Americans would cut Rommel off. He grunted deeply. "Yes," he said, "tell your boy that it will now be scrunch and punch." I also asked him what was happening and would happen to the Bey of Tunis. "'Obey' is what his name is now."

Diary   *May 4, 1943*

*I go down in the evening to Denham to dine and sleep with the Vansittarts. I find Van well enough, but getting deaf. We have a lovely pre-war dinner with trout, lamb, fruit and a bottle of Pomeroy '98. It is a lovely house with stately rooms and a stately butler.

Van feels that he is an aggrieved man. When I consider that he was head of his profession, received every honour, was given a peerage [in 1941], married a rich and lovely wife and is now a national figure I cannot understand this. There is in Van a deep underneath of real conceit. I like him enormously, but I fear that it is wounded conceit that makes him so bitter.*

H.N. to his sons   *May 8, 1943*

I was suddenly awakened five minutes after midnight by Mummy standing at the door. She had been listening to the midnight news. "Tunis," she said, not without a touch of drama, "and Bizerta are ours." That is how the news came to Sissinghurst. A gale blowing outside and my open windows straining at their catches; my door open against the light on my staircase; and Mummy standing there in her pyjamas enunciating these great truths.

I dined last Monday with Rob Bernays. He says that the mistake I make in the House is not to be formidable. "But, my dear Rob, I was not designed by nature to be formidable." "Well, take it from me, unless you become formidable, you will be overlooked." "But nobody can become formidable when he has been unformidable for 55 years." "You take it from me, Harold . . ." So I suppose something has got to be done.

Diary   *May 11, 1943*

*To the House. We have a Secret Session. Then Attlee gets up as Deputy Prime Minister [Churchill was in Washington] to make the Government statement on Tunisia. He achieved the impossible. He made the glorious campaign sound dull. Had he gone on for five minutes more the House would have had a *fou rire*. He stopped just in time.*

> The summer months saw the invasion of Sicily, the fall of Mussolini and the capitulation of Italy. The armistice was signed on the very day, September 3, when British troops landed in the toe of Italy, our first re-entry onto the mainland of Europe. The war which won the war was meanwhile being waged in Russia, where the Germans were retreating fast. H.N. was deeply involved in the disputes of the Free French in London, seeing as much of de Gaulle as of his opponents.

Diary   *May 13, 1943*

The Italians had announced that an important statement was to be made on their wireless at 9 p.m. It was made by General Vittorio Ambrosio, Chief of the General Staff. It was a perfunctory and formal explanation of defeat. But, according to the tape which we read at Brooks' at 11.15 he ended up "Viva il Re! Viva Italia!" Now the omission of Mussolini's name and the appeal to the House of Savoy is deeply significant.

Diary   *May 17, 1943*

Dine with Sibyl at Lord North Street. The Devonshires, Camroses, Rothermeres, D'Arcy Osborne [British Minister to the Holy See] and Desmond Morton [Personal Assistant to the P.M.] are there. Morton tells me that Monsignor Spellman [Archbishop of New York] had cast a spell over Churchill. He had told him exactly what he intended to say to De Valera. Churchill said, "I would not say that Monsignor; you will give the poor man a fit." "Far be it from me," replied the Archbishop, "to cause the death of any man, but if Almighty God should wish that De Valera lose his life on hearing the truth, I shall say many Masses for his soul." Osborne does not share this enthusiasm for Spellman who is much affected by the desire to please and who apparently gave the Vatican the impression that he was bitterly anti-British. We discuss the future of Italy and Osborne is convinced that there will be a great universal desire to get out of the war coupled with the realisation that Italy in her present condition must lose her Empire and will only exchange one form of occupation for another.

The latest idea is that we should give Libya to the Maltese.

Diary   *June 1, 1943*

Go to Chips' [Channon] house to meet Field-Marshal Wavell [Commander-in-Chief, India and later Viceroy of India]. A stocky man with one blind eye. I am reminded of the day when I was waiting in the ante-room of the Quai d'Orsay and there entered a square little man clasping an enormous portfolio. I thought, "That must be a sergeant in the Ordnance Department come with statistics for his chief." Then I thought, "What a remarkable face for a sergeant!" I then thought, "My God, it's Foch!" Wavell is rather restless and embarrassed. He talked to me about his book on Allenby in which he corrects or contradicts a statement I made in *Curzon*. I say I do not mind. What worries him, I think, is that Chips has also invited some of the wives of his staff. They do not fuse very well. That is what makes Wavell anxious and ill at ease.

H.N. to his sons   *June 9, 1943*

I had to go to a *conversazione* given by the Authors' Society. I arrived late and H. G. Wells was already talking nonsense in front of a microphone and a plate of biscuits. Gilbert Murray also spoke. Thereafter I mingled with my fellow authors. There was Rose Macaulay and G. M. Trevelyan and Elizabeth Bowen and Lady

Astor and Lindsay Drummond [publisher] and Arthur Koestler. The latter talked to me about Richard Hillary [Battle of Britain pilot and author of *The Last Enemy*]. He is editing a book about him or a collection of correspondence. This is always a guilty spot in me. I do not like heroes. I feel mean about all this, but I do not like the T. E. Lawrence brood. Koestler is intelligent on the subject. He thinks that Hillary would have become a great writer. He says that he was marred first by his amazing good looks, secondly, after his skin-graft [his face was terribly burnt when he was shot down], by his horrifying ugliness. But surely, surely, the man was a cad at heart, even as T.E.L. was a cad at heart. The literary temperament is only tolerable so long as it remains cowardly. Once it becomes courageous it is an unpleasant thing to meet.

Diary　　　　　　　　　　　　　　　　　　　　　　*July 14, 1943*

People are terribly optimistic. They say that the German offensive in the Kursk area has collapsed; that our troops in Sicily are meeting with no resistance and we shall be in Catania in three days, and Messina within a fortnight. They say we have beaten them in the air and over and under the sea; that they have no hope at all; that collapse will come. I admit that were I a German I should be feeling pretty glum. But I distrust optimism in any case.

H.N. to V.S-W.　　　　　　　　　　　　　　　　　*July 14, 1943*

I went down to the House for the Colonial Debate and felt that I should say something about African education. But somehow I felt that I could not do it. I have never before suddenly lost confidence in myself to that extent. I do feel it strange that a person of my experience is so much ignored nowadays. I suppose that the fact that I got into the Government (and in a post where I *ought* to have made good) and was thereafter discarded has created the impression that I am a dud. What I mind is that it has damaged my self-confidence. I don't want to drift into being an old buffer.

V.S-W. to H.N.　　　　　　　　　　　　　　　　　*July 15, 1943*

I am so glad you have written as you have, because for a long time I have suspected that something of that sort was going on in that curly-box [head]. It seems to me that your mind has never been more vigorous or more capable of canalisation, but that you are allowing it to run into many little rills, each of them clear and useful, but in the aggregate detracting from the power of the main stream. Let me tabulate your activities into two separate categories:

(1) *Marginal comments [Spectator].* Altogether admirable.
    B.B.C. Financially essential.
    Free French. Yes. Important. Hadji specially well-qualified.
    Your own books. You know what I feel about these.
    House of Commons. Well, obviously you must keep that on.
(2) *Endless committees and odd speeches and odd articles,* mostly undertaken because you cannot say NO.

To be constructive, I should like to see you scrap as much of No (2) as you can, and to devote yourself to *one* thing in their place. Personally I should like you to take up the re-building of England, both urban and rural. I think you have very special gifts in this direction, but I believe you have an idea that it is not sufficiently "public life".

Diary   *July 21, 1943*

I have breakfast at the Dorchester with Lord Baldwin. We sit at opposite ends of a tiny table, with a kipper in front of each of us. He is lame and slightly deaf, but I see no diminution either in his curiosity or his memory. He talks of Kipling [his cousin], and is trying to find out whether he ever refused the laureateship. Salisbury offered it to him; so did Asquith; did MacDonald also? He then talks of Ramsay and describes his last visit to him when he left in the funereal boat [MacDonald died at sea in 1937]. Ramsay was talking of all the books he meant to write and all the journeys he hoped to make. Baldwin knew all the time that he was a shattered man. He talks of human ambition and endeavour, and says that in his long life he has found always that in the end men and women are as good as one thinks them.

He then passes on to Winston. The latter had asked him to luncheon and given him three hours, telling him about all that was happening. "I went out into Downing Street," said Baldwin, "a happy man. Of course it was partly because an old buffer like me enjoys feeling that he is not quite out of things. But it was also pure patriotic joy that my country at such a time should have found such a leader. The furnace of the war has smelted out all base metals from him." He lives in a sort of pool or ambient water of forgiveness. He said that the only man he could never forgive was Beaverbrook.

I did not notice much change in old Baldwin. His nose has got more square and bulbous and now really looks like what Low [the cartoonist] made it look like years ago. His face is still that strange colour as if lightly dusted by ginger powder.

Diary   *July 25, 1943*

I had written my diary and gone to bed, leaving Viti as I hoped and believed recovering from her disease ['flu] in the North Cottage. But scarcely had I laid my head upon the pillow when I heard a strange sound below followed by Martha's [dog] familiar padding on the stairs. The door opened and there stood Viti dressed in her brown overcoat and an old Etonian sweater of Ben's. I was horrified, thinking for a moment that she had had delirium and was wandering in her mania. "Go back to bed at once," I said. But she said, "Mussolini has resigned."

She had been listening to Reginald King at the piano with his quintet when suddenly at 11.4 the programme was interrupted and a voice said "We interrupt this programme to say that the Rome wireless has announced the resignation of Mussolini."

Diary   *August 2, 1943*

We go to the village fête at Sissinghurst Place. All the village children dress up and there is one little boy who impersonates Montgomery riding in a tank. There are many side-shows. One of them is a dart contest in which people are invited to throw darts at large cartoon drawings of Hitler, Tojo and Mussolini. The Mussolini target does no business at all. Hitler and Tojo attract great crowds but people do not want to throw darts at Mussolini as they say he is "down and out". Really the English are an amazing race.

H.N. to Lady Violet Bonham-Carter   *August 28, 1943*

On my long journey to Edinburgh yesterday, I thought over the sad episode of the [William] Haley controversy [he was a candidate for the Deputy Director-Generalship of the B.B.C.]. Throughout my life (at Balliol, in diplomacy, in literature and even in politics) I have been dealing with people who, if they did not share my opinions, did share, or at least understand, my values. We may have differed as to the relative values of such virtues as truth, beauty, tolerance, fairness, generosity, courage, faithfulness and taste. But the assumption has always been that these were desirable virtues possessing a certain absolute validity. We took it for granted that to these ethical values certain intellectual values should be added – intelligence, wit, humour, knowledge – and the importance of these great things formed the "language" in which we discoursed. They were even more than that. They were the accepted currency with which we interchanged ideas. Suddenly I have found myself faced with a group of people who not only do not understand, but actually do not know, these weights and measures. It is as if for such current phrases of measurement as "$2\frac{1}{2}$ feet", "forty-two minutes", "eleven stone", "4/-", one used Siamese expressions indicating *yens* or *tickals* or whatever it may be. I feel in dealing with these men the same gap in communication as I do when I hear people talking about batting averages or football pools or racing form. I believe that they are honestly quite unaware of the standards which to us seem the axioms of life.

Thus even when we have reached agreement on some point, we have not really reached agreement. It is as if, having agreed with someone to meet him at the Travellers Club at 7.30, he supposed that one had fixed a meeting at Lyons Corner House at 11.45. I do not accuse them of dishonesty; only an honest lack of comprehension.

It is the absence of any sense of corporate function which renders the [B.B.C.] Board so contemptible a body. We are about to enter an age when all the old values will be called into question and many of the most precious of them discarded, not because they lack validity, but merely because they are old. We cannot hope that the Press as a whole will swim against the tide of vulgarization which will sweep in from the west. Only the B.B.C. can teach the public to think correctly, to feel nobly, to enjoy themselves intelligently, to have some conception of what is meant by the good life. Our responsibility is tremendous. I do not want to shirk that responsibility. And yet in seeking to convey it to my colleagues, I have to introduce words and concepts of which they have no understanding at all. They remain completely unaware of what we mean when we talk of the B.B.C.'s unerring instinct for the second-rate.

Diary   *September 8, 1943*

To Aldford House for our Greek Committee. The Greek Ambassador had telephoned to say that he would be late as he had been sent for by Anthony Eden. He arrives about 6.30 with his eyes shining like two stars. I go off and he accompanies me into the corridor. "It's all over," he says. "The Italians have surrendered unconditionally. Eden has just told me." "Is it to be published?" I ask. "Not till they are certain that Badoglio will broadcast to his people telling them to oppose the Germans."

What a day for the Germans! Stalino has fallen; they have lost nearly all the Donetz basin; and on top of it comes this dastardly stab in the back from Italy.

> *On October 14 H.N. left London for Sweden, by way of Edinburgh. Bad weather kept him in Scotland for four days and eventually he flew to Stockholm on October 19th. He lectured on behalf of the Ministry of Information. He returned on November 4.*

Diary   *November 10, 1943*

B.B.C. Board. I am warmly welcomed. We finish early and I walk with Violet [Bonham-Carter]. She tells me the details of Mark's [her son] escape. When the Germans arrived at Modena they divided the prisoners into eleven categories. Mark foresaw that they would move them in numerical order and thus got himself into the eleventh category, which would be the last. He thought at first of hiding in the sewer but it was really physically impossible. Then a man who had tunnelled a hole under the floor of his hut and covered it with boards said, "You can have my hole. I cannot manage to remain there more than two hours at a time." So Mark, with a Major in the Grenadiers, climbed down into the hole and remained there for 36 hours. The lack of air was agonizing, and he felt his heart would burst. They were stung by mosquitoes and Mark said, "If a mosquito can live in this, so can I." After three days in the hole they thought it might be safe to come up. The camp was basking in sunlight and not a soul was to be seen. They climbed the wall and jumped over. Some little Italian boys rushed at them whispering – "I Tedeschi I Tedeschi" – and surely enough the prison wall was being patrolled by German sentries. They mingled with the children and walked very slowly away. Mark had dyed his khaki trousers by pouring ink on them. They then started on their fifteen day trek, keeping to the hills and avoiding bridges and roads. They begged food from the peasants and were always given it. The only map they had was one torn out of Trevelyan's book on Garibaldi. As they came nearer to the front the peasants would tell them where the Germans were. On one occasion they were about to knock at the door of a cottage when they saw a field telephone wire in the grass. They knew that it was a German post. As they got closer to the line, they descended to the valleys foreseeing that the German gun-positions would be on the hills. The Germans whom they met took them for peasants. Then suddenly one afternoon they emerged from a wood straight upon an English gun-crew. They shouted in English. "By God! I thought you blighters were Jerries," said the corporal. "Then why," said Mark – his officer status returning to him – "Then why the hell did you not fire at us?"

Diary   *November 19, 1943*

I dictate letters in the morning and then go to the Dominions Office to meet Paul Evans and Bobbety Cranborne by appointment. They had said they had wanted to see me urgently. I had a suspicion what it was. My suspicion was correct. For after a long desultory conversation about my visit to Sweden, Bobbety says, "Would you undertake another trip?" "Where to?" I ask. "Australia." At first I said No – pointing out that I am a civilian of the old liberal school and that this might not go down. "You need have no feelings of inferiority," says Bobbety, "with the Australians about not fighting." "But seriously," he adds, "I really want you to go." "Well, if it's like that," I say, "I have only one answer. But Vita will never forgive you."

Anyhow that is that.

I lunch with Raymond [Mortimer]. I ask him as my dearest friend whether I should be cowardly in not defending Oswald

Mosley [released from prison on the day before] if he is attacked in the House. He says I should leave it to Morrison [Home Secretary] to defend his action and that I should be quixotic to rush into the breach over Mosley. I loathe feeling that I funk any moral obligation. But he says, "My dear Harold – nobody thinks you disloyal or cowardly – keep your powder for better causes." But there is something in me (my enemies call it "lack of judgement") which forces me to espouse hopeless causes.

I go to Pratts. I walk back feeling miserable about Australia. If the Government think I am any good why do they not give me a real job and not these potty little lecture tours?

Diary   *November 23, 1943*

Down to the House. We are prorogued. When I get there I find a procession of workers with banners protesting against the release of Mosley. Herbert Morrison makes a statement which I find admirable. He takes full responsibility for the release and says that he is not going to allow a man to die in detention. The House is really with him. But the *Daily Worker* has been stoking up the communists and there are demonstrations all over London.

I go to the Beefsteak with Rob. I tell him about Australia. He says (a) that I am mad to absent myself from Parliament at this moment; (b) that I shall be a ghastly failure in Australia. They will see in me all that they most dislike about the British.

Diary   *December 3, 1943*

I have a deputation of shop-stewards regarding the release of Mosley. It is quite evident that their resentment is deep, wide-spread and sincere. They are impervious to argument. Communist propaganda, if it has succeeded in nothing else, has certainly succeeded in destroying all confidence, not only in the governing class, but also the Labour leaders. This Mosley incident is more important than it may seem. It has widened the class breach. I see quite clearly now that I shall not stand a dog's chance in keeping my seat in West Leicester. The whole working-class will vote solid against me.

Diary   *December 30, 1943*

I go to Pratts and I meet Bobbety Cranborne. He says to me, "Halloa Harold! I gather I am seeing you tomorrow." I had heard nothing of this. He says that after full investigation they find that they cannot send me out [to Australia] except by sea, and cannot guarantee that they can get me back by air. This means that my CONDITION that I should be back by April cannot be fulfilled. Therefore he thinks I had better chuck the whole Australian idea.

When he indicated "NO" I felt a rush of relief and delight. So I never wanted to go at all. Or is it that my rush of delight was simply my relief about Vita's anxiety? I do not know. All I know is that I felt a definite pleasure thrill and not a disappointment sink.

The main military operations of the early months of 1944 were in Italy, where the Allies attempted to turn the German flank by landing a large force at Anzio. The Germans reacted quickly, and the manoeuvre failed. There was stalemate in Italy, as there was in Russia, for the rest of the winter. H.N. was in London, where German air-attacks were renewed in retaliation for Allied attacks on German towns.

Diary   *January 4, 1944*

I get a letter today from John Masefield, as President of the Incorporated Society of Authors etc. asking me why the B.B.C. have "banned" P. G. Wodehouse. If anybody we do not want to employ is regarded as "banned" then the B.B.C. will lose all freedom of selection. Moreover, there is no doubt that Wodehouse allowed himself, for a "consideration", to be used for broadcasts which were in the interest of the enemy [he had been interned by the Germans at the start of the war, and had broadcast from Berlin an account of his good treatment by them]. As such he is a traitor and should not be used. I do not want to see Wodehouse shot on Tower Hill. But I resent the theory that "poor P.G. is so innocent that he is not responsible". A man who has shown such ingenuity and resource in evading British and American income tax cannot be classed as unpractical.

Diary   *January 18, 1944*

*The House opens after the Xmas Recess. During questions there is a sudden gasp of astonishment and then the whole House begins to yell and cheer and wave their order papers. Winston strolled in [after his three-weeks absence abroad, and his recovery from pneumonia]. He flushes slightly, beams at the House, and then sits down. A tear trickles on to his flushed cheek which he wipes off. He answers questions afterwards. His voice is not as strong as it was.

He then comes into the smoking-room. I do not think he is looking really well. He tells how, on being flown from Tunis to Marrakesh, he finds that there is cloud cover and that the pilot is flying very low. "Can't we go higher?" he asks, "we shall bump into the Atlas at this height." "That is what I was afraid of, sir," replied the pilot, "but I have strict orders not to take you more than 2,000 feet." "Go up to 15,000 at once," said Winston.

Dine at the Dorchester with Sibyl. There are 30 people there. The clou of the evening is Archie Clark Kerr [British Ambassador in Moscow]. I had found the House this morning very fussed and bothered about (a) the Russian reply to Poland which suggests that they will not listen to any reason at all; (b) the *Pravda* report that we have been in secret conference with Ribbentrop. They fear that this means or indicates some desire to break with us and make a separate peace with Germany. It is thus of great value to talk to Archie whose good sense and sincerity I trust absolutely. He says (a) that the Russians will not make a separate peace. "I shall eat my hat" if they did. "No, No, Harold, that is not a thing to worry about." (b) That they very much want to "belong to the Club" and that we can have influence with them by playing that card. (c) That the Polish thing is just bloodiness and the Ribbentrop canard just oriental silliness.*

Diary   *January 29, 1944*

Our wireless has gone wrong and when (during a raid) Viti and I start fiddling with it there is a swish in the air and then two explosions which shake the cottage. Poor Martha [dog] gets in a terrible state and starts panting. We lift the curtain and see a white incandescent light outside which shortly turns to red. We go out into the rose garden and see a great blaze of fire at what seems to be the Hammer Brook bridge. As we watch, the fire engine with its bells clanging dashes along the road, Mrs Staples [their cook] comes to tell us that it was a bomber which crashed in flames, only missing the tower by a few yards.

Diary   *February 7, 1944*

I fear that Winston has become a liability now rather than an asset. This makes me sick with human nature. Once the open sea is reached we forget how we clung to the pilot in the storm. Poor Winston who is so sensitive although so pugnacious will feel all this. In the station lavatory at Blackheath last week I found scrawled up "Winston Churchill is a Bastard". I pointed it out to the Wing Commander who was with me. "Yes," he said, "the tide has turned. We find it everywhere." "But how foul," I said, "How bloody foul!" "Well you see, if I may say so, the men hate politicians." Winston a politician! Good God!!!

Diary   *February 9, 1944*

*I dine with Emerald Cunard. I recite my few Persian poems and would have gone on to Italian had it not been for the arrival of others. We go back to talking about poetry and the subject of Tennyson is raised. "But Harold dear," sayd Emerald, "pull yourself together; stop writing about French poets and diplomatists and give us a book on Tennyson." "Well, Emerald, I have done my best in that direction [in 1923]." She is absurdly embarrassed by this. I promise to send her a copy. Kenneth Clark rescues the situation by saying that my Tennyson book changed the attitude of his Oxford generation.

I come back by Underground. As usual it is crowded by American soldiers and each one has his girl. Now where the hell do these women come from? I suppose the East End. They are horrible to look at and I should imagine dissolute and diseased. Most of them are Jewesses. But what will the Americans think of our womanhood when they get back? I am all for a little promiscuity. But nymphomania among East End Jewesses and for such large sums of money makes me sick.

Kenneth [Clark] told me this evening that when at a Brains Trust recently he was asked whether the Russians had any good painters. He replied that it was a curious circumstance that although they had such gifted writers and choreographers and composers, they never produced a painter of the first class. He had many letters afterwards accusing him of being an enemy of the Soviet. Has the whole world gone mad?*

Diary   *February 10, 1944*

I lunch with [Lord] Camrose at the *Daily Telegraph*. Among the other guests is Sir Alan Brooke [Chief of the General Staff]. Brooke had gone over to Italy. He says that the terrain defies description. It is like the North-West Frontier; a single destroyed culvert can hold up an army for a day. He then went on to talk about the Germans. He says they are fighting magnificently. But that their strategy must be dictated by Hitler as it is all wrong. The Russian offensives indicate that he is short of immediate mobile reserves; the fact that he has had to reinforce Italy from the Balkans and Southern France indicates that he has not many reserves in Germany itself. He cannot hope to run four fronts – Russia, the Balkans, Italy and France. It does not look as yet as if the Germans are short of material. Our hopes that they would run out of oil have been disappointed. The morale of their troops is still admirable and only a slight change can be seen in the quality of the prisoners captured.

Diary   *February 16, 1944*

Go to supper with Rothermere. A discussion starts as to whether we should sacrifice lives in order to spare works of art. I say that we do not realize at all that works of art are irreplaceable whereas no lives are irreplaceable. If the war could be shortened by destroying Perugia then I might agree to do so. But I am not satisfied that the strategic value of fighting up through Italy justifies the enormous loss to civilization which it entails.

Diary   *February 18, 1944*

Miss Niggeman comes up to say that Vita is very upset about the bombing of Knole and broke down completely. It seems that it was a blaster bomb and that it crept round the house and broke windows in every part including that of her old bedroom. She minds terribly and the whole incident opens a sad wound.

Diary   *February 21, 1944*

*Stuart [Preston, a young American art historian] pulled slyly out of his pocket a review by Edmund Wilson in the *New Yorker*. He said, "Harold, are you one of those people who are hurt by criticism?" "Depends who it is by." "Well, you better have this," and he handed me a copy. It was, seemingly, a review of *The Desire to Please*, but was in fact a review of all my work. It said that my work was "unsatisfactory" and disappointing and that I had only written one good book – *Some People*. That I feel to be true. I mean that there is no inner divination in my books and sometimes a lack of muscle in my mind. But the reason he gives is not quite true. He thinks I am class-bound and inhibited. I think I am family-bound and should not wish, while Mummy [Lady Carnock] still lives, to write things which would cause her pain. But that is all I think. To suggest that I was "shocked" by Verlaine and Byron is to suggest something which simply is not true. But Wilson is a fine critic and I feel flattered that he should have devoted so much time to my books.*

Diary   *February 22, 1944*

I go down to the House early. It is packed. Winston gets up soon after noon. He is looking well again, but he has a slight cough. He begins quite abruptly with the words, "This is not a time for sorrow or rejoicing. It is a time for preparation, effort and resolve." He goes on to state our own contribution to the war-effort. He disclosed that we have lost 38,300 pilots and aircrew and over 10,000 machines since the beginning of the war. He forecasts reprisals by the Germans which have hitherto been "modest", but which will increase. He refers to the secret weapon [the V.1 and the V.2]. In describing how our air superiority is gradually asserting itself, he ends with the words, "There is a strange, stern justice in the long . . ." and then he sways his hands below the level of his waist ". . . long swing of events." He admits that the Anzio landing has proved a disappointment and was not carried out according to plan. He then refers to the new commands. The names of Eisenhower and of Alexander are warmly greeted; on the mention of Montgomery there is one isolated "Hear! Hear!"

Diary   *March 1, 1944*

Viti comes up [from Sissinghurst]. It is a joy to see her in my rooms. She likes my new pictures. Back to the House. I pick up Viti and go to Buckingham Palace for a tea party. It takes place in the hall and we do not go upstairs. The company is divided into two groups each side of the Propylaea, and the King and Queen stand in the middle. There are many foreign diplomatists whom they greet. I am taken to talk to the Princesses. Princess Elizabeth is a clear nice girl, with a most lovely skin. I talk to her about the Grenadiers. She is very keen about them [she was their Colonel-in-Chief]. I think Viti is amused, but I wish she had had time to be summoned to the Queen. She has to catch a train and I am rather impatient and train-fussy and drag her off. She looks so beautiful and distinguished. Nobody can compare to her. I go with her to Blackfriars Station.

I dine with James [Pope-Hennessy] at Rules and we go on to Pratts'. James cannot understand how it comes that I am so interested in politics. Pratts is a political kitchen. During the raid last Wednesday there was a committee meeting on. Suddenly there was a crash, all the lights went out, and the building rocked. Then the lights went on. "Well, gentlemen," said Eddy [Duke of] Devonshire, "I am not quite clear whether we elected that bugger or not."

It is sad on my return to see so many people sleeping on the tube platforms.

Diary   *March 10, 1944*

The Russians, this week, have launched three separate offensives in the Ukraine. They have, in one sector alone captured 500 tanks intact. It looks as if they managed to cope with the thaw while the Germans have been caught by it. Their ardour and skill are truly miraculous. When one considers that the Americans during the same week have made three devastating day raids on Berlin, one almost sympathizes with the Germans.

The miners' strike here continues and is creating much ill feeling. Public opinion at the moment is not good. They are exhausted by five years of war and do not stand things as well as they used to. The recent raids have created far more fear than the great blitz of 1940–1941. People dread another winter of war. But let us hope that the second front, when it comes, will again galvanize our energies.

H.N. to his sons   *March 19, 1944*

I went up to Leicester for my annual general meeting. I had to tell them what I should do if there were a General Election. I said that National Labour is over; that I would not go either Conservative or Labour; and that if they wanted to choose another candidate, they must let me know in time; otherwise I should stand as Independent with their support. So if they refuse to support me, I shall not fight the seat but stand somewhere else.

Diary   *March 27, 1944*

People seem to think that Winston's broadcast last night was that of a worn and petulant old man. I am sickened by the absence of gratitude. The fact is that the country is terribly war weary and that the ill-success of Anzio and Cassino is for them a sad augury of what will happen when the second front begins. The upper classes feel also that all this sacrifice and suffering will only mean that the proletariat will deprive them of all their comforts and influence and then proceed to render the country and the Empire a third-class State.

> On April 20, H.N. flew to Algiers for a speaking tour of North Africa.

Diary   *April 21, 1944*

I am warmly greeted [at Algiers] by Duff Cooper, who is I think delighted to see me. I am given luncheon – lobster and cold viands and vin rosé.

We dine with de Gaulle. It is getting dark, and as we enter the villa the white turbans of the Guard of Honour twinkle under the trees. Duff salutes gravely. We are received at the door by de Gaulle's a.d.c. The house is in the Moorish style, but is brilliantly lit by what is evidently an elaborate electric system just installed. We go in. De Gaulle greets me with what for him is almost warmth. Then I am greeted by André Gide, looking old and ill but as gay as a *perroquet*. Then Massigli [Commissioner for Foreign Affairs], and Bonnet (the Minister of Information) and Gaston Palweski [Chef du Cabinet]. The only other guests are [Albert] Marquet the painter and his wife. We go into dinner. Caviar eggs and sole and meringues. A good white wine. Very simple.

Massigli is enraged by the ban on diplomatic correspondence [imposed, that very day, by the British Government for security reasons]. He points out that it is all right for the other Allies, as they have their Governments in London. I have a long talk with de Gaulle. He is bitter about things, especially the ban. We go off early. I go to bed happy – not knowing whether today is yesterday or tomorrow.

Diary   *April 24, 1944*

I am woken by one of the batmen (who are in fact Mrs Ronald Greville's footmen heavily disguised in battle dress) bringing with him a huge glass of iced orange juice. I read an account of my lecture in the newspaper. Considering that they only print one sheet, they do me proud indeed. I then walk a bit in the garden. The roses are thick everywhere.

Duff comes back from his office and we drive in the smart ambassadorial car with flag flying to General Catroux's villa. He is Governor-General of Algeria and also one of the National Committee. He is most courteous. The ribbons on his tunic extend to four rows interrupted by many rosettes like the buttons on my wireless set. Duff and I had been somewhat apprehensive of this luncheon since the wireless this morning from Vichy had announced that Catroux's family had been arrested and would be held as hostages for any further Pucheu [Vichy Minister of Interior who had been executed on de Gaulle's orders] incidents. But Catroux shows no signs of anxiety or distress.

Catroux complains in a gentle way about the lack of discipline among the American troops. There are many "incidents". Our people, it seems, are better behaved. *"Vos Tommies aiment les enfants et les animaux. Ça nous touche."* I do my usual stunt of sticking up for the Yanks. But it is evident that the French here really hate them and dread their ignorant and amateurish interference in French affairs.

I go down to the University. The theatre is packed to the ceiling, but it is not a large theatre and the audience is nothing like as huge as it was yesterday. I lecture on "Proust and England". It was a lecture that I gave in 1936 in Paris when it proved a great success. But I can feel at once that they don't like it here. They do not like my making fun of their insularity; they do not really care about Proust.

Diary   *April 26, 1944*
                                                                Algiers

I go to see Harold Macmillan [Minister of State in Algiers], who arrived today from Naples. Harold greeted me with outstretched arms as if I had been his oldest and most intimate friend, which is not a fact. He showed me his reports on Giraud and de Gaulle. They are brilliantly written, but really brilliantly written, in the style of Macaulay. He describes how Giraud had every card in his hand and threw them away one by one. His only fault was lack of strength and his successive abandonment of his friends destroyed even his moral authority. His brain is nil. Of de Gaulle he wrote that he was conscious always that a Sieur de Gaulle had been one of Jeanne d'Arc's knights. This gave him that visionary and ecstatic attitude. Moreover he was deeply conscious of descending from a puritan and provincial milieu and this made him sensitive to ridicule.

H.N. to V.S-W.   *April 30, 1944*
                                          The British Embassy, Algiers

Oh My God! How I loved Tunis and how I revelled in walking in the footsteps of Niggs [who fought there a year before]. And how I longed for you to be there. I get irritated by people who are not interested in things. I rushed about like a spaniel, digging things out all the time. But the people there were rather indifferent.

Diary   *May 1, 1944*
                                                                  Algiers-Oran

We are to start at 7.30 a.m. and as I stand at the door with my luggage ready, a van arrives with two peacocks for Diana [Cooper]. They are carried off screaming loudly in the arms of two Italians.

Then we started off [from Algiers to Oran]. Our objective was Rélizane near Oran where I was to lunch and address the First Division *Blindée* of the French Army. We had arranged to be there by 12.30. But as we were skimming along the road at 11.0 there was a sudden sigh and our tyre went flat. We had no spare wheel and nothing to mend it with. We took off the tyre and examined the damage. The inner tube had a large rent. So there we sat. But eventually an American lorry came along. We thumbed them. They stopped and jumped off and with many jokes mended our tyre for us. They also gave us their rations. Nothing could have been more obliging or more gay than they were. But all this made us two hours late. Instead of arriving at 12.30 we arrived at 2.40. General de Vigier, who commands the Division, had made elaborate preparations. A banquet had been prepared in a tent erected over a swimming pool. And for my address a site had been prepared among the pine-trees. We were given a hurried and delicious luncheon. We then walked to the place where I was to speak. It was on the side of the pine-wood and some 800 officers and men had been drawn up in a semicircle.

I spoke to them without notes for some 45 minutes and they listened with extreme attention. Afterwards they crowded round me and asked questions. "Did I really think France would be treated as an equal after the war?" and so on. Pathetic and deeply moving it was to see those young clean faces and to note their anxiety. I spoke to them at length again and the General was delighted for me to do so. Then I was introduced to all the officers (including one of Giraud's sons) and we were given a drink before leaving. Of all the speeches I have ever made, that is the one which I shall never forget.

Diary   *May 18, 1944*
                                                                  London

We have a Secret Session about the hours of sitting. As it was not concerned with any essential war matter I may as well mention what happened. The Tories want to revert to our old hours, more or less, and sit from 2 to 9. The Labour people, who have wives cooking supper for them at Wimbledon and Wembley, wish to keep to our present hours. Behind it all there is a difference of principle as well as a difference of convenience. The Labour people tend to regard Parliament as a whole-time job and like to live at the House; the Tories regard it as a half-time job and like the morning free for other work. In fact the Tories are right, and the old system did diminish the professionalism of politicians and lead to a more worldly attitude, a more liberal attitude.

H.N. to his sons   *May 24, 1944*

I went to the House feeling rather hollow inside. Winston spoke for exactly one hour and a half. He went round the map of Europe and with amazing frankness told us of our relations with each of the Powers he named. To our surprise he went miles out of his way to shower roses and lilies upon Franco. To our regret he spoke of France, correctly, but in a cold, cold voice. He was as lucid as ever. There were here and there some of the old striking phrases. His humour and charm were unabated. But his voice was not thunderous and three times Members called out to him, "Speak up!" Then finally he sat down, and, as foreseen, 300 Members left for luncheon.

I bobbed up and my name was called. The first three minutes was a confusion of moving figures, and then the crowd cleared and I was left with about 100 Members on the benches. Winston sat there to my left, cocking his head forward, popping eyes up at me, as if to say, "What is the fellow going to say, poor chap?" But I managed all right and reproved him for his ill-treatment of small Powers and the snubs he gave to France. That was the theme set for criticism, and thereafter members of all Parties echoed my remarks. The French, of course, were delighted. Well, I bear many crosses, and the *Croix de la Libération* is not the least desirable.

On May 11, the day when H.N. returned from North Africa, General Alexander opened his offensive on the Italian front, which led to the capture of Rome on June 4. Two days later, the Allies landed in great force on the coast of Normandy, and on June 20 the Russians attacked in strength. Soon the Germans were in full retreat to Poland and Rumania. H.N. was lecturing to the Navy in its northern bases when he heard the news that Rome had fallen.

Diary　　　　　　　　　　　　　　　　　　　　June 5, 1944
　　　　　　　　　　　　　　　　　　　　　　　Scapa Flow

I come down to breakfast and find Colonel Simpson there. He looked up at me and said in his Caithness accent, "Heard the news? We entered Rome at 11 p.m. last night." Well, I never.

Diary　　　　　　　　　　　　　　　　　　　　June 6, 1944

I turned on the 9.0 a.m. news in the General Forces Programme – and heard to my excitement the following announcement: "The German Overseas News has just put out the following flash. 'Early this morning the expected Anglo-American invasion began when airborne forces were landed in the Seine estuary . . .'" I then wait till a later flash which says "The combined landing operations comprised the whole area between Havre and Cherbourg, the main centre of attack being the Caen area."

I go down to the House, arriving there at about ten to twelve. When I enter the Chamber, I find a buzz of conversation going on. Questions had ended unexpectedly early and people were just sitting there chatting, waiting for Winston. It was an unusual scene. He entered the Chamber at three minutes to twelve. He looked as white as a sheet. The House noticed this at once, and we feared that he was about to announce some terrible disaster. He is called immediately, and places two separate fids of typescript on the table. He begins with the first, which is about Rome. Alexander gets a really tremendous cheer. He ends with the words, "This great and timely operation," stressing the word "timely" with a rise of the voice and that familiar bending of the two knees. He then picks up his other fid of notes and begins, "I have also to announce to the House that during the night and early hours of this morning, the first of a series of landings in force upon the Continent of Europe has taken place . . ." The House listens in hushed awe. He speaks for only seven minutes.

Diary   *June 7, 1944*

Dine at the Beefsteak. Bruce Lockhart is there. He tells me that
there was terrible difficulty again between de Gaulle and Winston.
De Gaulle insisted upon being allowed to land troops in France.
Winston wrote him a letter saying, "The aeroplane which I placed
at your disposal will be ready to take you back to Algiers tomorrow."
Anthony [Eden] prevented this being sent. Then there was a row
about de Gaulle's broadcast. The Americans refused to drop
leaflets in his name over France. In the end all these difficulties were
surmounted, but only when Anthony had been dragged from his
bed at 4.0 a.m.

H.N. to his sons   *June 11, 1944*

You will want to know the general atmosphere during invasion
week. First, at Sissinghurst. It is literally dominated by aeroplanes.
All night they howl and rage above us. Then in daytime there is
also much activity: great fleets of bombers floating slowly above us
in the empyrean, their drone being a throb all round us. Otherwise
the trains run on time, the papers come the same, everything is the
same. We listen intently to the wireless at all hours.

In London it is different. There are people who ring up under the
illusion (a) that I have inside knowledge, and (b) that if I had it, I
should repeat it over the telephone. There is a continual crowd
around the ticker-tape in the House of Commons corridor. There
are all sorts of rumours buzzing through the smoking-room. And
there is the hourly expectation that Winston may make another
statement. Newspapers are snatched up the moment they appear
on the streets. People are relieved that it has begun. They scan the
weather a little more acutely than usual, and notice the direction of
the wind. But on the whole they are all amazingly calm.

Diary   *June 14, 1944*

There certainly have been mysterious rocket-planes [the V.1]
falling in Kent. The thing is very hush at the moment.

H.N. to V.S-W.   *June 15, 1944*

*Poor de Gaulle. He must have hated his longed-for visit to French
soil. It was very rough and he had a bad crossing. Then to find the

population dazed and bewildered and the little villages in flames cannot have been much fun for him.*

Diary   *June 19, 1944*

The German propaganda is making a great deal of its secret weapon [V.1] and putting out stories of the evacuation of London, of panic, of vast explosions and of a pall hanging over the city which does not enable the Luftwaffe to take photographs. I see no signs of all this. My train arrives on time, there are buses running as usual, and I can see no difference in the streets. One of the robot planes fell near the Law Courts and smashed many windows. Another fell in Tottenham Court Road. Another fell yesterday full on the Guards Chapel while there was a service. The worst effect is that it deprives people of sleep.

Diary   *June 25, 1944*

In the 9 o'clock news we hear that the Germans put out at 7.30 that Cherbourg had fallen. Nothing official. But reporters say that the Americans have entered the town. The doodle-bugs begin just before 9 and we hear five explosions all round us. The sixth seems to get away. The Spitfires on patrol circle around us all the time. I do not feel they are factors of protection: I feel they are elements of danger.

Diary   *June 28, 1944*

*Have a talk with Hinchingbrooke. He tells me that the Tory Reformers are getting into increasingly bad odour with the heads of the Conservative Party and that they are considering acquiring allies outside. What is my position and the position of National Labour generally? I say that Nat. Lab. as such has ceased to exist. I myself, were I free, would stand as a Liberal, but not being free I shall stand as Independent. I should never call myself a Tory. He asks whether I should be ready to attend their meetings. I say certainly I should if it were quite clear that I should be with them but not of them.

Have a talk with Brendan Bracken. He said that the Cabinet last night discussed the doodle-bug for three hours. Their main problem is that the blast effect is so devastating that countless little houses are rendered uninhabitable. There are as many as 235,000 such houses gone in the last fortnight.*

Diary *July 5, 1944*

Anthony [Eden] tells me about his bitter battles on behalf of de Gaulle. The Prime Minister had invited de Gaulle to come over here for the big battle of France. On June 4 Winston and he had gone down in a special train to near Portsmouth where they waited. De Gaulle and his party came there by car and Anthony went to meet them. They then lunched in the train and Winston produced champagne and drank to the health of France. Roosevelt had said that de Gaulle was not to be told the plan of operations but Winston ignored that, told him everything, took him across to see Eisenhower and forced the latter to show him the maps. Not one word of thanks from de Gaulle. Winston, feeling rather hurt, said to him, "I thought it only fitting that you should be present with us today." "I see," said de Gaulle glumly, "I was invited as a symbol." Viénot and Béthouard were in despair. Anthony was almost beside himself, feeling that Winston was deeply moved emotionally by the thought of the occasion, and that de Gaulle's ungraciousness would make him dislike the man all the more. Finally Winston asked de Gaulle to dine with him. "Thank you – I should prefer to dine alone with my staff." "I feel chilled," Winston said to Anthony.

Anthony went on to say that his great difficulty throughout has been that Winston is half American and that he regards Roosevelt with almost religious awe. Anthony does not share these feelings; he regards Roosevelt as an astute politician and a man of great personal vanity and obstinacy. Thus over this de Gaulle business Winston and Anthony have had terrible rows.

Anthony says that he cannot understand why the Germans have brought so many troops to the West. I say it is because they do not believe that the Russians will go outside what they consider their own borders. "But even the Germans can't think that," he said. "They must know more or less that the whole zones of occupation were settled in Tehran." He also thinks the war will be over soon.

"Luckily," he said, "we have now reached full agreement regarding the armistice terms. They are ready to be delivered at any moment."

Diary   *July 10, 1944*

I find that K.B.W. has been slightly blasted while I have been away. The panelling has been smashed again, the pictures fell down without breaking, and curiously enough this typewriter was twisted in its mechanism and had to be coached back to work again. Miss Niggeman devises a wonderful scheme by which the steel filing cabinet plus a mattress is put between me and my bedroom windows. I shall sleep more or less secure from powdered glass.

Diary   *July 21, 1944*

Hitler broadcast to Germany at 1 a.m. this morning to the effect that a bomb had been placed in his room by Colonel Graf von Stauffenberg, and that although one of his staff had been killed and others injured, he himself was unhurt. He adds, "What fate would have been in store for Germany had this attempt on my life succeeded is too horrible to think of."

Diary   *July 24, 1944*

At 4.45 this morning I am suddenly awakened by the sound of a flying bomb zooming over my head. As I hear it (a few seconds only) it cuts out and I know that it is about to descend. I bury my head in my pillow and then comes quite a small crash and no sense of blast through the room. But a second later I hear things falling and splintering in my sitting-room and I get up to look. The shutters have been thrown open and the iron bars smashed out. Only one pane is broken. All of my pictures have come down and two of them are broken. My lovely apothecary pot with lilies in it is also destroyed. I put on my great coat and go out into the court. They tell me that it has fallen in Essex Street. I notice a thick soup-like haze in the air and all today my eyes have been red and smarting. I go back to bed and sleep.

Diary   *August 5, 1944*

I had realised that today I must walk up and down the lime walk
considering what book I should write. I do not feel in tune for a
sequence to *In Search of the Past* since it all seems so meaningless in
face of current events. I think vaguely that I might do a book on the
Vienna Congress.

Diary   *August 15, 1944*

I turn on the 1 o'clock news and hear the bald announcement that
we have landed in the South of France between Nice and Marseilles.
The announcement is followed by the strains of the *Marseillaise*.

Diary   *August 23, 1944*

I am working at my notes on the Congress of Vienna and have just
reached the point where the Allies enter Paris. I look up and see it is
already 1 p.m. and I dash up to Viti's bedroom to listen to the news.
It takes some time before the juice gets through so I come into the
middle of the first sentence: ". . . fifty thousand armed men with the
assistance of many thousands of the unarmed population. By noon
yesterday all the official buildings were in the hands of the F.F.I.
[the Resistance]. Paris is free." I am so excited that I scarcely notice
that we have taken Grenoble.

   Viti rushes across to share the excitement. I have a hurried bathe
and am back in the dining room in time to hear the French 1.30 news.
They give it quite moderately. Miss Niggeman, who is down for the
day, manufactured a French flag and stuck it upon the greengages.
Mrs Staples [the cook] said, "How glad I am they did it themselves,"
which is characteristic of our deep spirit of generosity. All of us
(including Mrs Staples) have a glass of gin and toast the future of
France.

Diary   *September 8, 1944*

I take the 3.15 home [from London]. I find the proofs of my book
Friday Mornings. These are reprints of my articles in the *Spectator*.
I wish now that I had never agreed to publish them. They use up

paper which might have gone to some young writer publishing a new book. Silly of me.

It is evident that there is a pause in our advance. The Germans are beginning to recover from the shock and are resisting quite well on the Albert Canal, the Meuse and the Moselle. Meanwhile our armies are grouping for the second round – the Battle of Germany. Meanwhile, also, the Russians and Marshal Tito have cut off all the Germans in the Balkans.

Diary   *September 17, 1944*

At 1 o'clock we hear that we have landed a huge airborne army in Holland behind the German lines [at Arnhem]. It is the largest force ever sent by air.

Diary   *September 27, 1944*

Rob Bernays says, "I hope what I've heard is not true?" "What have you heard?" He says, "That you are thinking of going to the Lords." Now if he had heard this from Oliver Stanley or someone of that sort I should be quite prepared to believe that this was a tentative suggestion from on high. But I suspect that it is one of Sibyl's little plans. Anyhow I said, "I should love to go to the Lords but I see little prospect of it." He said, "But you never realise that you are a national figure" (pause) "of the s-s-s-s-s-second d-d-d-d-d-degree."

Diary   *September 29, 1944*

I cancel my engagements in the morning and concentrate upon what I am to say this afternoon. Winston had said that we would not recognise the Provisional Government [in France] until they were responsible to a "Legislative" Assembly. That taken literally means that only after a general election shall we accord recognition and that means two years from now. What he ought to have said is "Representative" assembly. I then go to the House. The Speaker (who is amazingly kind and useful – unlike old grouchy Fitzroy who kept one in uncertainty on purpose) tells me that he will call me after luncheon. I make a fairly good speech. But the value is that Anthony, in his reply, takes up two of my points and gives definite assurances. (1) Bulgaria will not be given Greek or Yugoslav territory; (2) The French Provisional Government will be recognised as soon as the Consultative Assembly has been turned into a Representative Assembly; (3) France will become an "equal and potent" partner in the reconstruction of Europe. These are important assurances. I am very pleased.

Diary   *October 4, 1944*

To the House. I find that people are really horrified at the collapse of the resisters at Warsaw and feel that Russia has behaved abominably. Moreover the idea is gaining ground that Russia is seeking to establish herself in the Balkans and has given up all idea of fighting the Germans in East Prussia. Anthony does not share this pessimism. But nonetheless distrust of the Russians is universal.

H.N. to his sons   *October 9, 1944*

At 5 p.m. Attlee rose to make a statement. He announced that he was glad to inform the House that Winston and Anthony had arrived safe and sound in Moscow. Now, such a statement, a year ago, would have provoked a burst of cheering especially from the Labour benches. But there was a hush and a mutter instead. I thought at first that this was due to the fact that Holy Russia is momentarily in disgrace for her conduct of the Warsaw business. But it wasn't that. It was merely that people are worried about Winston's health. It is difficult to conceive the personal affection which Winston enjoys among all Members of the House.

H.N. to his sons   *October 19, 1944*

I went to St Paul's for the service to commemorate the liberation of Athens. It was a service conducted jointly by the Church of England and the Greek Orthodox. For the Church of England there was the Bishop of London arrayed in a terrific cope, surrounded by the Dean and Chapter in purple and gold and accompanied by an orderly dressed in scarlet who carried his crozier. For the Orthodox Church there was my little friend the Archbishop of Thyateira, whom I know so well as a member of my Greek Relief Committee. On these occasions, when we meet under the chairmanship of Irene Ravensdale, it is a small round mousy prelate who sits there saying,

"Yes, Madame German: no, Madame German." But in St Paul's I was faced by the semblance of God the Father in all his majesty. Arrayed in gold, surmounted by a huge black head-dress, grasping a crozier in the shape of those walking-sticks we bought at Olympia, he sailed along majestically, his chin thrust out in vigour, the great amethyst cross on his bosom catching countless reflections from the lights, and his train carried by an elderly gentleman in a frayed white dressing-gown and pince-nez, who did not look like a Byzantine deacon or archimandrite, but like a shipping-clerk from Nauplia.

There we all were – the King of Greece, the Duchess of Kent, the Ambassadors and Generals and the Greek choir from Bayswater who were hidden behind a screen. The Bishop of London said, "Brethren, we are met today to return thanks to God . . ." and so on, all in a very Church of England voice. Then we knelt down and were told to give thanks unto the Lord our God, to which we replied in a general murmur, "It is meet and right so to do." I was becoming bored at this stage, and was startled from my day-dream by a loud ululation which echoed through the dome and sent the pigeons outside scurrying in panic. My little Archbishop of Thyateira had reached the microphone and let forth a loud Greek cry. A second time he yelled aloud through the microphone, and then from behind the screen the Greek Choir began intoning *Kyrie eleison! Kyrie eleison!* to which the British choir responded, "Lord, have mercy upon us", after which the Bishop of London took off his cope, handed it to his orderly, climbed the pulpit arrayed in lawn sleeves and delivered an address which was so inadequate as to be almost unbearable.

As I walked out, I felt my arm gripped from behind. It was the Lord Chancellor. "You and I, my dear Harold, could have devised that a trifle better, I think. A passage from Simonides, perhaps, or even a few words from the funeral oration?" God, what a toad and a worm Simon is!

Diary   *October 20, 1944*

*Go up to Leicester. I am taken out to the suburbs where a course is established for officers going to Germany on a Control Commission. I lecture to them on the "German Way of Life". I dine in the Mess afterwards and then listen to the 9 p.m. news. The Brigadier was called out but on his return he says, "Well, any news?" "No,

Sir, nothing of importance." "Steady on!" I say, "we heard of the capture of Belgrade, Aachen, Dubrovnik and the American landing in the Philippines." It wasn't liked. But I am always astounded at the ignorance of serving officers about anything not within their immediate orbit.*

Diary   *November 8, 1944*

The American election results come in all day and at 11 a.m. it is clear that Roosevelt has won. Tommy [Lascelles, the King's Private Secretary] tells me that the King was so delighted that he wished to send him a telegram. But Tommy suggested that it would be unconstitutional.

Diary   *November 14, 1944*

Anthony makes a statement in the House regarding his visit to Paris. Winston only gets back later in the day having been to visit the Vosges front in a dreadful snow storm. I have a talk with Anthony in the Lobby afterwards. He tells me that when they drove up to the Arc de Triomphe, the crowd did not recognise Winston in his Air Force uniform and that it was only when he came back and they saw him walking with de Gaulle that they realised who he was. I asked him whether de Gaulle was better as a host than as a guest and he replied "Yes, I *think* he was, but anyhow he was a very stiff host." He added that not for one minute did Winston stop crying and that he could have filled buckets by the time he received the Freedom of Paris. He said it was really amazing the way crowds sprang up wherever they went and the way they really yelled for Churchill as he has never heard any crowd yell before.

Diary   *December 8, 1944*

*I have to chuck all my engagements since there is a three line whip on the Greek situation. The Debate is opened at 11. Winston gets up. He is not good. He is like a spaniel who is diverted by the smell of a rabbit and dashes off wildly into the bracken. He keeps on being "drawn" by the Opposition. I am called at 3.22 and speak till 3.42. It goes well and I get more cheering than I have yet had. Then Anthony winds up in a really excellent way giving a most conclusive account of our attitude towards the Papandreou's [provisional Greek] Government.

In the smoking-room afterwards Winston comes across and congratulates me. He was especially pleased at my referring to [Count] Sforza as "an elderly peacock."*

Diary   *December 11, 1944*

*I have one of my rare outbursts of *wutanfall*. It all arose because rising early and going over to the Priest's House where I have to shave, I found that someone had taken away my razor blade. Thus I had to come all the way back to the South Cottage. And this convinced me how bitter it was to inhabit a house which was so cold and draughty and which entailed having to shave in a distant cottage and in the guest's bathroom. Sissinghurst is almost intolerably uncomfortable in winter.*

Diary   *December 21, 1944*

I am writing this diary when the telephone rings. A young man says that Ben was knocked down by a lorry on December 15 and injured his head. He is in hospital and they think he will be there for four weeks. No permanent injury reported.

Diary   *December 22, 1944*

*The news of Rundstedt's offensive [against the Allied line in the Ardennes] is slightly better this evening. He appears to have got 40 miles inside the American lines but has been halted on the flanks. Eisenhower has issued an order of the day to his troops saying that we must turn this defeat into a victory. The news from Athens is very bad I fear. All peace negotiations seem to have broken down and fighting is increasing in severity.

Viti is quite calm about Ben.*

Diary   *December 28, 1944*

It is the coldest Christmas we have had for 54 years. But it is bright and clear and bombers stream over on their way to Belgium.

The news is better. Winston has left Athens [he arrived on

Christmas Day], having been shot at by a sniper and used the expression "Cheek!" In the Ardennes and Belgium we seem to have held Rundstedt some seven miles from the Meuse and to have relieved Bastogne. The Germans are beginning to blame "the unprecedently fine weather" for their failure to achieve a complete break-through.

Diary   *December 31, 1944*

The end of 1944. A wonderful year marked by the most successful military operation we have ever undertaken. But a year in which internal dissension and distrust have much increased. A year saddened towards its end by Viti's arthritis, which I fear will become a permanent affliction. And by Ben's accident.

> *1945 began with some disappointments. Germany's offensive in the Ardennes, though eventually unsuccessful, created disharmony in the Allied command. Russia began to control the countries which she was overrunning in Eastern Europe, specially Poland. And there remained the question of Japan.*

Diary   *January 1, 1945*

Viti and I hear the new year in crouching over the fire in the dining-room. I turn on Berlin, the *Deutschlandsender*, and then Hamburg – and we get Hitler's horrible but quite unmistakable voice. The reception is not good and he gabbles off his piece so fast that I may have missed something. But it seemed to consist entirely about reflections upon Germany's fate if she loses her moral staunchness, about the fate of the satellites who have dropped out, about the strength of the Führung, on the need for unanimity, on the *sein oder nicht sein* theme.

Diary   *January 12, 1945*

*To Leicester. A trail of visitors. A man who wants me to get his boy to study dentistry, a man who wants my advice as to whether he should settle in the Bahamas, a man who wants me to allow

Jehovah's Witnesses to import their newspapers from the U.S.A., a man who is worried about the effect of Beveridge on friendly societies, and then three boys from Burma who are worried about their leave. They say that the Japs are brave but incompetent; in the jungle they are so frightened at night that they give away their position by calling out to each other. Rather exhausted by all this.*

Diary   *January 18, 1945*

There is a big debate opened by Winston on the war situation. He begins by warning us that he has a cold but in fact he is in as good form as I have ever seen him. In dealing with the question of un-conditional surrender he indicates that this will not mean the extermination of the German people. At this he takes off his glasses and swings round to the House, hitting his chest with his hand like an orang-outang. "We remain bound," he shouts, "by our own customs and our own nature."

Diary   *January 25, 1945*

I chuck my B.B.C. Board since we have a debate in the House on the reconstruction of the Commons Chamber. Winston made a short speech recommending the report. There is an amendment saying that we ought to have thrown the thing open to competition. In theory I agree that it is unimaginative and feeble to make a 1945 copy of an 1834 copy of an assumed Gothic original. But I do not see what the alternative is. We would be more incongruous if we adopted Charles II or Regency. Therefore the only alternative is modern. And modern, admirable though it is for hospitals etc., is not good as yet for domestic interiors. I make a speech to that effect.

Diary   *January 26, 1945*

Lunch at the Beefsteak with Christopher Sykes [the author]. He has been back to the area of the Ardennes to identify the bodies of his fellow paratroopers who were murdered in the woods by the Germans. It was a horrible business. He says the French peasants really love us mainly because they hate the Americans so much. I then go to Hatchards and send some art books to Ben.

Coming away I buy a copy of the *Evening Standard* and read

that Rob Bernays is missing in a 'plane over Italy [he had been on Parliamentary delegation to Italy, and his 'plane crashed over the Adriatic]. This knocks me silly. I go on to the House where I find gloom and apprehension. I gather from Anthony [Eden] that there is mighty little hope. I feel crushed by this. I go to bed feeling sore and sad about Rob. All my best House of Commons friends are now dead – Rob, Ronnie Cartland, and Jack Macnamara.

H.N. to V.S-W. *February 7, 1945*

There has been another 'plane accident. This time it occurred to one of the machines bringing the F.O. and War Cabinet staff to the Three Power Conference [at Yalta in the Crimea]. They lost their way and crashed near Lampedusa. About a third of them were rescued, but two-thirds were drowned. Moreover all the papers and maps are now at the bottom of the Mediterranean and it will cast a gloom over the Conference. It will do more than that. It will raise a stink in the House about War Transport. They say, of course, that in ordinary circumstances no airman would have taken the risk of flying in such weather, and that it was only the urgency of the thing that forced them to act dangerously. But all the same, if we cannot secure the safety of these key people, then nobody will travel after the war by British airlines. Already it is said that people prefer American pilots.

Diary *February 12, 1945*

Morgan Forster came round to the club. I found he was worried about the attitude which a progressive should adopt. He feels that in the Spanish issue it was clear where the right side lay and where the wrong. But he is not clear about Greece. Nor is he happy about Russian deportations in Poland. I say that it is a mistake to interpret Foreign Affairs in terms of right or left – but I do not comfort him.

Diary *February 15, 1945*

I go to the House and attend a Committee meeting about Polish deportees. There are about three escaped Poles there who tell us their stories. 1,230,000 Poles have been deported and only 9% of them got away afterwards. One really lovely woman tells us how her father, a bank manager, herself and her mother were put in cattle trucks and sent off to Kazan where they were made to work on the land and live with the Kalmuks. Her father disappeared. Another man tells us that he was in prison for eight months in Moscow on no charge. [J. B.] Hynd asks them what suspicion they had against them? The woman answers that she was a member of a Catholic Society called "The Daughters of the Virgin Mary", and they kept on bothering her to find out what political basis there was to this society. The other says she had travelled and learnt languages. They said to her, "But you cannot expect us to believe that anyone travels for anything but a political motive?" All this is convincing and profoundly disturbing.

Diary   *February 21, 1945*

Lunch at the Beefsteak. Gladwyn Jebb is there having returned from the Crimea Conference. Gladwyn says that at Yalta he and the staff were put in a sort of Convalescent Home which was crawling with bugs, and that Lord Moran [Churchill's doctor] came down with disinfectants in the hope of saving them from typhus. He says that President Roosevelt was an utterly changed man since he had last seen him. Not only did he look 20 years older, but that he was scarcely able to speak and that he reminded him of Ramsay Mac-Donald in the last year of his life. Gladwyn naturally defends the decisions of the Conference but disclaims all responsibility for what happened later in Cairo. It looks as if Winston had repudiated all our pledges both to the French and to the Jews.

Diary   *February 27, 1945*

I put on my new brown suit. Go down to the House fairly early. It is more crowded than I have ever seen it. Winston opens punctually at 12 and we adjourn for an hour at luncheon and he continues afterwards. He goes on to talk about the San Francisco Conference [which drafted the U.N. charter] and the general problems of the control of Germany. He then talks about Poland. He makes an extremely good case for arguing that Poland, in her new frontiers, will enjoy an independent and prosperous existence. But in his closing words before luncheon he rather destroys all this by saying that we will offer British citizenship to those Polish soldiers who are too frightened to return. The extreme Tories rush about getting signatures for an amendment expressing regret at the Polish provisions.

Buck De la Warr is there and I take him out for a drink. We are joined by Winston who, for once in his life does not seem to be in the least bit of a hurry. "Collins," he says, "you will give me a large brandy. I deserve it." He then shakes himself contentedly and begins talking. He is really very sensible. He says that he does not see what else he could possibly do. "Not only are they [the Russians] very powerful, but they are on the spot; even the massed majesty of the British Empire would not avail to turn them off that spot." Moreover, he said, it seemed to him a mistake to assume that the Russians were going to behave badly. Ever since he had been in close relations with Stalin, the latter had kept his word with the utmost loyalty. During the three weeks of the Greek crisis for instance, a single article in *Pravda* would have tipped the whole balance, but Stalin kept an obstinate silence which was of immense value to us. At the mention of Greece his whole face lit up, and he put his hand on my arm. "I have had great moments in my life," he said, "but never such a moment as when faced with that half-million crowd in Constitution Square [on February 14]. You will understand that." I asked him whether he thinks it would be indiscreet of me to say that the test of the Crimean resolution will be whether or not Mikolajczyk and Romer [the ex-Prime Minister and Foreign Minister of the exiled Polish Government in London] are invited to Moscow. He thinks for a moment and then says, "Yes, that would be a good thing. I could not say that, but you can." As he goes, he says, with his funny schoolboy grin, "I hope in your speech to-morrow you will not attack me very bitterly. I count you among my firmest friends."

H.N. to V.S-W.   *February 28, 1945*

I telephoned to you this evening to say that I had made my speech. I was fussed about it. I was not quite clear where my conscience was. Emotionally I feel for the Poles very deeply. As you know, I think the Russians imperialistic and unscrupulous. But on the other hand I really do believe that Winston and Anthony did save Poland from a fate far more terrible than might otherwise have been hers. I was absolutely sure in my own inner heart and mind that the Yalta decisions were not expedient only, but ultimately to the benefit of the Poles and mankind. So I supported these decisions with complete ease of mind and conscience.

I was called late in the debate on purpose and for that reason my speech will not *read* very well as it was replying to all manner of cross-currents which had been ebbing and flowing. Moreover my throat was very hoarse (too many cigarettes) and I spoke inaudibly. But apart from that, it was, I think the most effective speech I have made. Afterwards in the smoking-room Winston took his glass up from where he was sitting and crossed the room to sit beside me. He said, "Harold, you made a powerful speech. A most powerful speech. You swung votes. I thank you. I congratulate you. I give you" (and here he made a sort of offering gesture) "my congratulations. I only wish that I could also have given you one of my throat lozenges. Excellent they are. That horrible man, Lord Moran, who bullies the life out of me, prescribed them."

Darling, you don't think I am being boastful and silly do you? It is simply that when one is successful one feels warm inside, and you are the only person in the world to whom I can say these things without seeming silly or caring even if I do.

Diary   *March 1, 1945*

As we [Anthony Eden and H.N.] were walking to our seats through the tangle of the smoking-room we passed the *Evening News* spread out over the back of an arm chair. It bore the headlines "Tanks mass for Cologne". Anthony tapped it as he passed with the back of his fingers. "I think it is almost over, Harold." "What – the offensive?" "No – my dear – the WAR."

H.N. to his sons   *March 11, 1945*

On 2nd March, after the debate, I went to Paris. As I stepped ashore from the steamer at Dieppe, I bent down and touched the soil of France with a sacerdotal gesture. *"Monsieur a laissé tomber quelque chose?"* asked my porter. *"Non,"* I replied, *"j'ai retrouvé quelque chose."* I told this story to Jean Marin next day, and he relayed it on the *Radiodiffusion Française*. I am not quite sure that I was pleased by this.

Diary March 19, 1945

It has turned cold again. In the afternoon Viti and I tidy up Ben's room and then go to meet him. He comes by the 4.34. Mr Harvey [the station-master], hearing that a wounded soldier is to arrive, mobilises all the porters. They rush to his carriage and his tall thin figure emerges wrapped in dirty bandages. His plaster is right over his chin and up his back [he had broken two dorsal vertebrae]. He has a tremendous heavy dragoon moustache. But he seems to suffer no pain. He says that the last two and a half years have been among the happiest in his life. So that is a comfort.

Diary March 28, 1945

We have funeral orations for Lloyd George [who died two days before]. I meet Winston in the smoking-room and ask him whether the news is as good as it seems. "We have nothing in front of us," he says. But owing to the blackout on troop movements we do not know where people have got to and there are fantastic reports flying round. What we all dread is that the Führer will gather all his followers and S.S. and S.A. into the Bavarian highlands and surround them with all our prisoners of war. He will then say "Come on and do your damndest." If Patton could only get to Nüremberg in time he might prevent this plan.

I am elected Chairman of the Anglo-French Interparliamentary Committee.

H.N. to N.N. April 1, 1945

Ben and I came down here by the afternoon train. Like a wounded camel Ben stalked down the platform at Charing Cross. The train was crowded with people leaving for their Easter holidays. We found a carriage in which all the corner-seats were occupied, but in which two middle seats were vacant. Ben, with a wince of suffering nobly borne, lowered himself into the seat opposite me. Beside him was a Major-General covered in decorations. He gazed at Ben in a comradely way, as one soldier to another. Observing the pangs of agony which from time to time would pass over Ben's face, he addressed him politely. "Let us exchange places," he said. "I feel you might be more comfortable in a corner-seat." "I am sure I should," said Ben contentedly, and took his place. Not a word about thank-you or "Sir" or anything like that. Just a stricken warrior relapsing with relief into the comfortable seat vacated by an unstricken warrior. Ben closed his eyes for a moment, indicating gratitude and a momentary release from pain. The train started and at Tonbridge we got out. It was a disgraceful proceeding, since in fact Ben suffers nothing at all except an occasional itch.

H.N. to V.S-W. *April 13, 1945*

I woke up to hear the Composer of the Week, then Lift up Your Hearts and then the awful news about Roosevelt [who died from a stroke on April 12]. It is really a disaster. I feel deeply for Winston and this afternoon it was evident from his manner that he had had a real body-blow. Under that bloody American Constitution they have now to put up with the Vice President [Truman] who was actually chosen because he was a colourless and harmless man. He may, as Coolidge did [in 1923], turn out to be a person of character. But I have not heard any man say one good word in his favour. AND when one thinks of the problems ahead it is a misery that this has happened.

Diary *April 27, 1945*

I dine at the Grand [Hotel, Leicester] and listen to the news after-wards. It is pretty startling. The American and Russian forces linked up on Wednesday [April 25] afternoon at Torgau on the Elbe. Messages are relayed from Churchill, Truman and Stalin. It is odd to hear the latter's voice echoing through the lounge of the Grand Hotel. The Russians have completely encircled Berlin and taken Spandau and Potsdam. They are in the Tiergarten. The Germans insist that Hitler and Goebbels are still in the capital and it may in fact be true that they wish to do their final suicide act in Berlin. Thus the capture of Berlin means the end.

Diary *April 30, 1945*

It has snowed again very hard during the night and the lilac is weighted with great puffs of snow looking very odd. It is very evi-dent that we shall accept an offer of surrender from Himmler and that it may come at any moment. Meanwhile the news of Mussolini's murder is confirmed. He was caught near Como and murdered.

H.N. to N.N.   *May 1, 1945*

We had really dreadful photographs of his [Mussolini's] corpse and that of his mistress hanging upside down and side by side. They looked like turkeys hanging outside a poulterer's: the slim legs of the mistress and the huge stomach of Mussolini could both be detected. It was a most unpleasant picture and caused a grave reaction in his favour. It was truly ignominious – but Mrs Groves [H.N.'s housekeeper] said that he deserved it thoroughly, "a married man like that driving about in a car with his mistress."

I dined at Pratts. Lionel Berry was there (the son of Lord Kemsley) who told us that the German wireless had been putting out *Achtungs* about an *ernste wichtige Meldung*, and playing dirges in between. So we tried and failed to get the German wireless stations with the horrible little set which is all that Pratts can produce. Having failed to do this, we asked Lionel to go upstairs to telephone to one of his numerous newspapers, and he came running down again (it was 10.40) to say that Hitler was dead and Doenitz had been appointed his successor. Then Ben and I returned to King's Bench Walk and listened to the German midnight news. It was all too true. *"Unser Führer, Adolf Hitler, ist . . ."* – and then a long digression about heroism and the ruin of Berlin – *". . . gefallen."* So that was Mussolini and Hitler within two days. Not a bad bag as bags go.

Diary   *May 2, 1945*

I dine with Mrs George Keppel at the Ritz. I sit between Lady Moncrieff and Ava Anderson. I lean across to Cartier [de Marchienne, Belgian Ambassador in London] and say, "Well, Mr Ambassador, I saw you in the House this afternoon, expecting a statement by the Prime Minister which never came." "But it came tonight," said Ava. "What came?" And then she told me that Churchill had come in at 7.30 and told the House that the whole German and Italian forces in Italy and the Tyrol had surrendered unconditionally to Alexander. I get [Sir] John Anderson to repeat it carefully. I feel quite ecstatic. It is almost incredible.

Diary May 5, 1945

*Further German armies have surrendered and the patriots have
risen in Prague. Doenitz has announced that it is "senseless" to go
on fighting the Americans and ourselves, but that they must still
fight Russia.*

Diary May 7, 1945

3 p.m. and the news. It says that an hour ago Schwerin von Krosigk
[Doenitz's Foreign Minister] had spoken on the wireless from Flensburg [on the Danish border]. He has said that Germany was obliged
to surrender unconditionally, crushed by the overwhelming might
of her enemies. Ben and I dash off to tell Vita who is in the courtyard. The three of us climb the turret stairs, tie the flag on to the
ropes, and hoist it in the soft south-west breeze. It looks very proud
and gay after five years of confinement.

Diary May 8, 1945

*V.E. day. Lunch at the Beefsteak. Up till then everything had been
normal, but I then find the streets very crowded and people wearing
all manner of foolish paper caps and cheering slightly. When I
leave the club at 2.15, I find the roads packed. Trafalgar Square is a
seething mass of people with figures draped all over the lions. Whitehall is overflowing, but a few buses try to push their way through.
After the Cenotaph it is just a jam. I squeeze in behind a car and
manage to reach the House about 5 to three. I pause to recover myself in Palace Yard and regret to observe that I have torn a hole in
my new suit. The crowds are packed against the railing and the
mounted police have difficulty in clearing a path for the Government
cars. Then came the great strokes of Big Ben and thereafter an immense hush. From the loudspeakers in Parliament Square Winston's
voice booms out to all those thousands. It echoes on the Palace behind me so that I hear it doubly. He tells of the signature of surrender
and its impending ratification in Berlin. He is short and effective.
The crowd cheer when he finishes and when *God Save the King* has
been broadcast. But it is not frantic cheering.

I then enter the House. The place is packed and I sit on the step below the cross bench. I see a stir at the door and Winston comes in – a little shy – a little flushed – but smiling boyishly. The House jumps to its feet, and there is one long roar of applause. He bows and smiles in acknowledgement. I glance up at the Gallery where Clemmy [Churchill] should be. There is Mrs Neville Chamberlain there instead. And thereupon Winston begins. He repeats the short statement he had just made on the wireless ending up with "Advance Britannia" and then he lays his manuscript aside and with more gesture and emphasis than is customary to him, he thanks the House for its support throughout these years. He then proposes that we adjourn to the Church of St Margaret's Westminster. The Speaker then leaves his seat and the mace is fetched before him. He is in Court Robes with gold facings to his gown and his Chaplain and the Sergeant-at-Arms are also in full dress.

We file out by the St Stephen's entrance and the police have kept a lane through the crowd. The crowd are friendly, recognising some of the Members. I am with Nancy Astor who is, I feel, a trifle hurt that she does not get more cheering. We then have a service – and very memorable it is. The supreme moment is when the chaplain reads out the names of those Members of Parliment who have lost their lives. It is a sad thing to hear. My eyes fill with tears. I hope that Nancy does not notice. "Men are so emotional," she says.

We all go to the smoking-room. Winston comes with us. Passing through Central Hall he is given an ovation by the crowd. They clap their hands. A tiny little boy, greatly daring, dashes up to him and asks for an autograph. Winston solemnly takes out his glasses and signs. He then pats the delighted little boy on the head and grins his grin.

I have difficulty in getting to the Travellers afterwards as all the roads are closed. I eventually get there by going round by Berkeley Square. In the downstairs room we listen to the King's speech at 9. The words are excellent and he does not stammer too badly. Then off I go to a party at Chips Channon's after calling in at Pratts. I wish I had not gone to that party. The Amalienburg room is lit by candles and all the Nürembergers and Munichois were there. I sit with Sibyl and Ivor Novello and get away fairly soon. I walk all the way back to K.B.W. The search-lights have been turned on and make a cone of light above my head. The streets are absolutely packed with happy people, but there is not much drunkenness.*

Diary   *May 19, 1945*

*Viti affixes my map of the Pacific upon the board which hitherto
has carried my map of Central Europe. It is an odd effect to put
away all those little Nazi flags which I have been using all these
weeks.*

Diary   *May 21, 1945*

*Winston has asked the Labour Party to stay on until the end of the
Japanese war, suggesting a referendum to prolong the life of the
present Parliament. The Blackpool Conference which opened today
has rejected this by a huge majority. It looks therefore as if the
Election would take place in July. I am not at all sure that I do not
want Labour to win. I feel this would, on the whole, be more in
the national interest.*

> *Now that the war in Europe had been won, the Labour
> Party pressed for a General Election. H.N. found himself
> in an awkward position. The National Labour Party had
> ceased to exist. And while his admiration for Churchill
> was great, he refused to stand a Conservative, although
> the West Leicester Conservatives backed him. He there-
> fore stood, somewhat ambiguously, as the "National
> Candidate" in full support of Churchill. He knew from
> the outset of his campaign that his chances of winning
> were very slim. Polling Day was on July 5, and he was
> defeated.*

H.N. to N.N.   *May 27, 1945*

*I am frankly dreading the General Election. I dislike the falsity, the
noise, the misrepresentation, the exhaustion and the strain of the
whole thing. I dislike being abused and heckled. I have not the
combative instincts which lead some people actually to enjoy the
conflict. And, above all, I have no prospect of success. In normal
times, if things were quiet, I might possibly reap some reward from
the long and conscientious work I have put in at Leicester. But times
are not normal. People feel, in a vague and muddled way, that all

the sacrifices to which they have been exposed and their separation from family life during four or five years, are all the fault of "them" – namely the authority of the Government. By a totally illogical process of reasoning, they believe "they" mean the upper classes, or the Conservatives. Class feeling and class resentment are very strong. I should be surprised, therefore, if there were not a marked swing to the left.

I have loved my ten years at Westminster, and have found there that the combination of genial surroundings with useful activity is the basis of all human happiness. If I learn on July 26th that my political career is over (perhaps for ever), I shall accept it with philosophic resignation and devote such years as may remain to me [he was then 58] to serious literary work.*

H.N. to N.N.   *June 4, 1945*

My attitude towards my constituents in West Leicester has been that of a kindly doctor. I go and see them. I write them letters. I try to help them in their unhappiness and bewilderment, but always with the quiet, comforting (and, I dare say, slightly superior) manner of the doctor visiting his patients. Now I have to enter whole wards of patients, clapping my hands together and being comradely. Well, I just won't do it. I know that I am a good Member and that my family doctor attitude is not only sincere but authentic in me. Any other attitude is not authentic.

Diary   *June 15, 1945*

To the House at 11. We have prayers, and then just sit chatting till 11.20 when Black Rod knocks on the door. We all crowd into the House of Lords, but the entrance is too narrow to see anything and we stand and chatter outside. We then stroll back to the House. Finally the Speaker returns without the mace. He sits down at the Clerks' table and we file past him and shake hands. I then sadly leave the building. The police are very affectionate. My special friend who calls me taxis bids me fond farewell: "Good luck, Sir, and by God, you will need all of it in Leicester!" I shake his hand and leave the House, perhaps for ever.

I then take the train for Leicester.

H.N. to V.S-W.   *June 19, 1945*
                                                Grand Hotel, Leicester

The campaign opened yesterday. The first meeting was inauspicious.
It was in a slum quarter and the Communists were there. It was not
that they made a row exactly, and in fact they listened quite politely.
But then the questions began: "I wish to ask the Candidate why on
April 12, 1938 he voted against the proposal of the Labour Party?"
I naturally say, "What was that proposal about?" "Oh, I see you
have forgotten it." Then it turns out that it was something to do
with the Catering Bill. But I was rather amused when they said I had
no right to support Churchill since I had slavishly supported Chamberlain when he was in power. I must say this led to some protests
among the audience. One man got up and said that they didn't want
a chap who always talked about Czechoslovakia rather than the
wages of the poor. I was able to reply to this that if they had listened
to me about Czechoslovakia the war might have been prevented.
But all this is saddening in that it shows such a complete distortion
of the facts and an utter ignorance of motives and realities. One
ought to grow another skin and not mind. But I am one of those
people who are depressed and made miserable by ignorance.

Diary   *June 21, 1945*

*Small despair. I gather that Barnett Janner [Labour Candidate] has
been attacking me for living in a Castle. Poor Sissinghurst! I do
not like that dignified ruin to be dragged into my election.*

H.N. to V.S-W.   *June 22, 1945*

*The usual election day yesterday. Catholic deputation in the
morning. Then the small shopkeepers. Then the Farmers' Union.
The Catholic woman, who is one of my voters, and who is a dim
earnest little thing, says she is speaking for Janner and although she
has always voted Tory she will now vote Labour as she is a friend
of the poor. That is what I fear will decide the election. Everybody
agrees, more or less, that I am a better Member than is Mr Janner.
But they want to "give Labour a chance".*

Diary June 26, 1945

Vita arrives looking so lovely and graceful and gentle. We go on to a woman's meeting and V. makes a little speech. The women are enraptured.

The U.N. Charter is signed at San Francisco.

Diary July 5, 1945

Polling Day. A beautiful hot day and a cloudless sky. This is supposed to help me on the ground that Labour people turn out whatever the weather, whereas non-Labour people won't budge if it is overcast. I hear the Town Hall clock strike nine and know that the Election is over. About 9.30 we see policemen carrying away the boxes in which the votes will be stored until July 26 [to give time for the Service votes to be collected and counted].

Diary July 18, 1945
Sissinghurst

*Start on Chapter XIII [of *The Congress of Vienna*]. I have done some 68,000 words so far. Weed in my life's work [the lime walk].

At 4 we go to the station and Niggs arrives. He is looking thin and brown and far more handsome. It is a delight to have him back. We talk all evening and at dinner we open the bottle of Champagne we have kept. What he seems to have minded most was handing over the Russian collaborationists to the Russian forces.*

Diary July 24, 1945

I leave [Pratts] about 10.30 and am astonished to find a completely different London. For years I have crept out with my torch. Last night I emerged into a London coruscating with lights like Stockholm. My old way along the Embankment from the Temple Station, which I have traversed such countless times feeling my way between surface shelters and trees, was lit by a thousand arc lights. All these were turned up on July 15 when double-summer-time ended. I had not realised what a transfiguration had been created. And meanwhile all the sticky stuff [affixed to protect passengers from shattered glass] has been taken from the windows of the buses and the Underground and we shall no longer remember how we used to peep out through a little diamond slit in the texture to read the names of stations as they flashed by. One forgets these things at once.

Diary   *July 26, 1945*
                                                                    Leicester

We [Vita, Nigel and Ben] breakfast and then I pay the bill. In the hall an old gentleman in uniform mutters to me, "Bad luck: you are out – well out." I do not know who he is but imagine he must be some assistant to the Returning Officer.

It is thus with a heavy heart that I go to de Montford Hall. All the tables are set out and the counting has begun. I watch the piles being collected and it is evident that I am badly out. My own workers are sad but resigned as the counting continues.

At 11.15 the piles have been passed on to the platform and the Mayor, Alderman Minto, knocks on the rostrum and there is a sudden hush. He begins with the East [Leicester vote]. He then takes up another sheet of paper and announces Leicester West. I am standing in the body of the hall, and Viti is sitting at one of the tables to my right. He reads out: "Janner, 20,563; Nicolson, 13,348; Kirby, 4,639." There is slight cheering. Janner and I then go on to the platform. Janner makes his speech. He is not bad. He compliments me on the "decency and distinction" with which I have conducted my campaign. I second in a few words, saying that there is no bitterness in my sadness since I was indeed fortunate to have on so slight a majority represented West Leicester for ten years in the most historic of Parliaments. There is applause at this in which Janner's supporters join. I then come off the platform and am greeted by my disheartened supporters and also by many Labour people who say, "I only wish it had not been you."

The train is late and we only reach London at 6. On our arrival we are greeted by Elvira Niggeman and the 6 p.m. results. Churchill is out and Attlee has a clear majority! Nobody foresaw this at all. We have a drink and then motor down home. We get there just in time for the 9 p.m. news. Winston drove to Buckingham Palace at 7 and handed in his resignation. Attlee followed at 7.30 and was entrusted with the new Government. Winston has issued a statement expressing his gratitude for the support given him by the people of Great Britain in the dark years.

I go to bed with two aspirins – a rare performance on my part. I feel as if I had been run over by a tram, but mainly owing to physical exhaustion and nervous strain. I had never expected to win myself. But I feel sad at closing what has been a very happy chapter in my life and bidding farewell to Leicester and my beloved House of Commons.

Diary *July 29, 1945*

Last Wednesday [July 26] was indeed an unfortunate day, more so than I imagined. On that day the Temple treasurer gave me notice that I must evacuate No 4 King's Bench Walk by Christmas as they cannot afford, owing to the loss of premises during the war, to retain residential chambers for non-practising barristers. This is such a terrible blow that Viti has wisely kept it from me until I should have recovered slightly from my Leicester disaster.

Diary *August 1, 1945*

Robin Maugham [author, now Lord Maugham] rings me up. He had been round to No. 10 on July 26. Winston was in magnificent form and took his defeat with humour. He confessed that it was distressing after all these years to abandon "the reins of power." Someone said, "But at least, Sir, while you held the reins, you managed to win the race." "Yes," said Winston, "I won the race – and now they have warned me off the turf."

Somebody mentioned that I had lost my seat at West Leicester. Robin remembered the actual words Winston used and memorised them. "The House," he said, "will be a sadder place without him" – and then he paused – "and smaller." I believe that Winston really said that. And it pleases me more than anything.

PART III

1945–1964

The Labour Government had come to power under Clement Attlee, and H.N. had lost his seat in Parliament, never to gain another. He was now 58. He was greatly depressed by his defeat, although it was not unexpected. He returned to literature and journalism. During and after the period when the atom-bomb was dropped and Japan surrendered, he continued to write The Congress of Vienna *and his weekly article for the* Spectator. *He was still a Governor of the B.B.C.*

Diary August 6, 1945

The 9 o'clock news announces that we have split the atom. A long statement is read, drafted by Winston, explaining how the discovery was made. It cost £500,000,000 and took four years. They have used it today on a Japanese town [Hiroshima]. They cannot tell exactly what damage was done. They estimate that one atomic bomb equals 2,000 ten-ton bombs. It is to be used, eventually, for domestic purposes. Viti is thrilled by the atomic bomb. She thinks, and rightly, that it means a whole new era.

Diary August 8, 1945

I have a talk with Tommy Lascelles. He says that the King does not like the way the B.B.C. treat his constitutional position. Instead of saying "Mr Bevin was sworn in as Privy Councillor," they should say "The King held a council etc. . . ." He tells me that when Truman came to Plymouth [on his way back from the Potsdam Conference], all went very well indeed. Truman is short, square, simple, and looks one straight in the face. [James] Byrnes, the Secretary of State, is a chatterbox. At luncheon in the *Renown* Byrnes began discussing in front of the waiters the impending release of the atomic bomb. As this is Security Silence No. 1 the King was horrified. "I think," he said, "Mr President, that we should discuss this interesting subject over our coffee on deck."

Raymond [Mortimer] gives me a terrible talking to about my writing. He says I am too impatient. That I work with facility but do not distinguish between authorship and journalism. That I have never written a book, except that on my father, which is worthy of my gifts. He begs me to go through the [Vienna] Congress book in the mood of Flaubert, not allowing a single meaningless word, or a single unbalanced paragraph to pass.

Diary   *August 9, 1945*

The 8 a.m. news announced: (a) that the Russians have declared war on Japan; (b) that the Americans have dropped another atomic bomb, this time on Nagasaki.

Diary   *August 10, 1945*

I bump into Harold Macmillan who is without a coat or hat. He says, "What a pity that we could not keep on the old House and the Coalition until today. Then we could have had a final celebration." "Is there any news? I have heard nothing," I say to him, feeling foolish. "Yes," he answers, "the Japs have surrendered."

Well that is very odd. I have no feeling of elation at all. It seems remote. There is no sign of jubilation and I observe that the news-vendors have stacks of evening papers unsold and unasked for. I meet a small procession of American soldiers carrying Old Glory and followed by a very few urchins. It is not inspiring at all. But I do notice that we have adopted the idiot American habit of strewing the streets with bits of paper. [The actual ceasefire was announced by President Truman four days later; the final surrender was signed on September 2nd.]

H.N. to V.S-W. *September 26, 1945*

*I saw William Jowitt [the Lord Chancellor] at luncheon yesterday
and he told me that he had written me a long letter about my going
to the Upper House. I must say that his letter is as sympathetic and
tactful as it could be. Now that the matter has passed from the stage
of a Sissinghurst joke to the stage where it is being seriously dealt
with I think we should be very discreet about it. I don't want it to
get about either that I have asked for a Peerage and been refused, or
that they offered me a Peerage and I refused. Therefore if asked
about it I shall merely say that I don't feel free, owing to my previous
attitude, to join any of the two main Parties.*

Diary *September 30, 1945*

In the evening the boys abuse me for my literary style. They say that
I am so afraid of the obvious that I deliberately take refuge in the
recondite; they say that I so love extraordinary words that I introduce them without the slightest knowledge of their meaning. It is a
very agreeable conversation, and I love them dearly.

Diary *October 2, 1945*

Lunch at Beefsteak. Sit between the Belgian Ambassador and Esher.
Old Cartier [de Marchienne] is miserable because the cuisine in
Belgium is declining; this cuisine which was the finest in the world,
and superior (as I agree!) to the finest French cooking is based upon
the lavish use of butter. Now they have to use margarine. The tone
in which the old boy used the word "margarine" was replete with all
the loathing of the nineteenth for the twentieth century. It was a
crowded day at the Beefsteak, and William Jowitt, coming in late,
had to find a seat at the little side table which serves in extreme
cases as an overflow. "Observe that," said Cartier, "in what other
country in the world would a club like this allow the Lord Chancellor to take a seat away from the table: in what other country
would that happen quite naturally, without any of us regarding the

occurrence as unusual?" "In the United States," I say. "Certainly not," he answers. "If the Chief Justice came into a club in Washington a place would be found for him at the head and not at the bottom of the table."

Diary   *October 15, 1945*

Mr Elton of the British Council telephones to ask if I will go to Athens on October 24th. I say yes. God knows how I am to explain it to Viti who will be terrified of my flying. The accidents in the last three weeks have been something chronic.

H.N. left England for a lecture tour in Greece on October 25. He returned on November 4.

H.N. to V.S-W.   *October 30, 1945*
                                                              Athens

The political situation is bad, I fear. Everybody is frightened, and that makes them quarrelsome and irritable. They are frightened of the communists, frightened of the brigands, frightened of Tito and his Russian friends, frightened of the coming winter, frightened of inflation. Nor are these fears imaginary. They are all too real. I am terribly sorry for my dear Greeks. The tragedy is that after this long period of dictatorship and occupation, none of the younger men have had an opportunity of proving themselves in public life. And the older men are frightened or corrupt. I fear the situation is pretty hopeless really.

Diary   *October 31, 1945*
                                                              Athens

I have a discussion with Rex [Leeper, the British Ambassador] who is wondering what on earth he will do if the Government, in reply to his telegram yesterday, authorize him to "display greater activity". At 10.55 I go to see the Regent [Archbishop Damaskinos] at his office. I find the Regent sitting enormous, with his back to shuttered windows. We have coffee and cigarettes. After compliments of a very high order, the Regent tells me that the Royalists and the

Liberals are meeting this afternoon to agree upon a joint programme. I say that the economic situation is far more urgent than the political situation; he makes a helpless gesture indicating, "What would you?" He then embarks on a long disquisition about the political and economic claims of Greece. He says that the communists are not worthy of being regarded as Greek citizens since they take their orders from abroad. It is not a really satisfactory discussion.

Diary   *November 15, 1945*

I go to No 50 Albemarle Street to watch Peter Quennell and Jock Murray collate the Byron letters with the Prothero Edition [6 vols., 1904]. They wish to publish a compendium of the more important letters and find on examination that [William] Prothero left out many essential passages without indicating any omissions. It was strange to find myself in that room, with port and candles, and to hear John Murray's grandson or great-grandson read aloud the very letters which old John Murray in that very room had read to Scott and the rest.

Diary   *November 20, 1945*

I have an odd experience. I go at 10.30 to lecture to the young men who have just got into the Foreign Service under the new examination. What amuses me is that the lecture takes place in the former German Embassy [in Carlton House Terrace] which the F.O. have taken over. There are workmen removing the furniture which is to be sold, and as I arrive a huge safe is being lowered down from one of the upper windows. I talk to them about the qualities required of a member of the Foreign Service. I define the main quality as "reliability" and analyse its five components as truthfulness, precision, loyalty, modesty, and a sense of proportion. I have good questions afterwards. One young man asks me what one ought to do if a foreign official asks one whether some important fact is true. I say that if one doesn't know one should say "I have no idea at all." But if one does know one should say, "You ought not to have asked me that question." The session lasts for more than two hours and I think it was a success.

I dine at Sibyl's. Harold Macmillan, T. S. Eliot, Cyril Connolly, the Kenneth Clarks, the Julian Huxleys, [Sir Pierson] Dixon of the F.O. Harold says that we shall only with the greatest difficulty convince the work-people of this country that they have got to work. They have no conception of the realities of national wealth and have been taught that it is merely the profits of the rich. They think they can now be idle and that the Government will provide. He says, and I agree with him, that France will become a prosperous power long before we do.

Diary   *November 21, 1945*

I reach the mature age of 59. I go round to Neville Terrace [in South Kensington where he had taken a house] with my rake and spade. They have begun to cement the basement and have taken out some of the window frames. I rake the dead leaves rather sadly. There is a heavy fog which thickens towards afternoon and plunges London into complete darkness.

Diary   *December 3, 1945*

Guy Burgess comes in and I go across with him to the Reform. He tells me (on what authority I know not, but I suspect Hector McNeil [of the F.O. for whom Burgess was Private Secretary]) that Bevin has turned me down for the post of Chairman of the British Council and that in some way my peerage was involved in that appointment and that this also has disappeared. I am not sure how reliable this is.

H.N. to V.S-W.   *December 21, 1945*

This is the last letter I shall write to you from K.B.W. I confess that I mind leaving it more than one ought to regret any material severance. It has been such a large and important slice of my life from that morning in 1929 when you met me and turned on the light outside the door to show me delighted surprise within. Much worry and much anxiety and so much happiness these walls have seen. And now it will be turned over to people with hard hearts and heads who will not see the beauty of its ivory walls or know what privacy can really mean.

I hate it, darling. I dread Neville Terrace. I mind the change in my life, and having a new servant and having to bother about household things. Anyhow, that is my last complaint. Not one word more will there be.

Diary   *December 31, 1945*

What a year it has been! For me (in spite of my defeat at the General Election and my failure to acquire a peerage) a happy year. The worst blow has been leaving K.B.W. But all this fades into a greater surge of thankfulness that we have Nigel safe with us and Ben safe (I hope, but there is a fog) up in London. Never have I felt so acutely as in the last few days what a loving and united family we are. There is an underlying sense of harmony and love. It is perhaps the best thing that life can give.

I thus embark with thankfulness and faith upon my 60th year.

Diary   *January 6, 1946*

I do an article on Eleanor Rathbone [who died on January 2]. I am amused to realise that people will imagine I did this article in order to curry favour with her former constituents. As a matter of fact I had thought of doing it long before I thought of having to stand for the Combined Universities [the seat Eleanor Rathbone held, as an Independent, since 1929]. But this is what old Baldwin warned me never to worry about. "Never," he said, "allow yourself to worry for one instant about the attribution of false motive."

Diary   *January 7, 1946*

*Go to Pratts where luckily I find the Lord Chancellor [Jowitt]. I take the opportunity of saying to him: "Tell me, William, what would you do if you were in my position and were offered the nomination for the by-election in the Combined Universities?" He says, "Take it at once." He then tells me that Attlee had seemed very willing to give me a peerage and that he himself had expected to see my name included among those mentioned in last New Year honours. It was true that Lord Addison, the Labour leader in the H. of L., had shown some unwillingness, but that may not have affected Attlee at all. He felt bound, however, to say that if I fought the Combined Universities [as an Independent] and lost, then I would also lose all present chance of getting a peerage. "It is a difficult decision to make," he said.

I am amused by this predicament. I can scarcely refuse to try at least to get nominated for the Combined Universities. If I got in that would be splendid. But if, as is probable, I failed, then I should be in a worse position than before. I had got used to the idea of going to the Lords and had come to like it.*

H.N. to V.S-W.   *January 9, 1946*
                                          10, Neville Terrace, S.W.7

James [Pope-Hennessy] came in last night to see me. He found me sitting over my gas fire correcting my proofs [of *The Congress of Vienna*]. He said that the house was like a boarding house which had been turned into a reception centre for bombed-out people. No not even that. Bombed out Indian students. At any moment he expected to see a sleek black head looking over the banisters.

Diary   *January 9, 1946*

Ivone [Kirkpatrick, Deputy Commissioner of the Control Commission, Germany] tells me about his early experiences in Germany in June and July last when he with [Robert D.] Murphy [political advisor to the American Military Government in Germany] were representing the civilian side of the occupation.

There were two concentration camps for the Nazis, known respectively as the "Ash Can" and the "Dust Bin". He had visited them both. At the former all the Nazi leaders were interned. On his arrival he found it to be a large hotel surrounded with barbed wire with sentries at look-out posts. All the Nazis were out on the terrace sitting in basket chairs. They had been told to stand at attention when he and Murphy arrived and they did so obediently. Then after inspecting the kitchens and other accommodation, he sent for Goering who entered under the escort of a G.I. and stood sharply to attention. Ivone did not greet him by name. "You may sit down," he said. Goering was so bored that he was delighted to talk. He sat there for an hour. He was absolutely frank. Ivone asked him whether he thought the date chosen for the declaration of war was a good one. He said that although he had felt personally that Germany could get all she wanted without forcing us into war, yet take that Hitler was determined on a general war, the date of September 1939 was the correct date. Anything later or earlier would have been wrong. Ivone asked him what was the greatest mistake that Germany made. He answered in a flash, "Not invading Spain. If we had seized Gibraltar we should have won the war." He also said that it was our bombing of the centres of communication which brought on the final collapse.

Thereafter Ribbentrop was brought in. He was not frank at all. He denied everything.

He also told me that when the Americans entered Marburg an agitated little man ran out of the schloss there and asked to see the commanding officer. "I am the State Archivist," he explained. "I am in charge of the State archives. They contain the most vital historical documents and must be preserved at any cost." He told them that the castle contained all the Nazi documents but that there were other dumps in other places which he indicated. He begged them to collect the documents so that the whole collection might be complete. They did so. It never seemed to dawn upon the archivist that his duty as a German was to destroy these papers while the going was good: his only idea was that as an archivist he must preserve those papers at any cost and see they were complete in every particular. There were also at Marburg four coffins neatly sewn up in sacking – they contained Frederick the Great, William I, Hindenburg and Frau Hindenburg.

Diary   *January 28, 1946*

I dine with the Camroses. Senator Vandenberg and his wife are there. The Senator tells me that he had visited Roosevelt a week before he died, and that "the shadow of death was already on him". The Senator asked him whether, in view of his known anti-Russian attitude, it would be better if some less controversial figure went to San Francisco [the United Nations Conference in April 1945]. Roosevelt had replied, "No – I want you to go above all men and for that very reason. At Conference after Conference I have been forced to agree to things which I do not agree with in fear lest Russia should make a separate peace. She will now blackmail us again by threatening to withdraw from our League." Prophetic words!

Diary　　　　　　　　　　　　　　　　　　　　　*March 11, 1946*

I lunch at the Beefsteak and sit next to Barrington-Ward [Editor of *The Times*]. His view is that our working people will not work, not because they are temperamentally lazy, not because they dislike income tax, but because they have nothing to buy with what they earn. Once there are things in the shops then they will work well enough. I do not believe this. I believe that our lower classes are for some curious reason congenitally indolent; and that only the pressure of gain or destitution makes them work. When their profits are taken for income tax and they are insured against destitution their natural indolence comes to the surface.

H.N. to V.S-W.　　　　　　　　　　　　　　　　　*April 3, 1946*

I got a letter from the Post Master General saying that the Government would publish the list of new [B.B.C.] Governors this week. That means we have all got to go. I asked whether he would like me to go now or wait till July [when H.N.'s contract expired]. But in any case by that date I shall lose my £1,000 a year and I must think of some regular job. Nobody can in these days afford to lose £1,000 without noticing it. Luckily I have my head and hand and shall not starve apart from the fact that I married (a) an heiress; (b) a poet; (c) a best-seller – all of which sounds like trigamy.

Diary　　　　　　　　　　　　　　　　　　　　　*April 8, 1946*

I lunch at the French Embassy to meet Gafencu [former Foreign Minister of Rumania]. Gafencu says he has derived much relief and refreshment from his visit to London. There is such exhaustion and defeatism in other countries that it is an amazing discovery to find a country which seems self-confident, active and calm. He says that we are faced with a very grave Russian danger and that it is no use pretending it is not a danger. Russia is determined to create a unitary system in Europe. She is assisted in this by the fact that although her theories appeal only to a minority in every country, it is a very active, ruthless and unscrupulous minority. In Germany our great difficulty is that Russia can claim that her system would not be worse than any other, and that it is only under communism that Germany can attain her unity. Thus the sense of national unity (which is strong in Germany) is identified with communism; social democracy implied the division into zones. To combat this we must provide an alternative ideal; the only possible ideal is a federal Germany in a federal Europe.

Diary   *April 16, 1946*

I lunch at the Beefsteak with Desmond MacCarthy. I go to the flower show and buy many little things. In fact I am rather extravagant. I then go to the London Library and analyse *Punch* jokes from 1860 onwards [for his *English Sense of Humour*]. I see a man opposite me looking on with disapproval. I can see that he is thinking, "How strange that a man, obviously a man of education and even refinement can spend a lovely afternoon like this sitting in the reading room and poring over old volumes of *Punch*!"

I have a talk with William Jowitt. I say, "You remember that there was some suggestion that I should go to the House of Lords as an Independent? You remember you told me that Lord Addison did not like this idea and said that all Labour peers must be Labour peers? Well, I have thought it over and I would gladly accept the Whip." He said he thought that a wise thing to do. I said that I was heart and soul with the Government in its foreign policy and that I also agreed with its domestic policy. What worried me were the left-wing elements who seemed to me too revolutionary. "They are what worry all of us," he said. I did not feel that all my difficulties would be solved by my joining the Labour Party – nor did William. But anyhow I have taken the plunge and am rid (at some cost to my pride) of the incubus of being an independent. But no evasions will obscure the facts (a) that I have ASKED for a peerage; (b) that when I found I could not get one as an independent I then changed my party coat.

H.N. to V.S-W.   *April 25, 1946*

It is now confirmed that I fly with [Sir] George Clerk [at one time British Ambassador in Paris] to Nuremberg next week [to cover the trial of Nazi leaders for British and French journals]. I do dread it so. I know I am squeamish about this sort of thing, but I hate the idea of sitting all comfy in a box and staring at men who are certain to be hanged by the neck and who are in any case caught like rats in a trap. You know as well as I do that my feelings for Ribbentrop have always been cold feelings. But I do not want to see the man humiliated. And Schacht [Hitler's Finance Minister] was a friend of mine. I do not want to see him like a prisoner in the dock. Nor really do I want to see Germany in its present state. But I should never forgive myself if I shirked this opportunity.

Diary   *April 30, 1946*
                                                            Nuremberg

The colouring of the courtroom is dark brown relieved by heavy green marble surrounds to the several doors. The room is lit by slit-lights from above but there are alternative reflectors in position for illumination when photographs are taken. The room is far smaller than I expected; the dominant note is silence. The proceedings are carried out almost in a hush.

My gaze then turns to the dock. The defendants sit in the following order: Front row: Goering, Hess, Ribbentrop, Keitel, Kaltenbrunner, Rosenberg, Frank, Frick, Streicher, Funk, Schacht. Second Row: Doenitz, Raeder, Baldur von Schirach, Sauckel, Jodl, Papen, Seyss-Inquart, Speer, Neurath, Fritzsche.

They look drab, depressing, ill; they have the appearance of people who have travelled in a third-class railway carriage for three successive nights. It seems incredible that such a dim set of men should or could have done such huge and dreadful things. When one looks more closely one observes differences between them. Goering is the dominant figure. Clad in a loose light uniform without badges of rank, he leans his pasty face upon a fat pasty hand, and at times he will place the fist against his chin in the attitude of Rodin's *Penseur*. For so vast a man, although he is now shrunken, his movements are alert, rapid, nervous, impulsive. Beside him sits Hess – bearing a strong resemblance to the Duke of Rutland – apparently not attending much, opening a book occasionally which he holds on his knees, but not reading it with any attention, just glancing down as if it were something he happened to be holding in his hand.

Ribbentrop is much changed; his face is grey and thin; his soft collar flops; he closes his eyes and adopts a mask; he seems inarticulate, utterly broken.

Dr Dix, the leader of the Berlin bar, is making a long, rambling and to my mind ineffective speech in Schacht's defence. Schacht sits in the witness box opposite him. He is flanked by two young Americans in white helmets. Every hour, two other snowdrops appear from behind and silently take from their comrades the white batons of office, stepping into their place. At 3.15 there is a short recess. The German counsel rise from their seats and talk to their clients in the dock. They are carefully watched by the snowdrops as they do so.

When we begin again Schacht is asked questions by his counsel. He answers in a loud clear voice. He is completely master of himself and of his dates and facts. "Did you adhere to the Nazi _Weltanschauung?_" "I reject every philosophy which is not based upon true religion." "What was your true opinion of Hitler?" "A man of _diabolische Genialität_ [diabolical genius] . . . a man who may at the start have had fine ideas but who in the end became infected by the poisons which he instilled in the masses."

At 5.0 the Court rises. We drive back to [Sir Norman] Birkett's [one of the British judges] villa. He is carefully guarded. He has military policemen on his car and is followed by a jeep containing other red-caps armed with Tommy guns. Only gradually does he begin to talk about the trial. He says that the Nazi leaders would never have allowed themselves to be taken alive had they known that we should find such utterly damning documents.

Diary   _May 1, 1946_
                                                        Nuremberg

We go into the court room. This time we are in the Visitors' Gallery above the Press Gallery where we were yesterday. When we enter, Schacht is again being examined. He sits there, benign, confident, a complete master of his own defence. He remarks that Ribbentrop was one of the most incompetent men he has ever known. The latter drops his strained mask for a second and shakes his weary head.

At 11.15 there is an adjournment and we gather in Birkett's room. Colonel Andrus, who is Commandant of the prison, comes to fetch us. We start going round the prison under Colonel Andrus' guidance. The courts are connected with the adjoining prison by a long covered wooden passage, which twists and turns, and which has a duck-board floor. Our feet resound upon this floor as if it were a xylophone. The defendants as they walk to the court must hear either their own feet or those of their guards echoing upon this duck-board. For those whose lives are spared, that sound will echo till they die. Two-thirds of the way down this wooden corridor there is a gate leading to an exercise yard. There are lilac bushes in flower and the grass is worn by miserable feet.

We enter a prison gallery, identical with those I have seen at Brixton and Wormwood Scrubs. The only difference is that the prison smell is absent; it is replaced by the smell of beans cooking in tomato. The cells run along each side, and the names of the prisoners are attached outside. Andrus takes us into Sauckel's cell, and then to Ribbentrop's. They are made to clean the cells themselves and to fold their blankets. They have a bunk, a chair and a table. They have books and papers, and on their tables are pasted the photographs of their wives and children. In Ribbentrop's cell it was sad to see, not the accustomed prisoners' photographs taken at Margate, but Bond Street photographs of charming boys.

We saw the food, which was good. "Ah yes," said Colonel Andrus, "no mother has ever cherished her children as I cherish these men. I must keep them fresh for the last day." But he is not a gloating man; he is a nice, clever man, and humane.

He takes us to see the depository where the prisoners' luggage is kept. It is pitiable luggage. A fat suitcase of imitation leather belongs to Goering. It contained his particular drug. "We have suppressed that parcel," says Andrus, "and friend Goering has never been so healthy in his life." In a way, these waiting suitcases, gathered together as in a cloakroom at Victoria, were more expressive than anything else.

The court rises at 5. We have some tea in Birkett's room, and then drive with him to the *Heldenfeld*, or stadium, now called "The Soldiers' Field". I visit this scene of the great Nazi rallies with awe. It is a fine and tremendous erection, being a tremendous affirmation of the drama and power of the whole system. The huge eagle and swastika by which it was surmounted have been taken down, showing brick scars upon the stone plinth. We mingle with the crowd. The people glance at us, realise we are the conquerors, and look aside as if we were not there. If I were a Nuremberger I should feel nothing but undying hatred for those who have destroyed my lovely city. We see no scowls; merely a pretence of ignoring us.

Diary   *May 2, 1946*
                                                Nuremberg

Lord and Lady Lawrence [President of the Tribunal and his wife] come to dinner. Lady Lawrence tells me that the most dramatic moment in the trial was when they turned on a film showing the trial by Nazi justice of some wretched young man who had been involved in an attempt on Hitler's life. The judge yelled at him, pointing accusing fingers, shouting, "You beast! You brute! You traitor!" The sound of his objurgations echoed through the court room, rising in the end almost to a scream. Then the film stopped, the lights went up, and the gentle voice of Lord Lawrence intervened: "Please continue your examination, Dr Dix." The contrast between violence and calm was such that even the defendants moved uneasily upon their hard and narrow bench.

Diary   *May 28, 1946*

I dine with Mrs Randolph Churchill in her grand flat in Grosvenor Square. Everybody in dinner jacket and evening dress; the first time I have seen so uniformly pre-war a party. Raimond von Hofmannsthal [son of the poet and librettist of several of Strauss's operas] tells me that when he was a little boy he remembers Rilke coming to stay with his father. He was sent backwards and forwards with notes between the main house and the Gartenhaus in which Rilke lived. The purpose of these notes was to arrange between them the subjects which they would talk about during their afternoon walk. They were each of them too shy to meet without preparation.

Diary   *July 14, 1946*

In the evening we discuss the rumour that I am to succeed Duff as Ambassador in Paris. Viti says that any such idea would be quite intolerable. Ben says it would be convenient to stay at the Embassy. Niggs is all in favour of it. He says that he does not want me to end my life on a flat note; that I should be good at the job; that I should be mad to refuse. I am amused by all this, especially as the issue will never arise.

H.N. now went to Paris to report for the B.B.C. on the Peace Conference, which was to draw up the draft texts of the peace-treaties with Italy, Hungary, Rumania, Finland, and Bulgaria. The problems of Germany and Austria were not considered. The Conference met in an atmosphere of increasing antagonism between the United States and Russia: "Instead of open covenants openly arrived at," H.N. pointed out in one of his broadcasts from Paris, "we have open insults openly hurled."

Diary   *July 26, 1946*
                                                   Ritz Hotel, Paris

I believe that if we are very industrious and united we can make the B.B.C. reports from Paris as useful and influential as our reports during the war. The newspapers after the first days will become bored with the Conference which will drop out of the front page. It will be our business to keep public interest alive. I see no reason why, if the thing is carefully done, we should not teach the British Public that foreign affairs can be as interesting and as comprehensive as a test match. I am slightly startled by the size of my audience. I shall be speaking probably to 20,000,000 [people].

Diary   *July 29, 1946*
                                                           Paris

I walk across to the Luxembourg [for the opening of the Conference]. The roads are barred by gendarmes but we have passes. I am shown to a place bang in the centre of the front-row [of the gallery] from where I can see everything. The great theatre of the Senate is lit, partly by sunlight, and partly by spotlights. The delegations sit in the red plush stalls with little black book-rests in front of them; the presidential desk is on the stage, a vast Empire affair, and the interpreters sit in the orchestra. It is all like a first night at Her Majesty's or Covent Garden except for the absence of women in the stalls. People stroll in and take their places which are marked with the names of their countries on large placards. The minor delegates and experts enter first, making polite handshakes and bows. Then at 4 p.m. precisely the main delegates emerge from the back of the stage and walk across it, down the steps to the proscenium and then up among the stalls. Molotov and Vyshinsky stride across the stage with all the consciousness of power; Byrnes and his [American] delegation walk slowly and sedately with all the consciousness of great virtue; and then in trips little Attlee, hesitates on finding himself on the stage, tries to dart back again into the door through which he has come, and is then rescued by an official who leads him across the stage with a hand on his elbow. A lamentable entry. In fact our Delegation does not look impressive. How insignificant they look there in their red plush stalls! How different from Lloyd George and Balfour – how terribly different from Winston.

They all take their seats and the hum subsides. The *huissier* then shouts "Monsieur le Président," and Bidault [Prime Minister and Foreign Minister] walks in with neat little feet and takes his seat. Any dignity which the meeting might have had is completely marred by the photographers and cinema-men. They are everywhere. All the time American photographers creep about, now on the stage, now off the stage, flashing with their cameras. It might be Hollywood itself. In a somewhat rasping voice, Bidault opens the proceedings, making a short but conventional speech.

Diary   *August 4, 1946*
                                                              Paris

An unexpected and most undesired fame has descended upon me. I am Rip Van Winkle, the veteran of 1919, the only man in Paris who remembers the last Conference. It would seem in fact that, except for a dotard on the Brazilian delegation whose memory is unreliable, I am the only survivor of the former Peacemaking. The *New York Times* correspondent asks me to tell him differences . . . etc. etc. "Of course," he says, "there is a difference in personalities – they were giants in those days." "Balls," I say, "don't you believe it. Mr Byrnes, to my mind, is more effective than President Wilson; Bevin is certainly a stronger and finer character than Lloyd George; and old Orlando cannot be compared for force and capacity to Molotov; and in the circumstances Bidault is a far more suitable person than Clemenceau could ever have been." He is distressed by this remark.

To the [Hôtel] Scribe for my 6.15 talk. I then go into the recording room in order to hear Viti [who was broadcasting an appeal from Wales for the National Trust]. We arrive just in time to hear Vita announced as Miss VICTORIA S-W. I expect a row, but she does her piece with swan-like calm. Only at the end when she has to give her address does she fling into the initial "V" all the loathing which she has of her full name or of my name or of any name except V.S-W.

I go to see [Ernest] Bevin [Foreign Secretary] in the morning. I find him installed at a Louis XV table in an ivory-coloured room at the George V. He is most welcoming and genial.

He begins by saying polite things about my broadcasts. I say that it is difficult for me to put the Russian problem in its right perspective. He says that he has only just begun to understand how little we know of the Russians and how much our gaps in interpretation are due to the actual misemployment of words. For instance, when he first met Molotov, he once said to him, "Let us assume that as a basis of discussion." It was only later that he discovered that Molotov had interpreted the word "basis" as implying a fundamental agreement.

Unfortunately, however, Mr Byrnes (being a victim of his Press) has insisted on full publicity. That means that one can never think aloud without being overheard. That means that all real negotiation is impossible. I say, "But what about the Big Four meetings?" He chuckles at that. He says that the first one went splendidly, since he had prepared it in advance. But the second one was an absolute flop. "I have my instructions," began Vyshinsky. "Well," Bevin answered, "I have no instructions other than those which I give myself. Clearly therefore we are not discussing on the same level and I had better turn you over to my deputy." Vyshinsky blinked at that but he could go no further. Therefore the meeting broke up pending Molotov's return.

He thinks that the Russians are bitterly enraged with the Americans for having forced a show-down over Yugoslavia. He thinks that their insane proposal to transfer the UNO to Paris or Geneva was just a lunge back at the United States. He agrees with me that all this scoring points is lamentable.

None the less Bevin feels that we are getting on.

Diary   *September 10, 1946*
                                                   Paris

In the evening at 5.30 we motor out to Versailles for the reception given by Georges Bidault as President of the Provisional Government. The big courtyard is lined by mounted Gardes Républicains and by Goums and Spahis in their scarlet cloaks. On the staircase there are men dressed in liveries of the eighteenth century with wigs. Bidault receives us in the antichambre du roi and we pass through the Oeil de Boeuf into the Gallérie des Glaces. It is a lovely evening and the sun is pouring in. An absolutely superb Savonnerie carpet is on the floor and there are two vast buffets. I have short talks with many old friends. I stand in the window where I stood twenty-seven years ago after the signing of the Treaty of Versailles and look out on the ponds and canal turning green and purple in the sunset. In the Salon de la Paix there is a small orchestra playing Lully's minuets. When they stop playing one can hear the fountains plashing. When the darkness falls they turn on the flood-lighting. It is a scene of amazing magnificence and beauty. But the people look foul.

Diary   *September 28, 1946*
                                                   Paris

*I have to hurry a bit as I promised to receive Smuts at 12 p.m. at the Luxembourg. We go upstairs to the *studio des personalités* – a title which is typical of French protocol verbiage. I take the Field Marshal into the studio. I leave him. He has to record his B.B.C. talk for tomorrow. When he is gone, Venables [of the B.B.C.] again mops his brow. I ask him whether anything went wrong. "Yes," he says, "you know that white statue of a completely naked boy which stands in the *studio des personalités*? When the Marshal had finished speaking, he said in a loud voice to me, 'That young man does not seem to mind very much exposing his person.' I think and pray that this remark did not go out all over South Africa. But I am quite sure it was heard by all the engineers, officers, directors and typists in Broadcasting House. I shall have to give an explanation this evening."*

Diary   *October 1, 1946*
                                                                Paris

We put on the records [of the Nuremberg verdicts] at once. Eventually we could hear [Lord] Lawrence say, "Can you hear me now?" "Yes," said Goering. Then Lawrence said, "The defendant, Hermann Goering, having been found guilty on all indictments, is condemned by the International Military Tribunal to death by hanging." Then comes Hess who gets life imprisonment. Then Ribbentrop – "The defendant (hesitation on Lawrence's part) Joachim von Ribbentrop etc. is condemned to death by hanging." I cannot bear it. To sit there in that familiar room at the Scribe and to hear those men being bumped off one by one. I take off my earphones and rise to go. I see the glistening surface of the disk revolving pitilessly ticking off the lives of other men.

Diary   *October 16, 1946*
                                                                Paris

It all feels flat after the Conference closing down. Byrnes' attempt to impress Russia with the force of world opinion has only led Russia to believe that he sought to gang up the small States against him. It has convinced us that we cannot persuade Russia by argument, and that all we can do to her is to behave as well as possible and convince her by example. But much bitterness has been created. And much distrust.

Diary   *October 22, 1946*
                                                                London

I go to see Rab Butler who is to lead for the Opposition in the Foreign Affairs Debate this afternoon. He has obtained from Bevin the text of the opening speech. We go through it together. He is dreading what Winston will say tomorrow. He says that

Winston is a "magnificent animal" who has really no spiritual side at all. He fears he is going to trot out the bolshevik bogey and do much harm. They all wish that he was not their leader. Rab says that my talks from Paris have had "an immense effect". He thinks that for the first time they have induced the ordinary public to take an interest in foreign affairs.

Diary   *November 2, 1946*

I lunch at the Beefsteak. William Jowitt is there. He says he does not know what to do about the number of divorce cases. There are 40,000 ex-service men wanting divorce. His oath of office obliges him, not only to administer justice, but not to delay it. Yet he has neither the judges nor the court-rooms to cope with this accumulation. He feels that one ought to be able if there are no children, to obtain a divorce as easily as a dog licence. Yet that would entail legislation.

Diary   *November 21, 1946*

I reach the age of sixty. Until about five years ago I detected no decline at all in physical vigour and felt as young as I did at thirty. In the last five years, however, I am conscious that my physical powers are on the decline. I am getting slightly deaf and the passions of the flesh are spent. Intellectually, I observe no decline in vigour; I can write with the same facility, which is perhaps a fault. But I do not notice that my curiosity, my interest or my powers of enjoyment and amusement have declined at all. What is sad about becoming sixty is that one loses all sense of adventure. I am well aware, moreover, that I have not achieved either in the literary or political world that status which my talents and the hard work I have done and do might seem to justify.

Diary   *December 6, 1946*

My book on *The English Sense of Humour* arrives from the Dropmore Press. It is very excellently produced. Ben remarks with some astringency that the exterior is superior to the interior.

I return to Neville Terrace, do some dictation and then await my lecture [on the Lawrence portraits of the Congress of Vienna].

Elvira [Niggeman, his secretary] realises that I am nervous. "I have never seen your nervous before," she says. She is quite right. The reason is (a) that I do not like lecturing about subjects on which I am not an expert; (b) that I dread letting Ben [Deputy Surveyor of the King's pictures] down in front of his colleagues; (c) that I am uneasy at the presence of Queen Mary. Anyhow, V. and I drive to Burlington House. Queen Mary arrives on the tick accompanied by the Princess Royal. I give my lecture and it goes very well. I finish and step down from the platform. Queen Mary says, "Your lecture was too short." (It was 55 minutes.) "No lecture," I reply, "can be too short." "Yours was," she says. The Queen says she wants to see the pictures again and compare them to what I had said. We go from picture to picture and the Queen nods her head. She is specially interested in Lawrence's treatment of Alexander I's red face. She had not known about that before.

Diary   *December 9, 1946*

[Monday] Since I came down on Friday night I have (a) finished my article for *Contact*; (b) done my Marginal Comment; (c) done my talk for the Overseas Service; (d) done an article for the B.B.C. Yearbook; (e) done another talk for the European Service; (f) done my article for the *Figaro*; (g) done two reviews. I have also read two books. The bad weather has some advantages.

Diary   *December 10, 1946*

Ben tells me that the Palace have agreed to his becoming Editor of the *Burlington* [magazine, journal of the history of art; he remained Editor until his death in 1978].

Diary   *December 29, 1946*

In the afternoon I moon about with Vita trying to convince her that planning is an element in gardening. She wishes just to jab in the things which she has left over. The tragedy of the romantic temperament is that it dislikes form so much that it ignores the effect of colour. She wants to put in stuff which "will give a lovely red colour in the autumn". I wish to put in stuff which will furnish shape to the perspective. In the end we part, not as friends.

*The winter of 1947 was one of the severest on record, and
the nation suffered acutely. H.N., for once, was writing
no new book, occupying himself mainly with weekly
journalism. In February he joined the Labour Party,
hoping to begin a new political career in the Commons
or the Lords.*

Diary   *January 5, 1947*

It is really horribly cold. Raymond [Mortimer] reads my essay on
[English] humour and lays it down without a word and picks up
another book. When pressed, he says it is very bad and sham
philosophy and that I ought not to try my hand at that sort of thing.
I like that about Raymond. He never for one moment says what he
does not think merely out of affection or a desire to please.

Diary   *January 9, 1947*

I dine with General Jacob [Military Assistant Secretary to the War
Cabinet, 1939–46]. Jacob is full of talk and I enjoy my dinner. We
begin by discussing the present and future international situation.
I say that in five years from now we may find that France, Spain,
Italy, Germany and Greece have all gone communist. That the
smaller Western Powers are like rabbits in the python's cage. That
the whole of India is under communist direction and that we have
troubles in all our colonies and dependencies. At the same time
there will have occurred in this country a split between the present
Labour leaders (who take a patriotic or nationalistic point of view),
and their left wing (who take an international or Red Flag point of
view). The latter will, owing to the acute poverty of the country,
gain ground among the working classes. Thus if a conflict comes
between the U.S.A. and the U.S.S.R. we shall have a very active
fifth column in this country. The great bourgeois mass, terrified as
they will be by the prospect of atomic war, will wish only to please
Russia. The minority who sees that we must side with America will
be called "war mongers". And we shall thus lose our independence
and our Commonwealth. I say that this is what will *probably*
happen. To ignore this probability is to be both cowardly and
blind. To be frightened of it is to deny one's own soul. Because

nothing really happens which is as bad as the imagination forecasts. Time brings unexpected alterations. The danger may pass.

Diary   *February 12, 1947*

I go to the Historic Buildings Committee of the National Trust. There is no heat at all and we crouch round the table in fur coats and gloves. The electricity is cut off between 9 and 12 and 2 and 4. The black out is to be imposed. My God! What the poor people of this country have had to suffer in the last seven years!

Diary   *February 13, 1947*

The coal crisis is really disastrous. Our industry is at a standstill and it will take us months and months to recover from this disaster. There is a demand for vigorous leadership and of course all sorts of rumours. The most prevalent is that Attlee is going to retire in Bevin's favour. But I fear that Bevin is seriously ill – angina. He goes to Moscow with a doctor and a nurse. There was a leading article in the *Times* today which reached bottom for sheer pessimism.

Diary   *February 28, 1947*

I write a letter [applying for membership of the Labour Party] to the local Labour office. I am glad I have taken this difficult decision after all these months of worry and uncertainty. It will lead to a row at home. But this is the best moment, when the Labour Party are being banged on the head, to make my act of faith. It is NOT an impulsive act.

This decision will expose me to much obloquy, misinterpretation, ridicule and attribution of false motive. People will say I did this because I wanted to get a peerage. If I scrape my conscience I must admit that there is some truth in that accusation. I hate being out of Parliament. I do not want to fight an election. I should be at ease in the Upper House and able to do some good. If there were no prospect of my getting a peerage would I have done this? No. And if I do not get a peerage within a reasonable time will I fight an election as a Socialist? I might. What I will not do is abuse my former friends. I cannot get up and speak ill of Winston or Eden. Anyhow one thing is certain. I could never have become a Tory. It would be madness to become a Liberal. Therefore, becoming Labour is the only alternative to dropping out. That is not a noble motive. But what people will not know is that I am convinced that the only angle from which to fight communism is the Labour angle. The only thing that worries me is that my integrity is my most valued possession. Will this make people doubt my integrity? I do not think so. Because God knows my integrity is a solid thing with me; I am unambitious and devoted – I really am.

When I read the above again I say to myself, "You are making excuses, and very lame excuses, for yourself. That means that you are not spiritually at ease." No, not exactly that. It is the rows I dread; how it will hurt Vita and Mummy [Lady Carnock, aged 86]; the publicity that will follow. I wish I were more tough.

H.N. to V.S-W. *March 6, 1947*

I must break the fact to you that I have joined the Labour Party. I have done this because in the end it was inevitable and I had better do it when the night of misery is on them rather than when they are basking in the sun of popular acclaim. *I did it quite quietly by joining the local branch [Kensington]. They registered me as "H. Nicolson" and it is probable that there will be no publicity. I told Elvira who emitted a short sharp scream. I told the boys, who received the news in horrified silence.* I shall get a real scolding when I come down on Saturday. But I know I was right. *This is NOT (repeat NOT) an impulsive gesture. I have been worrying over it for months.*

Diary *March 13, 1947*

I go to see Mummy. She takes my having joined the Labour Party as a cruel blow. "I never thought," she said, "that I should see the day when one of my own sons betrayed his country." Freddy [H.N.'s brother] is equally indignant. "I suppose," he says, "you will now resign from all your clubs." They live such a sheltered life, poor people, that they see things out of proportion. But I hate hurting Mummy.

Diary   April 28, 1947

I do my wireless talk and my article for the *Figaro*. In the afternoon I weed. It is a cold but beautiful day and I am unhappy and distressed. I fear that my low blood-pressure is more serious than I imagined. It is not that I get unduly tired but that my work requires greater effort and my mind and memory do not display that resilience to which I am accustomed. I find myself having *Angst* about the future of the world and my own country. Subversive movements seem to be gaining a hold in industry; there is a succession of unnecessary strikes; the food and export situation is deplorable; and the energy that should be shown is not shown. When one adds to this the eternal disquiet caused by Russia, the dislocating tactics which they pursue, the lack of general confidence – all this inspires gloom.

I have got to make a speech to the Westminster Labour Party on Wednesday. I do not know what to say. My socialist convictions are purely academic and even negative. I hope by socialism to preserve our essential personal liberties. But I feel that I am being dragged in to the wake of the future; not that I am in the van. The awful thought gnaws like a rat at my conscience that I should have accepted being out of public life and done nothing at all. I feel a decline in energy and faith. I am in a bad mood.

I read Charles du Bos on [Benjamin] Constant. When he was young he suffered, or thought he suffered tortures of unhappiness and self-dispraisal. Now I when young was as happy and irresponsible as a lark. It is in my late age that happiness has become clouded. But if unhappiness comes to the young it gives them depth; coming at my age it confirms my superficiality. I am haunted by mental decay such as I saw creeping over Ramsay MacDonald. A gradual dimming of the lights.

Diary   May 9, 1947

I lunch at the Dorchester with Willy Somerset Maugham. Robin [Maugham] is there and Monroe Wheeler [of the Museum of Modern Art, New York]. We lunch in Willy's sitting-room. The telephone rings constantly: will he grant an interview? Will he give his autograph? Willy does not enjoy that sort of thing. "You at least k-k-k-know," he says, "my dear Harold, that I hate this f-f-f-f-fuss." It is a most agreeable luncheon and I am amused to observe that Robin is a trifle in awe of his astringent uncle. Then Emerald Cunard rings up and goes on talking, talking, talking. Willy, while he listens, makes to us gestures of despair and impatience.

Diary   *May 28, 1947*

I go to Sibyl's. I come into the room to find Osbert Lancaster there and a young man with his back to the window. He says, "Not recognise an old friend?" It is the Duke of Windsor. He is thin but more healthy-looking than when I last saw him. He has lost that fried-egg look around the eyes. He is very affable and chatty. I notice that he has dropped calling his wife "Her Royal Highness"; he calls her "the Duchess". I notice also that people do not bow as they used to and treat him less as a royalty than they did when he had recently been King. He takes all this quite for granted. I have an impression that he is happier.

The Duchess of Windsor then comes in. She also has much improved. That taut, predatory look has gone; she has softened. I have a talk with her alone. She says that they do not know where to live. They would like to live in England, but that is difficult. He retains his old love for Fort Belvedere. "We are tired of wandering," she says. "We are not as young as we were. We want to settle down and grow our own trees. He likes gardening. But it is no fun gardening in other people's gardens." Where can they live? They are sick of islands, otherwise they might go to the Channel Islands. They are sick of France. He likes America, but that can never be a home. He wants a job to do. "You see," she says, "he was born to be a salesman. He would be an admirable representative of Rolls Royce. But an ex-King cannot start selling motor cars." I feel really sorry for them. She was simple and sincere for the first time I have talked with her.

Diary   *June 10, 1947*

The Chinese Ambassador comes up to me and says nice things about my books. He asks me whether we in England were surprised by the long resistance put up by China. I say we were, as we had always supposed that the Chinese regarded war as an uncivilised practice, and soldiers as among the most despicable of mankind. He said that this was true, but they were fighting for their lives. "We have," he said, "a problem – I mean a proverb – in our country which says, 'Better to be a tile intact than a broken piece of jade'." "That is a very good proverb," I say. "I shall take a note of it," and I write it down in my notebook. "I wonder," I say, "whether your Excellency could repeat that proverb in Chinese?" He then screws up his face and begins with closed eyes. Then he stops. "No," he says, "I was mistaken in the problem. It is as follows: 'Better to be a broken piece of jade than a tile intact'."

Diary   *July 8, 1947*

To my dentist. I then lunch at the French Embassy, where Cyril Connolly, and I are invested with the Legion of Honour. We come in as usual, and the guests arrive. We hang about a bit and then [Ambassador] Massigli asks us to stand in a row. He then stands opposite us and makes an allocution. He does it very well, but I am overwhelmed by embarrassment. I feel angry with myself getting so shy about so simple an occasion. Then he motions to his staff and they advance with little medals on a tray. He then pins those on to us and gives the accolade – cheek against cheek. I hate it. Then champagne is produced and we have a *vin d'honneur* and then we lunch. I am annoyed at myself for having felt so clumsy and self-conscious.

H.N. to V.S-W.   *September 6, 1947*
                                                              Geneva

Yesterday I went to Lausanne and visited either the still existing, or now removed, [Benjamin] Constant sites. It is difficult to understand this sort of life at the end of the eighteenth century. Every member of the Constant family seems to have possessed at least two country houses outside the city as well as apartments both in Lausanne and Geneva. I suppose there were vineyards attached. They are some of them nice little villas with green shutters and dormer windows and terraces giving on the lake. But it is difficult to recapture the *train de vie*. Were there cooks in each of them and butlers and *femmes de ménage*? Or did they shut them up one at a time and transport the household. In each there is a fountain somewhere or a spurt of clear cold water from a pipe into a large stone trough. Each of these falls of water has a different note, and speaks, now sturdy, now mincing, in the voice it spoke to Benjamin all those long long years ago. But they can tell me nothing about how many cooks they had or gardeners.

Diary   *September 8, 1947*
                                                                  Geneva

I go to Coppet [the château owned by Mme. de Staël]. One walks down from the station past the wall of the park. The wall is only five feet high, and in the middle it is pierced by a grille. Just an ordinary railing it is, straight spikes alternating with wobbly ones. I expect it is through this railing that B.C. and Charlotte [de Hardenberg, whom he married secretly in 1808] had their clandestine interview.

From outside the château is both elegant and imposing. Brown tiles and woodwork of faded jade green. There is a fine forecourt with a cobbled approach.

There is a fine stone staircase to the first floor. A small anteroom and then the big *salon*, with tapestries and fine chairs dating from the time of Necker [Mme de Staël's father]. Next to it is a smaller room. It is lined with de Staël portraits – de Staël himself, Auguste [her son], Necker and his wife – and the Gérard portrait of Mme de S. The Vigée-Lebrun is also there. But I knew all these. What interested me more was a drawing of Mme de S. at the age of 14. There she sits very upright in a chair with her hands on her lap. Her hair is done very elaborately and powdered. One can see the ugliness of her mouth, the chubby cheeks, and the pert and brilliant eyes.

There is the library on the ground floor where they used to act their plays. The refreshments were handed in through the windows. Next to this huge room is what is called Mme de Staël's bedroom and beyond it what is called Madame Récamier's bedroom. The latter has a lovely Chinese wallpaper; and the former a heavy pompous bed. There is a show case cluttered with Mme de S.'s turbans and shawls. Red silk and yellow silk they are and some cashmere.

I forgot to say that the china at tea was blue china with an S and a baronial crown on it.

Diary   *November 9, 1947*

Read [Sir] Arthur Bryant on Pepys. It is odd how the English love a man who is not a humbug like themselves. To my mind Pepys is a mean little man. Salacious in a grubby way; even in his peculations there was no magnificence. But he did stick to his office during the Plague which is more than most men did. It is some relief to reflect that to be a good diarist one must have a little snouty, sneeky mind.

Diary   *November 10, 1947*

I discussed with Vita today the problem of my allocation of time. Now that I have dropped out of public life, I do nothing of any real importance. I do my "Marginal Comment" once a week; my *Daily Telegraph* reviews once a week; my *Figaro* once every other week; and my many broadcasts. I also have a succession of Boards and Committees [the National Trust, the National Portrait Gallery, the London Library, War Memorials and the Royal Literary Fund]. I find that I seem to have less time for my own work than when I was a Member of Parliament. These small diverse occupations interfere with my timetable. I should not engage in them, of course, were it not that they are my means of living. Why, being so hard-working, have I so little free time?

Diary   *November 11, 1947*

Come back and change and then go with Viti to the Royal College of Physicians where I lecture on "The Health of Authors". Niggs is also there. Lord Moran takes the chair. I ask him how Winston is. He says he is not well at all and that it was madness for him with such a bad cold, to go down to the House today. "Nothing will persuade him to take care of his health. Anyhow, I told him that in his present condition he would make the worst speech of his life." That evening I see a chap from the Commons who tells me that

Winston has made one of the most brilliant and powerful speeches he has ever made – about the House of Lords. What vitality that blessed man has got!

Diary   *December 3, 1947*

At 5.45 we drive in a lovely hired Daimler to Buckingham Palace. There is a party there for the Foreign Ministers Conference. As we enter the picture gallery, the delegations are grouped on the right and the non-delegations on the left. Tommy Lascelles comes up and says that Attlee wants to be introduced to Vita. I perform that ceremony. He is as gay and agreeable as ever. We then file into the Blue Room where the King and Queen and Queen Mary receive us. The King is in a good temper and grins in a friendly way. We then pass on into the White Drawing Room where there is a buffet. We lean against the buffet, have champagne cocktails and watch Molotov talking to the Queen. Winston appears in an old frock-coat which must have belonged to his father. His eyes have taken on an empty stare with a glaze such as only occurs in the eyes of much older people. He has long talks with Bidault and Molotov.

The King and Queen then bow and leave us. I am taken under the arm by Bevin and dragged to a seat. He is tired, having had to stand up for two long hours. He has a drink. He tells me that yesterday he had had a real heart-to-heart with Molotov in his (Bevin's) flat. He spoke as follows: "Now, Mr Molotov, what is it that you want? What are you after? Do you want to get Austria behind your Iron Curtain? You can't do that. Do you want Turkey and the Straits? You can't have them. Do you want Korea? You can't have that. You are putting your neck out too far, and one day you will have it chopped off. We know much more about you than you imagine. We know you cannot stand a war. But you are behaving in such a way that one day there will be a showdown. And you will have to give way in the end and lose your credit with your own people. You cannot look on me as an enemy of Russia. Why, when our Government was trying to stamp out your Revolution, who was it that stopped it? It was I, Ernest Bevin. I called out the transport workers and they refused to load the ships. I wanted you to have your Revolution in your own way and without interference. Now again I am speaking as a friend. You are playing a very dangerous game. And I can't make out why. You don't really believe that any American wants to go to war with you – or, at least, no responsible American. We most certainly do not want to. But you are playing with fire, Mr Molotov, and one day you will be badly burnt. And I don't see the object of it all. If war comes between you and America in the East, then we may be able to remain neutral. But if war comes between you and America in the West, then we shall be on America's side. Make no mistake about that. That would be the end of Russia and your Revolution. So please stop sticking out your neck in this way and tell me what you are after. What do you want?"

"I want a unified Germany," said Molotov.

"Why do you want that? Do you really believe that a unified Germany would go communist? They might pretend to. They would say all the right things and repeat all the correct formulas. But in their hearts they would be longing for the day when they could revenge their defeat at Stalingrad. You know that as well as I do."

"Yes," said Molotov, "I know that. But I want a unified Germany."

And that is all that he could get out of him.

Diary   *December 5, 1947*

Viti shows me a letter from the Prime Minister saying that she has got the C.H. I am overjoyed, but she takes it quite calmly. Benzie, when he arrives, has never heard of the C.H. and thinks it all ridiculous. Viti says it is my Civil Service mind which attaches importance to these things. But somewhere inside herself she is pleased, I think.

> *H.N. was now invited to stand as Labour candidate in the by-election which was impending at North Croydon. He accepted, with misgivings. The seat had been held by the Conservatives with a majority of only 607. They were as determined to retain the seat as the Labour Party was to capture it. H.N. hated the electioneering process, but campaigned conscientiously. He was defeated, but not ignominiously. V.S-W. played no part in the Election. She was lecturing in North Africa.*

Diary   *December 9, 1947*

Williams [Assistant National Agent of the Labour Party] rings me up from Transport House and asks whether I would take on the by-election at North Croydon. I say I must have time to think it over.

Diary   *December 11, 1947*

I am really perplexed to know what to do about this North Croydon business. I gathered from Frank Pakenham [Lord Pakenham, later Earl of Longford] he had expected my name to be on the list of those to be given a peerage in the New Year's Honours. Evidently I had been taken off the list at the last moment. Why? Is it because of Viti's C.H.? Or is it because Transport House said I was the chap to fight Croydon for them?

My perplexity takes two forms. One practical. If I refuse to fight this seat, then they will feel that I am not a good member of the party and I shall not be rewarded. If I fight the seat and lose honourably then all will be well. If I fight and win (which seems impossible) then it will be a tremendous triumph. But if I fight and lose badly, then I shall have missed both the lower and upper House. But my main perplexity is a moral one. If I refuse to do what they ask, I shall make it clear to my own conscience that I joined the Labour Party in order to get a peerage; and this will cause me such remorse that if offered a peerage I shall decline to accept it. I absolutely loathe fighting a by-election in circumstances of great publicity. I may make a muck of the whole thing. But the horror with which the prospect fills me is in itself an indication that I should undertake this horrible task.

[Later] But the crucial piece [of news] was at 3.15 when I went to see Williams at Transport House. I say that I will consent to meet the Local Committee on Thursday. I practically commit myself to fighting the seat if the local Committee adopt me which, I gather from Williams, they are certain to do.

Diary   *December 14, 1947*

Lord Baldwin has died. Poor old Baldwin. He was a man of little imagination and less vision, but he certainly had a gift for dealing with awkward situations as they arose. Generally his method was to evade them. But when he was forced to tackle them, as at the Abdication crisis, he did it very well. He was an agreeable, companionable man. He was really far more simple than he seemed. Or rather his simplicity appeared so naïve that many thought it was put on for effect: I do not think so. He enjoyed life and had certain excellent principles.

Diary   *January 4, 1948*

It is a sorrow to me that Viti is not more pleased with her C.H. I think that partly, in her modesty, she feels that she does not deserve it. But also the publicity involved annoys her, especially when they give her my name or associate me with her. I never quite understand why, when I am so proud of being associated with her, she should be so ashamed of being associated with me. Anyhow the whole business has made her, not happy, but irritable and nervous.

H.N. to V.S-W.   *February 25, 1948*
                                                                                       Croydon

Yesterday I had a horrible day. I had to go round with the *Daily Herald* photographer for feature pictures. Well, the first thing they wanted me to do was to visit an old Trades Unionist of 89 years of age. We drove up to his horrid little house. The old man was very ill in bed. He insisted upon getting up. He sat on the bed while the photographer dressed him. He panted terribly and I thought he was going to die. Then we sat him down in his armchair and I posed beside him. Suddenly he remembered that he had not brushed his hair and up he struggled again and poured a little oil into a tin and then dabbed the brush in it. Thereafter the photograph was taken.

　　Then I was dragged into a grocer's shop. A woman customer was dragged in to give more life to the group. I told her who I was. "Oh yes, I have often listened to you on the wireless. I should have voted for you had it not been for the Air Vice-Marshal [Bennett, Liberal candidate]. Such a raw deal that man has had – and a hero too!" So you see, I was right. Off I went again to a housing estate. The photographer in the excitement of the chase made me climb up a ladder of an unfinished house and interview the workmen doing the roof. I had to make explanatory gestures to them. Not my sort of thing at all.

H.N. to V.S-W.   *February 26, 1948*
                                                      Croydon

After a meeting last night a man came and entered into conversation.
"By the way," he said, "do your family object to your standing
Labour?" "Well, my mother said I had betrayed my country." He
was a Press Association man and all the papers this morning have
been ringing Mummy up. Oh my God!

H.N. to V.S-W.   *February 29, 1948*
                                                      Croydon

I actually enjoy canvassing, and it does good. That is one of the
advantages of being Labour. I have no hesitation in penetrating
into working-class homes, and they are so grateful and loyal. It
really moves me. I am so glad I belong to the Party now. I really
feel much more comfortable as a Labour man than I ever did as a
hybrid [National Labour]. There is a quality of mutual confidence
which is moving and rare. It was a lovely warm day at last, and the
whole thing seemed brighter and happier.

H.N. to V.S-W.   *March 4, 1949*
                                                      Croydon

*My God! It is dispiriting canvassing these dumb idiots. They have
no knowledge and interests at all. They are just sheep. One woman
evidently thought she was intelligent and that she could see higher
and further than her contemporaries and neighbours. She put on a
dreamy, visionary expression. "I want a MAN who can lead me!"
she said, gazing out towards the Surrey Hills which were still
shrouded in fog. "You mean Hitler?" I said. "Oh no – not 'im,"
she said. "I never could like his moustache. Silly I call it. I shall vote
for the Air Marshal. 'E seems to be my man." Idiot woman – it is
people like her who decide elections.*

H.N. to V.S-W.   *March 9, 1948*
                                                      Croydon

*This time tomorrow I shall have had my last meeting and deliver
my last speech. Probably in actual fact the last election speech I
shall ever thank God deliver. I long for that hour with sick longing.
I have not really enjoyed one moment of this election. The first few

days were true hell, partly because it was cold, partly because I felt ill at ease with my staff, partly because I had not discovered Ovaltine, but mainly because the election seemed to stretch in front of me as a long grey regiment of days. But now it is over and will shortly be an unpleasant memory.*

H.N. to V.S-W. [telegram to Tunis]   *March 12, 1948*

Beaten by twelve thousand. Oh my.

Diary   *March 12, 1948*
                                                        Croydon

I get to bed at 4.30 a.m. and am roused by the nice maid at 7.45 a.m. I get up and go down to breakfast. The old buffers are evidently delighted. One of them who came down later said rubbing his hands, "Well, what a result! What a triumph! Harris [the Conservative Candidate] has socked that cad Nicolson on the jaw!" "Shhh!" they answer, indicating me.

> *H.N. never received the peerage he hoped for, but he was invited to write the official biography of King George V, and this was to remain the central occupation of his life till its publication in 1952.*

H.N. to V.S-W.   *May 7, 1948*

I called in at the Roosevelt memorial [in Grosvenor Square, unveiled by the King in April]. The statue itself is a nightmare, but the surround with its two pools and the little fountains is quite successful. But how difficult the proletariat are! In principle I like to see such gardens thrown open to them. But they destroy the grass and there were little ragamuffins sailing cigarette cartons in the two pools. Yes, I fear my socialism is purely cerebral; I do not like the masses in the flesh.

Diary *May 28, 1948*

I had been expecting to be offered for the Birthday Honours the peerage which I nearly got in the New Year. But I have not had a word from Attlee and this means, either they are giving no peerages this birthday, or that my name is not among them. I am rather relieved really as I have *Benjamin Constant* to finish in the latter part of this year, and if they reform the House of Lords they are certain to make me a life-peer. I should prefer that in many ways. But I am amused to find in myself a fat grub of snobbishness. I have always hated the name "Nicolson" as being a common plebeian name. I don't mind it for myself, since "Harold Nicolson" is familiar and all right. But I hate it for Viti. Thus if I were made a real peer, I could change it to Cranfield. But if a life-peer, I could not change my name and "Lord Nicolson", and even more so, "Lady Nicolson" would sound absurd. Now really at my age I ought not to mind such things. And yet I am conscious of that grub or slug inside me. How little one knows oneself, even when one probes and pokes and is amused.

H.N. to V.S-W. *June 8, 1948*

This letter is about the "proposition" made to me yesterday by Tommy [Sir Alan] Lascelles [the King's Private Secretary]. I walked across the park to Buckingham Palace and entered by the side-door. I was at once taken to Tommy's room. He said the King had often spoken to him during the war about the need for an official life of George V. They had put it off from year to year. Then a few months ago the King had returned to the subject and said how important it was that this life should be written before Tommy and Owen Morshead [the Librarian at Windsor Castle] died. Tommy had therefore taken the opinion of five distinguished figures, and three of these five suggested me. He therefore told the King and the King said, "What do you feel yourself, Tommy?" And Tommy of course said that he would not have wished to put forward the name of an old personal friend, but that he agreed with the three elder statesmen. Then the Queen also agreed and Tommy was delegated to approach me.

At that stage I asked whether Queen Mary had given her assent.

He said she had not been consulted, I said I could not even consider the proposal unless she gave her consent. He said, "Very well, we shall ask her. If she objects, then we shall have to persuade her."

I then said that in principle I did not like writing biographies when I could not tell the whole truth. Tommy said – well I thought – "But it is not meant to be an ordinary biography. It is something quite different. You will be writing a book on the subject of a myth and will have to be mythological." He said that I should not be expected to say one word that was not true. I should not be expected to praise or exaggerate. All that I should be expected to do was to omit things and incidents which were discreditable. I could say as much in the preface if it eased my mind.

The idea was that I should be shown every scrap of paper that existed. I should have a table of my own in the library at Windsor and go down there three days a week. I should stay in Tommy's house if I wished to spend the night. Owen Morshead would help me. There was no hurry about the book – I could take four years if I liked.

I asked what about finance? He said that the King would not pay me anything at all, and that I should receive nothing from him even to meet secretarial expenses. All the King would do was to give me a table to work at, a cupboard to keep my papers in, and a free run of his archives. It was for me to make such arrangements as I could with my publishers.

Now what do you think? I see the balance-sheet as follows: *Advantages:* A definite task taking me three years at least and bringing a large financial reward. Access to papers of deep interest and importance. Close collaboration with charming people such as Morshead and Tommy. The opportunity of writing the history of my own times. Added to all of which I suppose is the compliment at having been chosen. *Disadvantages:* To have to write an "official" biography. The lack of charm in the King with whom I am dealing. My inability (and indeed my unwillingness) to poke fun at the monarchy. My not being allowed to mention discreditable or foolish things. My having to be mythological.

I told Elvira as she knew I had got an appointment with Tommy. She was delighted and as usual most intelligent. She said, "But it is just what you need – an anchor. It will keep you busy for three years and prevent you doing silly things like Croydon. People say that young men need anchors. That may be true – but people of later middle-age need anchors far more than the young." All of which, in a way, is true.

H.N. to V.S-W.   *June 9, 1948*

I write to Tommy and say "Yes". I shall not regret it.

Diary   *June 17, 1948*

I dine at the Persian Embassy. It is a big dinner for Bevin. He is in good form – noisy and vulgar. When the women go out he forces me to sit in the chair next to him which the Ambassador should have occupied. Bevin is so optimistic that he is unconvincing. He says that he pays no attention to all the attacks of the American press. What do they matter? After all, it is the principle that counts, and nobody is going to tell him that in principle it does not pay better to remain friends with 200 million Moslems than with 200 thousand Jews, "to say nothing of the oil." Not a discreet way to talk.

Diary   *July 22, 1948*

I go to Buckingham Palace for the Garden Party. I have a talk with Anthony Eden. He tells me that in his long experience he has never known such enthusiasm as he had during his visit to Berlin [at the start of the blockade]. There were crowds when he came out of the lecture hall, and they yelled and cheered. He was embarrassed, first because he does not like Germans, and secondly because he realised that it was an anti-Russian demonstration.

Nancy Astor is there and comes up to me in a crowd and says loudly, "The man who sold his soul." I ask why? She says because I joined the Labour Party in order to get the Embassy in Paris. I say (a) I hate Embassies and left the service in order to avoid one; (b) that Vita would never have enjoyed an Embassy and that this in itself would have made it impossible. She says, "Yes, you are right. I never thought of that." Then the other side of her comes out and she is charming. I really love that woman and admire her – but what enemies she must make among people who only see her silly sallies.

H.N. to V.S-W.   *September 9, 1948*

Poor Benjamin [Constant] was finished off today and this afternoon he goes to Constable. I feel quite sorry to say goodbye to him and to replace that gay companionship by such an old Thames pilot man. It will be fun being "In search of George" – but it will be hell writing the thing. I quite see that the Royal Family feel their myth is a piece of gossamer and must not be blown upon. So George VI will cut out all the jokes about George V.

> *On September 25 H.N. flew to Berlin to deliver four lectures at the request of the Foreign Office. It was a gesture of British solidarity with the Berliners during the Russian blockade.*

H.N. to V.S-W.   *September 26, 1948*
                                           Savoy Hotel, Berlin

Well this is tormentingly interesting but more horrible than anything you can conceive. A deep unhappy helplessness seems to brood over these ruins. My main impression so far is one of utter bewilderment. I have never felt quite so *stupid* in my life. Everything contributes to this. My cold (which is pursuing a normal course), the fact that I have forgotten my German, the fact that Hitler changed the monuments from one place to another, so that my sense of direction is completely misled, the fact that every now and then I recognise things for a second and that they then fade away into oblivion.

They picked me up for dinner and drove me out to a large villa in the Grünewald where there is a Press Club. They made me an honorary Member. It is pretty bleak I assure you. Only one bulb in the chandelier allowed to be on and of course no heating. The food was all British rations – not badly cooked. But there is a sense of living in a dugout.

It is far far worse than I expected. But it may be the shock of first impressions. It is like a moon landscape across which figures flit. Everything is almost unrecognisable. But what a deeply unsettling experience and how glad I am I came.

Diary   *October 1, 1948*
       London

The Berlin expedition was well worthwhile. It has taught me much. It has left me with my heart wrung with compassion and my nerves shattered. The future is really too terrible to contemplate.

H.N. to V.S-W.   *October 26, 1948*

How cold and lovely it was this morning. I walked about the platform of Staplehurst Station (since my train was late owing to coastal fog) and watched the leaves turning and thought how much NATURE had meant to me in life. Sissinghurst has a quality of mellowness, of retirement, of unflaunting dignity which is just what we wanted to achieve and in some ways have achieved by chance, I think it is mainly due to the successions of privacies: the forecourt, the first arch, the main court, the tower arch, the lawn, the orchard. A series of escapes from the world giving a progression of cumulative escape.

Diary   *November 7, 1948*

I do my review. I then try much to my fury to find quotations in my own books for Doubleday Doran's *Dictionary of Quotations*. It just doesn't work. I am not given to apophthegms. My gift is to explain things at length and convey atmosphere.

Diary   *December 1, 1948*

V and I come up in the fog. Our train is more than two hours late. I lunch with Willy Maugham at the Dorchester. We discuss, among other things, how it is that Cyril Connolly has managed to impose his personality upon his contemporaries. With scarcely any work at all he has managed to render himself an important literary figure. Willy says it is by sheer self-assurance. I say that Cyril is the natural parasite – he prospers on the labours of others.

Diary   *December 31, 1948*

For me it has in some ways been a bad year. My Croydon venture
was a misfortune. It shocked my Tory friends and it left upon the
Labour people the impression that my heart was not in it. The
peerage which I so nearly got last year has now it seems eluded me.
Nor am I feeling any younger. My deafness has increased slightly.
My political career (which was never very brilliant in any case) is
now closed forever. That is one of the worst things about getting
old. One ceases to believe the miraculous can ever happen.

But it is now evident that I have not been a successful man but a
failure; and this owing to lack of courage.

H.N. to V.S-W.   *January 7, 1949*

*My visit there [to Windsor] was a great success. I met Owen
Morshead who first showed me the [the King's] diaries. They are
really little more than engagement books and not at all revealing.
But they are invaluable for checking dates, etc. There is also those
extracts from Queen Victoria's diary which Princess Beatrice preserved. She burnt all the rest. Wicked old woman. Morshead tells
me he does not think the King or the Queen or even Queen Mary
will be difficult so long as I do not attack the principle of monarchy.
(Which I assuredly have no intention of doing.) But he fears that all
the old aunts will descend upon them and bully them. He says that
the difficult thing to treat will be his handling of his children. "The
House of Hanover, like ducks, produce bad parents – they trample
on their young."*

Diary   *January 20, 1949*

Nigel has got his friend [Jim] Rose of the *Observer* to offer me a
weekly article of 800 words on one book chosen by myself. This
would mean leaving the *Telegraph* and I should gain having to read
only one and not two books a week. Moreover it is quite evident
that the *Daily Telegraph* public is not one worth writing literary
articles for.

Diary   *February 27, 1949*

*Viti packs all day [for her lecture tour of Spain], and that saddens
me. After all, she is only going off for three weeks, I have plenty to

do and shall be busy, and it is childish to need her so much. But I know that I could not endure at my age to be separated from her for very long. I just could not bear it, and will not consent to it.*

Diary   *March 15, 1949*

I am alarmed to find a telegram waiting for me on the breakfast table. "Lectures in Barcelona cancelled arrive Dover 4.20 Thursday [March 17]. Please inform Sissinghurst all well love Vita." Now I do not believe all is well. I fear the strain has been too much for her and that she has broken down. I am worried but can only wait till Thursday.

I go to the [Army & Navy] Stores to get them to make into a suit the tweed that Nigel gave me. I say I want it double-breasted. The man is deeply shocked. "Surely not, sir; not in the country." I say I don't care a hoot and it must be double-breasted. "It will give you a Continental look, sir." "That is what I require. I have always wanted to be mistaken for an Austrian count."

Diary   *March 17, 1949*

I get back at 6 p.m. and at 6.15 telephone to Sissinghurst. Vita tells me she got 'flu at Granada. She wisely decided to cancel everything and come home.

Diary   *March 21, 1949*

I go to see Queen Mary at Marlborough House. She seems smaller than I expected, *has her back to the light, and I first took her for a lady-in-waiting. But I quickly recovered myself and we sat side by side.* She asked me whether I wished to put any questions to her. I said that in the course of my reading there would evidently be many things that puzzled me, but that for the moment there were very few things about which I was uncertain. For one thing, I found I had taken likes and dislikes as always happened when one steeped oneself in the life of an individual. I had acquired a great liking for Queen Olga of Greece [the King's aunt]. "Quite right too," she said. "The Queen was a second mother to him." Similarly I had taken a great dislike to Canon Dalton [Tutor to Prince George in 1871]. She was surprised by this at first. "The King was very fond of him," she said ruminatively. I said that I did not like the way he had written letters complaining of the naval officers and not allowed the Princes to consort with their fellow-midshipmen. She had never heard of his sneaking about the naval officers, which was wrong. The segregation of the Princes was even more wrong. But what she had against Dalton was that he never tried really to educate the Princes. It was disgraceful that "the King" had not been taught more. I asked her whether he could speak French really well. She did not quite like that question. "No," she said rather stiffly.

The King was by nature an immensely loyal man. He loved his old friends and servants. He was also extraordinarily truthful in that he never liked "going round and round", and at this she made a circular movement with her fingers.

She then turned to the question of his relations with his sons. She said that the real difficulty had been with the Duke of Windsor and never with "the present King", who always got on well with his father. I said that I had heard that he was good to the children when they were young; and good to them once they married; but that when they were young bachelors he was so terrified that they might fall into bad company that he nagged at them. She said this was true.

She added that "the present King" had been appalled when he succeeded. "He was devoted to his brother and the whole abdication crisis made him miserable. He sobbed on my shoulder for a whole hour – there, upon that sofa. But he had made good. Even his stammer had been corrected. And now he is so ill, poor boy, so ill." This in such a sad voice.

Diary   *April 17, 1949*

After tea, a great event happens. I actually begin writing *George V.* I am starting on the chapter dealing with the 1931 crisis as I want to have that chapter checked by people while still in the possession of their faculties. I do not get very far, but at least I have made a start.

After sunset I climb up the tower to pull down the flag. There is a great red glow in the west and the whole of Kent lies below me bathed in golden light. The garden looks so rich from the eminence – masses of blossom and daffodils among the dark of the yews. It truly is a most beautiful garden – so varied, so calm, so enclosed. It is a garden I should envy much if it belonged to someone else.

Diary   *June 10, 1949*

National Trust all day. We are getting more and more evidence that the present Government (or rather their supporters) do not like the Trust because it is managed by aristocrats working on a "voluntary" basis. One of the things I do not like about Socialists is their distrust of gratuitous public service. A man like [Lord] Esher, for instance, devotes his whole life to the furtherance and protection of the arts. But as he gives his services free, he is regarded with some suspicion by the doctrinaires.

Diary   *June 26, 1949*

I do my review of Bernard Berenson's *Sketch for a Self-Portrait*. Here again I have the conflict between sincerity and good feeling. He asks himself why he has not been able to inspire in others the confidence and affection he feels for them. Of course the answer is that he debauched his talent to make money and that he was harsh and selfish to his contemporaries. But he was good to young people and he did teach them all the zest for beauty. How can I insult a man of eighty-five? Yet by writing an adulatory review of him I am, I suppose, sinning against pure integrity. Raymond [Mortimer], in such a quandary, would not review the book at all. But under my dreadful time-pressure I cannot afford not to review a book which I have read with care.

Diary   *July 17, 1949*

I start writing the first chapter of my book on George V. I begin "Prince George was born at Marlborough House, London, at 1.30 a.m. on the morning of June 3, 1865." I gaze at the sentence in wonder, realising what a long journey I have to go before I reach his death. It is like starting in a taxi on the way to Vladivostok.

H.N. to V.S-W.   *August 17, 1949*

I fear I am getting rather down on George V just now. He is all right as a gay young midshipman. He may be all right as a wise old King. But the intervening period when he was Duke of York, just shooting at Sandringham, is hard to manage or swallow. For seventeen years in fact he did nothing at all but kill animals and stick in stamps.

Diary   *August 21, 1949*

I revise Chapter IV first part and try and go on with it but it gets sticky. One of my difficulties is dealing with Queen Victoria. Her words and phrasing and forms of thoughts are as old fashioned as a crinoline and her constant underlinings give a comic impression which is the last impression that I wish to convey. She had a wise and vigorous mind and was not really a comic figure at all, yet when one quotes her one appears derisory.

Diary   *September 24, 1949*

We are all feeling depressed about the Russian atomic bomb. We were told they would not have one for five years and they had got it in four. Does this really make so much difference? It may encourage the satellites to be more overweening, but it may also encourage Russia to be a little less nervous.

Diary   *October 4, 1949*

I spend the morning visiting York Cottage, the nest, the dairy, the gardens and the big house [at Sandringham]. There is nothing to differentiate the cottage from any of the villas at Surbiton. How right the Duke of Windsor was to say to me, "Until you have seen York Cottage you will never understand my father." It is almost incredible that this heir to so vast a heritage lived in this horrible little house for 33 years. It is now partly estate office and partly flats. But it is still untenanted in the upper floors and we went all over it. The King and Queen's baths had lids that shut down so that when not in use they could be used as tables. His study was a monstrous little cold room with a north window shrouded by shrubberies, and the walls are covered in red cloth which he had been given while on a visit to Paris. It is the cloth from which the trousers of the French private soldiers used to be made. On the walls he had some reproductions of Royal Academy pictures. The servants' rooms are mere attics with skylights. There is no garden.

Diary   *November 21, 1949*

My birthday. I am 63, damn it. It is a terrible shock to look forward to the gap of years to when I shall be eighty, and to realise that the same gap looking backwards brings me to a period which seems but yesterday.

Diary *January 4, 1950*

I had returned to me from Sandringham the proofs of section I of George V which I submitted for the comments of Queen Mary and the King. They are accompanied by a letter from Lady Cynthia Colville [Lady-in-waiting]. The corrections are very neatly tagged and marked. Apart from a few verbal misprints and so on, there are only two things they want me to omit. Anyhow I am lucky to have got off so well.

Diary *January 17, 1950*

Down to Windsor. I lunch with Owen Morshead. I suggested that there might come a moment when my conscience as a biographer became strained. What would happen if I found something which was really damaging to the King – for instance, a threat to abdicate if the Home Rule Bill were passed? My duty to the student would be to publish this; but if they asked me to cut it out? Could I resign my task? *Owen said rather primly, "Your first duty will always be to the Monarchy." At which all the contrariness in me surged up in a wave of sudden Republicanism.* I fear I have no mystic feeling about the Monarchy; I regard it merely as a useful institution.

Diary *February 2, 1950*

If I say the King has no power at all he may be hurt and say he is a mere cypher. But if I indicate that in any circumstances he can dissent from the advice of Ministers, then assuredly the radical press would claim that the Crown was too powerful.

Diary *February 3, 1950*

*I forgot to say that when waiting for my train at Waterloo the other day I ran into one of the French correspondents in London. He asked me where I was off to. I said I was going down to Windsor to study the archives. He asked whether he might enquire what was the subject of my new book. "Une biographie," I answered, "de

Georges V." He expressed surprise that there should be any documents at Windsor about any such person. Rather puzzled, I replied
that there was a whole room full of papers. "Quelle étrange per-
sonne," he said, "avec cette passion presque nymphomane pour les
hommes." I was much startled by this and then found he thought I
had said George Sand.*

H.N. to V.S-W.   *March 9, 1950*

I got into my huge Daimler and drove to the Travellers where I
picked up Raymond [Mortimer] and Clive [Bell] and James [Pope-
Hennessy]. In high spirits we went on to the French Embassy [for a
reception for M. Vincent Auriol, President of the French Republic].
James and I went to the buffet and had foie gras sandwiches and
champagne. There were masses of people there and James and I and
Clive stood at the back and watched while the King and Queen
came round and did *cercle*. It was amusing to see how some people
edged themselves into the front row. Then the King and Queen
retired to their own supper-room and we all started talking to
friends. While thus engaged a *maître de cérémonie* came to me and
said the President wanted to talk to me. *Grand ami de la France*.
So I was dragged through the two crowded salons into the ultimate
Royal (so Royal) supper-room and presented to Auriol. He is a
sweet and speaks with a strong accent – not exactly méridional but
regional. He said how sorry he was that I no longer wrote for the
Figaro. But I evaded that subject as I do not really want to start
writing for it again. Well, after an exchange of civilities, I shook
hands and was about to join the common herd when I heard a voice
say, "Just the man I want to see." It was the King. He talked to me
for about 20 minutes about the book. From time to time [René]
Massigli came up to interrupt, but the King ignored him. In the end
he said, "I seem to be neglecting my duties. I should like to talk for
hours about this. You must come and stay at Windsor." I had been
so interested in our conversation, that I had not noticed that there
were only about twelve people in the room – the Kings and Queens
and Presidents and so on. So I bowed my bow and then talked to
the Queen and to Princess Elizabeth, and then rejoined the
proletariat.

But no – I was seized by the arm and this was Winston. "So you
did not stand for your party – cowardice or conversion?" I said that

I had not stood because Niggs was standing. "Oh yes," he said, "Birmingham, wasn't it?" I said, "Leicester." He said, "Well, I knew it was a hopeless seat – beastly place, Leicester." [Churchill stood unsuccessfully as Liberal candidate for Leicester in 1923.] He then asked what the King had been talking to me about for all that time. I said it was the book. He said, "Oh yes, I remember. I want to talk to you about that. I have much information, very much information. Clemmie, remember to ask Harold for lunch one day." At that moment Attlee passed. "Well, Attlee," Winston said, "if we have many more parties like this, we shall be in a coalition together without noticing it at all." Then I went away. But doesn't it sound like something one has made up in one's bath.

Diary   *June 15, 1950*

I am horrified by the Labour Manifesto [refusing to join European community]. It will do immense harm abroad and shake any authority which we have left. It is a truly deplorable document. It means that Dalton, who sponsored it, cannot possibly succeed Bevin. I am deeply distressed by it. How I wish I had not been such an impulsive fool as to join the Labour Party. It was certainly the cardinal error of my life. But I cannot redeem it now.

H.N. to V.S-W.   *July 25, 1950*

I know you are right in thinking that I should make my book less documentary and more alive. I shall certainly try at later stages to introduce more vivid pictures of people and places. It may be that I have been so preoccupied with rendering the style and tone of the book of an equable surface (like linen) that I have refrained too austerely from any brocade. But I am sure that in a book of that length it would be a mistake to try and be "bright". One has just got to be intelligent.

Diary   *September 23, 1950*
                                                             Florence

A glorious hot day. At 4.30 we are picked up by the Berenson's chauffeur and driven all the way up to Vallombrosa where we stay the night. We are received by Nicky [Mariano, Berenson's secretary] and walk out to see the sunset where we find B.B. and Luisa

[Vertova, Berenson's assistant librarian, who later married Ben Nicolson]. They tell us they have received a telegram saying that Sibyl [Colefax] died in her sleep yesterday at 6.30 in the morning. We are shocked. At dinner B.B. is the gracious host. He talks well. He tells us about Rilke. "He must have been a very small man," said Vita. "Small?" said B.B. "Not in the least. He was my size. But I suppose you would call me small." He is neat and tidy but only about 5ft. 3. B.B. does not care for the moderns. He deplores Ben wasting his energies on the *Burlington*. He says that all the pioneer work of art criticism has been done long ago and that only finicky subjects remain. He says that there are so few English art historians that Ben is obliged to fall back upon foreigners, whose style is heavy and dull. He has a great belief in Ben. "There is," he says, "something very important at the bottom of that well."

Diary   *December 11, 1950*

At 11.45 a.m. Jim Lees-Milne picks me up with Jack Rathbone [Secretary of the National Trust] and we go down to Hertfordshire to see Bernard Shaw's house which he left to the Trust. We first go into the garden. A sloping lawn and rough grass intersected with a few rose-beds. A bank, with a statue of St Joan. A hut in which he worked. Everything as he left it. Postcards, envelopes, a calendar marking the day of his death [Shaw died on November 2, 1950], curiously enough a Bible and prayer book and Crockford's Dictionary, a pair of mittens. The grass path and the bed around the statue of St Joan are still strewn with his ashes and those of Mrs Shaw [who died in 1943]. The Trustees and the doctor got both urns and put them on the dining-room table. They then emptied the one into the other and stirred them with a kitchen spoon. They then went out into the garden and emptied spoonfuls of the mixture on to the flower-beds and paths. All this some fifteen days ago, but the remains are still there. Just like the stuff Viti puts down for slugs.

The house is dreadful and not really lettable. It will, moreover, be difficult to show to tourists as it is so small. It will be essential to keep the furniture exactly as it is and we shall have to send down a photographer. All his hats and coats and nailbrushes etc. are there. His long woollen stockings and his thick underclothes. The pictures, apart from one of Samuel Butler and two of Stalin and one of Gandhi, are exclusively of himself. Even the door-knocker is an image of himself.

Diary   *December 13, 1950*

Historic Buildings. We decide that we must accept Shaw's house morally and leave the discussion of finances to the Finance Committee on Friday. I am not happy about it. I do not think Shaw will be a great literary figure in 2000 A.D. He is an amazingly brilliant contemporary; not in the Hardy class.

Diary   *December 31, 1950*

So ends a horrible year with worse to come. I fear that the discomfiture of UNO in Korea is a bad portent. It indicates that although these international organisations can cope with small opposition, they become hesitant when the opposition is serious. We are all oppressed by a terrible sense of weakness and foreboding. We cannot count for one moment on France, Italy or Germany, and even the United States is afflicted with cold feet, taking the form of Hoover isolationism. The year closes in a mist of anxiety. We shall be lucky if we get through 1951 without a war.

How futile all my heavy work on George V seems in comparison to these gigantic ordeals and menaces! More and more do I cling, in almost desperate affection, to Viti, Ben, Nigel and my work and garden.

It is sad to become old amid such darkness.

Diary   *January 24, 1951*

I dine at Broadcasting House with Bertrand Russell and Lord Samuel, and afterwards we have a discussion upon "Why defend liberty?" Russell makes some good points. He says that the reason why communists are so zealous in pursuit of their own ideal is because they are a minority and because they are not quite positive it is true. Russell himself came to the conclusion that Marx's theory of values was bunk as early as 1895. He cannot conceive how any intelligent young man can be taken in by it. As for zeal – nobody has any zeal about arithmetic. It is not the vaccinationists but the anti-vaccinationists who generate zeal. Zeal is a bad mark for a cause.

H.N. to V.S-W.   *January 25, 1951*

I sent to Tommy Lascelles the piece I had done on the relations between King George and his children. I had put in everything I wanted to say, and expected him to cut something out. I did not want to submit to Queen Mary and the present King anything that would certainly be rejected, and thought that Tommy with his knowledge of the Royal mind could tell me what to modify and what would cause pain. But he telephoned to say there was nothing that he thought I ought to alter. They may be stung by it, but then that was just too bad. He also said that he had had a talk at Sandringham with Queen Mary and that she had spoken very highly of my book. "You may be sure," he said, "that you have her solidly on your side." Good.

Diary   *February 8, 1951*

Tommy Lascelles says that the present King never tells him actually what happened at interviews. The late King always sent for Stamfordham after he had seen a Minister and told him exactly what happened. Stamfordham then went off and wrote it down and sent his memorandum to the King to approve. The present King just says to Tommy, "Oh, he was optimistic as usual" or "He was worried about the coal situation" and never goes into detail. Therefore if George VI's life is ever written there will be no material at all.

Diary   *March 12, 1951*

I go round to see Mummy. She is half-conscious, but only recognises me when I shout at her, "I am Harold." She smiles so affectionately and murmurs, "My darling, darling Harold."

Diary   *March 23, 1951*

Good Friday. Gwen telephones at 7.50 a.m. to say the nurse says Mummy is dying and we better get round there soon. We have a hurried breakfast and walk to Tedworth Square. When we get there we are told she is just dead. She died at 8.10.

H.N. to V.S-W. *March 28, 1951*

Well, my dear old Mummy is no more than a handful of dust. I dislike having ceased suddenly to be anyone's son. It means that one is now definitely classed with the older generation and there is nobody older than oneself.

Diary *May 4, 1951*

I go to Waterloo and meet Viti. We then enter the South Bank Exhibition [the central feature of the Festival of Britain]. We are entranced from the first moment. It is rather a bore as we keep getting caught by the King and Queen, but nonetheless we enjoy it uproariously. It is the most intelligent exhibition I have ever visited. I have never seen people so cheered up or so amused, in spite of a fine drizzle of rain and a Scotch mist.

Diary *June 7, 1951*

I come back to Neville Terrace and am horrified to read headlines in the evening papers that Donald Maclean [head of the American department in the Foreign Office] and Guy Burgess [of the Far Eastern department] have absconded. If I thought that Guy was a brave man, I should imagine that he had gone to join the Communists. As I know him to be a coward, I suppose that he was suspected of passing things on to the Bolshies, and realising his guilt, did a bunk. During my dreams, his absurd face stares at me with drunken, unseeing eyes.

Diary *August 29, 1951*

A busy and useful day. In the morning I go to the B.B.C. and go through King George's broadcasts. His voice is so like the present King's. Very virile, rather bronchial, very emphatic. I notice the closed "o" as in "those"; it is what the B.B.C. call "off white" meaning thereby slightly cockney. I then go to the London Library and look up the actual texts of what I have just heard. I then go, after a quick luncheon, to St James' Theatre where I meet Viti and we see Olivier and Vivien Leigh in *Antony and Cleopatra*. The minor parts are very poorly played; the production excellent; Larry and Vivien good – she beautiful to look at, but not grand enough for so superb a part.

Diary   *September 19, 1951*

This morning at 1.20 p.m. I finish the last word of Chapter XXX and thus my life of King George V. I was first asked to do the book on June 7, 1948, but at that time I was finishing *Benjamin Constant* and did not get down to it till September. It has thus taken me roughly three years. I have enjoyed it immensely. It has been a most congenial task.

After tea I start on my "Author's Note". There are the genealogical trees to do, and the index and the illustrations and the proof revisions. But the main battle is over. I am satisfied. It was hard, hard work, but I think the result is pretty solid. I have a Gibbon feel.

Diary   *October 25, 1951*

We have a meeting of the sub-committee of the London Library to consider who is to be President. We decide to separate the posts of President and Chairman and to choose for the latter, not a man of eminence, but a man who will attend meetings. They therefore choose me. [H.N. remained Chairman until 1957.]

H.N. to V.S-W.   *December 5, 1951*

I went to a party for [Konrad] Adenauer [the German Chancellor]. He is looking well and young. He said that I had given him *viele freudige Stunden* [many happy hours] by *Public Faces*. It is always a matter of sadness to me that the books I take long to write never seem to attract anyone, whereas the ones I write in ten days or so seem to acquire fame immortal.

H.N. to V.S-W.   *December 11, 1951*

Do you know how much *Life* offer me for my article on Alexander the Great? They offer me 2,000 dollars which amounts to over £600.

Now that is more than I shall probably make over *George V*. Three years work compared to a fortnight's work. But I know it is not a logical point of view. I mean it is rather like Whistler when asked whether he felt justified in charging 100 guineas for a sketch that had taken him two hours to make replied, "Not two hours – a lifetime." Which is true in a way.

Diary   *December 25, 1951*

We give each other Christmas presents. I give Viti some bath towels (which I like, but she doesn't), some sherry glasses (which she doesn't like either), a flag [for the tower] (which she would have had to get in any case) and a new edition of *Larousse* (which she hates). Not a successful Xmas gift ceremony.

Diary   *January 2, 1952*

Horrible income tax demands and letters from my bank about overdraft. I am going to get into debt and have nothing to fall back on. I simply cannot work any harder than I do and it means that I shall have to cut down all my expenses. My financial position has always been precarious, mainly because I have no responsibilities other than for myself.

Diary   *January 11, 1952*

I get a letter from Tommy saying the King has no comments to make on Part IV so the thing goes off today to Constable's. FINISHED.

Diary   *February 6, 1952*
                                                              Bournemouth

It is about 11.20 in the morning. We draw up at the Central Committee Room to find Cowley waiting on the pavement with an expression of solemn anxiety. "Something terrible has happened," he says. "The King is dead." We are stunned, but almost at once we relate this national misfortune to the question of Polling Day at Bournemouth on this sixth of February 1952. Will the Conservative voters be too shocked to indulge in anything so mundane as voting? Will they jump to the conclusion that the Election is cancelled? How are we to let them know? Obviously all loudspeakers must be withdrawn from the streets. But the Labour people will have their voters gathered together in the workshops and they will vote in strength. Supposing no Tory voters come at all? Then Labour will win. In the shock of the moment these nightmares loom as large as the huge photographs of Nigel [on the hoardings]. He himself gets a little white. Viti suggests aptly that we should get on to the B.B.C. and persuade them to put out on the 1 o'clock news that the poll is still on.

I have to go back by the 12.40 train. Viti remains behind. At 7 I go to the Travellers. By that time I am convinced that Nigel will lose the seat. I pace the corridors of the Travellers up and down, waiting for a telephone call. It comes at 7.30. Niggs' voice. "It's not as bad as we feared. They started voting again after 3. About 60% of those who voted last time." I am much relieved.

Princess Elizabeth is flying back from Kenya. She became Queen while in a perch in a tree in Africa, watching the rhinoceros come down to the pool to drink.

Diary   *February 7, 1952*

I feel calmer this morning when I get up. But as the day passes my nerves begin to jangle again. To soothe myself I write a broadcast for tomorrow. I wait for the 1 p.m. news. I turn it on at 12.55 and get the weather report. While I am listening to that, Elvira, arrayed in deep mourning, dashes in with a piece of paper in her hand. "You have a son M.P.," she says and puts the telephone through. It is Viti at the other end. The figures are: Niggs, 22,480; Labour, 8,498; Liberal, 3,673; Independent, 1,692. Both the latter forfeit their deposits. Majority, 13,982. I am wild with relief.

I go to the Travellers for some tea. On the tape is the result of [the] Bournemouth [election] and Niggs' little speech. He claims to be the first M.P. to be elected in the reign of Queen Elizabeth II. How furious the great Elizabeth would be to know that she has been succeeded by this sweet girl.

Diary   *February 19, 1952*

Tommy says that there will be no Coronation this year. "Can't have Coronations," said Winston [once again Prime Minister], "with the bailiffs in the house." I get back about 11 p.m. and Niggs comes in at 11.30. He had enjoyed this the first of I hope thousands of days in the House of Commons. I go on working at my proofs till 1.30 a.m. and finish them. Bed at 2.

Diary   *April 24, 1952*

In the afternoon I have a discussion on the wireless with [Georges] Simenon. His wife came with him. She is like a Madonna in middle age and he clearly adores her. She manages all his business. He is a nervous excitable man, striding about the room puffing at his pipe. He does not speak English very well, but just well enough to get across to the Third Programme people. He tells me that he has written 300 books in his life, 148 of which are in his own name. He says he has decided to write one Maigret book a year and then leave time for more straight fictional works. He says his method is to soak himself in the atmosphere of a place for three days; then to soak himself in his main character; thereafter the plot and the minor characters form themselves. His identification with his main character is so intense that if the man is old, he himself for three days adopts the movements of a dotard. If the main character is a drunkard, he himself will start drinking hard. Then he writes in a fever for ten days and the book is finished. He says that the necessity of soaking himself in atmosphere and then writing about it is why he always moves from place to place. He is now writing a novel about American life. He will one day, when he knows us better, write about London. He says his son, aged 13, has never read a single book he has written. I rather liked both him and his wife.

Diary   *May 22, 1952*

Rab [Butler] drives me to the Albany. He is, as usual, very outspoken. He says that the difficulty is that Anthony [Eden] is assumed to be the heir apparent. He says that in any case Anthony has more appeal than he has, because Anthony has charm. I say I hope he will not seek to mimic charm, but remain reliable. He agrees. He says that Winston is so brave in war and so cowardly in peace; the Tory Government convey the impression of a wobble.

At the Albany I walk for the first time to C.1 [which was to be his London home until 1965].

Diary   *May 31, 1952*

Viti wakes me at 7 a.m. to say that Freddy [H.N.'s brother, 2nd Lord Carnock] is dead. I come up [to London]. I am met by a car at the station and drive straight to Sister Agnes' Home for Officers. I then go up to see Freddy lying there. He died in his sleep at 6.15 and without any pain or struggle. Poor old boy, it is such a wasted, lonely end.

I take the 4.38 home. It has rained today after a long drought, and the garden is fresh and beautiful. The roses are on the verge of being at their best. I walk with Viti in the garden after dinner when all the half-light plays on the flowers. It is peace unutterable, and in my heart there is great sorrow for Freddy. There ought to be relief, I suppose, that he is eased of all his loneliness and self-contempt, and that he died without suffering. But there is just sorrow at the thought of so wasted a life. I feel aching pity for him, and wish I were one of those who felt that he had been united with Mummy in some happy state. The mere fact that I want at this moment to find that sort of comfort convinces me more than ever that the belief in life-after-death is a human illusion.

Diary   *July 29, 1952*

Constable send round three copies of the revised and improved *George V*. It is excellently produced. I send a copy to the Queen and to the Queen Mother. After luncheon I go round to Marlborough House and am received by Queen Mary. She is getting older and toddles on her feet. But her mind is as clear as ever. She said two things which touched me. I was speaking of the King's outrightness, "Yes," she said, "he was sometimes too outspoken. We in our position have often to avoid answering indiscreet questions. I remember that I once had a Lady-in-Waiting who was a fool and used to ask indiscreet questions of my husband in the motor-car. He always answered exactly what he thought. I had to get rid of the woman." Then she said, when looking closely at the picture of Prince George as a young man, "How like he was to my poor silly son!" She stroked the book affectionately, and kept on murmuring, "Very well done. Very dignified."

Diary   *August 14, 1952*

King George V is published. There is a leader in *The Times* and in the *Manchester Guardian*, and an excellent review by Duff Cooper in the *Daily Telegraph*. All the other papers treat it as news. Seldom have I seen such prominence given to a single book.

Diary   *August 17, 1952*

There is an excellent review of *George V* by Kingsley Martin in the *New Statesman*. Also a really good one by [Lord] Samuel in the *Sunday Times*. A rather cross one by Walter Elliot in the *Observer*. But the whole effect is one of wide and lengthy adulation. How much of this is due to the very real respect that people have for King George? Never have I witnessed such a chorus of praise. I suppose I ought to feel elated. But somehow I am rather indifferent and do not experience any inner feelings of self-satisfaction.

H.N. to Sir Alan Lascelles   *August 31, 1952*

I have received two letters from you which I must now answer.

In the first, that of August 21, you were so good as to convey to me the congratulations of Her Majesty upon the excellent reception of my life of King George V. I am humbly grateful to the Queen for the interest she has taken in the book and for the appreciation which she has been gracious to express.

In the second – a private letter of August 22 – you envisage the possibility of my being offered the K.C.V.O., and you ask me whether my previous disinclination remains obdurate. I do not think that literary people should be accorded knighthoods, although, if you asked me to state rational grounds for this objection, I should be unable to do so. For snobbish considerations also, I do not want to change the shape of my own name or that of Vita. On the other hand, I quite see that, after the reception the book has received, the conferment of the C.V.O. would suggest to people that my biography had not been accorded full royal approval. To maintain my objections might be considered churlish and embarrassing.

I have discussed the matter with Vita, who is always so wise in such matters, and I now write to say that I should be honoured to accept a K.C.V.O. if it were offered.

Sir Harold Nicolson (as he was about to become) started his new book, Good Behaviour, *in October 1952. He was living during the week in London, and spent weekends only at Sissinghurst. He gave up his articles for the* Spectator *but reviewed a book a week for the* Observer, *and broadcast regularly on foreign affairs for the B.B.C. overseas service. His younger son, Nigel, now a Member of Parliament, was married in July 1953. And Ben, two years later.*

Diary   *November 5, 1952*

I turn on the wireless at 8 a.m. to hear Eisenhower's voice. It comes through the atmospherics of the Atlantic and the wild yells of his supporters. He is President-Elect. No details yet. Anyhow, thank God all that is over and that the U.S. can now become comparatively normal again.

We have a dinner at the House of Commons for the Brains Trust people. We discuss Eisenhower as President. Professor Goodhart [Master of University College, Oxford] says he will be good for NATO which is the rock to which we cling now that the UN is dead and done for. But what can he do in Korea? The electors will expect him to end the war, but he cannot do that without either abandoning the prisoners or bringing in new divisions from Formosa. In fact he is out on a limb. Goodhart says that he hopes Foster Dulles does not become Secretary of State, as he is deeply anti-British.

Diary   *December 30, 1952*

Up to London. Many letters, including a charming one from [Sir William] Haley, expressing regret at my abandoning Marginal Comment [the last of his 670 articles was published on December 26]. Of course, now that I have decided to do so, all sorts of ideas come into my head, and I regret being unable to express them.

Diary   *January 1, 1953*

My K.C.V.O. is published in the New Years' Honours and I get masses of telegrams. One that pleases me from Balliol. *It is all very embarrassing and I feel ridiculous and rather angry. How few people will realise how far far rather I should have received nothing at all!*

Diary   *January 3, 1953*

Why is it that I hate so much being congratulated on my K.C.V.O.? Partly natural shyness. Partly because it is embarrassing to express pleasure about something one loathes. And partly a conceited feeling that after all the work I have done in life, a knighthood is a pitiful business, putting me in the third eleven. I know that the K.C.V.O. is not supposed to be an assessment of my contribution to life, but rather a present from the Queen for a service rendered to the Monarchy. But other people do not realise that, and I feel as if I had got a fourth prize in scripture when I should have liked the Newcastle [Senior Classics Prize at Eton]. So one is really much more snobbish and vain than one imagined.

James [Pope-Hennessy] says that my diary is too boring for words and that there is no use going on with it. But it has become a habit, and is useful for reference. He thinks that no diary is of any value unless it expresses personal opinions, feelings and gossip, and recounts all that is said. I must try and render it less of an engagement book, as otherwise I agree that it is not worth the trouble entailed. So henceforward my diary will be an expression of deep internal thoughts and emotions. But no gossip. I do not think it right to record day by day all the turpitude or sexual aberrations of my friends. I love them too dearly for that.

Diary   *February 26, 1953*

I go to Buckingham Palace for an audience and investiture. I am introduced as Mr Nicolson. The Queen is standing by the fireplace and I advance and bow. She says not one word, but motions me to a faldstool that is ostentatiously standing in the centre of the room. Beside it there is a table with a scabbard and a sword. I kneel down and the Queen lays the sword, gently but quite firmly, first on my left and then on my right shoulder. I then rise and she gives me her hand to kiss. She then gives me the box containing the star, and says with a pleasant smile, "This is a personal present." Then she motions me to a chair and we sit down.

Diary   *March 4, 1953*

Niggs comes back holding out the *Evening Standard* with banner headlines, "Stalin has had a stroke and is dying". My God, what danger that means!

Diary   *March 24, 1953*

Queen Mary dies at 10.20, and Winston announces it in sobs at 10.45.

H.N. to Philippa Tennyson-d'Eyncourt   *April 1, 1953*
(Nigel's fiancée)

I am glad you are coming to Sissinghurst on Saturday, as it will give us time to get to know you and to break through the awful embarrassment inseparable from such introductions. You will find us shy, eccentric, untidy, but most benevolent. You will find Sissinghurst the strangest conglomeration of shapeless buildings that you ever saw, but it is an affectionate house and very mellow and English.

     Viti says that she asked you to call her "Vita", and you must call me "Harold". That is far simpler. I always called my own beloved father-in-law "Lionel", and it seemed quite natural after the first ten years or so.

Diary   *April 16, 1953*

I ask [Sir] Malcolm Sargent whether the musical profession is as mean and jealous as the acting profession. He says it is far worse. I really think that writers are the only people who do not wish to devour their competitors.

Diary   *May 6, 1953*

I lunch at the Austrian Embassy to meet the Queen of Spain [the daughter of Princess Beatrice and the wife of King Alfonso XIII of Spain]. She is unlike other royalties since she really is interested in the past. She began by saying that Queen Mary had given her a copy of my book and had said to her, "It is not only a true book, as you will see, Ena, but it is also beautiful." She tells me that at the age of five she had acted as bridesmaid to George V. She remembers it perfectly, mainly because she got into trouble. She had been told that she must keep quite silent, since nobody ever spoke in church. Then, when she heard the Archbishop beginning to read the prayers, she piped up, "But, Mummy, *that* man is talking." Queen Victoria told her afterwards that she had been "very pert". She also remembers that after the service there was a buffet at St James's Palace and that the children were in the corridor. An old gentleman with an odd collar and fur said, "I want to see the royal children play." They did not know what he meant and hung shyly, but Princess Patricia said, "He wants us to dance." So they danced in front of him up and down the corridor and he beamed at them. She now realises that it was Mr Gladstone.

She said that Queen Victoria never understood children and asked them so many questions that they became confused. She had a horrible bag of gold and coral out of which she would take sovereigns and give them to them. When it was too snowy at Balmoral to go out to Crathie church, she would give them Bible talks in her room. That was a great ordeal, as she always lost her temper with their stupidity. She can still recall her lovely girlish voice and that silver laugh. But no liberties were permitted. The Battenberg children, being resident family, were always given dull nursery meals – beef, mutton and milk-puddings – but visiting children were allowed éclairs and ices. Once, Princess Ena, in indignation at this, said as her grace, "Thank God for my dull dinner." Queen Victoria was enraged at this and punished her.

I enjoyed my conversation and returned to Albany meaning to record it. Elvira said, "Honours heap upon you." There was a letter from the Master of Balliol saying that I am to be elected an Honorary

Fellow. Only Niggs, and perhaps Viti, know that of all honours this earth can give, this is the one I most desire.

Diary   *June 2, 1953*

Coronation Day. We are called at 6 and walk round to the Travellers. There is television in the dining-room and we see the whole service quite beautifully. I am much moved. Then we have an excellent luncheon and go to our places on the stand. After a short wait the troops appear. There is a long pause while the Guardsmen wait in front of us and the rain pours down on their bearskins. This is due to the horse-artillery being unable to get their guns up the slippery slope of St James's Street. But off they move again and eventually comes Winston in his Garter robes waving his plumed hat and making the V sign, the Queen of Tonga immense and in an open carriage getting drenched, the Queen Mother and Princess Margaret, and finally the vast gold coach. The procession characteristically is ended by an ambulance for any horses that might get hurt.

Diary   *June 21, 1953*

Ben today made a strange remark while we were discussing what an effect a private school had on little boys, and how they separated their home from their school life. "It is an effect," says Ben, "which lasts all one's life. To this day I have a horror of rendering myself conspicuous or of seeming different from other people." Considering that his hair is like that of a gollywog and his clothes noticeable the other end of Trafalgar Square, this is an odd assertion. Yet it was made in absolute sincerity, and with that naiveté which is part of his compelling charm.

Diary   *July 4, 1953*

We process in robes into the City Hall [Newcastle-on-Tyne] where there are many graduands. I am the only honorary doctor and come first. I sit there in my robes and watch 300 men and women receiving degrees – not one of them that is not a monster of ugliness. How strange that the human nose and chin should be subject to such ungainly variations.

Diary   *July 16, 1953*

At the Beefsteak there is an American called Colonel Matthews. I beg him that when he returns to New York he will not encourage the idea that England is deluged under a flood of anti-American hatred. It isn't that. It is that we are frightened that the destinies of the world should be in the hands of a giant with the limbs of an undergraduate, the emotions of a spinster and brain of a pea-hen. He says, "The difference is that we are a democracy and you are not." What he really means is that they idolize the common man or woman and we only pay attention to the uncommon man. He is utterly unable to explain how [Senator Joseph] McCarthy's witch-hunting and book-burning can be reconciled with democratic principles. In fact he is a foolish man who thinks only in terms of small-town politics. I return distressed.

Diary   *July 29, 1953*

I go to Dartmouth House for the reception for Adlai Stevenson. It is packed. I am introduced to him, and he tells me that he has never forgotten how kind I was giving him luncheon and taking him into the House in 1939. I have no recollection at all of this incident. He is not as I thought him. A heavy man, with slim body, but heavy appearance, reddish face, alert eyes, a rather prancing manner – in fact a deception.

Diary   *July 30, 1953*

[Nigel's wedding-day.] We go in a car to St Margaret's. There is an awning and a large crowd. The church is already packed when we get there. All goes perfectly and we come out and walk down the aisle to Mendelssohn's silly tune. We drive off to Fishmonger's Hall. Everything there is magnificent and V and I stand beside the Tenny-son-d'Eyncourts shaking hands with troops of people. Ben makes a sweet little speech and we drink their health, and Niggs makes a speech in which he refers to our (his parents) happy married life. This brings a lump to my throat and tears to V's eyes. Then off they go in their little car to Sissinghurst.

I feel crushed and exhausted and sad. *I really believe that one can love a person so deeply that their happiness becomes far more important than one's own.* But I shall miss Niggs dreadfully.

Diary   *September 28, 1953*

The Americans, after three years of negotiation, have come to an agreement with Franco whereby they obtain bases in Spain. They are also obliging the Greeks to get rid of our naval mission and to have an American one instead. Gradually they are ousting us out of all world authority. I mind this as I feel it is humiliating and insidious. But I also mind it since it gives grounds for anti-American feeling, which is I am sure a dangerous and quite useless state of mind. They are decent folk in every way, but they tread on traditions in a way that hurts.

Diary   *November 1, 1953*

I read Virginia Woolf['s Diary]. She rightly says that to a diary one entrusts what is a mood rather than the expression of a continuous personality. There is nothing of her distinction, charm, and occasional affection and kindness in this diary. She seems neurotic, vain and envious. But it is fascinating nonetheless.

   I know well the mood that is entrusted to this diary. It is the time-table mood.

Diary   *November 19, 1953*

I go to hear T. S. Eliot speak on "The Three Voices of Poetry". The lecture takes place in Central Hall and I have never seen such a crowd for any literary lecture. They told me there were more than 2,500 people there and they remained silent throughout. I am on the platform and Norman Birkett takes the chair. Tom talks about his Three Voices – the voice of the poet talking to himself or nobody, the voice of a poet addressing an audience, the voice of a poet speaking through a dramatic character. He has much that is new to say. He says that for him inspiration is like matter that must be expelled in the form of a poem.

Diary   *January 18, 1954*

I read Paddy Leigh Fermor's essay on monasteries [*A Time to Keep Silence*] which is impressive. He is becoming an important writer.

Viti discovers that what I thought was a fine crop of myosotis is in fact salad. I weed it up sadly all afternoon. I read *Emma* [as background for his chapter on "Respectability" in *Good Behaviour*]. A happy day together – [one of] those beads on the necklace of my life that not even death or illness or madness or drink can destroy.

H.N. to V.S-W.   *March 10, 1954*

Did you feel very old when you got up this morning [V.S-W.'s 62nd birthday]? It is horrible this business about Time's Winged Chariot. It simply does not give us a chance at all. And I do want to get m.l.w. [my life's work – the spring-border] really perfect before I die, and I want to write five more books, and I want to see Jemima and Jasper [imaginary names for his unborn grandchildren] grow up, and, oh dear, what a lot of things I want!

H.N. to V.S-W.   *April 21, 1954*

*Well, I was wise to have had a car to meet me yesterday as there were no taxis at Cannon Street and a huge queue. But off I sailed magnificent and outrageous in my Daimler. I lunched with [Sir William] Haley, formerly D[irector] G[eneral] of the B.B.C.], and now Editor of the *Times* newspaper. I wanted him to join the Beefsteak as all his predecessors had, but he is too shy. "I am not," he said, "a clubbable man, and as you know am bad at general conversation." I always told you I liked Haley. He has such high ideals and does so adore the *Times*.*

Diary   *May 18, 1954*
Paris

I reach Paris at 6.10 p.m. and go to the Hotel Vendôme. Hugh Thomas [Ex-President of the Cambridge Union] comes to pick me up. We go to the Ritz for a drink and then on to Véfour. They say there are no tables free, and I am about to leave when I am caught by Jean Cocteau who insists on our having a table next to him. He is amusing and interesting. He tells me that he knew Alain-Fournier [the author who was killed in 1914 at the age of 28] well, and in fact they lived together for a few months. He has a little brass plaque let into the back of the bench at Véfour saying, "Here sat Jean Cocteau."

The next table has a similar plaque saying, "Here died Fragonard" [in 1806], and in fact he did die splosh into his plate.

Diary   *June 27, 1954*

I am depressed by my Manners book and wish I had never embarked upon it. In fact I am feeling old, deaf, stupid, with no new ideas. Nothing agreeable can happen in the future and the disagreeable things are large and numerous. This is just a mood.

H.N. to Juliet Nicolson [Nigel's daughter, aged seven weeks]
July 31, 1954

Now that you have been admitted into the Church [she was christened the day before] and had a paragraph all to yourself in the *Daily Telegraph*, you should be able, if not to read, then at least take in, private letters.

I thought it noble of you to remain quiescent while your god-father and godmother promised such glum things on your behalf. But I did not think it noble of you to sneak when I gave you a silver spoon and you went and bashed your own eye and forehead with it. It is foolish, in any case, to bash oneself with spoons. But it is evil for a girl about to be blessed by a bishop to sneak about her grand-father. You did not see the look your mother gave me. You did not realise the deep suspicion with which your nurse thereafter regarded me. (What an ass that woman was, flattering you like that; and how weak of you to respond with a grin to her blandishments.)

Will you tell your father that were I a Conservative, I should blush at the way they have behaved over Cyprus. "We cannot allow self-determination for Cyprus since it is a vital strategic base. We could not have remained in the Canal Zone, since, because it is a vital strategic base, it would have been bombed out of existence." Nothing shows up the Tories so badly as situations which they know to be false. It emphasises the falsity both of the situations and of the 1922 Committee.

And will you tell your mother that I really believe that you will have large eyes as lovely as she has and a character as sweet as hers, and that I really will not spoil you when you reach the age of 2, since

I detest spoiled children. And even if I do spoil you, I shall do so surreptitiously in order to avoid a look from her like the spoon-look.

H.N. to V.S-W. *September 16, 1954*

I took Richard Ward to Albemarle Street to see the Byron relics. Jock Murray, as always, was an angel and took so much trouble. He opened a drawer, saying to Richard, "It's Portugal, isn't it, that you go to next week?" "Yes, Lisbon." "Well, this may interest you ...," and at that he flung a huge tress of hair at Richard with a label on it in Byron's writing, "Lisbon – March 12, 1811". It was still quite fresh and brown. But what passes my understanding is how any woman could have allowed the English lord to take such a vast fid of hair away with him. It must have left the wench almost bald.

Diary *September 22, 1954*

We go to see Edith Evans in Christopher Fry's "The Dark is Light Enough". I can scarcely hear a word, which shows me how deaf I am becoming. But it seems a silly pretentious play to me, redeemed only by the excellence of Edith's acting. We come back and have supper with pink champagne. Edith Evans joins us and is charming. She, like all the older lot, regrets that young people are not trained sufficiently. She says her own training was rigorous and at times almost unendurable. Unlike most actresses, she says nothing unkind about other actresses, speaking with real warmth of admiration about Peggy Ashcroft.

H.N. to V.S-W. *September 30, 1954*

Tomorrow is a fiesta day [their wedding anniversary]. How little did I or you realise when we said "Till death do us part" on that October day [1913] at Knole that it would be so absolutely true. But what should I do without you? What should I do? I should be as lonely as a mouse in Santa Sophia. Just vastness and emptiness all around me. But I think one is wise not to brood on such disasters, and to live day by day grateful for each evening when it arrives without misfortune, accumulating a store of happiness on which to feed during the darkness and the cold. My sweet, what a store we have!

Diary   *October 12, 1954*

*Up to London. Masses of boring letters. I lunch at the Travellers with dear old Clive Bell. He had aged. He is writing a book about Virginia [Woolf, and others, entitled *Old Friends*] to undo the harsh impression left by Leonard [Woolf]'s edition of the diary.*

I take the chair at the Press Conference given by Chatham House in celebration of the completion of Arnold Toynbee's *A Study of History*, the last two volumes of which come out on Thursday [two further volumes were published later]. I make a speech in which I welcome "our more slender but no less weighty Gibbon". Not a smile does this quip evoke. I am hopeless at making an amusing speech, since my jokes never seem to the British public to be jokes at all. The only thing I am at all good at is making funeral orations. Anyhow, Toynbee made a speech and then they asked questions to which he replied with consummate charm and brilliance. One journalist asked him what purpose had impelled him to devote thirty-five years of his life to this single great work. Toynbee rose politely in his seat and replied with one word, "Curiosity." I like that sort of thing.

V.S-W.'s Diary   *November 29, 1954*

H. said that Nigel had sounded him on whether I would ever consider giving Sissinghurst to the National Trust. I said, Never, never, never! *Au grand jamais, jamais.* Never, never, never! Not that hard little metal plate at my door! Nigel can do what he likes when I am dead, but so long as I live, no National Trust or any other foreign body shall have my darling. It is bad enough to have lost my Knole, but they shan't take Sissinghurst from me. That at least is my own.

Diary   *December 1, 1954*

[Sir] Arthur Bryant tells me a nice story. His old tutor at Harrow, a Mr Mayo, told him that as a young master he had had to cope with a most unruly class. In despair he exclaimed, "I don't know what to do with you boys!", and a voice had answered him, "Teach us, Sir!" The voice came from a chubby imp with carrot hair – Winston Churchill. Mayo never forgot it.

Diary   *December 16, 1954*

Viti and I go to the Royal Literary Society where she reads her poems to an appreciative audience. Cecil Day Lewis is in the chair and is charming. Viti is asked for an encore and, rather bewildered, begins with the opening of "The Land". Then she suddenly realises that the word "Boeotian" is approaching, which she always forgets how to pronounce. So when she reaches it, she pauses and exclaims, "Harold!" in agony. So I say in a loud voice, "Boeotian!" The audience were much amused, but some of them thought it must be a put-up job.

Diary   *January 10, 1955*

Viti is late coming to dinner and when I go to fetch her I find she has slipped on the lawn and hurt her back. She was trying to get up. I produce a chair for her to climb up on. But I fear the weather and redoing the books in the Big Room have made her arthritis really dreadful. Her hand is all swollen. I cannot bear to think of her in pain.

H.N. to V.S-W.   *January 12, 1955*

I hated the idea of you sitting up there with Mademoiselle, and in pain with your back and hand. So I telephoned. You sounded sad at having lost your mobility and youth, but otherwise better. But it is horrible having this dragon eternally watching you and beginning to nibble and chew at you when the weather gets too damp or you move books. Dragons ought to know that women-of-letters are apt to move books frequently and ought to show more consideration. But I hate to think of you in pain. I mind that even more than you mind my being in taxis or aeroplanes.

Diary   *February 6, 1955*

I work at my Duff [Cooper] article [for the *Dictionary of National Biography*] and find it absurdly difficult. It is not my gift to compress

into tiny spaces. In fact it is more trouble to me than five articles.
It is like writing a chapter of Ezekiel on a sixpence.

Diary   *February 18, 1955*

There is heavy snow and Viti is late. I pick her up at her hairdresser
and then go to Buckingham Palace. In come Winston and Clemmie,
looking grand. Then the Iranian Ambassador. Then the Queen
Mother. Then the Queen and the Duke. And finally the Shah and
his wife. Then we pass into luncheon. Viti sits between [Sir Ivone]
Kirkpatrick and Winston. The latter is in his best mood and talks
gaily to her about history. On his other side is Madame Soheily [the
Iranian Ambassadress] and he recites Omar Khayyam to her. He
tells Viti that he is astonished to discover that we never had central
heating in this country from the day the Romans left until the day
the American heiresses arrived. After luncheon we stand around in
groups and Winston is very nice to me. He says, "It was sad you
leaving the House. You were developing into a good debater." He
looks far, far better than when I last saw him. The children then
come in and are very well-behaved and natural. Prince Charles
[aged six] crams his mouth with coffee-sugar; Princess Anne [aged
four] picks at it delicately.

H.N. to V.S-W.   *February 24, 1955*

*I lunched with Nigel and Philippa. We were discussing the ethics of
suicide and I said that if you died, I think I should kill myself. At
which, with wide-open eyes, Philippa said, "But you can't do that.
You have Juliet to think of, and both of us!" It was so spontaneous
and simple that it wrung my heart. And it is true in a way. But I
should not remain at Sissinghurst, but go and live in a little house
in Putney.*

V.S-W.'s Diary   *March 11, 1955*

Oh dear, this has been a dreadful day, or, rather, evening. H. got
up at 7.30 p.m. to have a bath while I made his bed, and came back
saying he had lost all power in his left hand and that his arm felt
numb. I looked at him and saw that his poor mouth was all twisted,
also his speech was so thick that I could only just understand what

he said. I feared that he had had a stroke, and rang up Dr Parish who confirmed it. He was perfectly clear in his mind and insisted on going on with the proofs of his Manners [*Good Behaviour*] book, which he had been doing all day. But he soon gave it up and said he would go to sleep.

I spent much of the night wondering how I could most tidily dispose of myself if he died, as I should not care to go on living without him.

Diary   *April 5, 1955*

I listen to the 6 p.m. news which tells me that at 4.30 Winston handed his resignation to the Queen, who was graciously pleased to accept it. I suppose the Queen will send for Anthony [Eden] tomorrow.

Ben is engaged on a book on a Flemish 17th century artist [Hendrick Terbrugghen] whose name is unknown to me. That is why he is off on this trip [to Holland]. But how very odd that he should never have mentioned it to V. or me! It is actually rude to be so reserved and uncommunicative and I feel annoyed with him. It is as if, taking no interest at all in our doings, he is determined to exclude us from taking any interest in his.

Diary   *April 13, 1955*

I am dictating to Elvira when the telephone rings and it is Vita. She had got a letter from Ben telling her that he is engaged to Luisa [Vertova]. Well I'm blowed! I telegraph to Ben and to Luisa. I pray that it will work out all right; I think it will. Anyhow, I am delighted.

H.N. to Philippa Nicolson   *April 17, 1955*

Vita's back is, so she says, better, but I doubt it [after she injured it three weeks before]. The x-ray makes it quite clear that she has cracked a bone called the "sacrum" (which is an idiotic name for any bone to have), and she ought to remain motionless until the crack fills up. But will she do anything of the sort? Of course she won't. She hates being fussed over, and I try to be tactful and just strew cushions in her path in the hope that she will lie upon them. But not she. Poor darling, she can't sit or even lie with comfort, and cannot do any writing at all.

Diary   *May 15, 1955*

I have a second small stroke. I had a good breakfast, came over to my room, and got up to take a book out of the shelf. I noticed that my fingers in the right hand were too numb to type, so I started rubbing them. I then thought I would go out for a breath of air and found my right leg was wonky. It felt as if my foot or shoe were cased in lead. I got out to my garden chair and could do no more. I staggered up to my bedroom and rang my bell for Mrs Staples [the cook] and she came. She summoned Viti who arrived looking rather white, bless her, and sent for Dr Parish. Parish took all the tests and said that it was probably an "arterial spasm" since it passed off so quickly. But he warned me that arterial spasms, if repeated, lead to clots, and clots to real apoplectic strokes. I must in future take things more easily. I realise that all this means I become a semi-invalid.

Diary   *May 22, 1955*

I decide that my next book will be on Sainte-Beuve. It is just what I want – a long spell of leisurely reading and not much travel or research, to which I am no longer up. So I get Ben to help me take down all *Les Causeries du Lundi* from a top shelf. I know that in all probability I shall not live to write such a book. But I hate not having a book on the stocks, and it cheers Vita up to see me have such confidence in my future. I don't think she was quite taken in, but she was touched by the experiment.

Diary   *June 19, 1955*

I wish to God I were well and able to have confidence in my own health. The bore of this apoplectic condition is that one never knows how bad one is. One feels perfectly well and then the fear of a stroke comes down on one for no reason. I do not notice that my mental or physical powers are in any way affected. I mean, I seem to read and write as well as I did before Portugal, but that may be an illusion. But the fact remains that at any moment I may pass out and become paralytic.

Diary   *August 8, 1955*
Florence

[Ben's wedding-day.] We drive to the Palazzo Vecchio. We stand
under the statue of David with his enormous hands and buttocks.
Signora Vertova and Luisa arrive. We go up to the Sala de Matri-
monio. It is a high room with early 18th century tapestries. Red gilt
and damask chairs, rather faded. Ben and Luisa sit in two larger
chairs in front, and Viti and Signora Vertova and the immediate
relations in a row behind. There are some twenty close relations and
friends present. The Councillor comes in by a side door. An old
gentleman with a tumbly beard, dressed in evening tails with a black
tie, and round his middle a huge *écharpe* of the national colours.
They sign registers and then the old boy starts an oration which goes
on for 45 minutes. In the end they have to pull his coat to get him to
stop. I cannot hear a word he says, but Viti hears him and is amused.
He makes *punchinello* gestures. He evidently much enjoys making
such a speech. Viti tells me afterwards that he warns Ben not to
behave either like Hamlet or Othello, and that Italians are more
espansivi than the English, and that he must kiss Luisa when he
leaves the house and again on his return. The audience titter slightly
at his jokes. He begins by calling Ben "Benedict", but it soon becomes
"Benedetto". To me, who hears nothing, it is not impressive, but
farcical. Then he presents Luisa with a bouquet on behalf of the
Commune and Ben with a book by Mazzini entitled *The Duty of
Man*. Everybody seems to have forgotten about the ring, and Ben
just shoves it on as an afterthought.

Diary   *November 9, 1955*

I dine with Baba [Metcalfe] to meet the Duke of Windsor. The Duke
is looking far fitter than he seemed when I saw him last time. He
chatters and chatters. He pretends to be very busy and happy, but I
feel this is false and that he is unoccupied and miserable. Poor
man, he is as nervous as ever. He has a vast cigar which he chews
and wets but does not even light and then lays aside. *Although he
must have talked to me for three-quarters of an hour without
stopping, there was nothing of any interest at all that he had to say.
But his memory is acute.*

H.N. to V.S-W. *December 1, 1955*

I am discouraged about Sainte-Beuve. I find *Port-Royal* really dreadfully dull, being uninterested in sin and redemption, and not caring
at all for the doctrine of Jansenism or la Mère Angélique. I have a
naturally pagan soul – *anima naturaliter pagana*. It is not that I am
wholly material or despise spiritual things. It is that I hate the idea
that God enjoys people mortifying the flesh and being inelegant.
And they were all such BORES. I always said it was a mistake to
embark on the biography of a man whom one does not respect or
like, but I thought the amusing side of S-B would carry me along.
But *Port Royal* has got me bogged. I don't want to publish a bad
book at the end of my life, and I may chuck the whole thing.

Diary *December 4, 1955*

Viti is finishing a [short] story and is furious at having to come across
to dinner. The difficulty with her is that if she is interrupted, she can
never start again. So instead of going to her tower after dinner, she
retires to bed at 9.15. I never know what to do about these things.

Diary *December 29, 1955*

The *Sunday Express* telephoned to ask me what was my main wish
for 1956. "Not," I said, "to be telephoned to by the *Sunday Express*
when I am busy."

H.N. to V.S-W. *January 25, 1956*

I have had an odd proposition made to me. Would I stand as candidate for the Professorship of Poetry at Oxford? It wasn't John
[Sparrow]'s idea – it emanated from some other quarter. It seems
now Cecil Day Lewis having completed his term of office, Enid
Starkie [Fellow of Somerville College] has put up W. H. Auden as
candidate. This has enraged the older members, as Auden shirked
the war and went to America. Thus they ask me to stand as his
opponent. Now, of course, my first instinct was to say "NO".
Partly because I am not a poet; partly because I do not like opposing
Wystan Auden; and partly because of my health. But I am always

carried away by the mention of Oxford even on a pot of marmalade, and it would be a great and glamorous honour. As for health, it means only one lecture a term, and that would not be a strain for me. The appointment lasts for five years and is purely honorific, although expenses are paid. So I said "YES", and now you will be cross with me. Anyhow, I expect they will choose Auden in the end and I rather hope they do. But, oh dear! I should like to be Professor of Poetry at Oxford!!!!!!!!

V.S-W. to H.N.   *January 26, 1956*

Oh dear, oh dear, FIDGET. Not content with being Chairman of the London Library, Vice-Chairman of the National Trust, Trustee of the National Portrait Gallery, D.Litt. of Grenoble University, President of the Anglo–Iranian Society, and God knows what besides, you must go and become Professor of Poetry at Oxford. Well, I do understand it; I really do. Anyhow, it is a great compliment to have been asked.

Diary   *January 29, 1956*

There is a nasty paragraph in the *Sunday Times* about the Oxford Chair of Poetry. It says that Auden is the best poet of the last 25 years, and that the post needs a poet and not "the urbane H.N." I wish to God I hadn't agreed to stand, as I hate this sort of controversy and rather agree that Auden would be better. It all comes, not exactly from my impulsiveness, but rather from a hatred of giving way to my old age and invalidism.

H.N. to V.S-W.   *February 1, 1956*

I had a nice dinner with Baba [Metcalfe]. The Oliviers were there and the [Douglas] Fairbanks. Vivien Leigh says that one of the things we don't realise about Shakespeare is how wonderful he is to act. "Shaw is like a train. One just speaks the words and sits in one's place. But Shakespeare is like bathing in the sea – one swims where one wants." I thought that a good metaphor.

Diary   *February 9, 1956*

John Sparrow telephones from Oxford to give me the result of the
election. The final figures are: Auden, 216; myself, 192; [Professor]
Wilson Knight, 91. John says that all the women dons and most of
the scientists voted against me. There was some excitement, and
slogans "Vote Auden" were chalked up on the walls of New
College. I am delighted by this result. What I feared and dreaded
was that either Wystan Auden would be beaten by me by a tiny
majority, thus enraging the undergraduates, or else I should be
beaten by a vast majority. As it is, my vote was most honourable
and there is no humiliating defeat, and youth gets what it wanted.
There is some disgust at Miss Starkie's violent propaganda. I am
glad we did no campaigning on our side and that it was never mentioned that Auden had run away to America. This imputation
would in fact have been wholly irrelevant.

H.N. to V.S-W.   *March 1, 1956*

It is unfortunate that Nigel always seems to espouse causes which
are unpopular [with his Party and constituency] – Israel, abolition
of the death penalty, Cyprus, and so on. He is too honest and progressive for those old Bournemouth tabby-cats. I hate that type of
person. He has had many letters referring him to the Old Testament
about "eye for eye and tooth for tooth". He can reply by referring
them to the Sermon on the Mount. I wish the Archbishops would
make a statement. I mean, they are glib enough to give their views
about disarmament or the UN or Mr Dulles, but here, where there
is a direct moral issue on which Christians seek for guidance, they
remain dumb.

Diary   *March 3, 1956*

*I revise Chapter III [of *Sainte-Beuve*]. I read vol. I of Winston's
History of the English-Speaking Peoples. It is like a series of essays
by good history students, interrupted by Winstonian comments.*

H.N. to V.S-W.   *April 24, 1956*

I am worried about the televising of Sissinghurst. It is so rare that
we differ on such things that when we do, each leans over backwards to please the other. But in this case I think your reasoning is

better than mine. I have a vague prejudice against (a) exposing my intimate affections to the public gaze; (b) indulging in private theatricals. But it is a garden matter, and in garden matters *voluntas deae suprema lex*. So I withdraw my objections. [V.S-W. later changed her mind to please him, and the garden was not televised.]

H.N. to V.S-W. *April 25, 1956*

My Labour friends told me that the dinner given by the Labour Executive to Bulganin and Khrushchev was a ghastly failure. Khrushchev made a speech saying that it was Russia alone who defeated Germany. George Brown, a Labour front-bench hearty, exclaimed, "May God forgive you!" Khrushchev broke off and asked the interpreter what he had said. It was translated. Khrushchev then banged the table and said, "What I say is true!" George Brown is not the mild type of Socialist. He replied, "We lost almost half a million men while you were Hitler's allies!" *Silence pénible*. And at the Speaker's luncheon yesterday George Brown went up with an outstretched hand to apologise, but Khrushchev put his hand behind his back and said sharply, "NIET." My friend told me that in a long experience of unsuccessful banquets, that will live in his memory as the most acid failure that he has ever witnessed. Apparently the Russians are furious at the undergraduates ragging them at Oxford and have told *Pravda* to say that it was a demonstration organised by fascist elements. Poor silly boys. I think they were rude in a way, but fascist, NO!

H.N. to V.S-W. *July 4, 1956*

I saw my old friend Alan Hodge, who now edits *History Today* [with Peter Quennell], and in the intervals helps Winston with his book. It will go down as far as the death of Queen Victoria, and they have got as far as 1815. He told me that Winston now stays in bed all morning. He has a tame budgerigar whom he calls "Toby", and who keeps fluttering about his bedroom. Winston is convinced that it talks. All other people think it merely twitters and chatters, but he is positive that again and again it repeats the cheerful phrase, "Sir Winston is very pleased."

*I think Joe Ackerley [the author and Literary Editor of *The Listener*] must have gone off his head. His book *Tulip* is disgusting.

I could hardly read it and shall certainly not review it. I was so shocked that I thought it must be Victorian inhibitions, so I asked Colin [Fenton, with whom he shared C.1 Albany] to read it. He was equally revolted. You see it is all about the functions of the body and spares us no detail at all.*

H.N. to V.S-W.   *July 12, 1956*

Eric [3rd Lord Carnock] came up to vote [yesterday] in favour of the abolition of hanging Bill. Charlie [Lord Sackville] and Sam [Lord St Levan] voted against. "Three uncles," Nigel snorted, "left the backwoods to vote, and only one of them voted the right way." But he was pleased that all the bishops but one were on his side.

H.N. to V.S-W.   *July 26, 1956*

I went to a party yesterday given by Bob Boothby. Nye Bevan was there, and talked to me about the "decay" of the present government. He attributes it entirely to Eden, who, he says, is much disliked, weak and vacillating, and in fact, hopeless. He was not talking as an Opposition leader, but as a student of politics. He said that in his experience the character of a government was determined by the character of the Prime Minister. To choose Eden had been a mistake, since he was not a strong man. He interfered with his colleagues and did not control them, and gave the impression to the House that he did not know his own mind. Now when I hear a man abused like that, I immediately wish to take his side. But I fear that it is all too true.

Diary   *July 27, 1956*

The Egyptians under Nasser have nationalised the Suez Canal. That is a pretty resounding slap in our face.

> *The crisis which stemmed from Nasser's action, and ended in the abortive attempt by Britain and France to regain control of the Suez Canal by force, profoundly affected H.N. His first reaction was that Nasser should not be allowed to escape unpunished for his behaviour.*

But as Anthony Eden's intention to resort to force became evident, he feared the consequences which in fact occurred.

Diary   *July 31, 1956*

Nigel says that most of the Tories are breathing fire and slaughter against Egypt, but that he expects that in the end "wiser counsels" will prevail. That means that under American pressure we shall enable Nasser to get away with it. I wish sometimes that we were less encumbered and more powerful.

Dulles is flying over to take part in Suez Canal discussions. It looks as if he were coming to urge us to pipe down.

Diary   *August 2, 1956*

Talks continue all day between Pineau [the French Foreign Minister], Dulles and Eden. It looks as if Dulles agrees with an international conference but disagrees with the use of force. The difficulty is that Nasser has not, so far as I can see, violated any International Treaty. What the treaties provide is that the Canal should be open in time of peace and war, not who should own the Canal. *It is highly inconvenient that a man like Nasser should have control of the Canal and be able to blackmail us by threats. It is also most unpleasant that his seizure may encourage other Arab countries to do the same.* But we cannot persuade the Americans that the situation justifies the use of force, and I am not abolutely sure myself whether we should use it or threaten it. In fact the Government have shown their accustomed irresolution and confusion of purpose.

H.N. to V.S-W.   *August 9, 1956*

In the midst of death we are in life. It was so absurd last night. We had people coming here to listen to Eden['s broadcast] – James [Pope-Hennessy], Lucien Freud, Hugh Thomas and Niggs. We heard the broadcast and then went into the sitting-room and discussed it. I left them to go to bed, and had not taken off my clothes when Ben telephoned to say it had begun [the birth of H.N.'s second granddaughter]. Then we got rid of our guests and I started to go to bed again. But I had only just got into bed when Niggs came in in his pyjamas and said it was a girl.

I spoke to Ben [this morning] who said, "I am just going round to visit my daughter." He will telephone me on his return from the nursing home, and I shall let you know how they both are.

What a relief! I was worried about Luisa. But it seems to have gone off in a flash, and there is Vanessa Pepita a citizen of the world. Ben was so relieved that there was not an inch left for regret at it not being a boy. I am disappointed, but do not wish to be rude to Vanessa so soon after her arrival.

Diary   *September 12, 1956*

I dine at the Beefsteak where I find many peers back from the House of Lords debate. They are a little shaken by the fact that Lord McNair [President of the International Court of Justice, 1952–1955] stated that we were breaking the Charter of the United Nations by moving troops in such a way as to constitute a threat of force. Shortly after I have got home, Nigel appears. He had returned from Oslo this morning and went straight to the House from the station. He was in time to hear the P.M.'s statement and Gaitskell's reply. Eden had brought out his Users' Association proposal [which called for co-operation between Egypt and the main users of the Canal on pilotage, signalling, etc.], and had indicated that if Egypt refused to co-operate, we and France, with the tacit approval of America, would use force. This led to an outburst in the House, the Tories cheering wildly and the Labour people shouting "Resign!" and "Warmonger!". I think Niggs is himself rather alarmed by this bellicose attitude, which he regards as bluff. No government could drag the country into war over the Suez Canal with the Opposition against them.

Diary   *September 15, 1956*

I go on with *Sainte-Beuve* and finish him at 12.20 this morning. I do not feel the usual feeling of elation, since I regard the book as bad, and as clear and overt evidence of my waning powers.

Nasser, as was expected, has refused the plan for a Users'

Association. He describes the proposal as an act of war. The Russians have issued a threatening communiqué saying that they cannot remain indifferent to war in the Middle East.

Diary   *October 30, 1956*

At 6 p.m. I turn on the news. Eden and Mollet [French Prime Minister] have addressed to Cairo and Tel Aviv an ultimatum summoning them to withdraw their forces ten miles from the Canal. This ultimatum expires in twelve hours, after which we shall take our own measures to enforce the decision and to·occupy Port Said, Ismailia and Suez. The House had received this announcement at 4 p.m. and Labour had protested that such action independent of the U.S.A. and UNO was a terrible gamble.

Diary   *October 31, 1956*

*Egypt has rejected our ultimatum, and Israel only accepted it on condition that Egypt does so also. The Security Council have, to a man, voted against us, and France and the United States have expressed strong disapproval. It really does look as if the Government had embarked upon a gigantic gamble.

Meanwhile, in the evening we learn that our bomber squadrons have left Cyprus for Cairo.*

Diary   *November 2, 1956*

There was such an uproar in the House last night that the Speaker had to suspend the sitting. The United Nations Assembly has voted with but five exceptions [Britain, France, Australia, New Zealand and Israel] ordering a cease-fire. Eden refused to tell Gaitskell what we would do [next]. There is a suggestion put forward by Canada that UNO should police the area, but it will take a long time before the police-force can be assembled, and meanwhile we and France will go ahead. The whole Egyptian bluff has been called good and proper. But that makes no difference. Success does not render a dirty trick any less dirty.

Diary   *November 4, 1956*

Anthony Nutting [Minister of State for Foreign Affairs] has resigned.
This is extremely important since it deprives backbench Members
of the excuse, "The Government must know best." Nutting knew
everything, and has yet decided that it is evil. The central fact remains that Eden has deliberately ignored the recommendation
passed by the overwhelming majority of the United Nations Assembly. This is a breach of law. I am not surprised that the House,
at their special meeting yesterday, should have burst into disorder.

I telephoned to Nigel at 9.15 this morning. He says that he can
scarcely, feeling as he does, vote for the Government. He was disgusted by the hypocrisy of Eden's broadcast. He says that he thinks
some twenty Tories will abstain, although this may mean the fall
of the Government.

The Russians have sent seven divisions into Hungary and are
closing in on Budapest with 1,000 tanks. But we have no right to
speak a word of criticism.

Diary   *November 10, 1956*

The analogy with the Munich crisis is curiously close. Even as people
then said, "Chamberlain has saved us from war," now people say,
"Eden has saved us from war," forgetting that we have been humiliated in the face of the world and broken our word. The sad thing is
that whereas at the time of Munich, we who opposed Chamberlain
were proved right in six months, it will never become utterly apparent how bad Eden's action was.

I read the Lytton–Virginia letters [*The Letters of Virginia Woolf
and Lytton Strachey*] and am appalled by their silliness, dirtiness,
and cattishness.

H.N. to V.S-W.   *November 21, 1956*

*It is no good pretending that I like being 70, because I loathe it. I
had a gay breakfast with heaps of telegrams and presents. Then the
bell rang and the knocker knocked and a lovely girl appeared with
an envelope which contained a cheque for £1,370 and a list of some
200 names. Really, I was overwhelmed. I am such an odd person.
I scarcely dare look at the list for fear it may contain names of
people whom I have long ceased to know. I simply loathe people

being asked to give me presents when they don't want to. This is not ingratitude, but a sort of disordered and diseased pride.*

Diary   *November 27, 1956*

I dine at the 200th Dinner of the 63 Club which is held in the Royal College of Physicians. The health of the guests is proposed by Sir Russell Brain [President of the Royal College of Physicians] and replied to by Douglas Woodruff [the author, Editor of *The Tablet*]. The latter says that my real claim to immortality will not be my books so much as my Diary. Poor Chap! If he only realised what a pitiable little engagement book it is.

Diary   *December 3, 1956*

In the House today Selwyn Lloyd announced that we are clearing out of the Canal forthwith. He claims that our action stopped a war and brought in UNO. I suppose some people will believe him.

Diary   *December 15, 1956*

Looking back at the Suez crisis, it seems strange to me that I should at the age of seventy have been so passionately moved by the whole business. Of course there was a personal interest in its effect on Nigel [who, by not supporting the Government, lost the backing of his Bournemouth East and Christchurch constituents]. But apart from that, the moral issues affected me as much as anything since Munich. My admiration for the Hungarians and my realisation of the immense importance of Russia suppressing by force a movement which was a patently working-class movement, were nothing like so intense as the shame and sorrow of the Suez incident. It meant much to me that a Prime Minister who had made his reputation by [his] moral courage should out of exasperation have violated his principles and told his country a series of shameful lies. It was a disappointment also to realise that my countrymen, in whose political good sense I had firmly believed, could prove as gullible and emotional as the Germans.

*On January 15, H.N. and V.S-W. went to the Far East,
the first of six successive winter voyages. H.N. later
revised his diary of this trip and published it under the
title,* Journey to Java.

Diary   *January 9, 1957*

I dine at the Beefsteak, and as I drive there my taxi-man says,
"Here's a pretty mess, the Prime Minister resigning like that." It
seems that Horace Evans had made a thorough examination, and
decreed that Eden could not live if he carried on. My only feeling is
one of profound compassion.

Diary   *January 10, 1957*

I go to the B.B.C., and the woman who works the lift says, "Well,
Macmillan is our new Prime Minister." The Queen had seen Winston and Bobbety [Salisbury], and come to this decision. It is sad
for the left wing of the Tory Party, since Butler was the leader of
young conservatism, but I daresay that in the circumstances it is
right.

H.N. to Nigel and Philippa Nicolson   *January 25, 1957*
                              M.V. *Willem Ruys*, near Cape Town

So far – (touch wood and indulge in all forms of sympathetic
magic) – everything has been perfect. It is a revelation to us to realise
that there really does exist such a phenomenon as spare time. In
this blessed void repose it doesn't matter one hoot whether today is
yesterday or tomorrow. I feel that my nerves have acquired a new
casing and that impatience is a vice that is slipping away from me.
Women can pause for quite a long time in gangways, chatting
amicably about the swimming bath, and I remain immune from
those spasms of rage which assail me in London. But I have not
been idle. I have read and annotated several books, and have
written an 8,000 word article upon the purpose of life. It is a Halcyon
existence, and I render thanks to those friends who rendered it
possible.

Diary   *March 17, 1957*

Slowly we tie up. At 9.40 a.m. we leave the *Willem Ruys* and step on
the shore of our native land through the same covered and illumined
gangway that we traversed on January 15. Since then we have
travelled more than 25,650 miles. V. has written 40,000 words of *La
Grande Mademoiselle* and I 60,000 of this diary with its inserts.

Diary   *April 2, 1957*

We motor to Buckingham Palace at 8 p.m. and pause for a while in
the Mall as we are too early, and then enter at 8.20 punctually. We
are met and escorted to the drawing-room upstairs; then lined up;
then the Queen and Prince enter; then dinner. I talk to Hugh
Gaitskell. He says that his Party is split over the atom-bomb question. He must not commit them to any definite rejection since he
may soon be responsible for the decision himself. It is the difficulty
of the Leader of the Opposition that his Party wish to oppose always
and do not realise that the leader has always to consider what
policy he would himself adopt if he were to become Prime Minister
tomorrow. *He is charming about Nigel, saying that it is so maddening that local associations have no idea of a man's true value in the
House. I am pleased by this.*

H.N. to V.S-W.   *April 16, 1957*

*Niggs is here and enjoyed lecturing in Berlin and Kiel. The Bourne-
mouth line is that he and those who felt like him ruined the Suez
operation by expressing doubts, and then murdered Eden. He says
that his constituents who were beginning to feel rather uneasy about
their attitude are now quite happy in the conviction that he is a
traitor and a murderer. On the other hand [Marshal of the Royal
Air Force] Sir John Slessor, who was with him in Germany, told
him that there is not a single senior officer in the services who does
not feel that the whole operation was a disaster.*

Diary   *May 1, 1957*

I attend the Royal Academy banquet. When Winston arrives, the
crowd in the courtyard cheer loudly. Winston is given a little chair
at the entrance to the main rooms where he sits looking rather
childish. On the wall in one of the rooms is a monstrous caricature

of him by Ruskin Spear R.A. which makes him look like a village dotard from the Auvergne. I cannot think how the Committee allowed it to be hung. The dinner is far better than the last time, having been done by Fortnum and Mason. There is unstinted champagne, port and brandy. Winston sits there looking very old, and there is a hint of dribble about his lips.

H.N. to V.S-W.   *June 13, 1957*

The B.B.C. Overseas people want me to take part in a broadcast justifying the West. I agreed to do so. The whole of modern civilisation, including the hydrogen bomb, derives from the Mediterranean basin, and the East is no good at all except at poetry and art. I despise everything east of Suez (including Suez itself), with the exception of the Chinese, for whom I have deep respect. My word, some of their carvings I saw at Spinks yesterday were magnificent!!!

H.N. to V.S-W.   *June 26, 1957*

Nigel's dining-club had the Prime Minister [Harold Macmillan] to dine. The P.M. was very frank with them and said that he simply could not think out any message to give the people. The masses now took prosperity for granted and did not realise that in the whole of history prosperity and full employment made for a rise in the standard, and therefore in the cost of living. The country simply did not realise that we were living beyond our income, and would have to pay for it sooner or later. Nigel was entranced by the intelligence and wisdom that he displayed.

Diary   *September 12, 1957*

I get up. I shave and wash and dress. I enter the sitting-room, and help myself to a sausage and pour out a cup of coffee. The telephone rings. "Yes?" I answer. A very young voice reaches me from the distance saying, "Harold, I have got a brother [Adam]." Then Niggs' voice intervenes, and explains that Philippa had a boy at 6.30 this morning. My delight at this news shows me how really worried I had been. I am so happy that I find myself singing.

Diary   *October 5, 1957*

I am woken up by V. bringing her portable wireless into my room, and saying that I must listen to the 8 o'clock news. It was announced before midnight that the Russians have released a satellite which is now circling the earth at tremendous speed giving out signals. The B.B.C. had managed to record the signals, and play them over to us – just ping, ping, ping, ping. I am annoyed that the Russians should have been the first to get away with this, since it will increase their scientific prestige. Damn them.

H.N. to V.S-W.   *October 9, 1957*

Mr Barker [an executive editor in Doubleday & Co.], lunched with me yesterday. They are proposing a series of world histories or "portraits of epochs", and want me to do the eighteenth century. I said I was too old and ill for that sort of thing and turned it down. But this morning I reflected (a) that I would in any case have a book on the stocks; (b) that the portrait of the eighteenth century would be far more interesting than reading the plays of Joanna Baillie [the poet and dramatist, 1762–1851, who was one of the figures H.N. intended to include in a book on minor nineteenth century writers]; (c) that it is physical and not mental effort that is bad for me; (d) that I might as well say yes. So when Elvira comes I shall telephone to Mr Barker and say I have reconsidered my attitude.

Diary   *October 19, 1957*

*I review Nancy [Mitford's] book on Voltaire [*Voltaire in Love*] and not too kindly. But there is a sort of bouncy vulgarity about her writing which jars my nerves.*

Diary   *November 24, 1957*

I have a rather meaningless review [for *Journey to Java*] in the *Observer* written by Alan Pryce-Jones, and a rather nasty one in the *Sunday Times*. I detect in both of them a feeling that the book is based on rather strained, and even false, merriment. I can see that in its intimacy and family allusions it may seem embarrassing to many, and it was certainly this that explains Tray's [Raymond Mortimer's] reserve on the subject.

H.N. to Philippa Nicolson   *December 24, 1957*
                                    S.S. *Reina del Mar*, near Venezuela

This is a marvellous boat – really exactly like a luxury hotel. Vita has most meals in her cabin as she has, until a few days ago, this recurrent fever and feels too limp to dress. She was up all yesterday without ill effects. She has been wonderfully patient and uncomplaining. Were it not for the constant anxiety I have been through, and for my loneliness, I have myself got much out of the journey – doing steady reading, taking notes for my book on the eighteenth century [*The Age of Reason*], bathing in the delicious swimming pool, gazing at the mountains of Jamaica and Cuba, and talking to Lady Magnus-Allcroft, who is married to Philip Magnus – a clever Oxonian and an excellent writer [of biographies]. She is a real person – obstinate and kind – and has been a friend to me during these dark days. I shall always be grateful to her.

Diary   *February 9, 1958*

*Wake up in Plymouth Harbour on a rather pleasant day. We wait some time in the ocean terminal but not as long as at Southampton last time. Reach Sissinghurst at 7 p.m. Too dark to see anything. I read some of my *Journey to Java* reviews. They are not too cruel considering that the reviewers are mostly young men and I belong to a vanished generation. Go to bed, but V. remains up in her tower late going through the accumulated letters.*

Diary   *March 19, 1958*

I write an article for the *Spectator* on the subject of Urbanity. In a
Beaverbrook periodical called *Books and Art* a young man writing
under the name of Humphry Clinker has accused me in two successive articles of being cultured, snobbish and urbane. I rather like
having the chance to answer him, although I do not really understand what his real grievance is. He says that "virtuosi" such as
Cyril Connolly and myself live in ivory towers and do not possess
the common touch or understand the dust and roar of life. We
should treat literature as a smart columnist treats life and should
not discuss general ideas but concentrate on personalities and be
more newsy. I say in my article that I am writing for an educated
public and not for an uneducated public and that it would be absurd
for me to put on a proletarian tone.

H.N. to V.S-W.   *May 14, 1958*

What a world we live in. The sense of authority has decayed and the
young revolt against the old and the irresponsible against the
responsible. I suppose something of the same sort occurred after
the French Revolution, but people were then mainly uneducated and
could not be driven to violence by propaganda. But here, simul-
taneously, we have the Lebanon on the verge of rebellion, the
French Algerians setting up a separate Government worse than
anything that happened in Ulster, and the Venezuelans spitting at
Mrs Nixon. The Americans are so deeply hurt when they discover
that they are not loved, and in truth I feel that the students of Lima
and Caracas have behaved rudely and wildly. It is all, I suppose,
due to the fact that the use of force is now prohibited and that
agitators like Nasser and his myrmidons can lash any crowd into
rage and excitement.

H.N. to V.S-W.   *September 10, 1958*

I said [to James Pope-Hennessy] that you and I might differ in political opinions but that we saw as one about VULGARITY which we
regard as "the enemy". Rich vulgarity like that of Mrs Simpson is
worse than poor vulgarity. In fact, when the latter descends to
hop-picker level, it is not vulgarity at all. I said that what had
shocked us was that he had half-admired the luxury of the Windsor

mill. He said that we had "feudal" conceptions and were class-conscious, whereas he had no class-consciousness at all. I said it was not snobbishness but fastidiousness. I think he was slightly impressed as he listens to what we say.

H.N. to V.S-W.   *October 8, 1958*

How dare you say that I pay no attention to your worries and troubles. I worry about them something dreadful. I devote far more time to thinking about wasps [V.S-W. was allergic to wasps' stings] than I do to thinking about Voltaire or Diderot. Only I keep quiet about it. You do know with half your heart and mind that you are always at the centre of my thoughts. But then you think that I ought to take some of the burden off you. Even when I go and get the Sunday papers from the big room, I am restrained and scolded. A crushed life is what I lead, similar to that of the hen you ran over the other day. But I love you more than anyone has ever been loved.

H.N. to V.S-W.   *October 16, 1958*

At noon I took a taxi to the German Embassy. I was waiting for the driver to give me change, when the portals of the house were flung open and out rushed a neat secretary who bowed low to me. The taximan must have been impressed. Then up I went to the Ambassador's private flat and the secretary bowed me in and left me alone. I started making amicable conversation, but the Ambassador said that he must first make an allocution and present me with my citation or *Verleihungsurkunde*. Then he made a set speech while I stood sufficiently stiffly to attune with my *visage de circonstance* but not exactly at attention, which might have seemed too military a pose. He then handed me a box containing *Das Grosse Verdienstkreuz mit Stern*. The Order consists of an enamelled dingle-dangle and a brass star. The *Verdienstkreuz* is awarded to distinguished men who have rendered services to Germany. I then went away clasping my *Verleihungsurkunde* and my blue box with the star against my chest, thinking how you would have turned on the gramophone record about, "I can't understand how you can possibly accept Orders from those horrible people who tried to destroy us."

Diary *November 4, 1958*

I look at the enthronement of Pope John XXIII on the television. He looks like a head-waiter at a Soho Italian restaurant. The ceremony is badly rehearsed and conducted. Acolytes rush about making signs to other acolytes or whispering in the ear of the Vicar of God what he is expected to do next. It is a great technical achievement to be able to send this living photograph from St Peter's to Sissinghurst, but I get into the train feeling all my anti-Catholic and anti-priesthood sentiments very active.

Diary *November 11, 1958*

Nigel and I lunch together. He is worried about what to do in the debate on the Wolfenden Report [which proposed to legalise homosexuality]. The mere fact that if he supports it he will seal his fate at Bournemouth makes him all the more eager to express his views openly and defy the consequences. All this is noble but inexpedient. Unfortunately [Professor] Freddy Ayer joins us, and Nigel asks him whether he thinks that the Government should lead or follow public opinion. Ayer is very positive – Government and Parliament must always be in advance of public opinion. That means a gulf fixed between the Member for Bournemouth East and his electors.

Diary *December 4, 1958*

I lunch in a private room at the Connaught at a luncheon given by David Astor [Editor of the *Observer*] for Igor Stravinsky. Stravinsky is a fan of mine and greeted me warmly. I sit next to him and he tells me how much he enjoyed *Some People*, and what a delight *Journey to Java* has been to him and his wife. I groan inwardly. "But of course," he adds, putting his hand on my shoulder, "your best book is your life of your father." I was overjoyed at that. He said that as a composer he admired technique, and that he felt my technique was superb. I swelled with pride. He said how much he envied us writers, who had finished our work when the book was published and bound. It was so different for a composer. His composition, when played at Buenos Aires or Melbourne, was entirely different from anything that he composed or intended.

Diary   *December 27, 1958*

*Vita shows me a passage from *Lolita* which she has finished. I cannot conceive a more lustful passage or of anything more calculated to corrupt. How Nigel can, for one moment, contemplate being associated with the publication of this book passes my comprehension. The whole business worries and perplexes me very deeply.*

H.N. to George Weidenfeld   *December 30, 1958*

*I am writing to you about *Lolita* which Vita and I have just read. We do not feel that its literary merits justify in any way the obscenity which underlies the whole book. Only one person in a million will feel that the book is really a moral or cautionary tale, or that it is anything but "corrupting" in the sense of the Obscene Publications Report. To the great mass of the public it will seem a salacious treatment of the very worst sort of perversion, a vice in which an extreme form of lechery confronts the extremest innocence. It will be universally condemned, and will give your firm the reputation, not of a courageous and "advanced" firm of publishers, but as a firm which specialises in obscene books. You may regard this as old-fashioned and puritan on the part of the public, but the vast mass of the public is puritan in these respects and there is no form of perversion which fills them with greater horror than that described with such relish in *Lolita*.*

Diary   *January 5, 1959*
                                                     Paris

As we leave Boulogne I wave at it, and Vita says, "Who are you waving at?" I reply, "I am greeting Sainte-Beuve." The waiter is pleased at this and smiles delightedly. What English waiter would understand an analogous greeting to Wordsworth? We reach the Gare du Nord an hour late and then dawdle round the ceinture. It is pelting with rain and when we get sudden vistas of the boulevards they are glistening under lights. The train slides past the lighted windows of tenement houses and we see brass chandeliers for a flash with red shades and the evening meal below them. Unknown lives. We dine and then go to bed.

Diary   *January 8, 1959*
                                           S.S. Cambodge [sailing to Japan]

A happy day at sea, and I start on Chapter I of my book on the eighteenth century, doing Saint-Simon, Louis XIV and the beginning of the War of the Spanish Succession. At 4 we pass Gavdos, the island off Crete. It has the peculiar look of crinkled tissue-paper.

Diary   *February 25, 1959*
                                              S.S. Cambodge, Colombo

The happiness of the day is clouded by a distressing episode. On entering the ship a Cingalese newspaper-man, whom I had just spoken to that morning before going ashore, rushes up to me. "Oh Sir Harold," he said, "I have been waiting for you four hours. I have a cable to discuss with you." I took him to my cabin and he undid his telegram. It ran something as follows: "Our Moscow correspondent reports that at Press Conference Guy Burgess stated that he asked Prime Minister for a safe conduct to England and back to Russia to see his mother who is seriously ill. Macmillan, when asked, said it was not for him to intervene: the Law must take its course. In subsequent conversation Burgess said that the only one of his former friends who had kept in touch with him was Harold Nicolson, who had written regularly. Please get in touch with Nicolson, passenger *Cambodge* arriving Colombo February 25, and ask him to confirm." I replied that certainly I had written to Guy since I felt sorry for him, as he had acted on impulse, and that my principle was not to desert friends in distress. But that I had written not one word which could not be published in any paper. I made him repeat this since I do not trust the accuracy of Cingalese reporters when faced with a scoop. God knows what he will say.

H.N. to V.S-W.   *April 14, 1959*

I had a charming luncheon at No 10. Delicious food and wine. We discussed what books had first influenced us. Debré [Prime Minister of France for whom the luncheon was given] (who is a nice *Ecole*

Normale type) said it had been *Le Livre de la Jungle* by Kipling. Nye Bevan said it had been *Le Rouge et le Noir*. So that was a fine interchange of Anglo-French compliments. I like the way we invite the Opposition leaders on such occasions. Both Gaitskell and Nye were there.

Diary   *June 24, 1959*

I go to Transport House and do the enclosed flash for the Labour Party. [It reads:] "Why should I, who have had a luxury education and lived a luxury life, vote Labour? Because I believe that they will do more than any other Party to secure equality of opportunity and to solve without violence the African problem, which may become the central problem of the next fifty years."

Diary   *August 7, 1959*

Lunch at the Garrick and am told that it is announced the Queen is to have a baby in January or February. What a sentimental hold the monarchy has over the middle classes! All the solicitors, actors and publishers at the Garrick were beaming as if they had acquired some personal benefit.

H.N. to V.S-W.   *November 3, 1959*

Niggs tells me that Nabokov told him that all his life he had been fighting against being influenced by *Some People*. "The style of that book," he said, "is like a drug." Well, I can assure him that *Lolita* is not likely to influence me. Niggs has taken a liking to Nabokov and above all to Mme Nabokov.

H.N. to V.S-W.   *November 18, 1959*

I lunched with the Swiss Ambassador at the Dorchester. The Cultural Attaché, who had arranged the luncheon, talked to me about the great conductors of the world and how the Philharmonia was about the best orchestra in the world and the Festival Hall without doubt the best theatre. I said I never went to a concert. He looked actually startled, as if he could not believe his ears and as if I had said, "It's no use your talking to me about books. I haven't read a book in fifteen years." I suppose my dislike of music must strike the cultured foreigner as an astonishing lack of taste or education.

H.N. to V.S-W. *November 27, 1959*

I had that bloody Keats–Shelley Committee. They mumble, and I am deaf. I ought never to be chosen as Chairman in my dotage, as I really do not hear properly and I can never recognise people or tell who they are. In fact, I am like an old discarded motor-car, fit only to be thrown on the dump outside Cleveland O! HI! Oh!

Diary *December 26, 1959*

In the afternoon vans arrive bearing Mr Maclure of the Columbia Broadcasting System, two French electricians and three others, together with vast trunks and suitcases. They establish their apparatus in the kitchen and dining-room and store-cupboard. I am sat down in a chair by the fire and the lights are turned on and adjusted. It takes from 5 p.m. to 7 p.m. Viti is enraged. I talk to Ed Murrow in St Moritz [for one of his *Small World* hook-ups], to Mrs Luce in, I think, Los Angeles, and to Chip Bohlen [American Ambassador to the U.S.S.R., 1953–1957] in New York. I do not see their faces (since the television pictures are put together later) but I do hear their voices, and we have a three-cornered discussion of the function of diplomacy. It seems to me to go rather well, but Viti is so angry that she gets bored. The lights, I admit, *are* rather a strain and the thing goes on far too long. But in the end they take a final shot of me, pack their many trunks, and sloop off into the night, where the wind howls across the fields and woods. I am not too exhausted but glad to get to bed. Viti feels I have been exploited, put-upon, taken advantage of, and maybe made a fool of.

H.N. to P.N. & N.N. *January 24, 1960*
S.S. Europa, Port Elizabeth

I cannot describe to you the horrors of Apartheid. I asked an Englishman how one pronounced the word and he said "Apart" and then "hate", and my God! Hate it is. It is far worse than anything that I had supposed. I was shocked when first landing at Durban to observe that all the seats along the esplanade (*all* of them, literally) were marked "For whites only". I was shocked, as I told you, when I found that in the vast Post Office at Cape Town there were counters for the whites and separate counters for the niggers. In fury at this, I queued up behind three niggers, but when my turn came the clerk said to me, "Sorry, Sir, you are at the wrong desk." So I had to pass on to the guichet marked "Whites only".

The Press came to see us as usual, and on this occasion it consisted of two women and a man who represented a liberal evening paper. What they told us was startling. Their letters are opened, their visitors noted, their telephones tapped and microphones concealed in their office. The girl was arrested for talking to a coloured fellow-student, and she would not be able to go abroad since they would refuse her a passport. They are anxious to see what the Prime Minister [Harold Macmillan] will say when he addresses the Legislature in Cape Town [on February 3; the famous "Wind of Change" speech]. He is bound to offend somebody, even by his omissions. They want him to say, "Well, leave the Commonwealth if you want to! You are a moral liability to us. But realise that if you do, you become a foreign country and will lose all the benefits of Empire preference."

You know how I hate niggers and how Tory Vita is. But I do hate injustice more than I hate niggers, and Vita screams with rage. She says it is like Hitler all over again and that these nice newspaper people who came to see us last night will end their days in a concentration camp. Fists of execration are raised on high. But truly, you have no conception how shocking it all is. The pure police state. How happy we are with our freedom and our Parliamentary questions! I could not live in this Nazi country in constant fear of the Gestapo.

Diary					*February 4, 1960*
					S.S. Europa, Somaliland

The radio news says that Macmillan made it absolutely clear [at Cape Town] that we disapproved of their racial policy. This was a courageous thing to do and I am delighted.

H.N. to V.S-W.					*March 17, 1970*

I had some American television men in during the morning and they interviewed me for a feature they are doing on Piccadilly. They asked me whether I did not feel embarrassed by the fact that the porters here wore "livery" and top-hats. I said I should feel much more embarrassed if they didn't and if people mistook me for a porter on my way out. I could see they thought me very snobbish and old-fashioned. They asked me whether the Albany was not a "privileged sanctuary". I said yes it was. I added that highly developed civilisations specialised in variety, whereas lower civilisations imposed uniformity. That was not a welcome remark.

Diary   *March 21, 1960*

I dine at the American Embassy. A small but select company – the Queen Mother, the Prime Minister and Lady Dorothy [Macmillan], the Chancellor of the Exchequer [Derick Heathcoat Amory], the Profumos [John Profumo, Army Minister] and Jeremy Tree. I sit between Mrs Whitney [the Ambassadress] and Mrs Profumo, and as the P.M. is on Mrs Whitney's other side, we talk across. He was delighted at having won the Oxford Election as Chancellor. He thinks the *Times* leader recommending [Oliver] Franks did the trick. He said that he regretted the Summit Conference being called "the" and not "a". He quoted me as having said that the greatest diplomatic asset was the passage of time – and that a regular series of Summit Conferences held, say, every four years, would prevent a breach and allow time to flow. He foresaw that in thirty years, if there was no war, Russia would become more bourgeois and the gap would narrow. He said that he hoped Khrushchev would remain in power as he was personally pledged to peace. He said that he had found de Gaulle much mellowed and very sensible. I thought him in wonderful form – wise and gay. I have seldom enjoyed a dinner more.

*I talked to Lady Dorothy about her visit to Rambouillet. She said it was evident that Mme de Gaulle was a poor *maîtresse de maison*. There were about forty men servants with silver chains, superb food, but no soap in their bedrooms, no paper-baskets and no writing material. It was so cold that she had to go to bed in a woolly. She asked Mme de Gaulle whether there was anything special she wished to do when she came on her State Visit to London, and she replied that she wished to visit Gorringes and Mrs Leo Amery, who is bed-ridden. She said that making conversation with Mme de Gaulle is like digging at clay with a trowel.*

Diary   *May 20, 1960*

I was worried last night about my budget. At breakfast I told Niggs that I must get a job as a hack-writer who wrote the history of City companies, and that I should have to ask a fee of £5,000, otherwise I should have to give up living in the Albany. He said, "Well, I must see what can be done about it." He then goes off to his office and returns in an hour to put a proposal to me from Weidenfeld. It is that I write the text of a vast album he is doing about Royalty – pomp and grandeur. I may take two years at it, do only 70,000 words, they will do the fuss about the illustrations, and I am to get £1,500 on signature of contract, £1,500 next year, and £2,000 on delivery of ms – £5,000 in all. Thus my dread of having to leave the Albany and alter my whole way of life is removed in 1½ hours. I go out at once and get a book on Monarchy out of the London Library.

Diary   *September 11, 1960*

We have done disgracefully at the Olympic Games. I have suffered so much from the athletic fetish that I am rather pleased. This is mean of me.

Diary   *October 29, 1960*

In the evening we listen to Vita on the Home Service doing a piece on the mistakes that past critics have made. She is furious as they refer to her as "V. Sackville-West, the well-known authoress". She had managed to persuade them not to call her "Lady Nicolson" or "Miss Sackville-West" or "Miss Victoria Sackville-West", but had omitted to warn them not to put "author" in the feminine. Imagine her rage, therefore, when she gets a letter from the Sevenoaks Urban Council asking whether they may christen one of their new roads "Nicolson Road". That is well enough in Stornoway or at Edinburgh, but not in Sevenoaks.

H.N. to V.S-W.   *November 1, 1960*

I did like your book [*No Signposts in the Sea*] so much. It seemed to me of such lovely texture and so moving. It was such a *decent* book

and all the three characters were ennobling and not degrading
characters. This will make the reviewers think it old-fashioned and
upper-class. But you and I prefer the upper-class to the middle-class
even as we prefer distinction to vulgarity. There is so much distinction in your book that it is like a lovely room or garden. Not one
ugly thing in it.

H.N. to V.S-W.   *November 9, 1960*

Did you listen to Nixon "admitting defeat" in the foyer of a Los
Angeles hotel? I am ambivalent about things. On the one hand I
have some prejudice against Kennedy because of his father, I don't
like candlesticks [Roman Catholics] in high positions, he reminds
me of Lindbergh, and I suspect him of wishing to have a tough
foreign policy and to worry about prestige. On the other hand he is
on the left, will be nicer to the negroes than to big business, and has
promised to appoint that nice Adlai Stevenson as Secretary of State.
So it works out 50/50 by me. Okay?

H.N. to V.S-W.   *December 8, 1960*

In the evening came the ceremony of unveiling the tablet to Duff
[Cooper]. We went down to the crypt [of St Paul's] and there were
many old friends. I should say about 100. I unveiled the thing and it
didn't stick as I feared. Then turning to the audience, I started, "I
have been asked to say a few words . . ." But it was at the wrong
state of the proceedings, and the Dean tugged at my coat whispering,
"I come first." So I stopped and returned, foolish-looking, to my
seat. Then the Dean did his stunt and I returned to the tablet and
again faced the congregation. "I have been asked," I said again, "to
say a few words." And this time my words remained uninterrupted.
My speech went well enough. Diana [Cooper] remained unmoved
but trembling. "Duff would so have hated it," she said to me afterwards, "if I had blubbed in public."

Diary   *December 29, 1960*

*I lunch at the Beefsteak with Tommy [Lascelles]. He agrees with
me that to broadcast the Queen's Christmas message on television
is a great error. It destroys the mystique of monarchy. He says that

when he was Private Secretary he tried to stop even the sound broadcast. We walk back together and Tommy gives me a sharp scolding for not being more traffic conscious. He says my conduct in crossing Piccadilly is unfair to bus drivers and motorists.*

Diary   *December 31, 1960*

I have a bad cough which keeps me awake till I hear the clock strike midnight and know that 1960 is gone.

Let it go indeed: it has been a beastly year. The rainfall between July and the end of the year has been heavier than for a century. The communist world has gained over the liberal world in every quarter of the globe from Laos to Cuba. The African situation is dreadful. Our own economic situation is only precariously prosperous. My *Age of Reason* has been criticised for misprints, misspellings, repetitions and careless writing. I know that it is because I am going gaga.

H.N. to N.N.   *January 29, 1961*
                                                    S.S. Augustus, Rio de Janeiro

There is an Argentinian girl on board, aged about twelve, to whom Vita and I have taken a fierce dislike and whose antics we watch with horror. She comes into the saloon doing the act, "Little girl in pink dress enters saloon of luxury liner". She then sits down and does the act, "Little girl, with finger on her chin, listens attentively to her mother". That passes into the act, "Little girl listens to the band with attentive appreciation". Then comes, "Little girl claps to show appreciation, nodding her head gracefully in the direction of the bandleader". Then we play Bingo, and there are several acts displaying little girl in expectation, little girl in disappointment, little girl in ecstasy of triumph, little girl, cheated of victory, indicates indifference to the triumphs of this world. Vita and I watch revolted.

H.N. to V.S-W.   *March 9, 1961*
                                                                     London

I had Kenneth Harris, my interviewer, yesterday [H.N. was recording four interviews on his life and opinions which were later published in the *Observer*]. He is an excellent interrogator, and makes one think about oneself. Why am I a Member of the Labour Party? Why indeed? I told him that I am a "liberal socialist" and that is true. I am sure that the vast outlay on the Health Service would not have been accomplished except under state socialism. But then I also believe in individualism. I fear my Labour side is due all too much to hatred of Tories, and this hatred has had bottles of real venom poured into it by the Bournemouth episode.

Diary   *March 16, 1961*

Kenneth Harris comes for his last instalment of interviews. We discuss the nature and purposes of culture. I lunch at the Greek Embassy. I get there too early and walk into the new American Embassy. The interior is superior to the exterior. The eagle on top hasn't got a beak, but the snout of a porpoise. I then go to luncheon. It is a luncheon of intellectuals to meet the King and Queen of Greece. After luncheon we go to the drawing-room. The Queen instals herself on the sofa and we are made to group our chairs in a semi-circle around her. She then delivers an hour's lecture on metaphysics, most of which I cannot hear, catching only such words as "electrons", "brotherhood of man", "objective and subjective", "materialism" and "atom-bomb". Freddy Ayer, with his exquisite manner, tries to intervene from time to time, but she sweeps him aside with a queenly gesture. I dare not catch anybody else's eye, since I fear giggles. But she does not cease until 4.15 and then says goodbye with a kind word for each of her exhausted audience.

Henry Moore tells me that Ben has not only saved the *Burlington*, but much increased its prestige internationally. I liked that.

H.N. to V.S-W.   *June 1, 1961*

I had a really interesting dinner with Harold Caccia [British Ambassador in Washington, 1956–1961]. He says that the great white soul of America is still blushing scarlet over Cuba [the failed Bay of Pigs invasion was on April 17]. He says that he has great confidence in Dean Rusk, but that Kennedy must "run himself in" before he can inspire confidence. He says it is not true to say that Kennedy "inherited" the Cuban situation. He wanted from the outset to show that he was a strong man determined to defend the Monroe

Doctrine, and plunged into the Cuban adventure on false information. He says the Americans do not blame Kennedy, who is still their red-headed boy, but that they put it all down to the "diplomatists", meaning thereby their information services. "Why can't we put a foot right?" they wail.

H.N. to V.S-W.   *June 21, 1961*

I lunched with Anne Fleming yesterday. The Kenneth Clarks were there, Diana Cooper, [Richard] Wollheim [Reader of Philosophy, University of London], and [Sir Solly] Zuckerman, who is Scientific Advisor to the Government. But Hadji is getting so deaf that he feels embarrassed at parties and becomes as inarticulate as his eldest son. I fear that the sun is setting in the west and that I have ceased to be a social asset and have become a liability. Moreover, not only have I ceased to hear, but I have ceased to speak. The old chatterbox has been shut down and the clasp has been set upon it. In fact, I did NOT shine or sparkle and I felt diminished. But I enjoyed my luncheon all the same and oo-er it was good. Scrambled eggs, cold sole and strawberries – but all of such quality that they were set high above most foods.

Diary   *July 15, 1961*

Viti and I go to Knole for luncheon. The Japanese deer are all around. They have much increased. We then go on to the house and meet Jacobine [the wife of Lionel Sackville-West who, in 1965, became the 6th Lord Sackville] on the way. We then visit the interior, seeing the furniture the National Trust have wrongly moved, and the Venetian Ambassador chairs, which have been regilded and which I do not think as awful as V. thinks. We look in at the North rooms which Lionel is redecorating for his habitation. We also go into the garden. The sunk-garden and pool are much improved. The rock-garden has wisely been swept away and the little orchard squares have been levelled out. Altogether it is more lovely than ever and Vita is happy there. We lunch. Charlie [Lord Sackville] is very very frail but perfectly compos.

H.N. to V.S-W. *August 9, 1961*

I went to the London Library and got a translation of the Koran. It passes my comprehension how so diffuse, repetitive and superficial a book can be compared to the Bible. It is because of the thinness of the teaching of Mohammed that I deride Moslem thought and despise Christians (and they are few) who become converts to Islam.

Diary *September 21, 1961*

A letter from Nigel saying that I must recast my Monarchy book since the foreign subscribers refuse to take it in its present form, in that it omits so much of importance and varies between commentary and history. What is really meant is that I am getting gaga and cannot really do such sort of books at my age. Poor Niggs! It must have been an unpleasant letter for him to write. It made me feel quite giddy at the prospect of the work of revision entailed.

Diary *September 22, 1961*

I am still feeling distressed by the obvious waning of my powers. I have not I fear been the same since I had my two strokes, and I am living on the fat of my former reputation. Vita consoles me, as always. She is not in the least annoyed with Nigel for ticking me off, and agrees that he is perfectly right.

Diary *November 21, 1961*

I am 75 years old. I am interviewed on "Today" on the Home Service. A shattered old bronchial voice discoursing on youth and happiness.

H.N. to V.S-W. *January 3, 1962*

*Now they have robbed us of the thaw I was waiting for. The streets of London are edged with brown slush. But the pavements are scraped clean and are now as dry as in July. Oliver Esher creeps with a stick saying he knows he is destined to break his hip and become bed-ridden. I said, "When you were young you would have said 'leg' not 'hip'. Your grandchildren will say 'femur' rather than 'hip'. Such is the progress and advance of science." "Yes," he said, "you and I are interested in the same things such as changes in vocabulary." *

On January 19 H.N., V.S-W. and her friend Edith Lamont boarded the S.S. Antilles for a cruise to the West Indies. In the train from Waterloo to Southampton, V.S-W. suffered a haemorrhage, the first indication of abdominal cancer. For over a month she concealed the fact from H.N. She told him that her tiredness and fluctuating temperature during the voyage were due to lumbago and bronchitis.

Diary   *January 19, 1962*

Called at 6.45. We leave the Albany and drive to Waterloo through dark, empty streets. The train leaves at 8.5 and we get to Southampton Docks at 10.40. Pass through passport and Customs easily. Go aboard the *Antilles*. I unpack and have a nap. Viti also has a nap.

V.S-W.'s Diary   *January 19, 1962*

Leave Albany at 7.15 and get the 8.5 at Waterloo, Edie [Lamont] meets us there. *Disastrous* journey. I am very worried and confide in E.

Diary   *January 20, 1962*

We are off to Bordeaux. It is already warmer. Viti sleeps or lies in her bunk most of the day because of her lumbago.

Diary   *January 27, 1962*
                                   S.S. Antilles, Martinique

Viti says she is better, but still has a slight temperature and stays in bed. I stay on board. In the evening her temperature goes up to over 100. I am, as always, sick with worry.

Diary   *January 28, 1962*
                                    S.S. Antilles, Barbados

Vita's temperature is down to normal, and the ship's doctor says that she can go ashore. I could not have believed it. When we get back, Vita is exhausted and her temperature is up to 101. I am worried again, but the doctor tells me to keep calm. *"Ne vous inquiétez pas, Monsieur."*

Diary   *February 1, 1962*
                                  S.S. Antilles, near Jamaica

Vita's temperature is down and her bronchitis is clearing up, but she is terribly weak and ill with all these injections they are giving her. She gets up for luncheon, but goes to bed almost immediately afterwards.

V.S-W.'s Diary   *February 15, 1962*

Thankful to be home. I feel really ill, and try to hide it from Hadji. The sooner I see the doctor the better.

Diary   *February 18, 1962*

I think Viti is better, but she never lets me know.

H.N. to V.S-W.   *February 20, 1962*

I am anxious to hear the result of the blood-test and I trust you to tell me the truth.

Diary   *February 23, 1962*

When I reach home, Viti tells me to prepare myself for a blow. She has had a haemorrhage and went up to London yesterday to consult a gynaecologist, who said she must go into hospital and be examined. I can see that Viti thinks it is cancer, and faces it with her usual courage. She is really heroic. The haemorrhage occurred in the train from Waterloo to Southampton on January 19. She did tell Edie, but she never told me, as she knew it would worry me. Her unselfishness is phenomenal.

The shock has a strange effect on me. It seems to sunder my life in two – the past being radiant with sunshine, and the present and future dark as night. Familiar objects (my pipe, my sponge, the book I have been reading) all seem like voices from the past. "Last time I handled you, all was sunlit."

Diary   *February 28, 1962*

Viti leaves home by the morning train. A car takes her from London Bridge to the Royal Free Hospital in Liverpool Road, Canonbury. Edie comes with her. The surgeon comes in while I am there. She says that until she opens things up, she cannot be sure whether it will be a "minor" or a "major" operation. If it is a major operation, Viti's life will be in danger for forty-eight hours. She is so gay and calm, seeking to ease my dread.

Diary   *March 1, 1962*

Dies irae. At 1.30 they telephone to say that Vita is "still in the theatre", and this fills me with horror. Then at 2.45 the surgeon telephones. "Lady Nicolson is now back in her bed and having a blood-transfusion. She stood the operation fairly well." "Did you do the major operation?" "Yes." "Did you find cancer?" "Yes." I feel like fainting, but drink some sherry.

During the afternoon there is a loud rap on the door. When Elvira opens it, she is confronted by a Grenadier in full uniform who hands her a letter. It is from Michael Adeane sending me a message of "sympathy and encouragement" from the Queen. This makes me feel better. At 6.30 I go to the hospital. V. had felt some pain, and they had given her dope and she was fast asleep. I go away with the picture of the oxygen and blood-transfusion apparatus hanging like gallows in my mind.

Diary   *March 20, 1962*

It is odd. Two weeks ago I loathed going to the hospital, as it was a *via dolorosa* and horrible to see her so weak and ill. But now every day she seems a little better, and it is a visit I look forward to. But she is still unable to read or eat or sleep.

Diary   *April 6, 1962*

Viti leaves the hospital at 10 and has a lovely drive in the Daimler ambulance down home. She is met by Edie, the doctor, Ursula [Codrington, secretary at Sissinghurst since 1959] and the household. She is not tired.

Diary   *April 23, 1962*

Easter Sunday. Philippa and Nigel appear unexpectedly with the children. He says that I sounded so miserable on the telephone when he rang last night, that they decided to come down. Juliet and Adam see Vita, and dance the twist in front of her. That amuses her. Then we go round the garden and Juliet dances about picking daffodils. Altogether a successful day, and for the first time since March 1, I feel almost happy.

Diary   *May 29, 1962*

The doctor comes to see Vita. He is worried about the slowness of her recovery, and feels that she really must undergo deep-ray treatment at Pembury. It will make her feel low and miserable, but it must be done. I am miserable and worried again. What a cursed year this is! Vita is depressed in the evening, and so, by God, am I!

Diary   *May 31, 1962*

Viti goes off in an ambulance to Pembury. She is there for a long time
and emerges exhausted. She returns about lunch-time, but refuses
everything but a bowl of soup. She sleeps soundly after luncheon,
but she is miserable, and so am I. It is a lovely day, which makes it
all the more intolerable.

Diary   *June 1, 1962*

Viti is so weak this morning that she is not strong enough to go to
Pembury. The doctor comes after breakfast. He says that I must face
the fact that there is little hope. He does not think she will suffer
much. I return to my room in a haze of fear. Niggs comes down late
at night.

Diary   *June 2, 1962*

It is a lovely morning. I get up early and walk round the garden.
V. is asleep, and I do not disturb her. Glen [the Labrador] dances on
the lawn with his brother, Brandy. I breakfast with Niggs, and then I
force myself to do my review of the composite book *Companion to
Homer*. I finish it about 12.30, and start reading the newspaper.
Ursula is with Vita. At about 1.5 she observes that Vita is breathing
heavily, and then suddenly is silent. She dies without fear or self-
reproach at 1.15. Ursula comes to tell me. I pick some of her favour-
ite flowers and lay them on the bed.

> *The funeral was three days later at Sissinghurst village
> church. Her ashes were placed in the Sackville crypt at
> Withyham.*

Diary   *January 1, 1963*

*More snow during the night. Horribly cold. Horribly unhappy. I
think drink is the only end for me. But Vita would not have liked
that cowardly escape. I must just go doggedly on and fortunately
I have such a dear family, so many friends, and such ardent tastes.
But I am very old and groggy.*

Diary   *January 12, 1963*
                            S.S. *Queen Mary*, sailing to New York

At 8.10 a.m. the Daimler comes and we drive to the station. I have a pullman, and painful memories of the last time I was there. Have breakfast in the train and get to Southampton in two hours. It is very painful seeing those escalators and green sofas again.

Diary   *January 18, 1963*
                                                         New York

I am not really in a fit state of health to go abroad alone: my legs are groggy and my sorrow unceasing. I wish I hadn't come.

Diary   *January 31, 1963*
                                                         New York

I lunch with [Leon] Edel at the Century Club and he shows me the portrait of the young [Henry] James. He is distressed how, in this third volume [of his biography of James], he will deal with James' homosexuality. He was a late-flowering bugger and the Boston puritanism retarded him until it was too late to get full satisfaction from it. Edel is an honest writer and is perplexed how to handle this problem. I advise him to treat it as a matter of course, making no apologies or evasions.

Diary   *March 1, 1963*

In the evening I go to see [Dr] Hunt. He says that once I recover from Viti's death I shall find my general health improve. At present I am still suffering from shock.

Diary   *April 10, 1963*

Niggs tells me that Philippa had a daughter at 2.15 this morning. Both are well. Baby weighs $7\frac{1}{4}$ lbs. I am so pleased that I forget to complete my shaving, but just sponge off the soap. As a result I have a bristle chin by luncheon. The baby is to be called Rebecca after my dog. How delighted Vita would have been.

Diary   July 7, 1963

It is surprisingly fine and sunny and I spend the day reading Greek on the lawn. I much enjoy going back and reading my old things. I am getting older every hour and feel rotten. It is curious that my consciousness seems perfectly alert, only I cannot express it and limp over a conversation.

> *H.N. now found little interest in keeping his diary. The entries became very brief; scarcely more than a note of where he spent each day. The last entry was on October 4, 1964: "Pick flowers for tomorrow [to take to London]. Otherwise do nothing but sit about. It is wonderfully fine weather."*
>
> *He died at Sissinghurst on May 1, 1968, aged 81.*

Index

Aachen, 275
Abdication crisis (1936), 105–8, 116,
   330, 340
Aberconway, Lord and Lady, *see*
   McLaren
Aberdeen, 104
Abruzzi, the, 119
Abyssinia, 80, 81, 82, 86, 88, 94, 97
Ackerley, J. J.: *Tulip*, 375–6
Action, 26, 27, 30, 31, 32, 33, 34
Adalia, 81
Addis Ababa, 94
Addison, Viscount, 303, 307
Adeane, Sir Michael, 404
Aden, 176
Adenauer, Dr Konrad, 350
Aeolian Hall, 244
Africa, 97, 109–11, 190, 202, 207, 213,
   248, 392, 398. *See also* French North
   Africa; Tanganyika; Uganda
Alain-Fournier (Henri-Alban Fournier),
   363
Alamein, El: battles (1942), 236, 237–8
Albania, 81, 148, 149
Albany, Piccadilly (H.N.'s London flat
   1952–65), 353–4, 359, 376, 395, 396,
   402
Albert Canal, 272
Albert, Prince, 224
Aldford House, 252
Aldrich, Chester, 68
Alexander, Field-Marshal Earl: Middle
   East command, 233, 236; Italian
   campaign, 260, 265–6, 285
Alexander I, Czar, 318
Alexander the Great: H.N. on, 350–1
Alexandra Palace, 145
Alexandria, 180
Alfonso XIII, King of Spain, 359

Algeria, 111, 262
Algiers, 240, 267; U.S. troops in, 238;
   H.N. in, 263–4; British Embassy,
   263
Allen, Bill, 28
Allenby, General, 247
Altmark, 173–4
Ambrosio, General Vittorio, 246
Americans, *see* United States of
   America
Amery, L. S., 150, 151, 171, 181, 228,
   395
Amory, Copley, 112
Amory, Derick Heathcoat (Viscount
   Amory), 395
Anderson, Ava, Lady, 285
Anderson, Sir John (Viscount
   Waverley), 285
Andrus, Colonel, 309–10
Anglican Church, 273
Anglo–French Interparliamentary
   Committee, 283
Anglo–French Parliamentary
   Association, 202
Anglo–German Naval Agreement
   (1935), 143
Anglo–Iranian Society, 373
Anglo–Polish Pact (1939), 148
Anne, Princess, 368
Anti-Comintern Pact (1936), 146
Antilles, S.S., 402–3
Anzio, 255, 260, 261
Apartheid, 393–4
Apéritif, 89
Appeasement, 144, 149
Aquitania, S.S., 76
Ardennes offensive (1944), 276, 277,
   278
Argyll House, 14

Arlen, Michael, 62–3
Arnhem, battle of (1944), 272
Asch, 134
'Ash Can', 304
Ashcroft, Dame Peggy, 365
Ashford, 200
Asia, 190, 207, 213
Asquith, H. H., (Earl of Oxford and Asquith), 24, 43, 184, 249
Asquith, Margot, 24, 96, 139, 141
Astor, David, 389
Astor, Nancy, Lady, 98, 100, 121, 149, 158, 235–6, 243–4, 247–8, 287, 335
Athenia, S.S., 163
Athens, 78; liberation, 273–4; crisis Christmas 1944, 281; H.N. in, 300–1; British troops evacuate, 208
atomic bomb, 297, 298, 342, 383
Attlee, Clement, (Earl), 183, 207, 226, 345; moves vote of censure (1935), 88; Abyssinia (1936), 97; talks with Chamberlain (1938), 123; Czech crisis (1938), 135, 137, 139; 'silly and charming', 145; dull, 169, 230, 242; Deputy Prime Minister (1943), 246, 273; wins 1945 election, 292, 297; willing to give H.N. peerage, 303–4, 333; Paris Peace Conference (1946), 313; rumoured retirement (1947), 320; introduced to V.S.-W. (1947), 327; awards her C.H., 328
Auchinleck, General Claude, 233, 238
Auden, W. H., 42, 56, 176, 178, 372–3, 374
Augustus, S.S., 398
d'Aumale, duc, 217
Auren, Mr, 222
Auriol, President Vincent, 344
Austen, Jane: *Emma*, 363
Austerlitz, battle of (1805), 122, 165
Australia, 81, 165, 228, 253, 254, 379
Austria, 100, 101, 103, 117, 119, 122, 312, 327; London Embassy, 359
Auvergne, 384
Ayer, A. J., 389, 399

Badoglio, Marshal, 252
Bagnold, Enid (Lady Jones), 24
Bahamas, 277
Baillie, Joanna, 385

Baldwin, Stanley, Earl, 104, 112, 130, 137, 196; Beaverbrook on, 14–15; and R.101 disaster (1930), 19; wins 1935 election, 86; National Government, 87, 91; Attlee's vote of censure (1935), 89; condolence to Queen Mary (1936), 90; dines with Lindberghs, 99; Abdication crisis (1936), 105–8; wife, 106; last statement as Prime Minister (1937), 113; on Churchill, 116–17, 249–50; Churchill on, 123, 217; 'a gutter snipe', 143; H.N. breakfasts with (1943), 249–50; advice from, 303; death (1947), 329–30
Balfour, A. J., 43, 212, 313
Balfour, Edward, 126
Balkans, the, 123, 204, 212, 258, 272, 273
Balmoral, 104, 359
Baltimore, 199
Banks, Mr, 68
Barbados, 403
Barcelona, 101, 144, 339
Barker, Mr, 385
Barrie, Sir James, 125, 177
Barrington-Ward, Robert, 182, 306
Bartlett, Vernon, 146
Basingstoke, 59
Bastogne, 277
Battenberg family, 359
Battle of Britain (1940), 190–4, 248
Baudelaire, Charles, 34
Baudouin, Paul, 204
Bavaria, 38, 283
Bay of Pigs, 399
Bayswater, 274
Beale, A. O. R., 16, 145
Beatrice, Princess, 338, 359
Beaulieu, 62
Beauvais, 19
Beaverbrook, Lord, 37, 57, 58, 81, 217, 387; employs H.N. (1930), 13, 22; H.N. meets, 14–15, 16–17, 26, 27, 39; Empire Free Trade, 14, 18, 24; character, 20–1; on New Party, 23–4, 39; offers H.N. editorship of *Evening Standard*, 26, 27; breach with H.N. (1931), 34; Macmillan on, 218; Baldwin on, 250

Beck, General, 155
Bedford Square, 145
Beefsteak Club, 135, 177, 182, 192,
    213, 224, 240, 254, 267, 278, 280,
    286, 299, 306, 307, 317, 361, 363,
    378, 382, 397
Beerbohm, Sir Max, 62
Belgium, 150, 165, 168, 182, 183, 186,
    276–7, 299
Belgrade, 275
Bell, Clive, 24, 344, *Old Friends*, 366
Bell, Vanessa, 206
Beneš, Eduard, 137, 139
Benghazi, 224
Bennet, Air Vice-Marshal, 330, 331
Bennett, Richard, 19
Berchtesgaden, 119, 132, 133, 135, 138,
    155, 268
Berengaria, S.S., 66–7
Berenson, Bernard, 103–4, 345–6;
    Sketch for a Self-Portrait, 341
Berkeley Square, 287
Berlin, 45, 93, 95, 119, 134, 154, 277,
    286, 309; H.N. returns from (1929),
    13; H.N. in, 34, 37–8; Lindbergh in
    (1936), 102; Gafencu in (1939), 149;
    R.A.F. raids, 192, 260; Wodehouse
    in, 255; Russians encircle (1945),
    285; in ruins, 285; blockade (1948),
    335, 336; Nigel lectures in (1957),
    383
Bernays, Robert, 110, 165, 177, 246,
    254, 272, 279
Berry, Lionel, 285
Besançon, 174
Béthouart, General, 269
Bevan, Aneurin, 218–19, 232, 242, 376,
    392
Beveridge, William: Report, 233, 239,
    243, 278
Bevin, Ernest, 297, 302, 313, 314–15,
    316, 320, 327–8, 335, 345
Biarritz, 39
Bibesco, Elizabeth, Princess, 144
Bible, the, 401
Bidault, Georges, 313, 315, 327
Binyon, Laurence, 244
Birkett, Sir Norman, 309, 362
Birmingham, 146, 198, 345
Bismarck, sinking of, 211, 212

Bizerta, 242, 245
Blackheath, 257
Blancagard, Professor, 175
Blenheim, 218
Blitzkrieg, 123, 155, 160, 164, 177, 185,
    189, 190–5, 197, 208, 217, 256–7, 261
Blixen, Karen, Baroness, 125
Bloomsbury, 193, 209, 213
Blum, Léon, 145
Blunden, Edmund, 244
Bognor, 214
Bohlen, Charles E. ('Chip'), 393
Bologna, 19
Bond Street, 310
Bonham-Carter, Mark 252–3
Bonham-Carter, Lady Violet (Lady
    Asquith), 139, 154, 224, 235, 250–1,
    252
Bonnet, Georges, 159, 262
Books and Art, 387
Boothby, Sir Robert (Lord Boothby),
    17, 132, 135, 140, 146, 159, 376
Borah, William E., 48
Bordeaux, 402
Bordein, 110
Boris, King, 124–5
Boston, 46–7, 79, 407
Bottomley, Gordon, 244
Boulanger, General, 199
Boulogne, 185, 390
Bournemouth: Nigel elected for (1952),
    351–2, 374, 381, 383, 389, 399
Bracken, Brendan, 125, 140, 183,
    189–90, 212, 235, 238, 269
Brain, Sir Russell (Lord Brain), 381
Brandy (dog), 406
Brazil, 313
Bremen, S.S., 54, 67, 156, 170
Bremerhaven, 156
Brest, 225
Brighton, 54, 92, 164
Bristol, 197
British Broadcasting Corporation, 42,
    211–12, 218, 220, 268, 352, 363;
    H.N. incurs enmity, 34; H.N.'s talks
    for, 13, 131, 134, 144, 192, 249, 312,
    314, 317, 318, 322, 352, 353, 356,
    382, 384, 401; Chamberlain's
    resignation broadcast (1940), 183;
    H.N. governor of, 214, 297; Dylan

Thomas asks for job, 216; Board, 218, 230, 251, 252, 278, 306; Empire Programme, 225; criticism of, 225, 251–2; 'bans' Wodehouse (1944), 255; Brains Trust, 258, 356; General Forces Programme, 266; Smuts broadcasts (1946), 315–16; Broadcasting House, 316, 347–8; Overseas Service, 318; Yearbook, 318; George V's broadcasts, 349; Third Programme, 353; records Russian satellite (1957), 385; 'Today', 401

British Council, 123, 300, 302

Brixton Prison, 310

Broadway, 49

Brockdorff-Rantzau, Count, 212

Bromley, 19

Brooke, Field-Marshal Sir Alan, 258

Brook's, 139, 222, 246

Brown, George, (Lord George-Brown), 375

Brownlow, Lord, 99

Bruce, Viscount, 81

Bruce of Clandeboye, 102

Brüning, Heinrich, 38

Brussels, 182

Bryanston Court, 96

Bryant, Sir Arthur, 326, 366

Bucharest: British Legation, 123–4

Buckingham Palace, 25, 111, 112, 124, 141, 260, 292, 318, 327, 333, 335, 358, 368, 383

Budapest, 380

Budberg, Moura, Baroness, 125

Buenos Aires, 389; U.S. Embassy, 96

Bulganin, Nikolai, 375

Bulgaria, 124–5, 202, 203, 272, 312; Foreign Office, 125

Burckhardt, Dr Carl, 168

Burgess, Guy, 222, 234, 302, 349, 391

Burlington House, 318

Burlington Magazine, 318, 346, 399

Burma, 278

Burne-Jones, Edward, 116

Burton, Sir Richard and Lady, 30

Butler, R. A. (Lord), 171, 216, 316–17, 353, 382

Butler, Samuel, 346

Byrnes, James (U.S. Secretary of State), 298, 313, 314, 316

Byron, Lord, 259, 301, 365

Caccia, Sir Harold (Lord Caccia), 399

Cadogan, Sir Alexander, 119

Caen, 266

Café Royal, 178

Cairo, 238, 280, 379; British Embassy, 238

Calais, 60, 185

Caledonian Market, 244

Cambodge, S.S., 391

Cambridge Union, 363

Camrose, Viscount, 215, 246, 258, 305

Canada, 19, 98, 106, 150, 163, 201, 234, 379

Cannes, 62

Canonbury, 404

Cap Dail, 103

Cap Ferrat, 62–3, 103, 128–30

Cape Town, 382

Caracas, 387

Cardiff, 197

Carlton Grill, 168

Carlton House Terrace, 301

Carnock, Eric, 3rd Lord (H.N.'s brother), 376

Carnock, Frederick, 2nd Lord (H.N.'s brother), 321, 354

Carnock, Lady (H.N.'s mother), 240, 245, 259, 321, 322, 331, 348–9, 354

Carnock, 1st Lord (H.N.'s father), 7–8, 13, 37, 72, 125, 298, 354

Carol, King of Rumania, 124, 141–2

Cartier de Marchenne, Baron, 285, 299

Cartland, Ronald, 140, 141, 153, 279

Cary, Robert, 195

Casa Mañana, 74–5

Cassino, 261

Castellane, de, 80–1

Castlerosse, Lady, 31

Catania, 248

Catering Bill (1945), 290

Catroux, General, 262

Cazalet, Victor, 112, 160, 167, 172, 177, 229, 231

Cecil, Lord David, 112

Cenotaph, 137, 286

Central Hall, Westminster, 224, 241, 287, 362

Chalon-sur-Saône, 174

Chamberlain, Neville, 123, 124, 136, 140, 141, 142–3, 149, 159, 171, 205, 225, 290; gout, 105; succeeds Baldwin (1937), 113; increasing control of Foreign Affairs, 117, 120, 121; relations with Eden, 122, 172; 'a clothes-brush', 127; H.N. 'anti-Chamberlain', 128; Czech crisis (1938), 130–8, 144; and Russia, 132; Berchtesgaden, 131, 133–4, 135; Munich, 138, 139, 144, 222, 380; no general election, 140; 'astonishing and perplexing', 145; Polish crisis (1939), 153, 157–8; depressed, 155; outbreak of war, 160; Churchill succeeds (1940), 163, 178, 183; lack of support, 164, 166, 167; 'dull as ditchwater', 169; Finland (1939), 170, 173–4, 176; Norway (1940), 179–80, 181–2; death, 196

Channel Islands, 323

Channon, Sir Henry ('Chips'), 98, 103, 116, 174, 247, 286

Chapel Royal, 90

Chaplin, Charlie, 31

Charles, Prince, 368

Charleston, 49–50

Chatham, 156

Chelsea, 14; Flower Show, 25

Chequers, 19

Cherbourg, 66, 266, 268

Cherkley, 24, 27

Chicago, 48

Chicago Sun, 231

China, 80, 213, 323–4, 384

Chopin, Frédéric, 99

Churchill, Clementine, 176, 210, 224, 237, 287, 345, 368

Churchill, Randolph (Winston's son), 222, 223, 311

Churchill, Lord Randolph (Winston's father), 327

Churchill, Winston S., 29, 35, 37, 87, 97–8, 104, 151, 153, 166, 167, 171, 180, 194–5, 201, 215–16, 218, 228, 229, 234, 235, 244, 245, 259, 265, 266, 284, 285, 290, 313, 344–5, 368,

375; appoints H.N. to Ministry of Information (1940), 8, 184; appearance, 14; *Marlborough*, 18; *My Early Life*, 18; *World Crisis*, 18; letters to Curzon, 59–60; Abyssinian crisis (1935), 81; Foreign Affairs Committee, 101, 115; Baldwin on, 108, 116–17; 249–50; congratulates H.N. on speech, 121; on Spain, 123; 'doing nothing', 126; meets Halifax, 132; Czech crisis (1938), 134–5, 136, 137–8, 139, 140; Churchill group, 141, 159; attacks Hore-Belisha (1938), 143; talks with Maisky, 147–8; in Paris (1939), 155; Polish crisis (1939), 157; declaration of war, 160; succeeds Chamberlain (1940), 163, 178, 183; First Lord of the Admiralty, 164; broadcasts, 173, 185, 188, 197, 213, 261; 'in perfect health', 179; Norwegian debate (1940), 181–2; on Dunkirk, 187; Bracken on, 189–90; on R.A.F., 191–2; and death of Chamberlain (1940), 196; refuses to state war aims, 199–200; on invasion of Greece (1941), 207; anti-Winston feeling, 209, 216, 222–3; Parliament bombed, 210; battle of Denmark Straits, 211–12; on Baldwin, 217; on Pearl Harbor, 219, 220; 'very grim', 221; Votes of Confidence, 223–4, 226; H.N. broadcasts on, 225; in Washington, 226, 246; de Valera on, 227; Tobruk, 231; Ismay on, 232–3; H.N.'s article on, 237; North Africa debate (1942), 239; 'adolescent', 242; and Spellman, 247; and Anzio, 260; relations with de Gaulle, 267, 269, 272; in Moscow (1944), 273; Greek crisis (1944), 275–6; Unconditional Surrender, 278; post-war policy, 280–2; death of Lloyd George (1945), 283; V.E. Day, 286; continues coalition, 288; defeat (1945), 292; atom bomb, 297; 'magnificent animal', 316–17; H.N.'s loyalty, 321; ill health, 326–7; Prime Minister again, 352–3; death of Queen Mary (1953), 358;

Coronation, 360; at Harrow, 366–7; resigns (1955), 369; *English-Speaking Peoples*, 374; Royal Academy banquet, 383

Churt, 43–4

Cincinatti, 50

Clandeboye, 102

Clark, Sir Kenneth, (Lord Clark), 151, 176, 210–11, 257–8, 302, 400

Clark, Reuden, 77

Clemenceau, Georges, 43, 166, 314

Clerk, Sir George, 307

Cleveland, 52

'Clinker, Humphrey', 387

Cliveden, 57, 100, 133, 136

Clydesdale, Lord, 209

Cocteau, Jean, 363

Codrington, Ursula, 405, 406

Colefax, Sybil, Lady, 14, 31, 60, 88, 89–90, 96, 99, 122, 129, 156, 167, 184, 208, 216, 256, 287, 301–2, 323; conversation with Mrs Simpson (1936), 105–6; broke, 189; plans for H.N.'s peerage, 272; death (1950), 346

Collins (publishers), 281

Cologne, 230, 283

Colombo, 391

Colston Leigh, 45

Columbia Broadcasting System, 211, 393

Columbus, 49

Colville, Lady Cynthia, 343

Combined English Universities (constituency), 32, 34, 303–4

Common Market, *see* European Economic Community

Commons, House of, *see* House of Commons

communism, 30–1, 32, 102, 122, 127, 254, 290, 300, 319, 328, 347, 349, 398

Como, 285

Companion to Homer, 406

Compiègne, 188

Comrade X (film), 214

Connaught, 220, 243, 389

Connaught, Duke of, 223

Connolly, Cyril, 170, 235, 301–2, 324, 337, 387

Conservative Party, 17–18, 26, 30, 98, 128, 140, 181, 213, 261, 268, 281, 289, 290, 338, 352, 364; Empire Free Trade, 15; Mosley urged to rejoin, 40; support for H.N. in Leicester (1935), 82; Central Office, 91; MacDonald and, 92; Churchill on, 123; 1922 Committee, 239, 364; on parliamentary hours, 265; H.N. could never join, 321, 399; wins North Croydon (1947), 328, 332; Suez, 377, 378, 380; left wing, 382

Constable (publishers), 42–3, 115, 336, 351, 354

Constant, Benjamin, 322, 324–5

Cookes, 15

Coolidge, President Calvin, 69–70, 284

Cooper, Lady Diana, 31, 88, 168, 264, 397, 400

Cooper, Duff (Viscount Norwich), 89, 151, 168, 245; Czech crisis (1938), 132; resigns, 139–40; Churchill group, 141; Minister of Information (1940), 184, 185, 189, 190, 191, 197, 201, 212, 213; Chancellor of Duchy of Lancaster (1941), 214; Cabinet Security Committee, 236; in Algiers, 261–2; Ambassador in Paris, 311; reviews H.N.'s *King George V*, 355; death (1960), 397

Cooper, Reginald, 34

Copper (chauffeur), 43

Coppet (Mme de Staël's house), 325

Cortez, Hernan, 53

Council Bluffs, 52

Coward, Noël, 99; *Private Lives*, 21; *Tonight at Eight-Thirty*, 89

Cowley, Arthur, 351

Cranborne, Lord (7th Marquess of Salisbury), 120, 134, 139, 140, 141, 253, 254

Cranbrook, 13, 15

Crathie, 359

Crawfurd, 84–5

Creevey, Thomas, 10

Crete, 391

Crimea, 279

Cripps, Sir Stafford, 224, 226, 229, 234, 235

Crockford's Clerical Directory, 346

Croft, Brigadier H. Page, 180

Cromwell, Oliver, 20, 181
Crookshank, Captain Harry, 194
Crossley, Anthony, 128, 140, 141
Croydon: H.N. candidate for (1947), 8, 328, 332
Cuba, 386, 398, 399
Cuernavaca, 74–5
Cunard, Emerald, Lady, 80, 96, 98, 112, 156, 257, 323
Curtis, Charles, 47
Curzon, Lady, 55, 57, 59–60
Curzon, Lord, 57, 59–60, 93
Cyprus, 364, 374, 379
Cyrenaica, 205, 221
Czechoslovakia, 97, 127, 130, 131, 132, 133, 134, 135, 138, 139, 140, 144, 286, 290

Daily Express, 13, 15, 94
Daily Herald, 17, 330
Daily Telegraph, 81, 96, 144, 164, 258, 326, 338, 355, 364
Daily Worker, 254
Daladier, Edouard, 138
Dalton, Hugh, 170, 345
Dalton, Canon John, 339–40
Damaskinos, Archbishop, 300–1
Danzig, 148, 152, 153, 157, 168
Dardanelles, the, 209
Darlan, Admiral, 239, 240
Dartmouth House, 361
Daughters of the Founding Fathers, 48
Daughters of the Virgin Mary, 280
David, J. L., 237
Davison, Mr, 80
Davy, Sir Humphrey, 144
De la Warr, Earl ('Buck'), 82, 91, 93, 99, 130, 133, 139, 140, 141, 143, 281
De la Warr, Diana, Countess, 93, 206
Debré, Michel, 391–2
Decon Brown's Point, 67–8
Dejean, Maurice, 204
Denham, 245
Denman, R. D., 92
Denmark, 177, 178
Dervishes, 110
Detroit, 51
Devonshire, 10th Duke and Duchess of, 246, 260

Dictionary of National Biography, The, 367
Dictionary of Quotations (Doubleday), 337
Diderot, Denis, 388
Dieppe, 234, 282
Dingwall, 90
Dix, Dr, 309, 311
Dixon, Sir Pierson, 302
Djibouti, 97
Doenitz, Admiral, 285, 286, 307–11
Donetz, 252
Dorchester Hotel, 200, 208, 215, 249, 256, 322, 337, 392
Doubleday Doran (publishers), 45, 337, 385
Douglas-Home, Sir Alec, *see* Dunglass, Alec
Dropmore Press, 317
Drummond, Lindsay, 248
du Bos, Charles, 322
Dublin, 200, 226–8
Dubrovnik, 275
Dufferin and Ava, 1st Marquess, 101
Dufferin and Ava, 2nd Marquess, 102
Duggan, Hubert, 141
Dulles, John Foster, 356, 374, 377
Dundrum, 226
Dunglass, Alec, 182
Dunkirk, 184, 186, 195
Durban, 393–4
'Dust Bin', 304

Eden, Anthony (Earl of Avon), 81, 122, 124, 133, 140, 146, 153, 172, 175, 180, 216, 252, 272, 273, 279, 281, 281, 282, 353; Minister without Portfolio (1935), 80; aims to prevent war, 93, 95; Abyssinian crisis (1936), 97; addresses Foreign Affairs Committee (1937), 114; Foreign Secretary (1937), 117; H.N. supports, 118; resigns (1938), 119–20; has 'sunk himself', 132; refuses to sign telegram to Chamberlain, 139; Eden group, 141, 149, 151, 163; in Leicester with H.N., 142; offer to join Cabinet (1939), 159; Dominions Office, 164; Balkans trip (1941), 204; and de Gaulle, 267, 269–70; Greek

crisis (1944), 275–6; visit to Berlin
(1948), 335; Prime Minister (1955),
369; Suez crisis (1956), 376–80, 383;
Macmillan succeeds (1957), 382
Edward VIII *see* Windsor, Duke of
Eisenhower, President Dwight D., 260,
269, 276, 356
Elizabeth, Queen Consort to George
VI, 94, 112, 127, 237, 260, 327, 333,
338, 344, 349, 354, 368, 395;
Baldwin's interview with, 113; H.N.
lunches with, 188; visits Sheffield,
198; at poetry-reading, 244; death of
George VI, 351
Elizabeth II, Queen, 344, 354, 368, 369,
382, 383; attends poetry-reading,
244; H.N.'s first impressions, 260;
accession (1952), 352; Coronation
(1953), 352, 360; *King George V*,
355; and H.N.'s K.C.V.O., 357, 358;
expecting baby, 392; Christmas
message (1960), 397; sympathy on
V.S.-W.'s illness, 404
Elliot, Walter, 80, 81, 133, 177, 210,
232, 355
Elton, Mr, 300
Empire Free Trade, 14, 18, 24
Emrys-Evans, Paul, 121, 123, 140, 141,
170, 253
Englewood, 68–74, 77
English, Mr, 92
Entebbe, 109, 110
Enterprise, H.M.S., 97
Erasmus, 116
Eregli, 81
Eritrea, 202, 207
Esher, Oliver, 3rd Viscount, 299, 341, 402
Etoile, 208
Eton College, 22, 200, 357
Europa, S.S., 156, 393–4
European Economic Community, 345
evacuation, 136, 165, 185, 200, 268
Evans, Dame Edith, 365
Evans, Sir Horace, 382
Evening News, 282
Evening Standard, 13, 15, 20, 22, 23,
24, 26, 27, 28, 30, 34, 278–9, 358

Fabre-Luces, 35
Fairbanks, Douglas, Jnr, 373

Falmouth, 21
Far East, 165, 221, 222, 223, 382
Farley (gardener), 114
Farmhill, 226
fascism, 30–1, 33, 34, 35, 43, 102, 197
Fenton, Colin, 376
Fermor, Paddy Leigh: *Time to Keep
Silence*, 362
Festival of Britain, 349
Fez, 64
Figaro, Le, 81, 113, 318, 322, 326, 344
Finland, 168–9, 170, 171, 173, 175–6,
312
Fisher, H. A. L., 56
Fishmongers' Hall, 361
Fitzherbert, Mrs, 105
Fitzroy, 272
Flanders, 187
Flaubert, Gustave, 298
Fleming, Anne, 400
Fleming, Peter, 177
Flensburg, 286
Florence, 224, 345–6, 371, 372
Foch, Field-Marshal, 247
Folkestone, 31
Foreign Ministers' Conference (1947),
327
Foreign Press Association, 143
Forster, E. M., 279
Förster, Gauleiter, 157
Fort Belvedere, 105, 106, 323
Fragonard, J. H., 364
France, 81, 82, 86, 95, 102, 103, 114,
119, 130, 131, 132, 133, 136, 143,
145, 154, 155, 165, 258, 265, 280,
265, 280, 323, 347; Free French, 8,
220, 229, 244, 246, 249; London
Embassy, 81, 306, 324, 344; Cabinet,
124; Polish guarantee (1939), 144;
Greek and Rumanian guarantees,
148; H.N. in (1940), 174–5; Army,
184, 186, 264; Germans occupy
(1940), 187–8, 195, 198–9; Allied
air offensive on (1942), 332;
American ignorance of, 262–3; de
Gaulle visits (1944), 267–8, 269;
Allies land in (1944), 271; Provisional
Government, 272, 273, 315; H.N.'s
return to (1945), 282; cuisine, 299;
recovery, 302; Gardes Républicains,

315; communism in, 319; Suez crisis (1956), 376–9; Revolution (1789), 387
France, 202
Franco, General Francisco, 101, 115, 144, 265, 364
Frank, 307–11
Franks, Sir Oliver (Lord Franks), 395
Frederick the Great, 305
Free French *see* France
Freemasons, 220
French Algeria, 387
French North Africa, 239
French Riviera, 101
Freud, Lucien, 377
Freud, Dr Sigmund, 80
Frick, 307–11
Fritzsche, Hans, 307–11
Froude, J. A., 116
Fry, Christopher: *Dark Is Light Enough*, 365
Fry, Roger, 191
Funk, 307–11

Gaer, Mr, 52
Gafencu, Grigore, 149, 150, 306
Gaitskell, Hugh, 378, 379, 383, 392
Galsworthy, John, 177
Gambetta, 166
Gandhi, M. K., 347
Garibaldi, 253
Garrick Club, 66, 208, 392
Garvin, J. L., 46
Gaudier-Brzeska, Henri, 24
Gaulle, Charles de, 240, 395; H.N.'s relations with, 8, 198–9, 202, 220, 221, 246, 261–2; dismisses Muselier (1942), 229–30; Macmillan's report on, 263; returns to France (1944), 267–8, 269
general elections, British: (1931), 32, 34; (1935), 82–6; (1945), 8, 288–91, 292, 297; (1951), 352
Geneva, 135, 315, 324
Genoa, 62
George IV, King, 105
George V, King, 20, 25, 90, 91. *See also* Nicolson, Harold: *King George V*
George VI, King, 108, 203, 260, 275, 327, 339, 349; accession (1936), 94;

Coronation (1937), 111; offers Baldwin earldom, 113; H.N.'s impressions, 188; writes to Churchill, 237; criticises B.B.C., 297; atom bomb, 298; unveils Roosevelt memorial (1948), 332; and H.N.'s *George V*, 333–4, 336, 338, 340, 343, 345, 351; death (1952), 351
Gérard, Baron, 325
Germany, 39, 97, 101, 114, 120, 127, 218, 219, 227, 244, 252, 258, 269, 278, 306–7, 312, 335, 347, 375, 383, 388; soul, 38; character, 52, 146, 180, 201, 381; appetites, 93, 130, 133; occupies Rhineland (1936), 94–5; Nazism, 102, 115–16, 126, 190–1, 255, 268; *Anschluss* (1938), 122, 128; occupies Sudetenland (1938), 131, 132, 134–5; military superiority, 143, 150; Ambassador, 143; invades Poland (1939), 148, 152, 157; Russo–German Pact (1939), 155; navy, 159, 209, 225; declaration of war (1939), 159–60, 304–5; invades Holland, 169, 183; propaganda, 172, 173, 268; invades Denmark, Norway (1940), 177–8, 179, 205, 207; and Belgium, 182–3; threatened invasion of Britain, 182, 185, 190, 200; invades France, 185, 187–8; Allied bombardment, 195; pact with Japan (1940), 195; overruns Bulgaria (1941), 202; and Greece, 207–9; in Balkans, 210; Wehrmacht, 212, 236, 285, 286; invades Russia (1941), 213, 217; declares war on U.S.A., 220, 221; Libyan campaign, 223, 224–5; in retreat in Egypt (1942), 236, 238; Stalingrad (1943), 242; retreat from Russia, 246, 248, 260, 266; V1 and V2, 259, 267, 268, 269, 270; Allied Control Commission, 274, 280, 304; Deutschlandsender, 277; S.S. and S.A., 283; Unconditional Surrender, 284–5, 286; London Embassy, 301, 388; U.S. military government, 304; concentration camps, 304; communism in, 319, 328; British Ambassador, 388; Gestapo, 394. *See*

also Battle of Britain; Blitzkrieg; Nuremberg
Gibbon, Edward, 350, 366
Gibraltar, 176, 208, 305
Gide, André, 262
Giraud, General, 239, 240, 263, 264
Gladstone, W. E., 43, 224, 359
Glen (dog), 406
Gloucester, Duke of, 157
Glyn, Sir Ralph, 86
Gneisenau, 225
Goadby, Sir Kenneth, 216
Godesberg, 134, 135, 136, 138, 139, 156
Goebbels, Josef, 127, 190, 213, 284
Goering, Hermann, 127, 210, 304–5, 307–11, 316
Goodhart, Professor A. L., 356
Gordon, General, 356
Gort, Field-Marshal Lord, 186, 188
Gott, Lieutenant-General E. H. E., 238
Goums, 315
Graham, Alan, 121
Granada, 339
Grand Canyon, 53–4
Grandi, Count Dino, 148
Greece, 39, 149, 202, 272, 362; French guarantee (1939), 148; British guarantee (1939), 154; Germans occupy (1941), 165, 205, 207, 208; Ambassador, 252; King, 274, 399; 1944 crisis, 275–6, 279, 281; H.N. in, 300–1, communism in, 319; Queen, 399; London Embassy, 399
Greek Orthodox Church, 273
Greek Relief Committee, 252, 273
Greenwood, Arthur, 100, 157, 158, 159, 207
Grenfell, Edward, 66
Grenoble, 174–5, 271; University, 373
Greville, Charles, 10
Greville, Mrs Ronald, 148, 193, 262
Grey, Sir Edward, 43
Griffiths, James, 212
Grosvenor Square, 80, 311, 332
Groves, Mrs, 285
Grunewald, the, 142, 336; press club, 336
Guards Chapel, 268
Gunston, Sir Derrick, 141
Gunther, John, 164

Hackwood, 59–60
Haldane, 172
Haley, Sir William, 250–1, 357, 363
Halifax, 3rd Viscount (Edward), 312, 133, 136, 142, 149, 169, 182, 230; succeeds Eden (1938), 118; conversation with Goebbels, 126–7; Norway, 174; 'a tired man', 180; Ambassador in Washington (1941), 199; and war aims, 200; broadcasts from New York, 211
Hall, Admiral Sir Reginald, 182
Hamburg, 101, 156, 170, 277
Hamilton, Duke of, 210
Hamlyn, Mr, 32
Hannon, Sir Patrick, 153
Hanover Terrace, 125
Harcourt, Brace (publishers), 79
Hardenberg, Charlotte de, 325
Hardy, Thomas, 347; *Pair of Blue Eyes*, 56
Harlech, Lord, 198
Harmsworths, 35, 37
Harris, Kenneth, 398–9
Harris, Mr, 332
Harris, Wilson, 200
Harrow School, 366
Harvey, Mr, 283
Hauptmann, Bruno, 70, 72–4
Hauptmann, Gerhart and Frau, 62
'Haw-Haw, Lord', *see* Joyce, William
Haxton, Gerald, 62
Heard, Gerald, 56, 178
Hebrides, 163
Helen of Argos, 244
Helsinki, 170
Hénaut, Jeanne, 34
Henderson, Arthur, 32
Henderson, Sir Nevile, 158
Her Majesty's Theatre, 312
Herbert, Sidney, 140, 141
Hess, Rudolf, 209–10, 307–11, 316
Heywood, Dubose, 49
Hicks, Joynson (Lord Brentford), 42
Hillary, Richard: *Last Enemy*, 248
Himmler, Heinrich, 285
Hinchingbrooke, Lord, 268
Hindenberg, 36, 37
Hiroshima, 297
Historic Buildings Commission, 347

History Today, 375

Hitler, Adolf, 36, 38, 93, 120, 126, 127–8, 132, 135, 136, 140, 156, 168, 175, 178, 193, 203, 208, 209, 213, 217, 219, 250, 258, 277, 283, 284, 308, 309, 311, 331, 375; and presidency (1932), 37; occupation of Rhineland (1936), 94, 95; *Anschluss* (1938), 117, 119, 122; Munich (1938), 131; Sudetenland, 133, 134; Chamberlain visits, 138, 139; invades Czechoslovakia (1939), 144, 146; Gafencu visits, 149–50; no designs on British Empire, 150; Nuremberg rallies, 152, 310; invades Poland, 157, 158, 163; compared to Napoleon, 165; contacts Duke of Windsor, 167; French surrender (1940), 188; and invasion of Britain, 189, 190, 191; Stauffenberg plot (1944), 270; death (1945), 285; alterations to Berlin, 336

Hoare, Rex, 124

Hoare, Sir Samuel, 86, 88, 149, 172

Hobhouse, Christopher, 35, 65, 77, 78

Hobson, Valerie, 395

Hodge, Alan, 375

Hodza, 135

Hofmannsthal, Hugo von, 311

Hofmannsthal, Raimond von, 311

Holland, 150, 165, 168, 169, 182, 183, 184, 272, 369

Holland, Lord, 14

Hollywood, 176, 313

Home Rule Bill, 343

Homer, 177

Hood, H.M.S., 211

Hood, Samuel, 214

Hoover, President Herbert, 48, 80, 347

Hopi Indians, 54

Hopkins, Harry, 228

Hopkinson, Austin, 142–3

Horder, Lord, 200

Hore-Belisha, Leslie, 143, 172–3, 232

Horizon, 170

Horne, Sir Robert, 87

Horner, Lady, 103

Horsbrugh, Florence, Baroness, 104

House of Commons: H.N.'s love for, 289, 293; Secret Sessions, 170, 190, 229, 239, 241, 246, 264–5

House of Lords: Commons occupies (1943), 240, 289; possible place for H.N., 299, 303–4, 307, 320, 333

Howard, Leslie, 176

Hungary, 133, 134, 152, 312, 380, 381

Hunt, Dr, 407

Huntington, Constant, 29, 66

Huntington, Gladys, 29–30

Hutchinson, Mary, 208

Hutchinson, St John, 208

Huxley, Aldous, 176, 178

Huxley, Sir Julian, 151, 194, 200, 219, 302

Hyde Park, N.Y., 218

hydrogen bomb, 384

Hynd, J. B., 280

Hyslop, Paul, 177

Iceland, 156

India, 165, 176, 213, 226, 228, 229, 319

Ingres, J. A. D., 237

Inskip, Sir Thomas, 142

International Court of Justice, The Hague, 378

International Military Tribunal, Nuremberg, 307–11, 316

Isherwood, Christopher, 176, 178

Islam, 401

Islington, 23

Ismailia, 379

Ismay, General Sir Hastings (Lord), 232–3

Israel, 374, 379

Italy, 114, 120, 122, 148, 155, 197, 205, 215, 247, 258, 265, 279, 347; Nicolsons on holiday, 18–19, 55, 59; H.N. and Mosley in, 34–7; invades Abyssinia (1935), 80–1, 82, 94, 99–100; Air Force, 116; distrust of Mussolini, 127; Munich (1938), 131; alliance with Germany, 132, 180, 184, 190; Army, 144, 238, 285; propaganda, 146; declares war on U.S.A. (1941), 220; General Staff, 246; surrender (1943), 246, 252, 312; communism in, 319

Jacob, General Sir Ian, 319

Jamaica, 386, 403

James, Henry, 407
Janner, Sir Barnett, 118, 290, 292
Jansenism, 372
Japan, 127, 221, 227, 228, 238, 277,
    278, 288; alliance with Germany,
    132, 165, 190, 195; Pearl Harbor
    (1941), 219; takes Singapore, 221,
    224; Unconditional Surrender (1945),
    297–8: H.N.'s trip to (1959), 391
Jarvis, W. B., 85, 118, 121
Jean, M. and Mme, 203
Jebb, Gladwyn (Lord Gladwyn), 118,
    280
Jehovah's Witnesses, 278
Jersey, Lady, 80
Jesuits, 220
Jews, 128, 150, 173, 220, 280, 335
Joad, C. E. M., 171, 172, 219
Joan of Arc, 263
Job, 150
Jodl, General, 307–11
John XXIII, Pope, 389
Jowitt, Sir William, 299, 303, 307, 317
Joyce, James, 29–30, 61; *Finnegans
    Wake*, 61, 150; *Ulysses*, 34, 61
Joyce, William ('Lord Haw-Haw'),
    172, 242

Kalmuks, 280
Kaltenbrunner, 307–11
Kampala, 109
Kauntze, 109
Kazan, 280
Keats–Shelley Committee, 393
Kedleston, 59
Keitel, Field-Marshal Wilhelm, 307–11
Kemsley, Lord, 285
Kennedy, President John F., 397, 399,
    400
Kennedy, Joseph (U.S. Ambassador),
    151, 174, 185, 203, 397
Kent, Duchess of, 274
Kent, Duke of, 157
Kenya, 125
Kenya, 110, 352
Keosseivanoff, 125
Keppel, Mrs George, 193, 285
Kerensky, 101
Kermanshah, 193
Kerr, Archibald Clark, 256

Keyes, Admiral Sir Roger, 140, 174,
    181
Keynes, John Maynard, Lord, 21, 24,
    46
Khartoum, 110–11
Khrushchev, Nikita, 375, 395
Kiel, 383
Kilvert, Francis, 9
King, Reginald, 250
King, William, 29
King George V, S.S., 199
King's Bench Walk (H.N.'s London
    home 1930–45), 13, 60, 91, 155, 182,
    192, 198, 208, 217, 236, 270, 285,
    287, 293, 302–3
Kinhoff, J. V., 51
Kipling, Rudyard, 14, 90, 116, 216,
    249; *Jungle Book*, 392
Kirby, J. A., 292
Kirkpatrick, Sir Ivone, 156, 304–5, 368
Knight, Professor G. Wilson, 374
Knights of the Round Table, 15
Knole, 13, 16, 46, 82, 258–9, 365, 366,
    400
Knuthsen, Sir Louis, 64–5
Koestler, Arthur, 248
Koran, the, 401
Korea, 327, 347, 356
Krosigk, Schwerin von, 286
Kuh, Fred, 203, 238
Kursk, 248
Kurusu, Saburo, 219
Kyllman, Otto, 115

Labour Party, 17, 26, 113, 114, 137,
    160, 180, 200, 205, 214, 254, 261,
    273, 303, 307, 351–2; Sunday
    Cinema Bill and Free Trade, 24;
    split with MacDonald (1931), 30;
    1931 election, 32; Mosley invited to
    lead, 40; and Finland (1939), 170;
    wartime coalition, 183, 288; and
    Beveridge Report (1943), 243; and
    parliamentary hours, 265; 1945
    election, 291, 297; H.N. joins (1947),
    319, 328–9, 331, 338, 399; Manifesto
    (1950), 345; Executive, 375; Suez,
    378–81; atom bomb, 383; H.N.'s
    flash for (1959), 392
Lady's Journal, The, 49–50

Lamont, Edith, 402, 404, 405
Lamont, Thomas, 68, 76, 77, 99
Lampedusa, 279
Lancaster, Osbert, 323
Lane, Allen, 166
Lane, John, 61
Langtry, Lily, 62–3
Lansbury, George, 81
Laos, 398
Larousse, 351
Lascelles, Sir Alan ('Tommy'), 275, 297, 327, 333, 335, 348, 351, 352, 355, 397, 398
Lateran Palace, 36
Lausanne, 324
Laval, Pierre, 86, 88, 199
Law, Andrew Bonar, 43
Law, Nigel, 122
Law, Richard (Lord Coleraine), 140, 146, 176
Lawrence, D. H. and Frieda, 44
Lawrence, Lord and Lady, 311, 316
Lawrence, Colonel T. E., 56, 125, 248; *Seven Pillars of Wisdom*, 177
Lawrence, Thomas, 317–18
le Bosquet, Audrey, 15
Le Havre, 238, 266
League of Nations, 8, 82, 93, 95, 100, 124, 168
Leatherhead, 27
Lebanon, 39, 387
Leeds, 198
Leeper, Allen, 78
Leeper, Sir Reginald, 78, 300
Lees-Milne, James, 60–1, 222, 346
Leicester, West: H.N. National Labour Member for (1935), 82–6, 115, 118, 142, 221, 274, 277–8; defeated (1945), 292, 293
Leigh, Vivien, 350, 373
Lenin, V. I., 150
Lewis, C. Day, 367, 372
Liberal Party, 26, 82, 137, 268, 321, 330, 352
Libya, 119, 149, 207, 218, 221, 223, 224, 225, 247
Liddall, Sir Walter, 138
Life, 351
Lima, 387

Lindbergh, Anne (*née* Morrow), 45–54, 68–74, 80, 94, 99, 102, 126
Lindbergh, Colonel Charles, 45–54, 68–74, 79, 80, 94, 96, 99, 102, 126, 208, 397
Lindbergh, Jon, 70
Lindsay, Elizabeth, 48, 50
Lindsay, Kenneth, 87, 96
Lippmann, Walter, 65, 151, 173
Lisbon, 365
Listener, The, 375
Litvinov, 135
Liverpool, 163
Livingstone, David, 109
Lloyd, Lord, 139
Lloyd, Selwyn, 381
Lloyd George, David, 24, 29, 81, 100, 157, 181, 183, 209, 242, 313; H.N. visits (1932), 43–4; and Curzon, 57, 59–60; congratulates H.N. on speech, 120–1; talks with Maisky (1939), 147–8; possible prime minister, 179–80; 80th birthday (1943), 241; death (1945), 283
Locarno Pact (1925), 94, 95
Lockhart, Sir Robert Bruce, 13, 88, 99, 267
Lodge, Henry Cabot, 14
London, Bishop of, 273, 274
London Conference (1930), 65
London Library, 57, 307, 326, 349, 350, 373, 396, 401
London University, 400
Londonderry, Lord, 93
Long Barn, 13, 15, 39, 60, 83, 94, 102, 126, 193
Longford, Lord, *see* Pakenham, Frank
Longworth, Alice, 48
Lords, House of, *see* House of Lords
Los Angeles, 31, 393, 397
Lothian, Lord, 195, 228
Louis XIV, King of France, 391
Louise (V.S-W's lady's maid), 40
Luce, Clare Booth, 393
Ludwig, Emil, 145
Lully, Raymond, 315
Lympne, 56
Lyons, 85, 174, 182

Macaulay, Lord, 263

Macaulay, Rose, 247–8
MacCarthy, Desmond, 29–30, 122, 307
McCarthy, Senator Joseph, 361
MacDonald, Berry, 23
MacDonald, Ishbel, 19
MacDonald, Malcolm, 23, 90, 91, 106, 120, 141, 201
MacDonald, J. Ramsay, 17, 36, 83, 87–8, 104–5, 116, 201, 249, 280, 322; 'my brain is going', 19–20; and circuses, 21–2; character, 22–3; Coalition Government (1931), 30; Abyssinia (1935), 81; offers post to H.N. (1936), 91–2, 93; thinks of resigning, 98; and Coronation (1936), 100–1; Abdication crisis, 106; Coronation (1937), 113; death (1937), 115
McEwan, Jock, 121
McLaren, Christobel (Lady Aberconway), 25
McLaren, Harry (Lord Aberconway), 25
Maclean, Donald, 349
Maclure, Mr, 393
MacMichael, Sir Harold, 109
Macmillan, Lady Dorothy, 395
Macmillan, Harold, 140, 153, 177, 179, 183, 301–2, 395; on party, 17–18; and New Party, 21, 23, 26; Eden group, 141, 149; Finland, 176; on Beaverbrook, 218; in Algiers (1943), 240, 263; Prime Minister (1957), 382; and Guy Burgess, 391; 'winds of change', 394
Macmillan, Miss (secretary), 157, 184
McNair, Lord, 378
Macnamara, John, 151, 279
McNeil, Hector, 302
Macpherson, 89
Madrid, 101
Maginot Line, 168
Magnus, Philip, 386
Magnus-Alcroft, Lady, 386
Mahdi, 110
Maidstone, 157
Maisky, Ivan (Russian Ambassador), 130, 146, 147, 153, 174, 205, 208, 210
Makarere College, 109
Malta, 176, 247

Manchester, 139
Manchester Guardian, 146, 355
Mandel, Georges, 175
Mar, 154
Marburg, 305
Marbury, Elizabeth, 45–6
Mareth Line, 244
Margaret, Princess, 244, 260, 360
Margate, 310
Margerie, Roland de, 203
Margesson, David, 23, 40, 104, 126, 147, 160, 170, 181, 182, 183
Mariano, Nicky, 345
Marin, Jean, 282
Marlborough, the, 133
Marlborough House, 339, 341
Marlborough, 9th Duke of, 55
Marlborough, Gladys, Duchess of, 55
Marne, battle of the (1914), 186
Marquet, Albert and Mme, 262
Marrakesh, 64, 256
Marseilles, 271
Martha (dog), 78, 250, 257
Martin, Kingsley, 42, 200, 242, 355
Martinique, 403
Marx, Karl, 347
Mary, Queen Consort of George V, 25, 90, 318, 327, 333–4, 338, 339–40, 343, 355, 358, 359
Marylebone, 194
Masaryk, Jan, 134, 139, 167
Masefield, John, 244, 255
Massawa, 207
Massigli, René, 75, 262, 324, 344
Matheson, Hilda, 42
Matthews, Colonel, 361
Maugham, Eliza, 129
Maugham, Robin, 2nd Viscount, 293, 322–3
Maugham, W. Somerset, 62–3, 103, 128–30, 176, 178, 322–3, 337
Maxton, James, 89
Mayo, C. H. P., 366–7
Mazzini, Giuseppe: *Duty of Man*, 371
Melbourne, 389
Mendelssohn, Felix, 361
Messina, 248
Metcalfe, Bob, 371, 373
Mexico, 66, 72, 74–5, 77
Mezières, 184

Michigan, Lake, 48
Middle East, 212, 226
Mikado, 219
Mikolajczyk, 281
Milan, 19, 36, 37, 100
Mills, Bertram, 21–2
miners' strike (1944), 261
Minorca, 123
Minto, Alderman, 292
Mitford, Nancy: *Voltaire in Love*, 385–6
Modena, 252
Mohammed, 401
Mollet, 379
Molotov, Vyacheslav, 313, 314, 327–8
Monaco, 103
Monckton, Sir Walter (Viscount Monckton), 214
Moncrieff, Mrs, 285
Monday Evening Club, 243
Monroe Doctrine, 399–400
Montesquiou, Robert de, 76
Montgomery, Field Marshal Sir Bernard, 250, 260; 8th Army, 233, 238, 242
Moore, Henry, 399
Moran, Lord, 280, 282, 326–7
Morgan, 84–5
Morgan & Co., J. P., 65, 68, 73, 75–6, 99
Morgan, Grenfell, 65
Morning Post, 37
Morocco, 59, 64, 81
Morpeth Mansions, 134
Morris, William, 116
Morrison, Herbert, 175, 200, 235, 254
Morrow, Anne, *see* Lindbergh, Anne
Morrow, Betty, 65–6, 67, 68–74, 75–6, 77, 102, 126
Morrow, Constance, 102
Morrow, Dwight, 65–6, 68–74, 75, 77
Morshead, Sir Owen, 333–4, 338, 343
Mortimer, Raymond, 42, 139, 177, 178, 253–4, 298, 319, 341, 344, 386
Morton, Desmond, 247
Moscow, 154, 155, 217, 256, 273, 280, 281, 320
Moslems, *see* Islam
Mosley, Lady Cynthia, 20, 23, 33, 57, 208

Mosley, Sir Oswald, 31, 33, 93, 208; New Party, 8, 20–1, 22–4, 28–9, 30, 32, 57; 1931 election, 32; in Italy with H.N. (1932), 34–6; Beaverbrook on, 39; offered leadership of Labour and Conservative parties, 40–1; Lloyd George on, 43; imprisonment, 253–4. *See also Action*; New Party
Munich: H.N. in, 60, 63; settlement (1938), 131, 138, 139, 142, 144, 156, 158, 164, 190, 222
Murphy, Robert D., 304
Murray, Sir Gilbert, 247–8
Murray, Jock, 301, 365
Murrow, Ed, 211, 230, 243, 393
Muselier, Admiral, 202, 229–30
Mussolini, Benito, 117, 138, 156, 158, 180, 218, 220, 250; Mosley and (1932), 36, 37; and Austria (1938), 119; Italians distrust, 127; Abyssinia (1935), 80–1, 82, 94, 99–100; Albania (1939), 148–9; fall (1943), 246; murder (1945), 285

Nabokov, Vladimir: *Lolita*, 390, 392
Nagasaki, 298
Nakuru, 110
Namier, Sir Lewis, 200
Naples, 17, 263
Napoleon, 101, 156, 165
Narvik, 178, 179, 181
Nasser, G. A., 376–81, 387
National Farmers' Union, 290
National Gallery, 205
National Government, 30, 32, 86, 91, 137
National Labour Party, 86, 87, 90, 92, 98, 104, 120, 201–2, 233, 268; H.N. Member (1935), 8, 82, 151, 331; no future, 91, 261; national support for, 92, 93; ceases to exist (1945), 288
National Liberal Party, 82, 84
National Portrait Gallery, 326, 373
National Trust, 314, 320, 326, 341, 346, 366, 374, 400
Nauplia, 274
Near East, 152
Necker, M. and Mme, 325
Nepal, 127

Nether Wallop, 196

Neurath, Baron Konstantin von, 307–11

Neville Terrace (H.N.'s London home (1946–52), 302, 304, 317, 349

New Mexico, 44

New Party, 8, 20–1, 22–4, 26–9, 30, 31, 32, 33, 34, 35, 40–1, 57

New Statesman, The, 42, 355

New York, 31, 44–6, 65, 66, 70, 76, 156, 211, 322, 361, 407

New York Times, The, 45, 313

New York Underground Railways, 74

New Yorker, The, 259

New Zealand, 379

Newark, 50

Newcastle-on-Tyne, 360

Next Day Hill, 68–74, 77

Nice, 62, 271

Nicolson, Adam (H.N.'s grandson), 385, 405

Nicolson, Benedict (H.N.'s son), 8, 13, 67, 69, 77, 85, 130, 144, 197, 250, 286, 303, 311, 347, 370; first sees Sissinghurst (1930), 18–19; holiday in Italy (1930), 18–19; unhappy at Eton, 22; visits Lady Sackville (1933), 54; H.N. worried about, 55; accompanies H.N. to U.S.A. (1935), 79–80; buys a Picasso (1940), 189; on Fry and Woolf, 191; on Connolly, 235; H.N.'s letters to, 236–7, 265, 267; military service, 236–7; accident (1944), 276–7; H.N. sends books to, 278; to Sissinghurst with H.N. (1945), 283–4; and return to King's Bench Walk, 285; in Leicester with H.N., 292; on H.N.'s literary style, 299; Deputy Surveyor of the King's Pictures (1946), 318; editor *Burlington Magazine*, 318, 346, 399; marriage (1955), 346, 356, 371; on private schools, 360; at Nigel's wedding (1953), 361; child, 377–8

Nicolson, Harold

Characteristics and Tastes: love of France, 8, 282; love of England, 8, 199, 201; feminine streak, 9; agile mind, 9; industry, 9, 96; diary, 9–10, 109, 202, 221, 381, 383, 408;

knowledge of German character, 13, 62, 165, 197, 205, 274; distaste for journalism, 13, 20, 22, 32, 41; happiness, 19, 34, 58; depression, 20, 32, 33, 34, 39, 46, 55, 59, 66, 164, 165, 169; sees both sides, 33; loathes fascism, 33; 'Mosley has done me harm', 34; loathes publicity, 37, 149; reckless, 37; 'I have made a fool of myself', 38–9; intellectual integrity, 55; New Year Resolutions (1934), 59; courage, 64; good memory, 64; not a political mind, 77; 'one of the leading writers of this age', 78; dislike of electioneering, 82, 118, 328; snobbish, 96, 103, 332, 387, 388; 'a good old tea-cup really', 100; sympathy for Germans, 135–6; fears defeat, 163, 164; on vulgarity, 173, 387; pacifist, 178; 'lacks virility', 215; thick skull, 216; homosexuality, 216; anti-clerical, 230–1, 388; 'I'm all for promiscuity', 257–8; and Jews, 257–8; 'Has the whole world gone mad?', 258; sense of failure, 317; and monarchy, 343; and afterlife, 354; on suicide, 368; and television, 374–5, 393, 394, 397–8; and Catholics, 388; dislike of music, 393; plays Bingo, 398; 'a liability', 400; and Islam, 401

Family life: birth, 7; childhood, 59; education, 8; marriage, 8, 19, 31, 58, 81–2, 205–6, 232, 306, 365–6, 388; sons, 8; King's Bench Walk, 13, 60, 91, 155, 182, 192, 198, 208, 217, 236, 270, 285, 287, 293, 302–3; decides to move, 13; buys Sissinghurst (1930), 13–14, 22; finances, 14, 22, 38, 39–40, 54, 57, 58, 83, 100, 164, 351, 396; holidays in Italy, 18–19, 55, 59; 'we have been so happy', 19, 81–2; Morocco, 59, 64; Cap Ferrat, 59–60, 103, 128–30; gardens, 60, 75, 97, 144, 148, 191, 197, 205, 318, 322; writes Will, 65; wins sweepstake, 76–7; near-escape (1923), 79; forbidden to fly, 79, 111, 300; death of Lady Sackville, 92; 50th birthday 108; admiration for V.S.-W.,

142, 235, 245; sails to France (1939), 154; sons criticise literary style, 299; Neville Terrace, 302, 304, 349; Albany, 353–4, 359, 376, 395, 396, 402; cannot bear to think of V.S.-W. in pain, 367; sorrow, 407; death of V.S.-W. (1962), 406–7; death (1968), 408

Political Attitudes and Career: diplomatic career, 8, 14, 37, 55, 59; 1919 Peace Conference, 8; Counsellor in Tehran, 8; and in Berlin (1927–9), 8, 13; and New Party, 8, 22, 23–4; National Labour M.P. for West Leicester (1935), 8, 82–6, 115, 118, 221, 274, 277–8; Ministry of Information (1940), 8, 184, 212, 213, 214; loses seat (1945), 8, 292, 293, 297, 303; Croydon election (1948), 8, 328, 329, 330–2, 334, 338; knighted, 8, 355, 356, 357, 358; return to England (1929), 13; joins *Evening Standard* (1930), 13, 22; broadcasts, 13, 131, 134, 144, 192, 249, 312, 314, 317, 318, 322, 352, 353, 356, 382; Macmillan includes in ideal Cabinet, 17–18; on Beaverbrook, 20–1; 'on the verge of politics', 22; edits *Action*, 26, 27, 30, 33; offered editorship of *Evening Standard*, 26; leaves *Standard*, 27, 30; New Party candidate for Combined English Universities (1931), 32; in Berlin, 34, 37–8, 336–7; in Italy with Mosley (1932), 34–7; in Paris, 34–5, 61, 168, 174, 175, 312–16, 317, 363–4; *Times* attack on, 37; and *Morning Post*, 37; U.S. lecture tour (1933), 39–40, 44–54; split with Mosley (1932), 41; offered literary editorship of *New Statesman*, 42; in Munich, 60, 63; Sevenoaks rejects H.N. as candidate, 78; crosses floor (1935), 82; maiden speech, 86, 89; MacDonald offers post, 91–2, 93; writes party policy statement, 96; Foreign Affairs Committee, 96, 101, 114, 118, 119, 123; in Africa, 109–11; and biography of MacDonald, 115;

'unfortunate speech on the Address' (1936), 117; rift with National Labour, 118; support for Eden, 118, 120; constituency vote of confidence (1938), 121; speaking tour of Balkans (1938), 123–5; 'Stand up, you brute!', 138–9; out of sympathy with government and party, 141; Munich speech (1938), 146; suggested Ambassador to U.S.A., 149; lunch with Queen Elizabeth, 188; speaking in Scotland, 196; suggested leader of National Labour, 201; review of situation (1939), 165; visits Maginot Line, 168; lecture tour of France (1940), 174–5; Governor of B.B.C., 212, 214, 297, 306; in Dublin, 226–8; involvement with Free French, 198–9, 202, 220, 221, 246, 261–2; breakfast with Baldwin (1943), 249–50; in Sweden, 252, 253; and Australia trip, 253–4, 255; relations with constituency, 254, 261, 274, 277, 288–91, 292–3; in Algiers, 261, 263–4, 265; and Oran, 264, 265; possible peerage, 272, 299, 302, 303, 307, 320, 329, 333; 'most effective speech', 282; in Paris (1945), 282; Anglo-French Interparliamentary Committee, 283; refuses to stand as Tory, 288; love for House of Commons, 289, 293; return to writing, 297; lecture tour of Greece (1945), 300–1; lectures to Foreign Office recruits, 301; turned down for British Council, 302; in Nuremberg, 307–11, 316; possible Ambassador in Paris, 311, 334; in Paris for Peace Conference, 312–16, 317; Royal Academy lecture, 317–18; joins Labour Party (1947), 319, 320, 321, 329, 334, 345, 392, 398; Historic Buildings Commission, 320, 347; hates being out of Parliament, 320; could never join Tories or Liberals, 321; speech to Westminster Labour Party, 322; socialist convictions, 322; Legion of Honour, 324; in Lausanne, 324; Geneva, 324–6; in Berlin (1948),

336–7; and Labour Manifesto, 345;
Chairman, London Library, 350;
doctorate, 360; in Paris, 363–4; and
Oxford Professorship, 372–4; trip to
Far East, 382; in Japan (1959), 391;
unveils Duff Cooper tablet, 397

Health: 'static, obese, and decaying',
38; brief illness (1934), 59; ear
trouble, 64–5; 'I do not need
Sanatogen', 97; growing old, 102,
302, 317, 342, 380, 401, 406, 407;
giddiness, 123–4; gives up smoking
(1941), 209; medical check (1941),
216; deafness, 317, 338, 371;
passions spent, 317; haunted by
mental decay, 322; strokes (1955),
368–9, 370, 401; ill health, 372; bad
cough (1960), 398; 'gaga', 401

Writings: JOURNALISM: 24, 27, 144,
164, 237, 303, 318, 326, 337, 341;
Contact, 318; *Daily Express*, 13;
Daily Telegraph, 144; *Evening
Standard* ('Londoner's Diary'), 13,
14, 17, 22; *Figaro*, 318, 322, 326,
344; *Observer*, 8, 338, 356; *Spectator*
'Marginal Comment'), 8, 141, 221,
271, 318, 326, 356, 357
BOOKS: *Age of Reason*, 385, 386,
391, 398; autobiography (projected),
59–60, 63, 64, 78; *Benjamin
Constant*, 333, 336, 350; *Congress of
Vienna*, 271, 291, 297, 298, 304;
Curzon, the Last Phase, 8, 39, 54,
55, 57, 64, 247; *Desire to Please*, 228,
231, 233, 259; *Diplomacy*, 58, 80,
135; *Dwight Morrow*, 65–75, 79;
English Sense of Humour, 307, 317,
319; *Friday Mornings*, 271; *Good
Behaviour*, 356, 363, 364, 369;
Helen's Tower, 101–2, 115; *In
Search of the Past*, 271; *Journey to
Java*, 382, 386, 389; *King George V,
His Life and Reign*, 8, 332, 333–5,
336, 338, 340–5, 348, 349, 350, 351,
354, 355, 356, 359; *Lord Carnock*, 8,
13, 72, 74, 298, 389; *Monarchy*, 396,
401; *Paul Verlaine*, 8; *Peacemaking*,
41, 42–3; *Public Faces*, 8, 41, 42, 43,
350; *Sainte-Beuve*, 374, 378; *Some
People*, 8, 41, 259, 389, 392;

Tennyson, 8, 257; *Why Britain Is at
War*, 166, 171
PLAY: *The Archduke*, 18
Nicolson, Juliet (H.N.'S granddaughter), 364–5, 368, 405
Nicolson, Luisa (*née* Vertova) (H.N.'s
daughter-in-law), 345–6, 369, 371,
378
Nicolson, Nigel (H.N.'s son), 8, 13, 67,
69, 85, 130, 197, 232, 245, 311, 338,
347, 358, 360, 378, 384, 405; first
sees Sissinghurst (1930), 15–16;
holiday in Italy (1930), 18–19; bored
with Eton, 22; appendicitis, 58;
Coronation (1937), 112–13; plants
willows, 144; H.N.'s fears for, 177;
easy birth, 193; H.N.'s letters to,
236–7, 265, 267, 382; military service,
236–7, 263; returns home (1945),
291, 303; in Leicester with H.N.,
292; on H.N.'s literary style, 299;
gives H.N. tweed, 339; Leicester
election (1950), 345; M.P. for
Bournemouth (1952), 351–2, 356;
marriage (1953), 361; children, 364,
385, 405, 407–8; Sissinghurst and
National Trust, 366; discusses
suicide with H.N., 368; and abolition
of hanging (1956), 376; and Suez,
377, 380; Gaitskell on, 383; and
Wolfenden Report (1958), 389;
Lolita, 390, 392; proposes Monarchy
to H.N., 396, 401; death of mother
(1962), 406
Nicolson, Philippa (*née* Tennyson
d'Eyncourt) (H.N.'s daughter-in-
law), 358, 361, 364, 368, 369, 382,
383, 386, 405, 407–8
Nicolson, Rebecca (H.N.'s granddaughter), 407–8
Nicolson, Vanessa Pepita (H.N.'s
granddaughter), 377–8, 405
Niggemann, Elvira (H.N.'s secretary),
164, 198, 258, 270, 271, 292, 318,
321, 334, 352, 359, 369, 385, 404
Nineteenth Century, 146
Nixon, Mrs, 387
Nixon, Richard, 397
Noel-Baker, Philip, 101
Norman, Sir Henry, 18

Normandy, 266
North Atlantic Treaty Organisation, 356
North Haven, 67–8, 79
North Street, 28
Northumberland, Duke of, 55–6
Norway, 173–4, 175, 177, 179, 180, 195, 205, 207, 208
Novello, Ivor, 287
Nuffield, Lord, 21
Nuremberg, 283, 287; Nazi rallies, 152, 310; war crimes tribunal, 307–11
Nutting, Anthony, 380

Obscene Publications Report, 390
Observer, The, 338, 355, 356, 386, 389, 398
oil, 223, 335
Olga, Queen of Greece, 339
Olivier, Sir Laurence, 18, 350, 373
Olympia, 21–2, 274
Olympic Games, 396
Omdurman, battle of (1898), 110
Oran, 264
Orlando, 313
Osborne, Sir D'Arcy, 246, 247
Oslo, 378
Osusky, M., 199
Ottawa, 201
Oxford and Asquith, Earl *see* Asquith
Oxford University, 26, 257, 372–3, 374, 375, 395; Balliol College, 8, 251, 357, 359–60; Christ Church Library, 116; New College, 374; University College, 356

pacifism, 171, 172, 173
Paddington Hotel, 125
Pakenham, Frank (Lord Longford), 329
Palace Yard, Westminster, 90, 112, 286
Palestine, 80, 97, 150. *See also* Israel
Palewski, Gaston, 262
Papandreou, George, 276
Papen, 307–11
Paris, 60, 69, 88, 247, 263, 307, 311, 342; H.N. in, 34–5, 61, 168, 174, 175, 312–16, 317, 363–4; Churchill in (1939), 155; bombed (1940), 182; liberated (1944), 271; Churchill and Eden in (1944), 275; Peace

Conference (1919), 8, 34, 43, 313; and (1945), 312, 313, 316
Parish, Dr, 369, 370
Park Lodge, 82
Partridge murder, 29–30
Pasadena, 51
Patricia, Princess, 359
Patrick, Mark, 146
patriotism, 199
Patton, General, 283
Paulus, Field-Marshal, 242
Peace, Charles, 29–30
Pearl Harbor, 219
Peel, A. G. V., 224
Pembroke family, 18
Pembury Hospital, 405, 406
Penguin Books, 166
Pepys, Samuel, 10, 326
Percy, Lord Eustace (Lord Percy), 54–5, 89
Persia, 42, 53, 213; London Embassy, 335
Perugia, 258
Pétain, Marshal, 199, 240, 242
Philadelphia, 79
Philip II, King of Spain, 29
Philippines, 275
Phoenix Theatre, 89
Piacenza, 19
Picasso, Pablo, 189
Pineau, Christian, 377
Pinero, A. W., 129
Plato: *Symposium,* 222
Plymouth, 154, 244, 297, 386
Poland, 133, 134, 152, 213, 266; British and French guarantee (1939), 144, 147, 154, 155; Army, 147; Ambassador, 157; Germany invades (1939), 157–9, 163, 164; Russia invades (1939), 165; Russian control, 277, 279–82; Government-in-Exile, 281
Pompadour, Mme de, 189
Pope-Hennessy, James, 204–5, 222, 260, 304, 344, 357, 377, 387–8
Popolo d'Italia, 36
Porgy (Heywood), 49
Port Elizabeth, 393–4
Port Said, 379
Portes, Hélène de, 203–4

Portofino, 60, 62
Portsmouth, 269
Portugal, 365, 370
Potsdam, 284; Conference (1945), 297
Prague, 144, 146, 286; British Minister in, 139
Pratt's Club, 123, 126, 218, 232, 254, 255, 260, 285, 287, 291, 303
Pravda, 256, 281, 375
Press Association, 331
Preston, Stuart, 259
Priestley, J. B., 146, 200
Prince Eugen, 211
Prince of Wales, H.M.S., 219, 220, 221
Princess Royal, 318
Profumo, John, 395
propaganda, 120, 146, 173, 176, 207, 209, 222, 228-9, 243, 268
Prothero, W. E., 301
Proust, Marcel, 55-6, 62, 64, 76
Provence, 31, 65
Prunier, Mme, 217
Pryce-Jones, Alan, 386
Pucheu, M., 262
Punch, 307
Putnam (publishers), 29
Putney, 368

Queen Mary, H.M.S., 407
Quennell, Peter, 235, 301, 375

R.101, 19
Radiodiffusion Française, 282
Raeder, Admiral, 307-11
Raikes, Sir Victor, 95
Rambouillet, 395
Rapallo, 62
Rathbone, Eleanor: H.N. on, 303
Rathbone, J. F. W., 346
Ravensdale, Irene, Baroness, 208, 273
Rayner, Brigadier Sir Ralph, 225
Rebecca (dog), 69
Récamier, Mme, 325
Reform Club, 302
Reina del Mar, S.S., 386
Reith, Sir John, 34
Rélizane, 264
Renown, H.M.S., 298
Repulse, H.M.S., 219
Reuter, 135

Reynaud, Paul, 155, 186, 203-4
Rhind, Cecil, 92
Rhineland, 94
Rhodes, Cecil, 14
Rhondda, Lady, 200
Ribbentrop, Joachim von, 135, 136, 154, 155, 158, 256, 305, 307-11, 316
Rilke, Rainer Maria, 311, 346
Rinder, Olive, 60
Rio de Janeiro, 398
Ritz, 203, 285
Rochester, 156
Rockefeller, J., 46
Rodin, Auguste: *Penseur*, 308
Roehm, 156
Roman Catholics, 213, 280, 290, 389, 397
Rome, 34, 35-7, 144, 265, 266; British Embassy, 36; German Embassy, 36; Palazzo Venezia, 220
Romer, Tadeusz, 281
Rommel, General Irwin, 221, 223, 225, 232, 245
Roosevelt, Eleanor, 228
Roosevelt, President Franklyn D.; 1st term (1933), 51, 52; 2nd term (1936), 117, 122, 136, 163, 172, 185; 3rd term (1940), 195-6, 199, 215, 218, 219, 228, 239, 269; 4th term (1944), 275, 280; death, 284, 305; memorial, 332
Roosevelt, President Theodore, 14, 48
Rose, Jim, 338
Rosenberg, Alfred, 307-11
Rothenstein, William, 17
Rothermeres, 37, 81, 240, 246, 258
Royal Academy, 342, 383
Royal College of Physicians, 326, 381
Royal Festival Hall, 392
Royal Free Hospital, 404
Royal Gallery, 210
Royal Literary Fund, 326
Royal Literary Society, 367
Royal Opera House, 312
Rubaiyat of Omar Khayyam, The, 368
Rubinstein, Artur, 99
Rules, 260
Rumania, 123-4, 147, 148, 149, 150, 154, 165, 203, 213, 266, 306, 312
Rumbold, Sir Horace, 38

Runciman, Lord, 137
Rundstedt, General von, 276, 277
Rusk, Dean, 399
Russell, Bertrand, 347–8
Russell, Elizabeth: *Enchanted April*, 60
Russia, *see* Union of Soviet Socialist Republics
Russo–German Non-Aggression Pact (1939), 154, 155
Rutland, 10th Duke of, 308
Rye, 49

Sackville, Charles, 4th Lord (V.S.-W.'s uncle), 78, 376, 400
Sackville, Edward, 5th Lord (V.S.-W.'s cousin), 139
Sackville, Jacobine, Lady, 400
Sackville, Lionel, 6th Lord (V.S.-W.'s cousin), 358, 400
Sackville, Sir Thomas, 16
Sackville, Victoria, Lady ('BM') (V.S.-W.'s mother), 40, 54, 58, 63, 67, 92, 93
Sackville-West, Victoria (Vita), 13, 40, 78, 130, 145, 157, 165, 172, 173, 184, 212–13, 260, 271, 286, 288, 311, 321, 326, 335, 337, 349, 352, 354, 360, 366, 368, 373, 385, 398, 400; marriage (1913), 8; buys Sissinghurst (1930), 15–16; holiday in Italy (1930), 18–19; MacDonald confides in, 20; to *Private Lives*, 21; bad back, 22, 369; Chelsea Flower Show, 25; gardens at Sissinghurst, 26, 144, 148, 318, 376; writes for *Action*, 30; bank loan (1931), 33; 'calm, comforting, and considerate', 38; finance, 39, 57, 83; U.S. lecture tour (1933), 44–54; impressed by Grand Canyon, 54; 'not a person one takes for granted', 58; in Italy (1934), 59; Cap Ferrat, 62–3; wedding anniversary (1935), 81–2; birthday (1936), 95; hates H.N. to fly, 79, 111, 300; refuses to help H.N.'s campaign, 82; in Algeria (1937), 111; on Sudetenland, 133; H.N.'s admiration for, 142; air raid warnings, 163; discusses war with H.N., 176; and the high spots in their life, 193; poetry-reading (1943), 244–5; and Ben's accident (1944), 276, 277; arthritis, 277; in Leicester with H.N. (1945), 292; thrilled by atom bomb, 297; broadcasts appeal for National Trust (1946), 314; Attlee introduced to, 327; C.H.,' (1947), 328, 329, 330; Spanish lecture tour (1949), 338–9; on Rilke, 346; *Antony and Cleopatra*, 350; Christmas (1951), 351; and H.N.'s K.C.V.O., 356; Nigel's wedding (1953), 361; 62nd birthday (1954), 363; poetry-reading (1954), 367; H.N.'s strokes (1955), 370–3; Ben's wedding (1955), 371; short story, 372; Far East trip (1957), 382; allergic to wasps' stings, 388; and *Lolita*, 390; and television, 393; Tory, 394; broadcasts (1960), 396; final illness, 402–6; death (1962), 406–7
WRITINGS: *All Passions Spent*, 18; *Family History*, 43; *Grande Mademoiselle*, 383; *Joan of Arc*, 96; *No Signposts in the Sea*, 396; *Pepita*, 96, 115; *Seducers in Ecuador*, 46; *Land*, 244; *Sissinghurst*, 244–5, 367
Sadleir, Michael, 42–3, 78
St Aubyn, Francis ('Sam') (Lord St Levan), 85, 376
St Aubyn, Giles, 144
St Aubyn, Gwen (H.N.'s sister), 60, 62, 69, 97, 111, 183, 348
St James's Palace, 359
St James's Theatre, 350
St Louis, 47, 48
St Margaret's Church, Westminster, 287, 361
St Michael, 67
St Moritz, 393
St Paul's Cathedral, 204–5, 217, 273, 274, 397
Saint-Simon, duc de, 391
St Stephen's Chapel, 210
Sainte-Beuve, C. A., 370, 372, 390; *Causeries de lundi*, 370; *Port-Royal*, 372
Salisbury, 5th Marquess of, 179, 182, 249, 382

Salisbury Plain, 210
Salmond, Air Marshal Sir Geoffrey, 19
Salonica, 148, 207
Samuel, Herbert, 81
Samuel, Lord, 347–8, 355
San Francisco, 51, 52–3, 241;
    Conference (1945), 280, 291, 305
San Francisco Examiner, 52
San Francisco Forum, 52
Sanders, Mr, 110
Sandringham, 127, 341, 342, 343, 348
Sandys, Duncan, 140
Santa Sofia, 365
Sarfatti, Signora, 36
Sargent, J. S., 46
Sargent, Sir Malcolm, 358–9
Sassoon, Sir Philip, 56
Sauckel, 307–11
Savehay, 23
Savoy, House of, 246
Savoy Hotel, 89, 139, 198
Scandinavia, 165, 179
Scandrett, Dick, 73
Scapa Flow, 266
Schacht, Dr H., 301–11
Scharnhorst, 225
Schiff, Miss, 71
Schirach, Baldur von, 307–11
Schloss St Martin, 103
Schmidt, Guido, 119
Schuberts, the, 36–7
Schuschnigg, Kurt von, 119, 122
Scinahan, Mrs, 51
Scotland, 101–2, 196, 209–10, 232, 252
Scott, Sir Walter, 301
Second Front, 234
Secret Sessions, *see* House of Commons
Sedan, 184, 238
Senhouse, Roger, 208–9
Sevenoaks Conservative Association, 78
Sevenoaks Urban Council, 396
Seyss-Inquart, 119, 307–11
Sforza, Count, 276
Shah of Iran, 368
Shakespeare, William, 373; *Antony
    and Cleopatra*, 350
Shaw, Charlotte, 25–6, 346
Shaw, George Bernard, 18, 25–6, 125,
    346–7, 373; *Back to Methuselah*, 25;
    Doctor's Dilemma, 26; *St Joan*, 26

Sheffield, 198
Shelley, Percy Bysshe, 216
Siam: King of, 62; Prime Minister, 220
Sicily, 238, 246
Siepmann, Charles, 42
Simenon, Georges, 353
Simon, Sir John (Lord Simon), 107,
    138, 149, 241, 274
Simonides, 274
Simpson, Colonel, 266
Simpson, Ernest, 88
Simpson, Wallis, *see* Windsor, Duchess
    of
Sinclair, Sir Archibald (Lord Thurso),
    123, 139, 154–5, 169, 170–1, 180
Singapore, 214, 221, 224, 225, 226, 229,
    230
Sissinghurst, 54, 59, 60, 80, 81, 86, 102,
    139, 145, 165, 169, 192, 245, 260,
    291, 299, 339, 358, 361, 386, 389,
    405; V.S.-W. buys (1930), 13, 15–16,
    22; garden, 26, 96, 97, 144, 148, 318;
    South Cottage, 157, 276; flag
    lowered (1939), 160; military
    presence (1942), 240; wartime
    atmosphere, 267; uncomfortable in
    winter, 276; flag raised (1945), 286;
    'Poor Sissinghurst!', 290;
    mellowness, 337; and National
    Trust, 366; and television, 374–5
Sissinghurst Place, 250
Sister Agnes' Home for Officers, 354
Sitwell, Edith, 244
Sitwell, Osbert, 244
63 Club, 381
Slessor, Sir John, 383
'Small World', 393
Smoke Tree Ranch, 53
Smolensk, 212
Smuts, Jan, 315–16
Smyrna, 193
Smyth, Dame Ethel, 46, 125
Socialism, 126, 341, 399
Society of Authors, 247–8, 255
Sofia, 124–5, 202
Soheilly, M., 368
Soho, 389
Somme, battle of the (1916), 186
South Africa, Republic of, 316, 393–4
South America, 18

South Bank Exhibition, 349
South Kensington, 302, 321
Southampton, 386, 401, 404, 407
Southwark, 156–7
Sovrani's, 17
Spahis, 315
Spain, 70, 75, 114, 120, 123, 144, 149, 208, 279, 305, 319, 338–9, 362; Civil War, 101, 114, 170
Spandau, 284
Spanish Morocco, 115
Sparrow, John, 373, 374
Spear, Ruskin, 384
Spears, Sir Edward, 122
Spears, Louis, 140, 141, 203, 204
Spears, Mary, 203
Spectator, The, 8, 141, 144, 149, 165, 176, 177, 178, 200, 221, 249, 271, 297, 356, 387
Speer, Albert, 307–11
Spellman, Monsignor, 247
Spender, Stephen, 17
spies, 185
Spinks, 384
Staël, Auguste de, 325
Staël, M. and Mme, de, 325
Stahremberg, Princess, 128
Stalin, Joseph, 154, 243, 284, 346, 358
Stalingrad, 236, 242, 328
Stalino, 252
Stamfordham, 348
Stanley, Sir Henry, 109
Stanley, Lady Maureen, 93, 126–7
Stanley, Oliver, 21, 23, 87, 99, 112, 132, 272
Staplehurst, 15, 157, 337
Staples, Mrs, 257, 271, 370
Star, The, 97
Stark, Freya, 144
Starkie, Enid, 372, 374
Stauffenburg, Graf von, 270
Stendhal: *Rouge et Noir*, 392
Stevenson, Adlai, 361, 397
Stockholm, 222, 252, 291
Stoke on Trent, 32
Stören, 179
Stornoway, 396
Stornoway House, 14, 16–17, 39
Strachey, G. Lytton, 37; *Letters*, 380
Strachey, John, 28, 29

Strand, the, 136, 192
Strauss, Richard, 311
Stravinsky, Igor, 389
Streatham, 40
Streicher, Julius, 307–11
Sudetenland, 131, 132, 133, 134, 135, 138
Suez Canal, 376–81, 383, 384
Suffolk, H.M.S., 212
Summit Conference, 395
Sunday Cinema Bill (1931), 24
Sunday Express, 39, 372
Sunday Times, 355, 373, 386
Surbiton, 342
Svevo, Italo, 29
Sweden, 175, 178, 222, 252
Swifts, 177
Switzerland, 81, 109–19, 165; Ambassador, 392; Cultural Attaché, 392
Swinton, 126
Sykes, Christopher, 278
Sylt, 176
Syracuse, 39

Tablet, The, 381
Tahiti, 75
Tanganyika, 109
Tangier, 63, 64
Taplow, 100
Tate, Mrs, 244
Taylor, A. J. P., 236
Taylour, Mrs, 15
Tedworth Square, 349
Tehran, 8, 269; British Legation, 8
Tel-Aviv, 379
10 Downing Street, 22–3, 134, 184, 214, 234, 237, 249, 293, 391
Tennyson, Alfred, Lord, 257
Tennyson d'Eyncourt, Sir Gervais and Lady, 361
Tennyson, d'Eyncourt, Philippa, *see* Nicolson, Philippa
Terbrugghen, Hendrick, 369
Thomas, Dylan, 216; *Portrait of the Artist as a Young Dog*, 180
Thomas, Hugh, 363, 377
Thomas, J. H., 36, 89, 97, 98–9, 140
Thompson, Dorothy, 215
Thomson, Lord, 19

Thor (dog), 68–9
Thyateira, Archbishop of, 273, 274
Tikki (typewriter), 65
Time and Tide, 200
Times, The, 37, 101, 136, 182, 306, 320, 355, 363, 395; *Weekly Edition*, 169
Tito, Marshal, 272, 300
Tobruk, 226, 230
Toby (budgerigar), 375
Tojo, Admiral, 250
Tokyo, 114
Toledo, 50–1
Tonbridge, 193, 284
Tonga, Queen of, 360
Torgau, 284
Tottenham Court Road, 268
Toulon, 81
Toynbee, Arnold: *Study of History*, 366
Trade Disputes Bill (1931), 23
Trafalgar Square, 136, 204–5, 286, 360
Transport House, 329, 392
Travellers Club, 78, 86, 154, 182, 251, 287, 344, 352, 360, 366
Tree, Jeremy, 395
Tree, Ronald, 142–2, 159, 196
Trenchard, Judge, 72
Trevelyan, G. M., 247–8, 253
Trieste, 30
Trinita dei Monti, 36
Tripoli, 242
Tripp, Lieutenant-General W. H. L., 212
Tristan, 150
Trondheim, 179, 181
Truman, President Harry S., 284, 297–8
Truth, 215
Tufton Street, 120
Tunis, 238, 245, 256, 264, 332; Bey, 245
Tunisia, 246
Turkey, 130, 149, 205, 209, 223, 327
Turner, J. M. W., 23
Tuthill, 85
Tyrol, 285

Uckfield, 78
Uganda, 109
Ujiji, 109

Ulster, 101–2, 387
Unconditional Surrender, 278, 284–5, 286
Underground, 257–8, 292
Union of Soviet Socialist Republics: Air Force, 126; Navy, 132; London Embassy, 146, 152–3; Army, 147, 284; Revolution, 147, 328; Russo–German non-aggression pact (1939), 154; Ambassador, 157; invades Poland (1939), 165; and Finland (1939), 168–9, 170, 171; Germany invades (1941), 212; and retreats (1942), 236; Ukraine, 260; hold on Poland, 277, 279–80; collaborators, 291; at war with Japan, 298; occupation of Germany, 306–7; Berlin blockade (1948), 335–7; atom bomb (1949), 342; invades Hungary (1956), 380, 381; satellite (1957), 385
United Kingdom: Admiralty, 174, 212; Air Ministry, 19; Army, 172, 182, 205, 221, 233, 236, 238, 240, 242, 244, 246; British Expeditionary Force, 185, 186, 187, 208; Cabinet, 116, 134, 135, 140, 142, 143, 159, 164, 177, 182, 183, 185, 187, 199, 200, 228, 237, 269, 279; Cabinet Security Committee, 236; Chiefs of Staff, 196; Civil Defence Committee, 210; Civil Defence Sub-Committee, 200; Colonial Ministry, 175; Commercial Service, 243; Consular Service, 243; Diplomatic Service, 243; Dominions Office, 126, 159, 164, 253; Fleet Air Arm, 211; Foreign Affairs Committee, 95, 96, 101, 114, 115, 118, 119, 121, 123; Foreign Office, 8, 27, 63, 76, 80, 81, 96, 117, 123, 138, 234, 243, 279, 301, 302, 336, 349; Foreign Policy Commission, 186; General Staff, 258; Home Defence Ministers, 187; Ministry of Information, 164, 174, 176, 184–214, 222, 252; Ministry of Supply, 218, 224; National Health Service, 399; Office of Works, 210; prisoners of war, 283; Privy Council, 106; Royal Air Force, 116, 126, 143,

191–2, 195, 196, 205, 225, 236;
Royal Navy, 131, 136, 148, 178, 180,
181, 182, 195, 205, 266; Treasury,
126, 194; War Office, 187, 213
United Nations, 280, 305, 315, 347,
374, 378, 379, 380, 381; Charter,
291; Security Council, 379
United Press, 238
United States of America: H.N. and
V.S.-W.'s lecture tour (1933), 39–40,
44–54; Depression, 44–5; Senate,
47–8, 52; Ulysses banned, 61; H.N.
in, 65, 66–72, 72–4, 79–80; Air
Force, 232, 260; State Department,
77; vulgarity, 98; English in, 176,
178, 374; Royal Visit, 150; Congress,
172; enters war (1941), 220, 221;
Churchill in (1942), 222; Army, 227,
236, 238, 266, 268, 276, 284, 305;
Constitution, 284; anti-British
feeling, 230; atom bomb, 297, 298;
Spanish bases, 362; London
Embassy, 395, 399
Users' Association, 378–9

Valera, Eamon de, 106, 200, 227–8, 247
Vallombrosa, 345
Van Loon, Henrik, 45–6
Vandenberg, Senator Arthur H., 305
Vanderbilt, 45–6
Vansittart, Sir Robert (Lord), 80, 96–7,
99, 122, 130, 174, 245
Vardar Valley, 148
Vatican, 61, 247, 389
Venables, 315
Venezuela, 386, 387
Venice, 101
Verlaine, Paul, 259
Versailles, 34, 60, 315; Treaty (1919),
60, 94, 212, 315
Vertova, Luisa, *see* Nicolson, Luisa
Vertova, Signora, 371
Vichy, 262
Victoria, Queen, 104, 224, 338, 342,
359, 375
Victoria, Lake, 110
Vienna, 122, 128, 202; Congress of
(1815), 317–18
Viénot, Pierre, 269
Vigée-Lebrun, 325

Vigier, General de, 264
Villa Mauresque, 62–3, 103, 128–30
Villa Medici, 36
Villa Torlonia, 36
Villefranche, 103
Virgil, 56
Virginia, 244
Vladivostock, 341
Voigt, Frederick, 146
Voltaire, 385–6, 388
Volts, 31
Vyborg, 170
Vyshinsky, M., 313, 314

Wales, 235, 314
Waley, Arthur, 244
Walker, 110
Wallace, Barbara, 143
Wallace, Euan, 126, 143
Walters, Sir John Tudor, 21
Wandsworth Prison, 118
War Memorials Commission, 326
Ward, Penelope Dudley, 125
Ward, Richard, 365
Warsaw, 273
Washington, D.C., 47–8, 49, 51, 69–70,
79, 80, 114, 149, 195, 199, 226, 244,
246, 300, 399
Waterhouse, Captain Charles, 85, 86,
194
Waterloo, battle of (1815), 218
Wauchope, Sir Arthur, 80
Wavell, Field Marshal Lord, 247
Weald, 94
Wedgwood, J. C., 180–1, 182
Weidenfeld, George, 390, 396
Weizmann, Dr Chaim, 150
Wellington College, 8
Wells, H. G., 24, 31, 125, 167, 168,
247–8
Wembley, 265
West, Rebecca, 200; *Black Lamb and
Grey Falcon*, 222
West Leicester Conservative
Association, 82, 121
West Leicester Women's Conservative
Association, 114
Westminster Abbey, 90–1, 112–13
Westminster Hall, 90–1
Westwood, 15

Weygand, General, 199, 200
Wheeler, Monroe, 322–3
Whistler, J. M., 351
White Lodge, 92
Whitehall, 136–7, 286
White's, 214
Whitney, Mrs, 395
Wight, Isle of, 36
Wilde, Oscar, 17, 38, 103
Wilhelm II, Kaiser, 174
Wilhelmshaven, 225
Willem Ruys, M.V., 382, 383
Williams, 329
Willkie, Wendell, 195–6, 200
Wilson, Edmund, 259
Wilson, Sir Horace, 136, 149, 171
Wilson, Woodrow, 43, 313
Wilton, 18
Wimbledon, 191, 265
Winant, John G. (U.S. Ambassador), 203, 216–17
Windsor, Duchess of, 105, 112, 145, 167–8, 323; H.N. meets, 89–90; H.N. dines with, 96, 128–30; dines with King, 96, 98; King's obstinacy over, 101, 108, 116; 'third-rate American', 104; H.N. sorry for, 106; vulgarity, 387–8
Windsor, Duke of (Edward VIII), 88, 89–90, 98, 145, 167, 188, 323, 340, 342; obstinacy over Mrs Simpson, 101, 108, 116; H.N. dines with, 96, 128–30, 371; dines with Lindberghs, 99; terrible accent, 104, 129; Abdication crisis, 105, 106, 107; Queen Mary on, 355

Windsor Castle, 333–4, 338, 343, 344
Windt, 109
Withyham, 406
Wodehouse, P. G., 125, 255–6
Wolfenden Report, 389
Wolkoff, Miss, 185
Wollheim, Richard, 400
Wolmer, Viscount, 140
Wood, Sir Kingsley, 126, 172
Woodruff, Douglas, 381
Woods, Mrs, 94
Woolf, Leonard, 206–7, 366
Woolf, Virginia, 191, 206–7, 362, 366; *Letters*, 380
Woollcott, Alexander, 96
Wordsworth, William, 390
Wormwood Scrubs, 310
Wren, Sir Christopher, 204–5
Wright, Dr Almroth, 26
Württemberg, 38
Wylie, Editor of *New York Times*, 45–6

Yalta Conference (1945), 279, 280, 281–2
York Cottage, Sandringham, 342
Young, Allan, 28, 29
Young, Esther, 28
Young, G. M., 167
Yugoslavia, 165, 202, 205, 222, 272–3, 315

Zoological Society, 194
Zuckerman, Sir Solly, 400